Psychological Anthropology for th 21st Century

This book provides a comprehensive introduction to psychological anthropology, covering both the early history and contemporary state of the field. Eller discusses the major themes, theories, figures and publications, and provides a detailed survey of the essential and enduring relationship between anthropology and psychology. The volume charts the development, celebrates the accomplishments, critiques the inadequacies, and considers the future of a field that has made great contributions to the overall discipline of anthropology. The chapters feature rich ethnographic examples and boxes for more in-depth discussion as well as summaries and questions to support teaching and learning. This is essential reading for all students new to the study of psychological anthropology.

Jack David Eller is Associate Professor (Emeritus) of Anthropology at the Community College of Denver, USA. An experienced teacher and author, he is the author of the major introductory textbook *Cultural Anthropology: Global Forces, Local Lives* (third edition, 2016). His other titles for Routledge include *Introducing Anthropology of Religion* (second edition, 2014), *Cultural Anthropology: 101* (2015), *Culture and Diversity in the Unites States* (2015), and *Social Science and Historical Perspectives* (2016).

Psychological Anthropology for the 21st Century

Jack David Eller

Routledge
Taylor & Francis Group

LONDON AND NEW YORK

First published 2019
by Routledge
2 Park Square, Milton Park, Abingdon, Oxon OX14 4RN

and by Routledge
711 Third Avenue, New York, NY 10017

Routledge is an imprint of the Taylor & Francis Group, an informa business

British Library Cataloguing-in-Publication Data
A catalogue record for this book is available from the British Library

Library of Congress Cataloging-in-Publication Data
A catalog record has been requested for this book

ISBN: 978-1-138-59378-7 (hbk)
ISBN: 978-1-138-59376-3 (pbk)
ISBN: 978-0-429-48927-3 (ebk)

Typeset in Goudy
by codeMantra

Printed and bound in Great Britain by
TJ International Ltd, Padstow, Cornwall

Contents

Figures, boxes, and table

Figures

Boxes

Table

Introduction

When I started my doctoral education in anthropology in the early 1980s, psychological anthropology had fallen into disfavor, if not disrepute. The excesses and oversimpifications, along with the unkept promises of previous incarnations—known by such diverse and overlapping names as culture-and-personality, cognitive anthropology, and cognition and culture, among others—had largely led anthropologists to turn their back on the psychological anthropology of the first half of the twentieth century and to move on to other questions, theories, and methods. Yet fascinating new ideas and approaches were on the horizon, and psychological anthropology was on the verge of a rebirth.

From its very inception, anthropology has been thoroughly enmeshed with psychology, whether that concerns the characteristics of alleged "primitive mentality" versus the universality of mental processes; the effects of child-rearing and social experience on personality; or the role and variability of perception, memory, learning, etc. in culture. Many members of the first generation of anthropologists or field researchers were trained psychologists or psychoanalysts (and/or physicians), and many others collaborated with specialists in those fields while sometimes undergoing analysis themselves. Most of the important anthropologists of the twentieth century—from Franz Boas and Bronislaw Malinowski to Clifford Geertz and Claude Lévi-Strauss—asked psychological questions or offered insights that were relevant to the psychological side of society and culture. Anthropologists further incorporated psychological techniques, including tests of perception and intelligence, into their fieldwork. Most recognized that a complete understanding of humans as social and cultural beings would require consideration of the human mind and its relation to the evolved human body. Even scholars who appear to have shed the focus on mind or psychology, such as Pierre Bourdieu, still contributed to the investigation of tacit (unspoken and perhaps unspeakable) and embodied knowledge, and Dan Sperber's suggestions about the spread and "catchiness" of certain ideas have been adopted for the cognitive-evolutionary theory of religion and culture generally and more widely for the production of "viral" ideas. Meanwhile, anthropology has ventured with intriguing and important results into other psychological territory, such as emotions, dreams and altered states of consciousness, personhood, and mental illness.

Psychological Anthropology for the 21st Century is the first comprehensive text to encapsulate both the early history and the contemporary state of the subdiscipline. It provides a detailed survey of the essential and enduring relationship between anthropology and psychology (matters of personality, mentality, character, mind, cognition, and so forth) from the very earliest days of anthropology until the present. Beyond chronicling the rise, practice, (often scathing) critique, and subsequent decline of theoretical schools and research agendas, the book describes some grand themes that have characterized not only the subdiscipline but also the entire enterprise of anthropology, including the racialist and racist attitude that infected the field and much of Western thought in the late nineteenth and early twentieth centuries (and that, depressingly, still persists too often in the twenty-first). We also see psychological anthropology change or mature as its focus shifted from personality or character to more profound issues of knowledge and cognitive process. Finally, we underscore the intimate mutual influence of anthropology on the one hand and allied fields like philosophy and linguistics on the other. Combining the questions of knowledge and language, we stress the gathering consensus that language is not a perfect model or metaphor for knowledge or mind (knowledge-as-statements, mind-as-grammar, or culture-as-text) since not all knowledge or mentation is verbal or propositional but is rather "practical" and embodied.

As with any writing project of manageable scale, it is not possible to cover every topic of interest and relevance in this book. Even in the chapter on emotions, an explicit choice is made to concentrate on a few emotions—anger, fear, and love—on the assumption that this treatment establishes the prospect for an anthropology of any and all emotions. As one of the reviewers of the final manuscript accurately commented, there are other topics that deserve attention, from pain and hope to well-being, and indeed, every psychological subject could be, should be, and probably has been investigated through a cross-cultural and ethnographic lens. At the same time, some of the scholars discussed in the book may not exactly qualify as, or identify themselves as, psychological anthropologists, but that is precisely the point: psychological anthropology is not a sharply bounded subset of anthropology but a perspective that emerges from and flows into many corners of the discipline, taking many forms. The selection of subjects in this book is mine alone and in no way exhausts the actual and potential achievements of psychological anthropology. Readers are encouraged to search out other relevant subjects and perhaps even add to the growing psychological anthropology literature.

Ultimately, *Psychological Anthropology for the 21st Century* charts the development, celebrates the accomplishments, critiques the inadequacies, and considers the future of a field that has made great contributions to the overall discipline of anthropology and that plays a crucial role in anthropology's mission to become a comprehensive science of human nature and diversity.

Structure and features of the book

Because *Psychological Anthropology for the 21st Century* is both historical and topical, it is divided evenly into two parts, covering these two terrains. The opening five chapters are roughly chronological, beginning with the first chapter on psychological interests in anthropology from the 1800s to the 1920s. The second chapter covers the famous culture-and-personality school from the 1920s to the 1940s, and the third chapter continues that examination for the period from 1945 to the 1970s, when participants took stock of a half-century of work, even as the school was losing momentum. The fourth chapter surveys the "cognitive turn" in anthropology in reaction to the older approach, including ethnoscience or cognitive anthropology and Lévi-Strauss's structuralism as well as Leslie White's concurrent rejection of psychology in favor of "culturology." The fifth chapter brings us up-to-date with presentations on symbolism, practice, and embodiment.

The second, topical part is comprised of five chapters on specific contemporary areas of research in psychological anthropology. These include self and personhood, emotions, dreams and altered states of consciousness, mental illness, and cognition and neuroanthropology.

Because the goals of the two parts are so distinct, the structure of the associated chapters differs somewhat:

- each of the first five chapters opens with a chronological list of major figures and publications, and closes with a summary of the accomplishments and shortcomings of the respective scholars and schools
- each of the second five chapters opens with a list of key questions broached in the study of the particular subject and closes with a summary of the findings and results of the respective research.

All of the chapters also feature extensive and rich ethnographic examples, both classic and cutting edge, and multiple boxes for more in-depth ethnographic or conceptual discussion.

Final remarks

Psychological Anthropology for the 21st Century is the product of over thirty years of research and teaching, beginning with an individual major in college labeled "Patterns of Human Experience," continuing through a doctoral dissertation titled *Culture and Subjectivity: On the Theory of the Individual in Culture*, and culminating in this project. It is my hope, and the hope of the kind reviewers who evaluated the original proposal for the book, that it will reinvigorate psychological anthropology, secure the subdiscipline's value in the past and the present, and stimulate further interest in the psychological achievements of anthropology while promoting interdisciplinary dialogue and research between anthropologists; psychologists; other scholars, like neuroscientists and artificial-intelligence designers; and practitioners, like psychiatrists and social workers—who themselves are increasingly aware of the cultural component in illness and treatment.

A note on verb tenses

Anthropologists have struggled, perhaps more than other social scientists, with the temporal dimension of our research and writing. We have often been guilty—and have castigated ourselves—for putting our findings in the "ethnographic present," that is, using the present tense, even when our fieldwork was performed in the past and when the information we convey refers to a bygone era (for instance, "The Warlpiri do this" or "The Yanomamo believe that"). The problem also arises when citing the work of other scholars, whose books and articles may have been published last year or more than a century ago. There is obviously no simple, universal solution to this dilemma: we cannot merely put all verbs in the past tense or the present tense. In this book, where the time frame is not perfectly obvious, I have made the arbitrary decision to phrase data or quotations in the past tense (e.g. "Geertz said") if they were published more than ten years ago (approximately before 2007) and the present tense (e.g. "Coolidge and Wynn emphasize") if they are less than ten years old.

Part I

The development of psychological anthropology

Chapter 1

Psychology in the formation of anthropology

Key figures:
Edward Burnett (E. B.) Tylor (1832–1917)
Sigmund Freud (1856–1939)
Lucien Lévy-Bruhl (1857–1939)
Franz Boas (1858–1942)
William Halse Rivers (W. H. R.) Rivers (1864–1922)

Key texts:
Primitive Culture (1871)
How Natives Think (originally published as *Les fonctiones mentales dans les sociétés inférieures*, 1910)
The Mind of Primitive Man (1911)
Totem and Taboo (1913)
Sex and Repression in Savage Society (1927)

The eminent twentieth-century anthropologist Claude Lévi-Strauss wrote that anthropology, more specifically ethnology or the description and analysis of humankind's diverse cultures, "is first of all psychology" (1966: 131). We hope that he is wrong as this would make anthropology redundant or reduce it to a branch of another discipline, and indeed, he is wrong as anthropology has a different mission and different methods than psychology. Yet anthropology and psychology have been close companions since the 1800s, when both fields began to coalesce into their modern forms. Many of the early contributors to anthropology were professional psychologists, and many early professional anthropologists asked explicitly psychological questions while borrowing psychological theories and tools, like intelligence tests and Rorschach inkblots.

Especially in the United States but also in France and Germany, psychological concerns have pervaded anthropology and continue to do so; in fact, they may do so more today than at any time since the 1970s. American cultural anthropology in particular has actually spawned a number of specializations and subdisciplines, from psychoanalytic anthropology to culture-and-personality to ethnoscience or componential analysis to cognitive anthropology and neuroanthropology. The heyday of psychologically oriented anthropology was probably the 1960s and 1970s, when Francis Hsu (1972b: 6) proposed a new and more inclusive name for the subdiscipline—*psychological anthropology*.

Over the past century, anthropology has constructed, critiqued, transcended, and some-times strenuously rejected this sequence of psychologically focused schools or theories, but psychological anthropology is not just the story of one failed and discarded paradigm after another. First, psychological anthropology from its inception offered an alternative to other dominant approaches, such as functionalism and structural functionalism. Second, even in its failures or excesses, each wave or generation of psychological anthropological thought can claim its accomplishments and insights, and has left its mark on the discipline. Third and ultimately, psychological anthropology speaks to the deepest issues of human culture and of the human individual, recognizing the essential connection or interpenetration of the two. In this way, it seeks to fulfill the promise of anthropology to be a true science of humanity and not mere antiquarianism or the collection of cultural oddities.

Setting the question

Everyone (well, almost everyone) can agree that culture and the individual are intimately linked: culture shapes individual thought, feeling, and behavior, while individual action produces and reproduces cultural ideas, norms, relations, and institutions. It is of course possible to investigate cultural and social phenomena without appeal to psychology—just as it is possible to study, say, mathematics without referring to brain processes, although to be sure, doing math requires brain processes—and most ethnographic research makes no specific mention of it. However, culture only exists because of certain evolved human men-tal capacities and tendencies (see Chapter 10), and, as psychologists have also discovered, human psychological processes are not independent of culture—are not "precultural"—but are reciprocally influenced by social experience.

What then is psychological anthropology? Hsu gave a very broad answer, asserting that it includes any work

> by an anthropologist who has a good knowledge of psychological concepts or by a mem-ber of another discipline who has a good knowledge of anthropological concepts [By this definition, psychologists or neuroscientists doing cross-cultural research are in effect psychological anthropologists.]
> Any work that deals with the individual as the locus of culture
> Any work that gives serious recognition to culture as an independent or a dependent variable associated with personality [that is, culture may be explored as cause or effect of personality factors]
> Any work by an anthropologist which uses psychological concepts or techniques or by a scholar in a psychological discipline which provides directly pertinent data in forms which are useable by anthropologists.
>
> (1972b: 2)

Among the most persistent topics in psychological anthropology, particularly in its early to mid-twentieth-century manifestation, have been

> (a) the relation of social structure and values to modal patterns of child rearing, (b) the relation of modal patterns of child rearing to modal personality structure as expressed in behavior, (c) the relation of modal personality structure to the role system and pro-jective aspects of culture [i.e. art, myth, religion, etc.], and (d) the relation of all of the foregoing variables to deviant behavior patterns which vary from one group to another,
>
> (2–3)

including mental illness and altered states of consciousness, like dreams and trance.

Finally, acknowledging that anthropologists are not the only scholars interested in social influences on thought or in cross-cultural differences in cognition, Hsu contrasted psychological anthropology with social psychology in the following ways:

1 Psychological anthropology is cross-cultural in approach from its inception while social psychology has traditionally drawn its data from Western societies
2 Social psychology is quantitative and even, to a certain extent, experimental in orientation, while psychological anthropology has paid little attention to research designs and only lately awakened to the need for rigor in the matter of hypothesis formation and of verification
3 Psychological anthropology deals not only with the effect of society and culture on psychic characteristics of individuals (a basic concern of social psychology) but also with the role of personality characteristics in the maintenance, development, and change of culture and society.

(12–13)

Admittedly, these distinctions are not as sharp today as they were half a century ago: some psychological research is truly cross-cultural, even ethnographic, while some anthropological research is quantitative and methodologically rigorous.

Defining "culture" and "personality"

In the noble and ambitious calling of psychological anthropology, a major obstacle has been deciding on and defining key terms for identifying and differentiating the collective and the individual, the external and the internal, the social and the mental, variables of behavior. The initial decades of the twentieth century, as we will soon see, leaned heavily on the concepts of "culture" and "personality," although especially in regard to the latter, many rival, overlapping but not synonymous, terms vied and still vie for a place in the discourse, including "mentality," "mind," "character," "self," "person," "cognition," and so forth. Neither anthropologists nor psychologists are entirely unanimous on the meaning of these terms nor, therefore, on their interrelation.

Beginning with culture, anthropologists recognize Edward Burnett (E. B.) Tylor as probably the first scholar to give an anthropological definition of culture in his 1871 *Primitive Culture*, where the opening sentence of the book reads, "Culture or Civilization, taken in its wide ethnographic sense, is that complex whole which includes knowledge, belief, art, morals, law, custom, and any other capabilities and habits acquired by man as a member of society" (1958: 1). The noteworthy features of this definition are its reference to mental content like knowledge and belief, its emphasis on acquisition or learning, and its appreciation of social membership—and thus, potentially, the differences in knowledge, belief, and learning in different societies.

Others have defined culture in similar but varying ways. In his 1963 *Culture and Personality*, Victor Barnouw characterized it as

the way of life of a group of people, the configuration of all of the more or less stereotyped patterns of learned behavior which are handed down from one generation to the next through the means of language and imitation.

(1973: 6)

Ralph Linton, one of the champions of culture-and-personality analysis at mid-century, characterized culture as "the configuration of behavior and results of behavior whose component elements are shared and transmitted by the members of a particular society" (1945: 32), reflecting a Tylorian view; emphasizing the place of the individual in culture, Linton went on to state that "real culture" is the sum of the behavioral configurations of all the members of a society (in other words, add up all the individuals, and you have "culture"), while the "culture construct" is a creation of the anthropologist who intuits (if not invents) "the mode of the finite series of variations which are included within each of the real culture patterns and then uss this mode as a symbol for the real culture pattern" (45). In a later summary of the field, Anthony Wallace rephrased his definition of culture to designate "those ways of behavior or techniques of solving problems which, being more frequently and more closely approximated than other ways, can be said to have a high probability of use by individual members of society" (1964: 6).

Assuredly, there are many other definitions of culture, some stressing thought and others stressing action, some including material objects and others not. If anything, the situation is even more fraught when it comes to the subject of personality—for which one might substitute (and many have substituted) mind, character, or other words. Barnouw considered personality to be "a more or less enduring organization of forces within the individual associated with a complex of fairly consistent attitudes, values, and modes of perception which account, in part, for the individual's consistency of behavior" (1963: 10). Wallace defined the term simply to mean "those ways of behavior or techniques of solving problems which have a high probability of use by one individual" (1964: 7), but Linton expanded considerably on the concept; for him, personality referred to

> the organized aggregate of psychological processes and states pertaining to the individual. This definition includes the common element in most of the definitions now current. At the same time it excludes many orders of phenomena which have been included in one or another of these definitions. Thus, it rules out the overt behavior resulting from the operations of these processes and states, although it is only from such behavior that their nature and even existence can be deduced. It also excludes from consideration the effects of this behavior upon the individual's environment, even that part of it which consists of other individuals. Lastly, it excludes from the personality concept the physical structure of the individual and his physiological processes. This final limitation will appear too drastic to many students of personality, but it has a pragmatic, if not a logical, justification. We know so little about the physiological accompaniments of psychological phenomena that attempts to deal with the latter in physiological terms still lead to more confusion than clarification.
>
> (1945: 84)

For his part, Robert LeVine made an effort to unpack the term a bit, asserting that personality "is the organization in the individual of those processes that intervene between environmental conditions and behavioral responses," adding that it consists of many variables, such as "perception, cognition, memory, learning, and the activation of emotional reactions—as they are organized and regulated in the individual organism" (1973: 5). Articulating the concept further, he distinguished between "observable behavioral consistencies" which he called "personality indicators"; the underlying psychological complex of "motivational, affective, and cognitive components and multiple forms of expression" which he called "personality dispositions"; and the structured "personality organization" in which those dispositions are embedded (9).

The relationship(s) between culture and personality

Given the imprecision of its two fundamental terms, it is little wonder that anthropologists (and others) disagree about the actual relationship between culture (or shared, public processes and content) and personality (or individual, internal processes and content). British social anthropologist S. F. Nadel, for instance, was quick to insist that scientists

> may take it for granted that there is some connection between the make-up of a culture and the particular personality (or personalities) of its human carriers. Yet in taking this connection to be a simple and obvious one, so simple and obvious that one can be inferred from the other, we run the risk of arguing in a circle
>
> (1951: 405)

—in fact, probably two inverse circles: one in which culture causes personality and the other in which personality causes culture.

LeVine hypothesized that observers had advocated at least five different positions on the question of the relationship between culture and personality or, more generally and less argumentatively, between culture and the individual. First were those positions that were frankly disinterested in, if not hostile to, the issue of personality/individual altogether. Among these are Alfred Kroeber's view of the "superorganic" nature of culture—that is, that culture has its own level of reality *apart from and above* the individual—and the "culturology" of Leslie White, who believed expressly that anthropology should be the study of culture and not of the individual (see Chapter 3). Alongside Kroeber and White, LeVine counted the symbolic interactionists who explained behavior in terms of meanings and situations, both external to the individual; we might add the behaviorists, who considered personality as at best a "black box" of unknown and unknowable factors and at worst an academic fiction, and at least some Marxists, who viewed individuals as less relevant than—even as mere instantiations of—class and economic relations.

Second, LeVine posited the "psychological reductionists" for whom culture could and should be explained (away?) simply in terms of personality: in the reverse of anti-personality theories, psychological processes and forces are real, and "culture" is a mere epiphenomenon of that internal world. LeVine indicted Freudian psychology as the "major contemporary reductionism" (1973: 48) for claiming to find the root of sophisticated cultural matters like art and religion in child-rearing practices and, even more reductively, in psychological (or biological) drives and mental structures like the id, ego, and superego.

Ironically, this psychological reductionism was influential in anthropological studies of culture and personality, many of which took the form of LeVine's third position, which he dubbed the "personality-is-culture" view. He claimed that prominent practitioners of culture-and-personality anthropology, like Margaret Mead and Ruth Benedict, "rejected the conceptual distinction between culture and personality" (53); in an anthropological cliché, culture for them was nothing more than "personality writ large" (see Chapter 2).

For a fourth contingent, including anthropologically informed psychologists and psychiatrists like Abram Kardiner, personality was intermediate between the so-called primary institutions of culture (like the family) and the secondary or more abstract cultural institutions of politics, religion, and so on (see Chapter 3). Finally, LeVine maintained that there was a fifth camp of theorists who took a "two systems" approach to culture and personality, seeing "personality and sociocultural institutions as two systems interacting with each other":

> Each system is comprised of interdependent parts and has requirements for its maintenance. Both sets of requirements make demands of individual behavior, the personality system for socially valued performance in the roles that are institutionalized in the social structure. Stability in the interaction of the two systems is attained only when their respective requirements are functionally integrated by standards of role performance that permit the individual to satisfy his psychological needs and meet sociocultural demands at the same time.
>
> (58)

Anthropologists Melford Spiro and A. Irving Hallowell are associated with this view.

In the end, LeVine represented the five models with simple equations stipulating the avowed relationship between culture (C) and personality (P):

Anti-personality	$C \rightarrow P$ (or in extreme cases, just C without any P)
Psychological reductionism	$P \rightarrow C$
Personality-is-culture	$P = C$
Personality-as-mediation	$C1 \rightarrow P \rightarrow C2$
Two systems	$P \leftrightarrow C$

(59)

BOX 1.1 BRITISH SOCIAL ANTHROPOLOGY

While American cultural anthropology has had an abiding interest in psychological matters, British social anthropology was traditionally relatively disinterested. Strongly and overtly influenced by Émile Durkheim's sociology, British social anthropology was much more committed to "social facts" than its American counterpart. In fact, social anthropologists like Alfred Reginald (A. R.) Radcliffe-Brown doubted the utility, if not the very possibility, of studying either personality *or* culture. He asserted that one

> cannot have a science of culture. You can study culture only as a characteristic of a social system… If you study culture, you are always studying the acts of behavior of a specific set of persons who are linked in a social structure,
>
> (1957: 106)

rendering the mental realm irrelevant.

Physiological psychology: body, race, and mind

It is an underappreciated fact that psychology and anthropology both emerged around the same time (in the mid-to-late 1800s) and often shared practitioners but that both originally had their roots in biological and even medical sciences. Psychology, or what Gustav Fechner in 1860 deigned to call "psychophysics," initially grew out of investigations of the nervous system; other founders of the science, like Hermann von Helmholtz and Paul Broca, were also researchers in nerve and brain physiology and function, and

Wilhelm Wundt (1832–1920), who founded the first psychology laboratory, attempted to measure sensory perception and thought itself (with his so-called "thought-meter") and penned a volume titled *Principles of Physiological Psychology*. The second source of early psychological exploration was mental illness, as in the work of Jean-Martin Charcot, who directed the French hospital of La Salpêtrière, where he studied not only spinal cord injuries, multiple sclerosis, and Parkinson's disease but also hypnosis and hysteria. Sigmund Freud began his career in neurology before going on to clinical psychology and ultimately his theories of mind and culture.

Anthropology was likewise conceived as a "natural science of man" before it became a cultural science. In his 1863 *Introduction to Anthropology*, Theodore Waitz asserted that the field "aspires to be the science of man in general; or, in precise terms, the science of the nature of man" (1863: 3), which should "study man by the same method which is applied to the investigation of all other natural objects" (5). Armand de Quatrefages, a nineteenth-century lecturer, explained that this meant that the anthropologist should study mankind "as a zoologist studying an animal would understand it" (quoted in Topinard 1890: 2). Paul Topinard summed up late nineteenth-century thinking when he declared that anthropology was "the branch of natural history which treats of man and the races of man" (1890: 3). Thus, anthropology was the name of the more inclusive science, including but not restricted to a branch of *ethnology* that examines the world's diverse human populations to describe their "manners, customs, religion, language, physical traits, and origins" (8–9).

More than a century previously, Carolus Linnaeus (1707–78) had inaugurated the natural-science study of humanity. In his 1740 *Systema Naturae*, he divided the human species into four subtypes, which were eventually labeled Homo europeaus, Homo afer, Homo americanus, and Homo asiaticus. Each category—or what we would today call "race"—was characterized by skin color but also by (alleged) behavioral habits and personality tendencies, often in shockingly insulting ways.

BOX 1.2 LINNAEUS'S RACES OF MANKIND

Linnaeus described his four types of humanity as:

Homo europaeus (European/Caucasian): "white, sanguine, muscular. Hair flowing, long. Eyes blue. Gentle, acute, inventive. Covered with close vestments. Governed by laws."
Homo afer (African): "black, phlegmatic, relaxed. Hair black, frizzled. Skin silky. Nose flat. Lips tumid. Women without shame. Mammae lactate profusely. Crafty, indolent, negligent. Anoints himself with grease. Governed by caprice."
Homo americanus (Native American): "reddish, choleric, erect. Hair black, straight, thick; nostrils wide; face harsh; beard scanty. Obstinate, merry, free. Paints himself with fine red lines. Regulated by customs."
Homo asiaticus (Asian): "sallow, melancholy, stiff. Hair black. Eyes dark. Severe, haughty, avaricious. Covered with loose garments. Ruled by opinions"
(quoted in Slotkin 1965: 177–8)

For good measure, he added two purely imaginary species: Homo ferus (a hairy and mute being that walked on all fours) and Homo monstrosus (a monstrous race of nocturnal cave dwellers).

Others, writing before the dawn of modern anthropology, proposed other biological/racial schemes, like Johann Friedrich Blumenbach. In his 1770 *On the Natural Variety of Mankind*, he also announced four races—African, American, Asian, and "Caucasian," a term he introduced, later adding Malayan as a fifth entry. These races were, unsurprisingly, not only different but unequal: he judged Caucasians as both the original or "primeval" form of humanity and the most beautiful, and non-Caucasian strains were explained as a product of "degeneration" from this primary and ideal type.

The typologies or racial classifications of humans that appeared before modern anthropology and that were inherited by the discipline were purportedly based on real, empirical physical differences. Accordingly, much of nineteenth- (and even early twentieth-) century science was directed toward documenting these differences. One of the main methods of what has been called "scientific racism" was *anthropometry*, literally "man-measure." Anthropometry was and is a practice of measuring the bodies of human beings for the purpose of describing individual and collective physical characteristics—and, more importantly for many of its practitioners, of discovering the biological basis for supposed psychological differences between the races in terms of intelligence, temperament, morality, and so forth.

Many physical features were measured and cataloged, but of central importance were the ones that presumably indicated "primitiveness" or mental inferiority. For example, "facial angle" reflected the protrusion of the lower face and jaw on the assumption that more "primitive" races had more protruding faces (like dogs or monkeys), while higher races enjoyed flatter faces. Longer arms and legs also signaled primitiveness. No doubt the most important measurements were brain volume and cephalic index, the latter a ratio of the width and depth of the head. Surely, these scientists reckoned, larger brains with a higher index indicated greater intelligence and rationality. Physical traits, especially those of the head and face, were even seen as evidence of more complex and specific personality or psychological failings, such as immorality, criminality, or insanity. An entire parallel science of eugenics developed beside scientific racism, with the project to improve the intelligence and morality of the species (Figure 1.1).

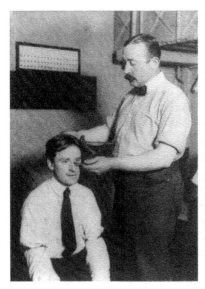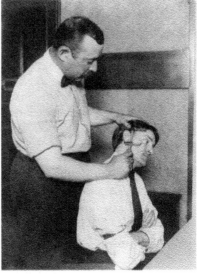

Figure 1.1 Nineteenth-century anthropometry measured human physical traits to establish differences between types (especially races) of humans; *Library of Congress.*

BOX 1.3 CESARE LOMBROSO: ANTHROPOLOGICAL CRIMINOLOGY

Cesare Lombroso (1835–1909), a medical doctor and criminologist, devised a theory of "anthropological criminology" (or what we might call "racial profiling" today) on the basis of physical characteristics or defects that he claimed were diagnostic of deviant personality and behavior. In his learned view, criminals were throwbacks to a more primitive kind of humanity, a phenomenon that he termed "criminal atavism." Certain bodily traits were common to criminals, "primitive" humans, and prehistoric mankind, including long arms, sloping foreheads, misshapen faces and heads, and protruding faces. Such physical deformities were the visible evidence of personality or character deformities, like stupidity, immorality, impulsiveness, egotism, and cruelty. Ideally then, a criminal or other social inferior could be detected by sight and perhaps even at birth.

It should not be difficult to see that this brand of physiological psychology was more (and less) than science but also what Eric Wolf (1994) pinpointed and critiqued as a "bio-moral" project, that is, a system to *justify* social inequalities—like slavery or colonial conquest—on the basis of putative biological and psychological differences and inadequacies. Social policies followed suit, from prohibiting interracial marriage to the selective sterilization of "inferior types" to rejections of attempts to educate or uplift disadvantaged races since apparently they were congenitally incapable of higher intellectual and moral functioning.

One example of this reasoning can be found in the work of Stanley Porteus (1883–1972), an Australian psychologist and inventor of the Porteus Maze Test of intelligence. He conducted intelligence and personality tests on "delinquent" and "feeble-minded" boys in 1915, determining that most of the boys were several years behind in their mental and moral development. He then applied his research to remote Australian Aboriginals, which he reported in a series of papers and in his 1931 book *The Psychology of a Primitive People.* Although he accepted that many of the aspects of traditional Aboriginal culture were clever adaptations to a harsh natural environment, he concluded that traditional life had left a deleterious brand on the Aboriginal mind. Mental development in Aboriginal children was normal, even rapid, early in life but was then followed by "a marked slowing-down mental development…characteristic of the Australian race" (1933: 32). Further, they suffered from poor rote memory from listening and a lack of abstract intelligence matched only "by the abilities of the feeble-minded of our race" (34), not to mention "the common racial characteristics of indolence, shiftlessness, and lack of foresight" (1917: 38). Consequently, he predicted "the improbability of marked advancement in civilization of the Australian race" (1933: 34) since it is "very difficult indeed to educate them beyond about the fourth grade" (1917: 38).

Folk psychology and the question of the primitive mind

Although modern-day psychology is usually associated with the individual and internal/mental processes, while anthropology is assumed to concentrate on collective and public/social ones, we have seen already that this division is by no means absolute today nor was it true of the disciplines in their formative years. Not only were and are anthropologists interested in psychological questions, but psychologists were and are interested in cultural ones.

As far back as the late 1700s, historian Johann Herder (1744–1803) had suggested that each *Volk* (German for folk, people, or nation) had its own unique qualities, genius, or even soul or spirit. Herder used such phrases as *Nationalgeist* (national spirit), *Seele des Volks* (soul of the people), *Geist der Nation* (spirit of the nation), and *Geist des Volks* (spirits of the people) to capture this collective peculiarity which was, to him, inexpressible and invaluable. The spirit of a people was to be found in its art, its literature, its philosophy, its folklore, etc., depending on the particular society. This emphasis on, even obsession with, a nation's identity and cultural patrimony led directly to an interest in national or group beliefs, behaviors, and accomplishments, that is, to "culture" in the anthropological sense. This, in turn, led to an attempt to identify the group/collective processes which gave rise to national cultures, that is, a *Völkerpsychologie*, a "folk psychology" or "psychology of a people," in contrast to an "individual psychology" (Diriwachter 2004: 87–8):

> That is, the study of psychology was also to include the products of collective mental processes of peoples identified as a unified body (e.g. the Germans), distinctly separate from others (e.g. the French). Individual psychology was limited to the focus of the capabilities of one person.
>
> (88–9)

One of the great early psychologists became one of the great proponents of *Völkerpsychologie*: namely, Wilhelm Wundt, mentioned earlier. In an 1888 article, he defended research into national psychology:

> Just like it's the objective of psychology to describe the actuality of individual consciousness, thereby putting its elements and developmental stages in an explicatory relationship, so too is there a need to make as the object of psychological investigation the analogous genetical and causal investigations of those actualities which pertain to the products of higher developmental relationships of human society, namely the folk-communities (*Völkergemeinschaft*).
>
> (quoted 96)

However, in the case of *Völkerpsychologie*, standard (especially experimental) psychological methods would not suffice; rather, it was necessary to employ a comparative method, to do "historical comparisons," to examine the products of these collectivities and collective minds. For Wundt, then, *Völkerpsychologie* was not a strictly psychological enterprise but "in essence a social-developmental discipline: social because it predominantly moves within societal dimensions; and developmental because it also needs to examine the different steps of mental development in humans (true psychogenesis), from underdeveloped to higher cultures" (97). He even attempted to construct an outline of this historical-developmental process from "primitive man" to "the totemic era" to "the ages of heroes and gods" to "the development of humanity":

> Each stage has its own unique characteristics that mark the achievements of the group under examination. For example, while primitive man is said to be closest to nature, comparable to wild animals, the man of the totemic era is already distinguished by a realization of the possession of a soul. In fact, the totem itself is the manifestation of a

soul, either the soul of an ancestor or the soul of a protective being, often in the shape of an animal.

(98)

In the late 1800s and early 1900s, many scholars went beyond the notion of unique "national minds" to ponder whether all humans of all nationalities, races, and societies shared the same thought processes and mental abilities. Did "primitive peoples," in a word, think like "modern" (read: "Western") people, or did they have a decisively different (and inferior) mind? What were Western travelers and intellectuals to make of the fact that native peoples around the world seemed to believe and do things that were, to "civilized" eyes, strange, irrational, and often demonstrably false?

On one side of the debate were those who defended the *psychic unity of humankind*, that is, the position that humans everywhere had similar psychology, even if their minds produced diverging or contradictory results. One of the earliest to stake this claim was Adolf Bastian (1826–1905). After traveling around the world and spending four years in Southeast Asia in the 1850s and 1860s, he concluded that the innate and universal processes of mind generated "elementary ideas" or *Elementarkgedanken* (what Carl G. Jung, a follower of Freud, might later call "archetypes") that were found in all places and times. However, because of local historical and environmental/geographical forces, these universal ideas might be expressed differently in different populations as "ethnic" or "folk" ideas or *Völkergedanken*. For Bastian, as for Herder and Wundt, a group's folk ideas could be discovered in its folklore, art, mythology, and so on, but underneath this variation were recurring themes. One crucial implication from this perspective was the importance of conducting "investigations of the most isolated and simple societies," that is, doing what anthropologists would come to endorse as fieldwork and ethnography. Bastian was committed to the view that the ideas of "primitive" or "natural" humans "grow according to the same laws" as those of Westerners but that their "growth and decline are easier to observe, since we are looking at a limited field of observation which could be compared to an experiment in laboratory" (quoted in Penny 2002: 23).

Around the same time, an even more seminal figure was advancing a similar conclusion. In his aforementioned 1871 *Primitive Culture*, E. B. Tylor began by enunciating that "the condition of culture among various societies of mankind…is a subject apt for the study of laws of human thought and action" (1958: 1). Surveying such disparate topics as emotion, language (including proverbs, riddles, and nursery rhymes), counting, and religion (myth, ritual, and, most famously, his concept of "animism"), he argued for the continuity of human thought, even if different groups were at different levels of development of their knowledge and understanding. For instance, Tylor reasoned that "the language of civilized men is but the language of savages, more or less improved in structure, a good deal extended in vocabulary, made more precise in the dictionary definition of words"; however, "development of language between its savage and cultured stages has been made in its details, scarcely in its principle" (445–6). Religion too, from the most rudimentary myths and ceremonies to the glories of European Christianity, revealed consistent thought processes operating below the surface. Further, refuting the scientific racism of his day, Tylor saw no reason to introduce race into the analysis of mind and action: everywhere he looked, he encountered "similarity and consistency" of "character and habit" (6), making it "both possible and desirable to eliminate considerations of hereditary varieties or races of man, and to treat mankind as homogeneous in nature, though placed in different grades of civilization" (7).

BOX 1.4 E. B. TYLOR: PSYCHOLOGICAL ORIGIN OF RELIGION

For Tylor, religion itself had a psychological origin. The most basic form or expression of religion in his view was belief in spiritual beings, and this idea arose as a reaction to certain mental experiences, such as dreams, visions, hallucinations, and trance or out-of-body experiences. Prehistoric individuals naturally speculated that the source of these uncanny occurrences, Tylor reasoned, was that some part of a person was separate from—even detachable from—their body, so that dreams, visions, etc. were authentic experiences by this immaterial part, perhaps of other people's immaterial parts (see Chapter 8). This disembodied component of a human being (and maybe some or all other beings) is "spirit," the first religious idea and the foundation of all subsequent religious ideas.

One other early supporter of the psychic unity position was James George Frazer (1854–1941), a student of comparative mythology and the author of *The Golden Bough*. Frazer opined that the religious beliefs and stories of all societies demonstrated common motifs (including half-human, half-divine beings and dying gods) and that those motifs were often related to cultural practices, like agriculture, or to natural phenomena, like the solstices. More, he judged that religion and magic were not so irrational after all but evinced rational if erroneous thinking; primitive (and religious) people use the same processes of thought, but they merely start from false premises and thus reach false conclusions. Later psychological anthropologist Richard Shweder put it this way: "All people are applied scientists. 'Primitives' are just not very good at it. That, in a nutshell, is Tylor's and Frazer's view of the relationship between the 'primitive' mind and the 'modern' mind" (1980: 70).

BOX 1.5 HADDON AND CORT: EARLY STUDY OF "PRIMITIVE" COGNITION AND PERCEPTION

One of the assumptions, if not stereotypes, of "primitive" cognition was that native peoples, although deficient in logic, were advanced in sensory perception. It was frequently claimed that indigenous people (sadly, probably like animals) possessed highly developed senses of sight, hearing, and smell. Indeed, one of the first formal ethnographic expeditions had the express psychological mission of testing "primitive" perception. The Torres Straits Expedition of 1898 was led by Alfred Cort (A. C.) Haddon, a trained biologist and zoologist, to study the inhabitants of the islands between Australia and Indonesia. He recruited three medical doctors plus an experimental psychologist and neurologist, William Halse Rivers (W. H. R.) Rivers (1864–1922). The team collected all sorts of data during their comparatively brief sojourn in the islands, but Rivers, who had investigated color vision, optical illusions, and other aspects of perception in his psychology lab at Cambridge, seized the occasion to study the natives in regard to visual acuity, color vision, color blindness, after-images, contrast, visual illusions, auditory acuity, rhythm, smell and taste, tactile acuity, weight discrimination, reaction times to visual and auditory stimuli, estimates of time intervals, memory, muscular power, motor accuracy, and a number of similar topics.

(Berry et al. 2002: 197)

He disproved that Torres Strait Islanders had extraordinary vision, but he did notice one tantalizing difference in visual perception. Rivers administered the Müller-Lyer illusion (see the following) to natives of Murray Island (and later to Todas of India) and found that they were less susceptible to the illusion than Westerners, that is, they judged the length of lines more accurately. (See Chapter 3 for continuations of perception experiments.) Years later, although Rivers turned increasingly to anthropology and ethnographic fieldwork, he affirmed that "the ultimate aim of all studies of mankind...is to reach explanation in terms of psychology...by which the conduct of man, both individual and collective, is determined...by the social structure of which every person...finds himself a member" (1924b: 1). Indeed, today, Rivers is more celebrated in the annals of cross-cultural psychology than in anthropology.

The Müller-Lyer illusion: Westerners tend to misjudge the length of lines depending on the direction of the arrows on the lines (Figure 1.2).

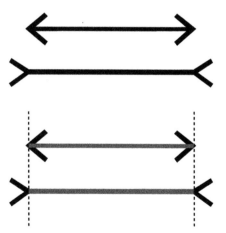

Figure 1.2 The Müller-Lyer illusion.

On the opposing side of the debate over diversity in human thought processes were the advocates of a distinct (if not defective) "primitive mentality," of which Lucien Lévy-Bruhl (1857–1939) is the arch-representative. In his 1910 *Les functions mentales dans les societes inferieures* (literally, "Mental Functions in Lower/Inferior Societies" but published in English under the inoffensive title *How Natives Think*), Lévy-Bruhl laid out an elaborate case for the incommensurability of the primitive and the modern mind.

Contrary to Bastian, Tylor, Frazer, and Rivers, Lévy-Bruhl bluntly asserted that "primitives perceive nothing in the same way as we do.... Primitives see with eyes like ours, but they do not perceive with the same minds" (1966: 30–1). He also rejected the Frazerian claim that natives were just bad scientists: myth and magic, for instance, "do not appear to originate in the desire for a rational explanation; they are the primitives' response to collective needs and sentiments which are profound and mighty and of compulsive force" (14–15). So, primitives were slaves to traditional and collective thoughts and feelings, unlike Western freethinkers. But more, those traditional and collective "representations" (as he called them, probably following Durkheim's use of the term) had certain deep flaws:

> The collective representations of primitives, therefore, differ very profoundly from our ideas or concepts, nor are they their equivalent either. On the one hand...they have not their logical character. On the other hand, not being genuine representations, in the strict sense of the term, they express, or rather imply, not only that the primitive actually has an image of the object in his mind, and thinks it real, but also that he has some hope or fear connected with it, that some definite influence emanates from it, or is exercised upon it.... I should say that this mental activity was a *mystic* one.
>
> (24–5)

This takes us to the essence of Lévy-Bruhl's characterization of "primitive mentality." Reality for the primitive mind, he posited,

> is itself mystical. Not a single being or object or natural phenomenon in their collective representations is what it appears to be to our minds. Almost everything that we perceive therein either escapes their attention or is a matter of indifference to them. On the other hand, they see many things there of which we are unconscious.
>
> (25)

—by which he meant, indubitably, that they do not exist. Rocks, trees, and other natural objects "readily assume a sacred character in virtue of their supposed mystic power" (27), which the rational mind denies. In a word, the primitive mind was, he said explicitly, a *prelogical* mind, one that did not make all the distinctions that a logical mind can and must make. The prelogical, primitive mind, to start, is incapable of cause-and-effect thinking, sometimes failing to recognize the causal relationship between events and sometimes assuming a noncausal, magical relationship. It cannot think abstractly, and it is indifferent to contradiction. Most profoundly and problematically, it functions according to a principle that he called the "law of participation." At bottom, this means that the primitive mentality does not sufficiently distinguish between self and not-self, between one object and another object, or even between different kinds of objects or phenomena. A natural object like a tree, or a cultural object like an Australian Aboriginal *tjurunga* (a sacred board or stone, with or without incised markings), may be part of a human person—or a person in its own right. Or a physical object may have or be a spirit at the same time; as logicians say, the law of participation violates the "law of exclusion" that X cannot be not-X at the same time. Finally, the law of participation grants a kind of transmission or "communication of qualities (through transference, contact, projection, contamination, defilement, possession, in short, through a number of varied operations) which, either instantaneously or in the course of time, bring a person or a thing into participation with a given faculty" (83). Frazer had noted something similar in what he dubbed "sympathetic" and "contagious" magic: in the former case, resemblance (say, between a voodoo doll and an intended human victim) could cause an effective connection, and in the latter case, contact between two objects (say, a person and a bit of their hair or fingernail) could have the same effect. But whereas Frazer explained this as clever but faulty reasoning, Lévy-Bruhl interpreted it as a fundamental inability to comprehend how the world works.

Later in life, Lévy-Bruhl retracted his most extreme assertions about primitive mentality, acknowledging, among other things, that modern Western individuals sometimes make associations based on resemblance or contagion (e.g. talking to photographs or holding onto possessions of a departed loved one) and accepting the dual quality of certain objects (e.g. that a wafer could be a wafer and the body of Christ simultaneously). But such analysis continued on despite his retraction, as in the work of renowned psychologist Lev Vygotsky. In a collection of essays ominously titled *Ape, Primitive, Man, and Child* (Luria and Vygotsky 1992), first published in 1930, he reiterated that "primitives" suffered from lack of abstraction and metaphor in their language and thought. For that reason, they were burdened with concreteness and detail, which prevented them from reaching higher levels of literacy, numeracy, and logic. And Vygotsky made these accusations with abundant references to Lévy-Bruhl's work.

Franz Boas, psychological anthropologist

"One of the chief aims of anthropology is the study of the mind of man under the varying conditions of race and environment" (1901: 1), wrote Franz Boas in the opening sentence of his article "The Mind of Primitive Man." Widely regarded as the father of American cultural anthropology, Boas studied psychology (or "psychophysics") and geography before becoming a protégé of Bastian and turning to anthropology in the waning years of the nineteenth century. He was also a tireless critic of racial explanations of cultural and psychological differences, especially in three publications between 1901 and 1911—the essay cited earlier, a book by the same title, and an article conspicuously called "Psychological Problems in Anthropology" (Boas 1910).

In the earliest of these writings, Boas weighed the two competing options—that possibly "the minds of different races show differences in organization; that is to say, the laws of mental activity may not be the same for all minds" or that

> the organization of mind is practically identical among all races of man; that mental activity follows the same laws everywhere, but that its manifestations depend upon the character of individual experience that is subjected to the action of these laws
>
> (1901: 2)

before coming down solidly on the experiential side. Forcefully, he declared that "there can be no doubt that in the main the mental characteristics of man are the same all over the world" (3). Granting that there might be differences in brain size between the races, he still maintained repeatedly in the article that the "functions of the human mind are common to the whole of humanity" (5), even if "the degree of development of these functions may differ somewhat among different types of man" (6). But where there are differences between "primitive" minds and "civilized" ones, his position was firmly that any dissimilarity "in the mode of thought of primitive man and of civilized man seems to consist largely in the difference of *character of the tradition material with which the new perception associates itself*" (7, emphasis added). In other words, it is *culture*, the shared and transmitted *content* of thought—or, in simple terms, experience—rather than the underlying *processes* of thought that separate various populations of humans. For a cautious anthropologist,

> the development of *culture* must not be confounded with the development of *mind*. Culture is an expression of the achievements of the mind, and shows the cumulative effects of the activities of many minds. But it is not an expression of the organization of the minds constituting the community, which may in no way differ from the minds of a community occupying a much more advanced stage of culture.
>
> (11, emphasis in original)

Boas reiterated these points in his 1910 essay, stipulating first that anthropology "deals with the biological and mental manifestations of human life as they appear in different races and in different societies" (1910: 371). The three questions of the science, consequently, concerned the origin of "human types" (the eventual province of physical or biological anthropology), the historical development of culture (the realm of cultural anthropology), and "the psychological laws which control the mind of man everywhere, and that may differ in various racial and social groups" (371). Indeed, he charged what he called "anthropological psychology" with the duty "of looking for the common psychological features, not in the outward similarities of ethnic phenomena, but in the similarity of psychological processes so far as these can be observed or inferred" (375–6). He did not discount all deviations between "primitive" and "civilized" mentality: for instance, he allowed that ideas and concepts are separated or combined in a "peculiar manner" in the mind of "primitives" (376) and that for them, concepts and categories "have never risen into consciousness, and that consequently their origin must be sought not in rational, but in entirely unconscious processes of the mind" (377)—a foreshadowing of the influence of Freud in anthropology (see the following and later chapters). Ultimately, Boas pronounced, the "primary object of these researches would be the determination of the fundamental categories under which phenomena are classified by man in various stages of culture" (377).

Boas's position is most fully articulated in his 1911 book *The Mind of Primitive Man*, a significant portion of which is dedicated to the speciousness of race. Recognizing that "in many quarters the popular view still prevails that all psychological tests reveal an organically determined mentality," or more specifically, "a biological oriented psychology" (1938: 30) and most odiously, a race-based psychology, he set about to dismantle this claim completely. "Ethnological material," he said, "does not favor the view that different human types have distinct personalities," refuting the contention that "the habits of life and cultural activities are to any considerable extent determined by racial descent" (129). Simply put,

> personality so far as it is possible to speak of the personality of a culture will *depend upon outer conditions that sway the fate of the people*, upon its history, upon powerful individuals that arise from time to time, upon foreign influences.
>
> (129–30, emphasis added)

Boas went so far as to address particular planks in the "primitive mentality" platform (mentioning Lévy-Bruhl by name), such as lack of impulse control, inability to concentrate, and prelogical thought. On the subject of impulse control, Boas insisted that taboos, gender segregation, and other cultural restrictions were proof of curbs on impulsiveness, while allegedly weak concentration could be dismissed as boredom with the artificial situations and incessant questions posed by fieldworkers. As for the prelogical quality of "primitive" thought, Boas wrote,

> This conclusion is reached not from a study of individual behavior, but from the traditional beliefs and customs of primitive people. It is believed to explain the identification of man and animal, the principles of magic and the beliefs in the efficacy of ceremonies. It would seem that if we disregard the thinking of the individual in our society and pay attention only to current beliefs that *we should reach the conclusion that the same attitudes prevail among ourselves that are characteristic of primitive man.*
>
> (135, emphasis added)

This did not mean that no psychological or cognitive differences between human groups exist at all but that such differences as we can verify empirically are to be attributed to "individuals and family lines" (138) and, in the final analysis, to experiential (including cultural) influences and not to the mind or brain.

Sigmund Freud, anthropological psychologist

> It is largely due to Sigmund Freud that we understand the importance of these forgotten incidents which remain a living force throughout life the more potent, the more thoroughly they are forgotten. Owing to their lasting influences many of the habits of thought and traits of personality which we are all too ready to interpret as due to heredity are acquired under the influence of the environment in which the child spends the first few years of its life. All observations on the force of habit and the intensity of resistance to changes of habit are in favor of this theory.
>
> (Boas 1938: 143)

So stated Boas in 1911, when Freudian theory was still relatively new and, frankly, unfinished. Sigmund Freud (1856–1939) had published his first major book, *The Interpretation of Dreams*, only in 1900, and most of his major theoretical statements were yet to come. Nevertheless, his impact was clearly already felt in anthropology, and this impact would persist for decades—for many anthropologists and other social scientists, to this very day.

Freud's thinking unfolded gradually over the course of more than four decades, so it is difficult if not incorrect to assert what *the* psychoanalytic theory was. He began his career, like many other psychologists in the late 1880s, in neurology and medicine, doing experimental/surgical, clinical, and academic work. In 1885, he apprenticed under Charcot in France (see earlier), where Freud learned of the therapeutic value of hypnosis. He incorporated the technique into his treatment of patients in Vienna, developing what one of his patients called a "talking cure," during which they would discuss their symptoms and feelings while hypnotized. Soon abandoning hypnosis in favor of what he named "free association" or speaking freely about whatever was on their minds, he came to the determination that their psychological complaints seemed to be tied to thoughts of which they were unconscious or to experiences that they had actively forgotten (referred to as "repression").

By the first years of the twentieth century, Freud had arrived at what he called psychoanalysis, which he regarded as effective for treating neurosis and especially "hysteria," which could often be explained and cured as a translation of psychological or emotional trauma into physical symptoms like paralysis or blindness. The unknown, forgotten, or repressed mental content could also express itself in dreams (and later, he found, in jokes, slips of the tongue [hence, "Freudian slips"], and all the little and innocent behaviors that he called in a 1901 book "the psychopathology of everyday life"), leading to his landmark 1900 study of dreams.

It was in *The Interpretation of Dreams* that many of Freud's bedrock concepts were enunciated. A preliminary structure of the mind was proposed, featuring a conscious, preconscious, and unconscious component. He also identified two distinct mental processes operating in all people, primitive and civilized alike. The first was the *primary process*, functioning on the basis of wish fulfillment, pleasure-seeking and pain-avoidance, and "magical thinking," that is, the mind believing that merely thinking or wishing makes it so. The primary process is the principle of the unconscious and therefore of children (and, he and others would go on to say, of "primitives" and neurotics). The *secondary process*, a more mature way of thinking, works on what Freud would eventually call the *reality principle*, understanding cause and effect, and adapting itself to the (sometimes painful) realities of life. Finally, as he had opined in writings for several years, most overtly his 1898 "Sexuality in the Aetiology of Neuroses," at the foundation of much psychopathology, if not of most ordinary life, was sexuality— including childhood sexuality, a rather shocking declaration at the time.

Hence, Freud summarized his analysis of dreams by announcing that the "interpretation of dreams is the royal road to a knowledge of the unconscious activities of mind" (1965: 647). This was about all that was known of Freudian theory at the time of Boas's essays and book on mind. It would not be until 1915 that Freud would offer his further thoughts on instincts; he would only transcend his ideas about the pleasure principle, suggesting a "death" or disintegration principle, in 1920, and his now-familiar mental structure of ego, id, and superego would not be formulated until 1923. Before those books, though, Freud would show another dimension of his psychological curiosity and of the potential of psychoanalysis by applying his models to cultural phenomena, such as art, religion, and the very origins of society.

Specifically, his *Totem and Taboo*, subtitled "Some Resemblances/Points of Agreement between the Mental Lives of Savages and Neurotics" and released in 1913, would reverberate through anthropology and the social sciences. On the first page of that epochal book, Freud surmised that in contemporary "primitive" or "savage" peoples, we see "a well-preserved picture of an early stage of our own development," and if so,

> a comparison between the psychology of primitive peoples, as it is taught by social anthropology, and the psychology of neurotics, as it has been revealed by psycho-analysis, will be bound to show numerous points of agreement and will throw new light upon familiar facts in both sciences.
>
> (2001: 1–2)

For this purpose, as his title indicates, he chose two characteristic notions from "primitive" societies—totems and taboos—and naturally and necessarily, he borrowed data from anthropologists, such as James Frazer's 1910 *Totemism and Exogamy*; Andrew Lang's 1905 *The Secret of the Totem*; and, most notably, Baldwin Spencer and F. J. Gillen's 1899 *The Native Tribes of Central Australia*, the latter of which would also be crucial for Durkheim's contemporaneous sociological theory of religion.

Of all primitive taboos, the one most interesting to Freud was the incest taboo, which he seized upon to imagine the very origin of human society itself. Evaluating and rejecting sociological and competing psychological theories for the existence of totemism (that is, the association of individuals and groups with a particular plant and animal species, which is frequently subjected then to taboos against killing or eating that species), Freud advanced a view based on the rule of exogamy (i.e. marrying outside one's own family or group), which is nothing more than an elaboration of the incest taboo. But why there should be such a deep and universal "horror of incest" (2001: 144) remained to be explained. The only possible answer for Freud was something equally if not more deep and universal, namely, the Oedipus complex. Named after a character in ancient Greek literature, Freud's Oepidus complex maintains that every male child secretly desires his mother and would if he could kill and replace his father; at the same time, the boy fears that his father will kill or at least castrate him (the equally infamous "castration anxiety").

Freud reasoned that the Oedipus complex is not only at the root of individual (male) psychology but at the root of human sociality itself. By a circuitous route, he concluded that the totem animal is a substitute for a prehistoric father and that all of society stems from an original Oedipal drama. In the beginning, before there was orderly society,

> there is a violent and jealous father who keeps all the females for himself and drives away his sons as they grow up…. One day the brothers who had been driven out came together, killed and devoured their father and so made an end of the patriarchal horde. United, they had the courage to do and succeeded in doing what would have been impossible for them individually. (Some cultural advance, perhaps command over some new weapon, had given them a sense of superior strength.) Cannibal savages as they were, it goes without saying that they devoured their victim as well as killing him. The violent primal father had doubtless been the feared and envied model of each one of the company of brothers: and in the act of devouring him they accomplished their identification with him, and each one of them acquired a portion of his strength. The totem meal, which is perhaps mankind's earliest festival, would thus be a repetition and a commemoration of this memorable and criminal deed, which was the beginning of so many things—of social organization, of moral restrictions and of religion.
>
> (164–5)

After the great crime that lies at the foundation of all society, the men vowed never to kill a father again, sacrificing in his place the symbolic totem animal. Further, and to the point of Freud's opening question, they agreed not to hoard their daughters and sisters among themselves but to marry them out to other families in exchange for wives from those families—establishing the first incest taboo, exogamy, marriage exchanges, and hence regulated society.

Anthropologists would exploit psychoanalytic thinking extensively, becoming more, not less, reliant on it over the next several decades. Many anthropologists applied psychoanalysis in their research, and some actually became trained psychoanalysts; at the same time, some psychoanalysts conducted anthropological fieldwork of their own, like Géza Róheim and his 1925 *Australian Totemism: A Psycho-analytic Study in Anthropology*. In sum, we can say that among the specific—and largely positive—effects of Freudian theory on the discipline are:

- attention to the ways in which social experience shapes individual character, that is, a fundamentally developmental or constructionist perspective on personality
- focus on childhood, child-rearing practices, and family relations
- awareness of the central importance of sexuality specifically and embodied experience in general

- search for clues to personality and mind in cultural evidence, such as dream content, art, and myths
- cross-cultural testing, in the field, of supposedly universal psychological phenomena, including but not limited to the Oedipus complex.

BOX 1.6 BRONISLAW MALINOWSKI: TESTING FREUD IN THE FIELD

Bronislaw Malinowski (1884–1942) is generally seen as the equivalent of Boas in British social anthropology and not as a central figure in psychological anthropology. However, more so than the structural functionalists who succeeded him (like Radcliffe-Brown, mentioned earlier), he did emphasize the role of the individual in his own brand of functionalist theory. Generally, he believed that culture functioned to fill the needs of individual members of society, which was true even or especially for religion. In analyzing the religion of the Trobriand Islanders, he noticed that when navigating the ocean out of view of shore, the natives tended to indulge in religious behavior, but when sailing near land, they did not. He reckoned that open-water travel was much more dangerous, and therefore, religion served the human psychological need for safety and a sense of control over circumstances. Emphasing not safety but control, Malinowski explored the subject of religion and magic in relation to gardening in his major ethnographic study of Trobriand culture, his 1922 *Argonauts of the Western Pacific*, and in his 1935 *Coral Gardens and Their Magic*, supporting Tylor and Frazer's view that natives were practical-minded and rational, even when they engaged in "irrational" acts like magic. Trobriand gardening, indeed all of Trobriand life, was shot through with magical incantations and rituals, but Malinowski fully appreciated that magic alone, without realistic knowledge and practice of planting, weeding, and sowing, would leave people starving to death. (We might also consider this a case of Freud's primary process [magic] coexisting with secondary process [rational action in response to reality].) Malinowski wrote, for instance, that along with garden magic,

> soil, rain, proper work, are given their full due. None the less, no one would dream of making a garden without the full magical performance being done over it. Garden magic is thought to make just this difference, which a man hopes for from 'chance,' or 'good luck'.... So we see that, in all these cases, magical influence runs parallel to and independently of the effects of human work and natural conditions. It produces these differences and those unexpected results, which cannot be explained by any of the other factors.
>
> (1984: 421)

More importantly for present purposes, Malinowski was one of the first, if not the first, to engage Freud and *to test Freudian theory in the field*. In 1929, he produced a study of Trobriand sexuality, clearly beholden to Freud's accent on sex in the formation of culture and character; in the preface to the book, sex researcher Havelock Ellis wrote,

> the genius of Freud...has given an impetus to the study of the sexual impulse and to its possible manifestations even in the myths and customs of savages. To these developments Dr. Malinowski is fully alive. He was even prepared at one time

to be much more nearly a Freudian than we can now describe him. Today he is neither Freudian nor anti-Freudian; he recognizes the fertilizing value of Freud's ideas, and he is prepared to utilize them whenever they seem helpful in elucidating the phenomena under investigation.

(1929: xi)

But he was also prepared to submit Freud's ideas to the court of ethnographic fact and to criticize or reject them if necessary.

Hence, Malinowski's 1927 *Sex and Repression in Savage Society*. Granting that psychoanalysis "has given to the study of mental processes a concrete turn," one that "had led us to concentrate on child psychology and the history of the individual" as well as "the unofficial and unacknowledged sides of human life" (1927: viii), he nevertheless revealed that he found himself "less and less inclined to accept in a wholesale manner the conclusions of Freud" (ix). The case in point was his core concept of the Oedipus complex, which for the psychologist was universal and inevitable. Malinowski discovered a defect in Freud's thinking on the matter: rather than universal—but oddly consistent with broader psychoanalytic theory—the conventional Oedipus complex might be conceived as a particular intersection of psychological processes and socially determined childhood experience. First, Malinowski asserted that psychoanalysis

is essentially a theory of the influence of family life on the human mind. We are shown how the passions, stresses and conflicts of the child in relation to its father, mother, brother and sister result in the formation of certain permanent mental attitudes or sentiments towards them, sentiments which, partly living in memory, partly embedded in the unconscious, influence the later life of the individual in his relations to society.

(2)

This is a fair assessment of the psychoanalytic project. But when we introduce the anthropological fact "that *the family* is not the same in all human societies" (3), it suddenly becomes possible that the standard Oedipus complex is *one possible psychosocial outcome but not the necessary or only one*. Malinowski proceeded to demonstrate this point by comparing Trobriand family and society to Western family and society. The crucial difference is matrilineal kinship or "mother-right" in the Trobriands. In matrilineal kinship systems, the child belongs to the mother's kin group; the father is a less central male figure in the child's life, that role being played by the mother's brother. In places like the Trobriand Islands, the father "is thus a beloved, benevolent friend, but not a recognized kinsman of the children. He is a stranger, having authority through his personal relations to the child, but not through his sociological position in the lineage" (10). In short, the father is not the threatening, frightening character that he is in patrilineal and patriarchal societies. Chronicling the psychosexual development of the Trobriand child, in the context of a freer sexual culture where there is "nothing suppressed, nothing negative, no frustrated desire forms a part of" feelings toward parents (75), it becomes incumbent "not to assume the universal existence of the Oedipus complex, but in studying every type of civilization *to establish the special complex which pertains to it*" (82, emphasis added). In other words—and this is the very hallmark of anthropology—what Freud described may not be a universal psychological force but *a culturally specific one*, and anthropologists may uncover other different culturally specific complexes when (universal) psychology confronts (particularistic) culture.

Interestingly—and frustratingly to some anthropologists—Malinowski did not thereby jettison Freudian theory. Of the psychohistorical drama of the first father-murder and the invention of the incest taboo, Malinowski insisted that it "has in itself nothing objectionable to the anthropologist" (159), still placing great value on psychoanalytic ideas about sexuality, instincts, and the unconscious. All the same, he offered his own discussion of how presumably innate and universal psychological drives and instincts are groomed by culture in specific ways. In the final analysis, if there are universal instincts or emotions, they "can be trained, adjusted, and organized into complex and plastic systems" (236), yielding variations of personality and mentality depending on social experience.

Summary: achievements and shortcomings

Psychology and anthropology were born at virtually the same moment in history. They share many of the same ancestors, and as siblings, they regularly collaborated and continue to collaborate. In the first generations of psychological anthropology (roughly mid-1800s to approximately 1927), the discipline had some notable accomplishments:

- It recognized a vital interconnection between society/culture and personality/mind.
- It began and largely completed the detachment of psychological questions from race, bitterly critiquing assumptions about racial mental inequalities.
- It established without much doubt the psychic unity of humanity.
- It commenced the project of collecting quantitative cross-cultural data on cognition and perception.
- It proved that, whatever aspects of psychology may be innate and universal, individual and group character is shaped by social experience (in the family and beyond) and cultural content (specific beliefs, values, institutions, etc. of societies).

This early version of psychological anthropology still suffered from a number of limitations, including:

- It lacked a sophisticated theory of personality and learning.
- It was not yet quantitative; in fact, little research was yet conducted specifically on early-life experiences and personality qualities for the purposes of demonstrating any link between the two.
- It was too preoccupied with racial questions; it also still talked in terms of "primitive" or "savage" personality or mind.
- It was too beholden to one psychological model (Freudian psychoanalysis).

Chapter 2

The early culture-and-personality school

Key figures:
Edward Sapir (1884–1939)
Ruth Benedict (1887–1948)
Abram Kardiner (1891–1981)
Ralph Linton (1893–1953)
Margaret Mead (1901–78)
Cora Du Bois (1903–91)

Key texts:
Coming of Age in Samoa (1928)
Patterns of Culture (1934)
Sex and Temperament in Three Primitive Societies (1935)
The Individual and His Society (1939)
The People of Alor: A Social-Psychological Study of an East Indian Island (1944)
The Psychological Frontiers of Society (1945)
The Cultural Background of Personality (1945)

"The year 1927 may be taken as the beginning of the codification of the culture and personality position in anthropology," opined Francis Hsu (1972b: 366), based on the publication of an essay by Edward Sapir titled "The Unconscious Patterning of Behavior in Society" and drafted for a symposium on the unconscious (Child 1927). As Hsu stated,

> Sapir's paper, probably the first major piece of theoretical writing in the culture and personality tradition, set, or at least prefigured, the frame of reference of later anthropological work in this area. This frame of reference was predominantly psychological rather than biological: it implied that the fundamental, and often unconscious, organizations of individual behavior which are conventionally labeled "personality" are molded, not by physical constitution, but by a combination of cultural milieu and individual experience.
>
> (Hsu 1972b: 366)

This approach to anthropological investigations of psychology or mind shows the clear mark of Boas, and indeed many of its leading practitioners were students of his.

It will also be recalled that 1927 was the year that saw Malinowski's *Sex and Repression in Savage Society*, which we might regard as one of the last entries in the old psychological anthropology paradigm. As Hsu's characterization suggests, the late nineteenth- and early twentieth-century debate on primitive mentality versus psychic unity had been settled to the satisfaction of the younger generation in favor of unity, and the battle that Boas and others had waged against biological (that is, *racial*) explanations of mind had been won (at least in professional anthropology circles, if not yet among the general public). In fact, 1927 also gave the world Paul Radin's *Primitive Man as Philosopher*, in which yet another student of Boas argued passionately that "primitive" societies produced the same range of temperaments and abilities as "civilized" societies, including thoughtful, articulate individuals who deserved to be recognized as philosophers of their own cultures. Thus, if we seek an end-date for the first foray into psychological matters and a start-date for a new paradigm, 1927 will suffice.

For approximately a generation (from roughly 1927 to 1945), a group of scholars built a theoretical and empirical school of thought that came to be called "culture-and-personality"; the following generation expanded and elaborated this approach for another two or three decades, as we will see in the next chapter. Looking back on its work, Victor Barnouw evaluated the culture-and-personality school as

> an area of research where anthropology and psychology come together—more particularly where the fields of cultural and social anthropology relate to the psychology of personality.... Serving as a bridge between ethnology and psychology, the field of culture-and-personality is concerned with the way in which the culture of a society influences the persons who grow up with it.
>
> (1963: 3)

In fact, one of the features of the school was a collaboration between anthropologists and psychologists and psychiatrists, as we will discuss later. Finally, in his own summary and retrospective of the school, Anthony Wallace expressed that it was

> guided by two assumptions about the field of anthropology itself: first, that it is the business of anthropology to develop a scientific theory of culture; and second, that any theory which pretends to explain, or to predict, cultural phenomena must include in its formulations non-cultural phenomena. Many of these latter non-cultural phenomena can be subsumed under the general rubric of "personality."
>
> (1964: 1)

As we will discover in this chapter, culture-and-personality anthropologists posed and set out to answer some of the key questions in psychological anthropology, such as the effect of childhood and child-rearing on personality, the principle personality traits in any culture, the relationship between social institutions (not least language) and personality, and the nature of personality deviance or "abnormality."

BOX 2.1 DUDLEY KIDD: "SAVAGE" CHILDREN

Although in the opening years of the twentieth century, childhood was beginning to become a central concern in both anthropology and psychology, Dudley Kidd maintained in 1906 that he was unable to locate one English-language book on children in indigenous or "savage" societies. He offered to fill that gap with a study of "Kafir" (a particularly unfortunate term, literally Arabic for "unbeliever") children in South Africa. His book, which was less academic ethnography than colonial-era travelogue, contained chapters on birth and infancy, "the dawn of self-consciousness," "the inter-dentition period," "the development of the faculties," play, and work. Like so many observers mentioned in the previous chapter, he believed that the process of mental maturation and the achievement of self-consciousness among non-Western people "is not only sometimes retarded, but also frequently arrested at a very imperfect stage. The process seems rarely to be continued after adolescence," at which time "the sexual life overshadows nearly all of his other interests" (1906: 58). The result was a personality characterized by "aggressive self-assertion," "inordinate vanity," and "self-satisfied indolence," one "so unreflective, so full of animal spirits, so satisfied with the world and lives so utterly in the passing moment" that a Kafir adult "may be a very troublesome and unpleasant creature to manage as a laborer or houseboy: his indolence and stupidity may be very irritating at the moment" (5–6). Happily, their good nature offset some of these deficits. Yet, in a description of typical "primitive mentality," Kidd concluded that "a Kafir may not have a clear consciousness of a 'self'" (65), tends to confuse the self with objects and possessions and even with his own shadow, and actually does not feel pain.

The field study of childhood and personality: Margaret Mead

Margaret Mead (1901–78), probably the best-known of all cultural anthropologists, was a student of Franz Boas and her senior contemporary Ruth Benedict (see the following), receiving a master's degree from Columbia University in 1924. After criticizing racial intelligence testing in her 1926 paper "The Methodology of Racial Testing: Its Significance for Sociology," she produced what many regard as the founding document of culture-and-personality anthropology, analyzing childhood and child-rearing practices on the island of American Samoa. *Coming of Age in Samoa* (1928) featured a foreword by Boas in which the mentor confessed that, although much ink had been spilled on speculations about cultural practices, values, and institutions on the one hand and psychology or mentality on the other, "up to this time hardly any one has taken the pains to identify himself sufficiently with a primitive population to obtain an insight into these problems" (1928: xv). This was precisely what Mead did, and Boas praised her research for confirming "the suspicion long held by anthropologists, that much of what we ascribe to human nature is no more than a reaction to the restraints put upon us by our civilization" (xv) (see Figure 2.1).

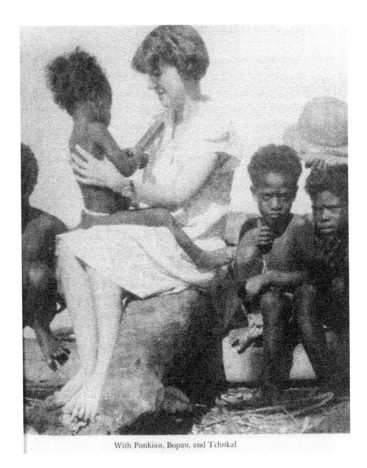

With Ponkiau, Bopau, and Tchokal

Figure 2.1 Margaret Mead, whose *Coming of Age in Samoa* helped launch the early culture-and-personality school of anthropology *Fotosearch/Getty.*

The subtitle of Mead's book, "A Psychological Study of Primitive Youth for Western Civilization," reveals her motivations for the research and the publication. Her question concerned adolescence, an age category that had only recently come to prominence as a theoretical concept (and a social problem) in G. Stanley Hall's 1904 two-volume *Adolescence: Its Psychology and Its Relation to Physiology, Anthropology, Sociology, Sex, Crime, and Education.* Hall had described adolescence as a period full of "storm and stress," distinguished by "rapid fluctuations of mood" (1904, v.1: xv) and even "semicriminality" (v.1: 404), during which "the wisdom and advice of parents and teachers is overtopped, and in ruder natures may be met by blank contradiction" (v.2: 79). But, Mead wondered, "Were these difficulties due to being adolescent or to being adolescent in America?" (1928: 5). That is, was the tempestuous and rebellious period of adolescence a universal thing or, like the Oedipus complex for Malinowski, culturally specific?

Mead reasoned that the only way to approach this problem was from the outside, as it were, examining a society very different from the United States and using it as a sort of natural laboratory. She focused on the young girls of Samoa, recording their childhood experiences in the context of Samoan social organization. For instance, she found that children did not always live in the homes of their biological parents. Also, social rank was very important, but individual achievement was not stressed. Surprisingly, the community "ignores both boys and girls from birth until they are fifteen or sixteen years of age" (74), and "in most Samoan villages a girl will be ceremonially ignored until she is married" (21). On the other hand, from a young age, girls were charged with responsibility for their younger siblings, introducing them to adult duties early in life. Unsurprisingly, "No very intense friendships are made at this age" (61)

What most caught Mead's eye was the sexual freedom available to Samoans, young and old. Although they were taught avoidance of boys in their first decade, by the age of sixteen or seventeen, the girls "have lost all of their nonchalance. They giggle, blush, bridle, run away" (87). As for premarital chastity, "Samoans regard this attitude with reverent but complete skepticism and the concept of celibacy is absolutely meaningless to them" (98). Nor was romantic love valued: "Romantic love as it occurs in our civilization, inextricably bound up with ideas of monogamy, exclusiveness, jealousy, and undeviating fidelity does not occur in Samoa" (105).

The ease with which Samoan girls navigated the transition to adulthood, and the lack of restriction and guilt in regard to their sexuality, implied for Mead that sexuality was not the traumatic source of mental maladjustments that it was for Freud's society. "Familiarity with sex, and the recognition of a need of a technique to deal with sex as an art, have produced a scheme of personal relations in which there are no neurotic pictures, no frigidity, no impotence" (151). As for her original question, Mead concluded that, with a few exceptions,

> adolescence represented no period of crisis or stress, but was instead an orderly developing of a set of slowly maturing interests and activities. The girls' minds were perplexed by no conflicts, troubled by no philosophical queries, beset by no remote ambitions. To live as a girl with many lovers as long as possible and then to marry in one's own village, near one's own relatives and to have many children, these were uniform and satisfying ambitions.
>
> (157)

Mead closed her book with ruminations about the implications of these discoveries for her own society, with its stormy adolescence, sexual rigidity, and ample neuroses. No mere academic exercise for her, the comparison of American and Samoan childhood and personality taught her that we could learn much from them:

> Realizing that our own ways are not humanly inevitable nor God-ordained, but are the fruit of a long and turbulent history, we may well examine in turn all of our institutions, thrown into strong relief against the history of other civilizations, and weighing them in the balance, be not afraid to find them wanting.
>
> (233)

Needless to say, Mead's data and assertions have come under criticism from other anthropologists, most savagely by Derek Freeman, whose 1983 *Margaret Mead and Samoa: The Making and Unmaking of an Anthropological Myth* accused her of bad research and of being the victim of a hoax concocted by imaginative Samoan girls. Here, we do not aim to assess her work but to recognize its influence in the budding field of culture-and-personality.

She followed up *Coming of Age in Samoa* with her 1930 treatise *Growing Up in New Guinea*, subtitled "A Comparative Study of Primitive Education." Based on six months of fieldwork in the Manus village of Peri, she used the book as another occasion to consider how "each human infant is transformed into the finished adult, into the complicated individual version of his city or his century" (1930: 1). And, surveying the experiences and training of the Manus child, she once again set about "to study the educational process, to suggest solutions to educational problems which we would never be willing to study by experimentation upon our own children" (5). The upshot was an emphasis on how "education" shapes personality—and how American and Western societies might reform their educational processes to make better and healthier personalities.

One of the most consequential findings from her Manus fieldwork was a direct challenge to Lévy-Bruhl's notion of mystical participation in the "primitive" mind and more specifically to Tylor's belief that "animism" was the primordial version of religion. Based on observations of children and the collection of more than 32,000 of their drawings, Mead declared that there was "no evidence of spontaneous animistic thought in the uncontrolled sayings or games of these Manus children" (1932: 180). To be precise, she

> found no instance of a child's personalizing a dog or a fish or a bird, of his personalizing the sun, the moon, the wind or the stars. I found no evidence of a child's attributing chance events, such as the drifting away of a canoe, the loss of an object, an unexplained noise, a sudden gust of wind, a strange deep-sea turtle, a falling seed from a tree, etc., to supernaturalistic causes.
>
> (181)

Animism seemed, instead, more common in adults than in children, strongly suggesting that it was not a natural tendency in the "primitive" mind but rather a taught and learned cultural habit.

The third volume in Mead's trilogy of trendsetting writings was her 1935 *Sex and Temperament in Three Primitive Societies*. Here, she asked a question that had not previously been posed: are gender personalities universal or culturally particular? For this purpose, she took advantage of the proximity of three New Guinea tribes within a hundred-mile range of each other—the Arapesh, the Mundugumor, and the Tchambuli. With a chapter on each society (the first by far the longest and the third extremely short), she reported,

> In one [Arapesh], both men and women act as we expect women to act—in a mild parental responsive way; in the second [Mundugumor], both act as we expect men to act—in a fierce initiating fashion; and in the third [Tchambuli], the men act according to our stereotype for women—are catty, wear curls, and go shopping, while the women are energetic, managerial, unadorned partners.
>
> (1963: i)

In other words, as with adolescence, Mead disputed "the cultural assumptions that certain temperamental attitudes are 'naturally' masculine and others 'naturally' feminine"; rather, two of her three tribes "have no idea that men and women are different in temperament" (xiii). Most simply phrased, "the personalities of the two sexes are socially produced" (310) and are therefore no more determined by biology than is intelligence or mentality determined by race.

BOX 2.2 MARGARET MEAD AND GREGORY BATESON: BALINESE CHARACTER

After her epochal personality research in Samoa and New Guinea, Mead's next project was more extensive fieldwork on the Indonesian island of Bali with her new husband Gregory Bateson. Two years of participant observation yielded a unique document: their *Balinese Character: A Photographic Analysis*. Many visitors have remarked on what a visual feast the Balinese land and people are, and Bateson and Mead took advantage of the new technology of photography to chronicle behavior and the acquisition of that behavior in children. "This is not a book about Balinese custom, but about the Balinese," they wrote, "about the way in which they, as living persons, moving, standing, eating, sleeping, dancing, and going into trance, embody that abstraction which (after we have abstracted it) we technically call culture" (Bateson and Mead 1942: xii). Bateson and Mead covered such topics as spatial orientation, learning, parenting, stages of child development, body orifices, and the integration and disintegration of the body in dance and trance, precociously appreciating that Balinese ideas, personality, or mind could not be studied in isolation from Balinese bodies (see Chapters 5 and beyond for the current anthropological emphasis on embodiment and embodied knowledge). For instance, they stressed that childhood learning was less verbal than active and participatory, a kind of apprenticeship in Balinese culture:

> Learning to walk, learning the first appropriate gestures of playing musical instruments, learning to eat, and to dance are all accomplished with the teacher behind the pupil, conveying directly by pressure, and almost always with a minimum of words, the gesture to be performed.... The Balinese learn virtually nothing from verbal instruction and most Balinese adults are incapable of following out the three consecutive orders which we regard as the sign of a normal three-year-old intelligence.
>
> (15)

Social hierarchies and rigid formalities marked the experience of Balinese child and adult alike. Notably, after a comparatively indulgent early childhood, between the ages of three and six, the youth began to withdraw from other people emotionally and physically, and "once established, his unresponsiveness will last through life" (33). This lack of emotional affect was evident even in marital and love relationships, in which "the romantic excitement steadily dies down after the first encounter," and the lovers' "brief, unreal ardor cools" (37). In sum, they posited that Balinese people learned to live "in a state of dreamy-relaxed dissociation, with occasional intervals of non-personal concentration—in trance, in gambling, and in the practice of the arts";

> Fear and absolute confusion will arise if he does not know the day, the directions, and the caste of those whom he addresses, but he has such sureness of movement within a known place that his acts require only a tithe of his attention. He is vulnerable, but deft and gay, and usually content. Always a little frightened of some undefined unknown, always driven to fill the hours, so empty of inter-personal

relations, with a rhythmic unattended industriousness, he follows the routines laid down by calendars and the revelations of those in trance, relaxed at the center of any world of which he knows the outlines.

(47–8)

Most of the book provided visual representations of these alleged social and mental states. In the early era of culture-and-personality studies, there was something of an anthropological industry in Balinese character studies, including Jane Belo's "The Balinese Temper" (1935–6) and "Balinese Children's Drawings" (1937)—Belo was a student of Mead—and Kurt Eissler's "Balinese Character" (1944), published in the journal *Psychiatry*.

Configurations of culture and personality: Ruth Benedict

Between Mead's three books, and influencing at least the third explicitly, came arguably the most popular anthropology book ever written. Ruth Benedict (1887–1948) was fourteen years older than Mead, a student of Boas and then, after she joined the faculty of Columbia University, a teacher of Mead. Benedict added a more articulate theoretical base to Mead's relatively nontheoretical writings and advanced a stronger version of equivalence between culture and personality (Figure 2.2).

Benedict's thinking in her 1932 article "Configurations of Culture in North America" and in her pivotal 1934 book *Patterns of Culture* conspicuously owes much to Oswald Spengler's model of history and to the Gestalt school of psychology. In his *The Decline of the West*, Spengler proposed, as Benedict understood it, that each

> culture has taken a certain direction not taken by another, it has developed beliefs and institutions until they are the expression of this fundamental orientation, and the full working out of this unique and highly individualized attitude toward life is what is significant in that cultural epoch.

(1932: 3)

This resembles Herder's *Volksgeist* idea and Wundt's *Völkerpsychologie*, as seen in the previous chapter. We might say that every culture has its distinct "pattern" while following a long-term historical pattern or life cycle of birth, growth, maturity, and decline. Gestalt psychology (from the German for "shape" or "form") reinforced this perspective from another angle, focusing on the wholes of which specific perceptions or traits were only a part. These two sources suggested to Benedict a holistic approach to culture that placed particular cultural traits into more-or-less integrated patterns or configurations. As such, similar traits across cultures might have different meanings or significances and might be connected and used in different ways.

Accordingly, as she explained in her article and elaborated further in her book, every culture—including and maybe especially "primitive" cultures—has or is a configuration of elements (which is why her model is sometimes labeled "configurational"). More,

> Cultural configurations stand to the understanding of group behavior in the relation that personality types stand to the understanding of individual behavior.... It is recognized that the organization of the total personality is crucial in the understanding or even in the mere description of individual behavior. If this is true in individual psychology where

Figure 2.2 Ruth Benedict, one of the founding figures of the early culture-and-personality school. *Library of Congress.*

individual differentiation must be limited always by the cultural forms and by the short span of a human lifetime, it is even more imperative in social psychology where the limitations of time and of conformity are transcended. The degree of integration that may be attained is of course incomparably greater than can ever be found in individual psychology. *Cultures from this point of view are individual psychology thrown large upon the screen, given gigantic proportions and a long time span.*

(1932: 23–4, emphasis added)

BOX 2.3 RUTH BENEDICT: CULTURE IS PERSONALITY WRIT LARGE

Benedict's position, sometimes encapsulated in the aphorism that "culture is personality writ large," is a good example of LeVine's model of **C = P**, in which culture *is* personality, only on a different scale.

The subject of Benedict's more fully realized treatment of culture and personality, *Patterns of Culture*, is "the fundamental and distinctive cultural configurations that pattern existence and condition the thoughts and emotions of the individuals who participate in those cultures" (1934: 55). In this view, we could justifiably say that personality is to the individual what culture is to the society. Indeed, personality is like culture in a number of ways. Both personality and culture are regular and organized: "A culture, like an individual, is a more or less consistent pattern of thought and action" (46); ideally, both a personality and a culture become more internally consistent and more fully integrated over time. Further—and this is a crucial aspect of Benedict's argument—any particular personality and any particular culture contains a selection of the total set of human traits; no personality or culture can manifest all that is human, but neither can all human potential be expressed in any one personality or culture. In regard to personality, she referred to the "great arc of possibilities" that is the whole spectrum of thoughts, beliefs, values, and feelings: "we must imagine a great arc on which are ranged the possible interests provided either by the human age-cycle or by the environment or by man's various activities" (24). We could liken this great arc to a piano keyboard: every human potential, like every note, is held by it, but any particular culture only "presses" certain "keys," played together as "chords," thus making the music of each culture, built out of the same potential sounds, different and hopefully consonant.

Benedict supported her position with three case studies of cultures, each supposedly displaying an identifiable configuration of style of culture that is also seen in the personality of its members. The Pueblo Indians of New Mexico she captured in one word—Apollonian, a term employed by the philosopher Friedrich Nietzsche in his study of ancient art and culture to designate the qualities of calm, sobriety, rationality, and self-discipline. The Dobuans of New Guinea were, in a word, paranoid:

> They are lawless and treacherous. Every man's hand is against every other man.... In a strict sense [the society] has no legality...because the social forms which obtain in Dobu put a premium upon ill-will and treachery and make of them the recognized virtues of their society.
>
> (131)

The Kwakiutl of the northwest coast of North America, finally, were christened Dionysian, the opposite of the Apollonian Pueblos. Dionysian, another Nietzschean term, conveys passion, intensity, excess emotion, and even irrationality. Benedict found this tendency in Kwakiutl religion as well as economics, especially in the famous ritual destruction of property known as the potlatch.

Benedict granted that not all societies could be summarized in a single word or ever achieved these degrees of integration and configuration. More importantly, the most integrated and patterned societies included individuals who did not conform to the pattern. Surely the "vast proportion of all individuals who are born into any society always and whatever the idiosyncrasies of its institutions, assume, as we have seen, the behavior dictated by that society" (254). But there are always some individuals who cannot or will not internalize the norms and values of the group and who are therefore branded "abnormal"—but *abnormality is culturally relative*. For instance, being calm and reasonable was normal for Pueblos but would be abnormal for Dobuans, and being paranoid and treacherous was normal for Dobuans but would be abnormal in most societies. Consequently, there is no personality trait that is abnormal-in-itself, only those traits that are judged abnormal in a group, that "have received no support in the institutions of their culture" (270). And in the final analysis, "the range of normality in different cultures does not coincide" (275). (For much more on culture, abnormality, and the special kind of abnormality categorized as "mental illness," see Chapter 9.)

BOX 2.4 GREGORY BATESON: IATMUL PERSONALITY AND ETHOS

The first decades of culture-and-personality anthropology was a period of groping for terms and concepts to communicate its ideas and theories. Some scholars, like Mead and Benedict, used the word "personality," having largely jettisoned the nineteenth-century language of "mentality." Others found "personality" inadequate, either because it was too inclusive or too exclusive. In his 1936 ethnography of the Iatmul titled *Naven*, Gregory Bateson suggested the term "ethos," which was understood as "the culturally standardized system of organization of the instincts and emotions of individuals" (1936: 220). In good culture-equals-personality fashion, Bateson then added that "any pervasive characteristic of the cultural structure can be referred to peculiarities of the Iatmul mind; that, in fact, we are here dealing with the cultural expression of cognitive or intellectual aspects of Iatmul personality" (220). One advantage of Bateson's analysis was that it allowed for the coexistence of more than one ethos in a single society. And he reasoned that in Iatmul society (and most if not all societies) "each sex has its own consistent ethos which contrasts with that of the opposite sex" (198). The male ethos was characterized by "pride, self-assertion, harshness, and spectacular display," while the female ethos demonstrated "a sense of reality" that was cooperative, "easy and 'natural'" (198). (These of course sound much like conventional Western gender stereotypes.) Interestingly, *Ethos* was adopted as the title of the journal of the Society of Psychological Anthropology. Meanwhile, Morris Opler proposed the concept of "themes." For Opler, a cultural theme was a "dynamic affirmation," "a postulate of position, declared or implied, and usually controlling behavior or stimulating activity, which is tacitly approved or openly promoted in a society" (1945: 198). Actual behavior was the expression of cultural themes. Usefully, though, unlike a single personality or an ethos or two, a culture might and ordinarily does offer multiple themes, which may be disparate and on occasion actually incompatible with one another. Thus, personality and the behavior that emanates from it, for Opler, could not be reduced to one or two patterns.

Why cultural anthropology needs the psychiatrist: Edward Sapir

If we make the test of imputing the contents of an ethnological monograph to a known individual in the community which it describes, we would inevitably be led to discover that, while every single statement in it may, in the favorable case, be recognized as holding true in some sense, the complex of patterns as described cannot, without considerable absurdity, be interpreted as a significant configuration of experience, both actual and potential, in the life of the person appealed to.

(Sapir 1934: 411)

So wrote Edward Sapir (1884–1939), the most psychologically sophisticated of the first generation of culture-and-personality anthropologists and yet another student of Boas. Sapir, also an accomplished linguist (see the following), concurred with Mead and Benedict that scholars of culture cannot "ignore the individual and his types of interrelationships with other individuals" (411) and that the "more fully one tries to understand a culture, the more it seems to take on the characteristics of a personality organization" (412). He even granted that many if not most dimensions of culture "are discoverable only as the peculiar property of certain individuals," but he significantly modified the simplistic C=P equation by insisting that individuals "cannot but give these cultural goods the impress of their own personality" (412). Laurence Kirmayer, in a commentary on Sapir's construction of culture and personality, contended that "Sapir was sharply critical of the notion of culture as 'personality writ large' popularized through the work of Ruth Benedict" (2001: 25).

Sapir staked out his position not only on culture and personality but on the central relevance of psychiatry to the anthropological enterprise in two papers at opposite ends of the 1930s—his 1932 "Cultural Anthropology and Psychiatry" and his 1938 "Why Cultural Anthropology Needs the Psychiatrist." In the former, while he praised recent attention to the individual in culture, he objected to the fact that, as is quite clear in the work of Mead and Benedict, it is "what all the individuals of a society have in common in their mutual relations which is supposed to constitute the true subject matter of cultural anthropology and sociology" (1932: 229). Variations between individuals—differences within or from the configuration or the standard character—were hardly dealt with beyond the category of "the abnormal" and hardly could be dealt with if personality was imagined as a microcosm of culture and culture as a macrocosm of culture (as some followers of mainstream culture-and-personality anthropology literally stipulated). Early culture-and-personality scholars have been caricatured as promoting an "any individual is a perfect sample of culture" perspective, but it is not an extreme caricature.

Sapir argued for the specificity and thus the diversity of individuals in culture. "The true locus" or site of culture and its myriad processes, he wrote,

> is not in a theoretical community of human beings known as society, for the term "society" is itself a cultural construct which is employed by individuals who stand in significant relations to each other in order to help them in the interpretation of certain aspects of their behavior. The true locus of culture is in *the interactions of specific individuals* and, on the subjective side, in *the world of meanings which each one of these individuals may unconsciously abstract for himself from his participation in these interactions.*
>
> (236, emphasis added)

In the end, the "culture" of any two individuals may be "significantly different, as significantly different, on the given level and scale, as though one were the representative of Italian culture and the other of Turkish culture" (237). Therefore, the anthropologist must consider the "personal meaning of the symbolisms" for specific individuals in a society.

Sapir developed his agenda further in his second essay. The jumping-off point is a memorable remark by James Owen Dorsey in his *Omaha Sociology*. In describing Omaha society and culture, Dorsey repeatedly commented that a particular informant named Two Crows doubted, denied, or claimed no knowledge of particular facts; for instance, on the subject of sections or clans, some interlocutors said that there were four, but "Two Crows seemed to doubt them" (1884: 237), and when it came to a particular hairstyle, Two Crows did not deny it but seemed to "know nothing about it" (238). Dorsey realized, but subsequent anthropologists, including members of the culture-and-personality school, seemed to overlook, that

> he was dealing, not with a society nor with a specimen of primitive man nor with a cross-section of the history of primitive culture, but with a finite, though indefinite, number of human beings, *who gave themselves the privilege of differing from each* other not only in matters generally considered as "one's own business" but even on questions which clearly transcended the private individual's concern and were, by the anthropologist's definition, implied in the conception of a definitely delimited society with a definitely discoverable culture.
>
> (Sapir 2001: 3, emphasis added)

Moreover, Two Crows and his kind are not just dissenters from some ideal cultural consensus; they may be innovators in the future culture of the group. "If we get enough Two Crows to agree," Sapir grasped, "we have what we call a new tradition, or a new dogma, or a new theory, or a new procedure":

> What starts as a thoroughly irresponsible and perhaps psychotic aberration seems to have the power, by some kind of "social infection," to lose its purely personal quality and to take on something of that very impersonality of custom which, in the first instance, it seemed to contradict so flatly.
>
> (4)

And there lies the relation to psychiatry for Sapir. In his earlier paper, he described psychiatry as the field that diagnoses and possibly cures behavioral deviations of the individual. But (a) all individuals deviate from the cultural configuration, the ideal personality, and the purportedly common knowledge of the society to some extent, and (b) what is a deviation at one moment in time may be the new norm at a future moment. So, the anthropologist should not discard individual difference within culture and certainly should not condemn it as "abnormal" or "insane." Instead, the anthropologist should take a cue from psychiatry and give special consideration to such exceptions. Sapir's insight was, then, that

> any individual of a group has cultural definitions which do not apply to all the members of his group, which even, in specific instances, apply to him alone. Instead, therefore, of arguing from a supposed objectivity of culture to the problem of individual variation, we shall, for certain kinds of analysis, have to proceed in the opposite direction. We shall have to operate as though we knew nothing about culture but were interested in analyzing as well as we could what a given number of human beings accustomed to live with each other actually think and do in their day to day relationships.
>
> This mode of thinking is, of course, essentially psychiatric.
>
> (6)

BOX 2.5 GÉZA RÓHEIM: PSYCHOANALYTIC FIELDWORK

One sure sign of the mutual necessity of anthropology and psychiatry was the fact that a number of early culture-and-personality articles, like Sapir's own 1938 essay, were published in the journal *Psychiatry*. Another is the adoption by psychiatrists of anthropological methods, including conducting long-term fieldwork in "primitive" societies. Probably the best case of this multidisciplinary research is Géza Róheim, whose *Australian Totemism: A Psycho-analytic Study in Anthropology* was published in 1925, before the culture-and-personality school fully flowered. Róheim was an orthodox psychoanalyst and supporter of Freud's cultural and historical theories. Freud urged him to sojourn in central Australia to collect data confirming Freud's propositions in *Totem and Taboo* about the Oedipus complex and the psychosexual origins of culture. In 1929 Róheim spent time at the mission station of Hermannsburg, gathering information on dreams, sexual activity, child play, and myths and ceremonies. Among the products of his research were an essay, "Animism and Religion" (1932) and two books, *The Riddle of the Sphinx* (1934)—an obvious reference to the ancient Greek tragedy of Oedipus—and *The Eternal Ones of the Dream: A Psychoanalytic Interpretation of Australian Myth and Ritual*. Predictably, Róheim believed that Australian Aboriginal culture and religion, regarded by many as the most primitive in the world, justified Freud's theories. For instance, the much used and abused concept of animism was for him a projection of the Oedipus complex onto nature and the landscape. In *The Riddle of the Sphinx*, so titled because Aboriginals indisputably, in his reading, suffered from the Oedipus complex, he went much further, asserting that culture itself was exactly "the sum of all sublimations, all substitutes, or reaction formations, in short, everything in society that inhibits impulses or permits their distorted satisfaction" (1934: 216)—in other words, a perfect Freudian neurosis. Someday, Róheim speculated, there would be a completely psychoanalytic anthropology, which would be the one true anthropology.

Beyond a doubt, Róheim and those who followed Freud closely fall within LeVine's model of P→C, culture being a product, epiphenomenon, or even symptom of personality or psychic processes.

Anthropologist and psychiatrist in collaboration: Abram Kardiner

Interestingly, one of the prime movers of the early culture-and-personality school in its second decade was not an anthropologist but a psychiatrist, trained and analyzed by Freud himself. Abram Kardiner (1891–1981) helped found the psychoanalytic movement in the United States and, more importantly for our purposes, started the New York Psychiatric Institute in 1930, which held seminars on psychological and cultural topics. Among those who were invited to participate were anthropologist Ralph Linton, who became a close collaborator and contributed the bulk of the ethnographic data for Kardiner's first major book, along with Cora Du Bois and James West, who provided information for his second.

In conversation with anthropologists, Kardiner became the center of a neo-Freudian interpretive tradition and of a nascent psychoanalytic anthropology such as Róheim envisioned. Kardiner was the convener and chief voice in two formative publications, *The Individual and His Society* (1939) and *The Psychological Frontiers of Society* (1945). Each of the volumes features two or more extended case studies of specific societies written by one or more anthropologists and then analyzed by Kardiner as well as general theoretical and conceptual discussion. The material in the earlier book begins with brief presentations on Trobriand, Zuni, Kwakiutl, Chuckchee, and Eskimo societies before launching into full-chapter studies of the Marquesan islanders and the Tanala of Madagascar, authored by Linton. The later book holds full-length case studies of the Comanche (based on data from Linton), the Alorese (from Cora Du Bois's revolutionary research; see the following), and an anonymous America city called Plainville (by James West).

The theoretical statement by Kardiner in *The Individual and His Society* is less robust than in its sequel. He began by acknowledging, as is especially critical for Freudians, that the "study of psychology must begin with the biological characteristics of man" (1939: 3), the most pressing of which is the long period of immaturity and dependency that is human infancy and childhood. Humans must, therefore, organize themselves to care for these frail little individuals, and children must adapt themselves to those social conditions. The key unit of social organization for Kardiner was the "institution," which he defined as

> any fixed mode of thought or behavior held by a group of individuals (i.e., a society) which can be communicated, which enjoys common acceptance, and infringement of, or deviation from which creates some disturbance in the individual or the group.
>
> (7)

Any particular culture, then, "acquires its conformation and specificity from the uniqueness of its institutions" (7). The psychoanalytic/anthropological task accordingly became, first, to "describe the institution, which, for example, interferes with an impulse" (impulses held to be those undeniable but repressible or sublimatable unconscious drives or instincts) and, second, to:

describe the effects of this interference on the individual with respect to
a   changes in the perception of the impulse;
b   modification this makes on the executive functions;
c   feelings to those who impose it;
d   unconscious constellations formed by this series of conditions;
e   relation of these unconscious constellations to the actual behavior of the individual;
f   relation between those constellations to *new* institutions (or neurosis).

(20–1)

At the top of his concerns were family structure, along with childhood bodily disciplines (especially anal and sexual control), curbs on aggression, training for adult roles, and so forth.

Significantly, Kardiner divided cultural institutions into two classes, primary and secondary, with the primary ones being "older, more stable, and less likely to be interfered with by vicissitudes of climate or economy"; they included "family organization, in-group formation, basic disciplines, feeding, weaning, institutionalized care or neglect of children, anal training, and sexual taboos" (471). Secondary institutions, more derivative and malleable than their predecessors, were such things as "taboo systems, religion, rituals, folktales, and techniques of thinking" (471). The Freudian premise of the book and of the entire psychoanalytic approach to culture was that if "primary institutions create certain constellations, then secondary institutions in society must satisfy the needs and tensions created by the primary or fixed ones" (476).

Between the primary and secondary institutions, however, stood the individual or the personality, which was a product of primary institutions but a producer of secondary ones.

Kardiner's technical term here was *basic personality structure*, defined as the "group of psychic and behavioral characteristics derived from contact with the same institutions," which he distinguished from *character* as "the personal variant of the basic personality structure" and from *ego* or "the total personality as subjectively perceived" or what we might call *self* (21). Under the heading of basic personality structure, he placed "techniques of thinking, or idea constellations," the "security system of the individual," "super-ego formation" or internalized control (e.g., senses of shame or guilt), and "attitudes to supernatural beings" which were stand-ins for attitudes toward parents (132).

We can represent the relationship between primary and secondary institutions ("culture") and basic personality structure ("personality") as follows:

primary institutions → basic personality structure → secondary institutions

---

BOX 2.6 ABRAM KARDINER'S THEORY OF PERSONALITY

Kardiner's theory of the construction and intermediary role of personality is the epitome of LeVine's model of $C1 \rightarrow P \rightarrow C2$.

The Psychological Frontiers of Society is a further test and refinement of Kardiner's theory and concepts. Providing the foreword for the volume, Linton defined basic personality as "that personality configuration which is shared by the bulk of the society's members as a result of the early experiences which they have in common"; surprisingly, perhaps, he added,

> It does not correspond to the total personality of the individual but rather to the projective systems or, in different phraseology, the value-attitude systems which are basic to the individual's personality configuration. Thus the same basic personality type may be reflected in many different forms of behavior and may enter into many different total personality configurations.
>
> (Kardiner 1945: viii)

How that affects the utility of the concept in anthropological analyses is a point worth pondering.

In the preface, Linton expressed his belief that "in stable societies the basic personality type and the culture configuration tend to reinforce and perpetuate each other" (ix), essentially concurring with Mead and Benedict. And the link or the locus of culture for the individual was evidently "biography" (11) or the individual's lived experience, which is once again presumably sufficiently similar throughout the society to warrant the assumption of a shared basic personality structure. In Kardiner's refined language here, primary institutions were the "specific influences [that] were brought to bear on the growing individual" (23), molding his or her personality. Digging deeper into the array of primary institutions and allied practices, Kardiner stressed maternal care (with the inevitable feeding, weaning, and sphincter control), emotional bonding, discipline and punishment, sexual regulation, sibling relations, training for adult roles, social changes that accompany puberty, and marriage (27). The fundamental goal for anthropology as for psychology and psychiatry consequently was to describe the primary institutions of a society and then to understand how they shape a particular personality system which, in turn, projects secondary institutions like religion, art, and folklore. Kardiner confidently or hopefully argued that "if we know how the basic personality is established, we can make certain predictions about the institutions this personality is likely to invent" (29). However, like Sapir, Kardiner conceded that a culture does not manufacture a single personality or character for every member of society. Instead, his basic personality structure "only indicates a certain range and certain modalities within which great differences can arise, depending on 'constitution,' the specific characters and fortunes of the parents" (228). In other words, even the best psychoanalytic-anthropological analysis left considerable room for personality slippage.

BOX 2.7 BIOGRAPHICAL STUDIES

A concrete understanding of how personality or character is formed and how it functions in social relationships and institutions, as Kardiner recognized, implied a necessarily "biographical" approach in anthropology and psychology. Some observers, like Mead, embedded brief accounts of specific individuals' life-histories in their published work, and others like Cora Du Bois (see the following) used biographical materials extensively to search for connections between childhood experiences and adult personality. Other scholars went further, offering book-length biographies or autobiographies of individual members of non-Western and "primitive" societies. One of the earliest examples is Paul Radin's 1926 *Crashing Thunder: The Autobiography of an American Indian*, followed by Walter Dyk's 1938 *Son of Old Man Hat: A Navajo Autobiography*, Clellan Ford's 1941 *Smoke from Their Fires: The Life of a Kwakiutl Chief*, and, most famously, Leo Simmons's 1942 *Sun Chief: The Autobiography of a Hopi Indian*. Simmons overtly intended his autobiography of Don Talayesva to be more than the chronicle of one man but to be a tool for "developing and checking hypotheses in the field of culture and its relation to personality development, or of the individual and his role in cultural change" (1942: 1). Yet even Simmons admitted in the closing pages of the book that "it may be that an extensive life history is so extremely complex that it cannot be analyzed as a single unit in which all the variables are properly accounted for" (385). Indeed, after nearly four hundred pages of adventures, it is difficult to discern a direct link between Don Talayesva's childhood and his adult character. For this reason, and because the stars of (auto)biographies tended to be exceptional if not deviant individuals, many anthropologists have despaired over the worth of the biographical approach. This caution, though, has not precluded an industry in anthropology of biographical studies, such as Marjorie Shostak's renowned 1981 *Nisa: The Life and Words of a !Kung Woman*, which continues to this day. Biographies may not answer all questions about culture and personality, but they do invariably illustrate how culture and history are encountered by an individual—always in unique and unpredictable but theoretically informative ways.

Beyond basic personality and toward a scientific study of culture and personality: Cora Du Bois

Cora Du Bois's 1944 *The People of Alor* ends our tour of the first phase of the culture and personality school of anthropology, but it could just as easily and appropriately open a survey of the second phase. In time and in outlook, it stands at the fulcrum of the old and comparatively impressionistic approach and a more technical and scientific endeavor.

Kardiner and his peers in anthropology left us with the concept of basic personality struc-ture, which was presumed to be shared within a community based on common childhood experiences of certain key institutional practices; this conclusion was derived from mostly qualitative data that were not usually collected specifically for the purpose at hand. Du Bois (1903–91), the youngest of the founding generation of culture-and-personality anthropolo-gists and a full generation younger than Sapir and Benedict, although she was a contributor to Kardiner's work, also conducted her own independent research and offered results that rivaled the psychoanalyst.

As she revealed in her preface, she had been involved in the psychiatric study of person-ality formation in American society since 1935 and had joined Kardiner's New York semi-nar in 1936. These interests, as well as her employment in government service during World War II (see Chapter 3), led to her fieldwork on the island of Alor, at the southeastern tip of Indonesia. There she undertook research intentionally to test the basic assumption of culture-and-personality anthropology, and specifically of psychoanalytic anthropology, namely,

> whether there was indeed a demonstrable relationship between the personalities of adults within a group and the socio-cultural milieu in which they lived. If such a rela-tionship were found to exist, its explanation was presumed to lie in the consistency of life experiences ranging from the earliest child-rearing practices and relationships to the reinforcing effects of adult institutions and social roles.
>
> (1960: xviii)

For this purpose, she deployed an unusually robust battery of methods. Almost two hundred pages of the final report were dedicated to ethnography of Alorese culture and society, with a focus on childhood. She described childbirth beliefs and practices, early childhood training (as always, with an eye on feeding, toilet training, sexual and other disciplines, and sleep-ing arrangements), youth and adolescence, marriage and adult sexuality, and adult behavior (status, conflict, economics, etc.) before turning to religion. Kardiner closed this section of the study with a chapter on "personality determinants in Alorese culture."

Two further parts of the book, totaling more than four hundred pages, marshaled a variety of other kinds of evidence. First among these were biographies of eight particular individu-als, each case followed by a psychological analysis by Kardiner. The second set of data came from an assortment of formal psychological tests done on Alorese children and adults, who were subjected to the Porteus Maze Test (see Chapter 1), a nonverbal measure of intelligence, planning, and foresight. They were also asked to perform word associations, an obviously verbal task. Children's drawings were solicited, collected, and analyzed. Last but not least, people were given the Rorschach test, in which inkblots are presented and individual re-sponses are sifted for clues to personality or character. (The Rorschach test was to become a standard tool of psychological anthropologists in the field; see Chapter 3.)

The results of all this energy were not kind to the conventional claims and concepts of psychological and psychoanalytic anthropology. "It is not astonishing," Du Bois wrote, "that the undertaking failed to reveal any very high degree of consistency between the aspects investigated" (xviii)—although it perhaps should have been astonishing and alarming to advocates of more simplistic culture-equals-personality, "culture-is-personality-writ-large" positions. Even Kardiner, reflecting on the biographies, had to confess that each person "is a highly individual character. Each has some features of the basic personality structure, but each is in turn molded by the specific factors in his individual fate" (548). Further, there was no straightforward, one-to-one correspondence between childhood experiences and adult personality or character.

All of this led to Du Bois's most significant theoretical innovation, which was to replace the concept of basic personality structure with a new notion—*modal personality*. Asserting first that without a doubt "the people living within any one society are not identical"—in other words, that it is untrue that there is a single universal group personality or that any individual is a perfect sample of the society—she proposed "modal personality"

> to designate central tendencies in the personalities of a *group* of people studied by means of more or less objective and cross-culturally applicable tests as well as by means of observation and autobiographies. Modal personality was not an explicative concept. It was a purely static and descriptive one.
>
> (xix, emphasis in the original)

To be accurate, modal personality is a *statistical* concept, utilizing as it does the technical term "mode," the most commonly-occurring value or point in a data-set. As a statistical fact, it only can (or should) be arrived at from a detailed set of quantitative social and psychological data, not just an impressionistic or incomplete overview of the society. Further and most consequentially, there is no *a priori* claim as to exactly *how* common the modal personality is: it might apply to ninety percent of the population, or it might describe only a plurality (say, thirty or forty percent) of the people. Finally, as in any array of data, modal thinking implies that there is a *range* of personalities, not one or maybe even a few personality types.

Nonetheless, as we will see in the next chapter, the idea of a few types or a single type of personality survived and in fact was put to work on large modern societies like Russia, Japan, and the United States as much as, if not more than, small "traditional" ones.

BOX 2.8 EDWARD SAPIR: LINGUISTIC RELATIVITY HYPOTHESIS

It is more than a little surprising that, although it is a major part of culture—and of the interaction between anthropologists and members of a society and ultimately of the presentation of anthropological knowledge in books and essays—language received limited attention in the early culture-and-personality school. This would change soon and dramatically, as will be evident in Chapter 4 and the subsequent chapters, when language becomes a central preoccupation and indeed paradigm of culture and of the knowledge that individuals carry in their minds or personalities.

The first anthropologist to put serious thought into the question of language was Edward Sapir, who was, we noted earlier, a linguist in addition to if not before an anthropologist. In 1921 he wrote an introductory text on language, which covered all of the formal aspects of language but also speculated on its relationship to thought. Language, he reckoned, "is primarily a pre-rational function. It humbly works up to the thought that is latent in, that may eventually be read into, its classifications and its forms" (1921: 15). While he held that language is only "the outward fact of thought on the highest, most generalized, level of symbolic expression," he also pondered, "what if language is not so much a garment as a prepared road or groove" of thought? (15). Later in the book he made a much stronger stand: "Language and our thought-grooves are inextricably interwoven, are, in a sense, one and the same" (232), although he equally forcefully denied that language was determined by race or deterministic of culture. A mere eight years later, Sapir's own thinking had evolved more in the direction that would be come to be called *linguistic relativity*. In a 1929 essay, "The Status of Linguistics as a Science," he opened by noticing an increased interest in language and linguistics in many social science disciplines, from anthropology and psychology to philosophy. In fact, language "is becoming increasingly valuable as a guide to the scientific study of a given culture. In a sense, the network of cultural patterns of a civilization is indexed in the language which expresses that civilization" (1929: 209). This is because language "is a guide to 'social reality'": "We see and hear and otherwise experience very largely as we do because the language habits of our community predispose certain choices of interpretation" (209–10). This perspective was building toward the first and one of the clearest and most often-quoted statements of the linguistic relativity hypothesis, that language

> powerfully conditions all our thinking about social problems and processes. Human beings do not live in the objective world alone, nor alone in the world of social activity as ordinarily understood, but are very much at the mercy of the particular language which has become the medium of expression for their society. It is quite an illusion to imagine that one adjusts to reality essentially without the use of language and that language is merely an incidental means of solving specific problems of communication or reflection. The fact of the matter is that the "real world" is to a large extent unconsciously built up on the language habits of the group. No two languages are ever sufficiently similar to be considered as representing the same social reality. The worlds in which different societies live are distinct worlds, not merely the same world with different labels attached.
>
> (209)

This idea of the power of language over cognition and over perception itself was advanced and articulated by Benjamin Lee Whorf (1897–1941), a student of Sapir at Yale University in 1931 and himself a lecturer in anthropology at Yale in 1937. Sapir inspired Whorf's interest in Native American languages, and much of his subsequent work concentrated on the Hopi (southwest Native American) language. His teacher's influence and the impact of studying a radically different language like Hopi can be felt in a 1936 paper on Hopi verbs (anthologized in a posthumous collection of his writings), where he argued that

> language first of all is a classification and arrangement of the stream of sensory experience which results from a certain world-order, a certain segment of the world that is easily expressible by the type of symbolic means that language employs.
>
> (Carroll 1956: 55)

In another essay composed the same year, he insisted that the Hopi language, like every language, "conceals a metaphysics" (58) or a particular way of understanding the world, which can be captured in its verb forms or other grammatical categories; for instance, he maintained that Hopi offered no words or other linguistic rules for referring to time but that it did feature grammatical forms for assertion (e.g. the "reportive" for reporting facts, the "expective" for anticipation, and the "nomic" for statements of general truth) and modality or mood (e.g. the "quotative" for repeating someone else's words, the "inhibitive" for conveying when the subject is prevented from achieving the effects noted in the verb, the "potential," the "indeterminate," the "advisory" for uncertainty, the "concessive" for conceptual validity rather than empirical factuality, the "necessitative" for things that are natural or inevitable, etc.) that are not found in English. The external world is what it is, but, as he posited in a 1940 article on the Shawnee language, "different languages differently 'segment' the same situation or experience" (162), drawing speakers to attend to certain dimensions of reality and minimize or disregard others. In his words, humans "dissect nature along lines laid down by our native languages" (213); "Each language performs this artificial chopping up of the continuous spread and flow of existence in a different way" (253). The very act of "thinking itself is in a language" (252) and can never be totally freed from it. Language, in short, digs the "thought-grooves" that Sapir mentioned: it is not that it is impossible to think outside the grooves but that it is much easier and automatic to think within them. The linguistic relativity hypothesis, also known as the Sapir-Whorf hypothesis, thus can be stated in this simple form postulated by John Carroll: "the structure of a human being's language influences the manner in which he understands reality and behaves with respect to it" (23). The hypothesis has been the topic of extensive subsequent research and continues to be a powerful if controversial idea.

Summary: achievements and shortcomings

The years between 1927 and 1945 were a productive period for what was called then and since the culture-and-personality school of anthropology. Among its accomplishments we can count:

- It successfully moved beyond the nineteenth-century problems of "primitive mentality" and the race determination of mental processes.
- It firmly established a connection between (external) culture and (internal) character and personality, even if not a simple or linear connection.
- It conclusively documented that different cultures produce different personality types.
- It secured an anthropological interest in childhood and the formative experiences that theoretically shaped adult personality.
- It inaugurated a tradition of conducting fieldwork for the express purpose of studying childhood and/or personality.
- It built strong bridges between anthropology and psychology, sometimes in the manner of interdisciplinary cooperation and sometimes literally in the person of individuals who were qualified in both disciplines.
- It experimented with various research methods, from institutional analysis to (auto) biography and psychological testing.
- It began to hone the terminology and the conceptual and theoretical models of the field.

At the same time, as critics were quick and often brutal to point out, there were a number of grave problems with culture-and-personality anthropology as practiced in its opening decades:

- It was reliant on a small number of dominant individuals who shared similar training (especially emerging from the classrooms of Franz Boas) and whose ideas were mutually supporting.
- Many of its concepts and theories were based on fieldwork that did not specifically target psychological questions, hence the data used for its purposes was not always sufficient for its cause.
- Much of the data were general and qualitative rather than quantitative, making it difficult if not impossible to derive causal conclusions and make meaningful comparisons.
- It promoted relatively simple concepts of common personality (and had not even quite settled on its concepts, whether personality, character, ethos, themes, or what have you) that tended to homogenize personality traits in a society, when what was really called for was ethnographic attention to the specifics and diversity of personality in any group.

The late culture-and-personality school

World War II changed many things, including anthropology and the social sciences in general; the long Cold War that followed it continued to alter the interests and methods of social scientists. Many anthropologists contributed to the war effort, putting their area expertise and methods at the service of knowing the enemies of America and Western Europe, and devising successful military and social policy. Ruth Benedict and younger anthropologists, such as Geoffrey Gorer and Clyde Kluckhohn, were recruited by the Office of War Information, and Cora Du Bois held a position in the Office of Strategic Services before moving on to head the research unit of the U.S. Army's Southeast Asia Command. A number of anthropologists worked for the Office of Naval Research and, after its formation in 1956, the Special Operations Research Office, a program designed to "seamlessly meld social scientific expertise with the operational concerns of army officers" (Rohde 2013: 4).

The militarization of anthropology had (and has again, with the deployment of social scientists in the U.S. Army's Human Terrain System in Iraq and Afghanistan) a sizable effect on the questions that anthropologists asked and the publications they produced. And in a broader way, the professionalization of anthropology and other social sciences, along with frustrations and disappointments with the qualitative and generalistic approaches of the early culture-and-personality school, led to a revolution in methodology by the next generation of scholars, who conducted more quantitative research in an effort to make their findings more scientific, more causally powerful, and more politically relevant.

As we noted at the end of the last chapter, Cora Du Bois's 1944 book on Alorese culture and personality stands at the close of the old psychological anthropology and the opening of the new. For convenience sake, though, we will take 1946 as the unofficial birth date of the second phase of the culture-and-personality school, the year when Ruth Benedict's *The Chrysanthemum and the Sword: Patterns of Japanese Culture* appeared. That book, as the subtitle indicates, still reflected Benedict's previous commitment to cultural "patterns," but it also inaugurated a new kind of study with a new kind of purpose. By the late 1960s or early 1970s, anthropologists were taking stock of the whole culture-and-personality project, suggesting that the enterprise had both ripened and exhausted itself, giving way to other forms of anthropology that either developed or disregarded the prior psychological orientation.

National character or the study of complex societies

Commencing during and immediately after World War II, the language of psychological anthropology shifted subtly from the study of "personality" to that of "character." Two other shifts accompanied that change. First, anthropologists increasingly applied their concepts and methods not to "primitive" or traditional/indigenous societies but to large, complex, modern societies and countries like the United States, Japan, or the Soviet Union. Second, as an explanation for the former, the uses of anthropological knowledge became increasingly political and, as acknowledged earlier, military. In fact, Margaret Mead, still very much active in the culture-and-personality scene, wrote in 1953 that this new wave of "national character" studies took "both their form and methods from the exigencies of the post-1939 world political situation" (1953: 642) because "in today's world, nation-states are of paramount political significance, and a great many activities of individuals and groups, both in domestic and in international settings, are conducted in terms of national values" (660).

National character can be understood as the basic personality structure or modal personality of a mass, politically centralized society, and the groundbreaking book in the postwar study of national character was Benedict's *The Chrysanthemum and the Sword*, a study of Japanese character published just after the war ended. The first sentence announced the book's intent: "The Japanese were the most alien enemy the United State had ever fought in an all-out struggle"; as she went on to specify, because the Japanese did not belong to Western civilization and did not share its "conventions of war," a major problem for war planners was "the nature of the enemy. We had to understand their behavior in order to cope with it" (1972: 1). For instance, why would Japanese pilots fly suicide missions into Allied warships, and why would Japanese soldiers fight to the death rather than surrender? And what was this strange loyalty to the Japanese emperor? Benedict claimed to find clues in the child-rearing practices and cultural values of Japan, boiling Japanese national character down to two different and in some ways contradictory patterns or, in Opler's terms, "themes" or, in Bateson's terms, elements of "ethos," symbolized by a flower and a weapon:

> Both the sword and the chrysanthemum are a part of the picture. The Japanese are, to the highest degree, both aggressive and unaggressive, both militaristic and aesthetic, both insolent and polite, rigid and adaptable, submissive and resentful of being pushed around, loyal and treacherous, brave and timid, conservative and hospitable to new ways. They are terribly concerned about what other people will think of their behavior, and they are also overcome by guilt when other people know nothing of their misstep. Their soldiers are disciplined to the hilt but also insubordinate.

(3)

Of course, Benedict's analysis came too late to contribute to the war effort, although it could be useful during the postwar occupation of the vanquished foe. But by the late 1940s, the United States and Western democracies had other problems to solve and other ghosts to exorcise. Not only were the Soviet Union and, in 1949, Communist China perceived as mortal threats to the West, but scholars (and many members of the general public) in the liberal world were perplexed and horrified by the rise of totalitarianism in their own societies. What malignant forces shaped the character of a Hitler? An industry of characterological studies of the Führer cropped up, but the bigger and more unsettling question was what was it in the national character of the Germans, or the Italians or the Japanese for that matter, that made them follow such leaders?

BOX 3.1 CHARACTEROLOGICAL STUDIES

It was not only despicable figures from recent history who got a characterological treatment in the second half of the twentieth century nor was it only anthropologists who indulged in such examinations. Erik Erikson, a neo-Freudian psychologist who extended Freud's developmental-stage thinking to the entire life span, drafted two character studies of major world-historical individuals: one on Martin Luther, the founder of Protestantism (*Young Man Luther: A Study in Psychoanalysis and History* [1962]) and one on Mohandas (better known as Mahatma) Gandhi, the advocate of nonviolent resistance to colonialism in India (*Gandhi's Truth: On the Origins of Militant Nonviolence* [1969]).

National character studies became all the rage for about a decade as anthropologists tried to help scholars, political leaders, and the public comprehend rival states and why ordinary citizens would capitulate to, if not warmly embrace, communist and authoritarian regimes. Victor Barnouw calculated that ten or more such books were published by anthropologists between 1942 and 1953 (1973: 220). Francis Hsu was one of the most committed champions of national character, illustrated by his 1953 *Americans and Chinese: Reflections on Two Cultures and Their People*. As Hsu revealed, his motivation for the comparison was at least partly personal, being a person of dual cultural heritage: "I am a marginal man" (1972a: xiii), born in China and transplanted to the United States. Over more than four hundred pages, he contrasted Chinese and American character through historical, cultural, and psychological evidence, concluding that

> Chinese and American ways of life may be reduced to two sets of contrasts. First, in the American way of life the emphasis is placed upon the predilections of the individual, a characteristic we shall call *individual-centered*. This is in contrast to the emphasis the Chinese put upon an individual's appropriate place and behavior among his fellow-men, a characteristic we shall term *situation-centered*. The second fundamental contrast is the prominence of emotions in the American way of life as compared with the tendency of the Chinese to underplay all matters of the heart.
>
> (10, emphasis in the original)

Sagely, Hsu also recognized that along with central cultural focus, Chinese or American culture each faced its own self-inflicted problems or, in his terms, "dilemmas," as a consequence of its key values. The greatest problems for Americans, he believed, "tend to occur in the domain of human relationships," which are prone to "atomization and explosiveness" based on "bitter struggles between individuals and between groups" (315). Chinese "weaknesses," in his words, consisted of "the absence of any significant or sustained compulsion to change existing institutions, to alter the material environment, or to labor in the realm of the abstract" (315–6).

Meanwhile, the Japanese continued to attract their share of analysis, not only for their wartime behavior but for the changes that the society was undergoing in modernization and the rise of a middle class. However, special energy went into investigation of the main nemesis of Western democracies—the Soviet Union. Research into the propensity of the Russian people to submit to communism led to the high point, or low point, of national character studies: Geoffery Gorer and John Rickman's 1949 *The People of Great Russia: A Psychological Study*. Gorer's name in particular is associated with the notorious "swaddling hypothesis," which some readers assumed or hoped was a parody of national character thinking. Apparently quite soberly, they averred that their goal was "to establish a connection between the attitudes toward political authority and their prototypes in the familial situation" (1962: 213), which is entirely consistent with the culture-and-personality approach. They then forwarded the hypothesis that swaddling, or wrapping a baby very tightly, was the root of Russian and therefore of Soviet communist character. This swaddling practice, they opined, "was painful, as inhibiting spontaneous movements of the limbs and that the infant responded to this pain with rage" (215), contributing to "infantile depression as a result of exhaustion from unassuaged rage" (218). To be sure, other societies practice swaddling to various degrees, but Gorer and Rickman held that Russian swaddling was especially intense and long-term such that "Russian babies can scarcely move any part of their bodies except their eyes," explaining why "Russians use their eyes so eloquently" (225). Presumably then, adult Russians were so tired and depressed, so accustomed to passivity and yielding to authority, that a Lenin or Stalin could substitute for their *babushka* (to which Gorer and Rickman explicitly refer) and surrender their will to such a leader (Figure 3.1).

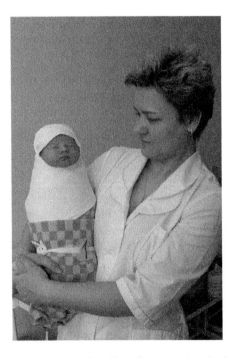

Figure 3.1 Swaddling was claimed by Geoffrey Gorer to be the key to Russian national character © Bystrova et al. CC BY 2.0.

BOX 3.2 THE STUDY OF CULTURE AT A DISTANCE

A problem that complicated and potentially threatened to undermine the anthropological study of nations like the Soviet Union and Communist China, or of wartime Japan, was that conducting participant observation in hostile countries was virtually impossible. But in-person, on-site fieldwork was the accepted standard of anthropological research, which means either that studies of belligerent societies could not be done or that they had to be done in another way. Many anthropologists referred to and adopted the method of "study of culture at a distance," based on whatever resources the researcher could access from outside the target society. Benedict's work on Japan was admittedly done at a distance, and a number of anthropologists struggled to make a virtue out of this vice. In 1953, Margaret Mead and Rhoda Métraux published their *The Study of Culture at a Distance*, ostensibly a "manual" for conducting such inquiries and significantly a project financed by the Office of Naval Research. Assembling contributions from participants in the Columbia University Research in Contemporary Cultures program, the manual summarized "methods that have been developed during the last decade for analyzing the cultural regularities in the characters of individuals who are members of societies which are inaccessible to direct observation" (1953: 3). Yet more ominously, Mead and Métraux disclosed that the emphasis on national character "has been dictated by an interest in the role of nationally originating behavior in warfare, policy making, domestic educational and morale-building campaigns, and so on" (4). The specific methods they surveyed included interviewing migrants from these off-limits countries; analyzing written and oral literature as well as films (from folktales and children's stories to newspaper articles and novels); and psychological and "projective" tests, like Rorschach inkblots or Thematic Apperception Test cards (see the following). All of this material could be concatenated into a picture (what Mead and Métraux called an "end linkage") of the society and its character without ever stepping foot inside the country.

Anthropologists and other social scientists also turned their sights on American culture and character, as in Geoffrey Gorer's 1948 *The American People: A Study in National Character*. His decidedly psychoanalytic angle assessed the immigrant experience of American society—and even the violent separation of the original colonies from England—as a loss or rejection of the father figure, leaving Americans inherently suspicious of authority. Ironically, by the 1950s, competing scholars expressed alarm at the creeping authoritarianism in the United States, most fully articulated in Theodor Adorno et al.'s *The Authoritarian Personality*. This landmark study united multiple researchers and multiple methods to investigate prejudice and ethnocentrism in what they called "the *potentially fascistic* individual, one whose structure is such as to render him particularly susceptible to anti-democratic propaganda" (1950: 2, emphasis in the original). In terms that are as applicable today as they were more than a half-century ago when they were written, the authors determined that the authoritarian personality was plagued with rigidity and moralism, intolerance of ambiguity, pseudoscientific or anti-scientific beliefs, suggestibility or gullibility, lack of introspectiveness or ability to reflect on and evaluate their own thoughts, and unrealistic conceptions of means-ends connections (461). David Riesman, Nathan Glazer, and Reuel Denney's 1950 *The Lonely Crowd* and William H. Whyte, Jr.'s 1956 *The Organization Man* painted equally somber portraits of postwar American character.

After less than two decades, the impetus of national character studies was largely spent: Barnouw maintained that between 1960 and 1973, only two new anthropological titles were published on the subject, and he cited a 1967 literature review that declared the era of national character studies to be at an end. But academic and pragmatic studies of national character did not fade completely, as evidenced by Brigadier General Washington Platt's 1961 *National Character in Action—Intelligence Factors in Foreign Relations* and Alex Inkeles's 1997 *National Character: A Psycho-Social Perspective.*

Comparative study of child-rearing: the Six Cultures Study

From its very inception, the culture-and-personality school had been passionately interested in childhood as the crucial period of culture acquisition and the formative period of personality. Margaret Mead's inaugural 1928 *Coming of Age in Samoa* concentrated on childhood and adolescence, and even anthropologists who were not fundamentally concerned with personality, such as British social anthropologists Raymond Firth (1936), E. E. Evans-Pritchard (1940), and Meyer Fortes (1938), could hardly avoid children in their research and writing.

Following Mead's lead, Dorothea Leighton and Clyde Kluckhohn released their analysis of Navajo children in 1948, based on ethnographic observations and psychological tests, including the Rorschach, the Thematic Apperception Test, and the Goodenough Draw-a-Man Test (see the following). But these and similar projects proved to be less than revealing and less than scientifically useful. Part of the problem was that each study tended to focus exclusively on one society and to employ concepts and methods that made comparison difficult. In other cases, as in Kardiner's volumes discussed previously, psychological conclusions were often extracted from fieldwork that was not originally conducted with psychological questions in mind.

Consequently, an interdisciplinary team of anthropologists and psychologists set out to correct these failings and to put the comparative study of childhood on more stable footing. The result was a mammoth undertaking, the Six Cultures Study of Socialization project, spearheaded by John W. H. Whiting (1908–99) and his wife Beatrice (1914–2003), both anthropologists, and psychologist Irvin L. Child. John Whiting had previously published his own ethnography of childhood in a "primitive" society, *Becoming a Kwoma: Teaching and Learning in a New Guinea Tribe* (1941), and together with Irvin Child, he produced *Child Training and Personality: A Cross-Cultural Study* in 1953. In this co-authored book, they performed a cross-cultural survey (see the following) of seventy-five societies, rating them on initial indulgence of the child and severity of socialization methods, and relating those childhood experiences to adult behavior systems, including oral, anal, sexual, dependence, and aggressive behaviors.

BOX 3.3 SOCIALIZATION

Interestingly, although "socialization" became a central concept for psychological anthropology in the 1950s, and it remains—along with or replaced by "enculturation"—a key term in the anthropological vocabulary, the term was not common in the first decades of anthropology. For instance, it does not occur at all in Boas's treatise on primitive mind, and it is found only once in Mead's Samoa study, in reference to the role of dance in "the education and socialization of Samoan children" (1928: 117). It appears three times in Benedict's *Patterns of Culture*: once in the table of contents, once in reference to Zuni (Native American) society as a "socialized culture" (more suggesting "collectivist" or "group-oriented" than the modern anthropological use of the word), and only once in its more contemporary usage.

While *Child Training and Personality* was awaiting publication, Whiting and Child were plotting their next ambitious step—a simultaneous and systematic field study of several societies, collecting comparable data for meaningful analysis. In preparation, Whiting led a seminar for anthropologists and psychologists in which the participants designed a standard research protocol for all of the field researchers to follow; it was circulated in typescript form in 1953 as the fifty-some page *Field Manual for the Cross-Cultural Study of Child Rearing*. (More than a decade later, Whiting and his colleagues drafted a more extensive manual, *Field Guide for a Study of Socialization* [1966], featuring summaries of research topics and methods as well as more than fifty hypotheses for testing.) Whiting's original vision was to send out one hundred research teams, but since that was quickly understood as impractical, he settled on six.

Robert LeVine, one of the participants in the pioneering project, recalled decades later how it came to fruition. It was financed by a Ford Foundation grant of $350,000, the equivalent of $2.6 million dollars in 2006, and inspired by two academic programs: Yale University's Institute of Human Relations and Harvard University's Department of Social Relations. The project was first known formally as "A Study of Socialization in Five Societies" (a sixth society was later added), built around a year of fieldwork and two years of data analysis. LeVine writes that

> the socialization project was initially conceptualized not as exploratory or inductive but instead as testing the validity of the theory of culture and personality constructed at Yale by Whiting and Child, based on thinking by [psychologist] John Dollard and others. The theory incorporated Clark L. Hull's behavior theory (largely based on habit-formation experiments with laboratory animals), Bronislaw Malinowski's functional theory of culture, and Sigmund Freud's psychoanalytic conception of development and psychodynamics. Whiting had studied with Hull and Malinowski as a postdoctoral fellow at Yale, 1938–1939. He and his wife Beatrice had been psychoanalyzed by Earl Zinn, an analyst trained at the Berlin Psychoanalytic Institute.
>
> (LeVine 2010: 514–5)

Six teams were formed and sent to the following field sites:

- Robert and Barbara LeVine—Nyansongo (Kenya)
- Leigh Minturn and John Hitchcock—Khalapur (India)
- Thomas and Hatsumi Maretzki—Taira (Okinawa, Japan)
- Kimball and Romaine Romney—Juxtlahuaca (Mexico)
- William and Corinne Nydegger—Tarong (the Philippines)
- John and Ann Fischer—"Orchard Town" (northeastern United States)

Upon return from the field, Beatrice Whiting took the principal role in analyzing the voluminous data and in assembling the resulting book, *Six Cultures: Studies in Child Rearing* (1963).

Six Cultures was a tome of over one thousand pages, essentially six ethnographies under one cover. Each case study was organized into two parts—Ethnographic Background and Child Training—with roughly similar sections in each part. The ethnographic background surveyed daily routines; the economy; social organization; marriage; religion; disease and medicine; education; recreation; and, in some instances, politics. Under the all-important heading of child training, the cases reviewed pregnancy and childbirth; infancy; weaning; preschool and school age; and, sometimes, adolescence and/or initiation. However, despite shared protocols, the material was not perfectly synchronous.

A surprisingly short introduction preceded the case studies, presumably penned by Beatrice Whiting, which explained the genesis of the project, specified nine "behavioral systems" for description, and laid out two hypotheses from the *Field Guide*. The nine important behavioral systems were "succorance, nurturance, self-reliance, achievement, responsibility, obedience, dominance, sociability, and aggression" (Whiting 1963: 7). The two hypotheses, directly related to aggression, were (1) "that permissiveness on the part of parents for teasing behavior should be reflected in the increase of observable unprovoked aggressive behavior on the part of children and adults" and (2) "that children will be less apt to retaliate to aggression if parents and socializing agents punish any expressiveness with regard to anger" (10). The latter of these seems rather self-evident, and the former is verging on tautological.

In addition, the introduction set forth a model of the links between the natural environment or ecology, "maintenance systems" (what Kardiner would have called primary institutions), child-rearing practices, and child and adult personality. The model basically suggested the following (Figure 3.2):

Ecology → Maintenance systems → Childrearing practices → Child personality → Adult personality

economy	work	crime
social structure	games	suicide
	fantasy	leisure activity
	sayings	religion
	recreation	disease theories
	world concepts	folk tales

(based on Whiting 1963: 5)

Figure 3.2 Links between ecology, "maintenance systems," child-rearing practices, and child and adult personality.

The volume offered no analysis at the close of the case studies.

LeVine reminds us that the six ethnographic cases were published individually a few years later; yet he also concedes in retrospect that the sprawling research and book "yielded incomplete or inadequate data" (2010: 517), and it is difficult to draw any substantial conclusions from them. Nevertheless, the participants continued to mine and extend the material over the ensuing years, as in Minturn and Lambert's *Mother of Six Cultures: Antecedents of Child Rearing* (1964) and Whiting and Whiting's *Children of Six Cultures: A Psycho-cultural Analysis* (1975).

In the same journal issue that featured LeVine's reflections on the historic project, Carolyn Edwards and Marianne Bloch evaluate the long-term impact of the Whitings's work and their concept of culture. Finding obvious value in the Whitings's basic but hardly revolutionary assertions, they conclude that "the Whiting model for psychocultural research is not commonly included today in texts or reference articles, but it still exerts influence in contemporary psychology and anthropology" (Edwards and Bloch 2010: 490). Contemporaneous with the Six Cultures project, many more field studies of childhood and child-rearing were conducted, including Hamed Ammar's 1954 *Growing Up in an Egyptian Village*, Hildred Geertz's 1961 *The Javanese Family: A Study of Kinship and Socialization*, E. T. Prothro's 1961 *Child Rearing in the Lebanon*, and B. Kaye's 1962 *Bringing Up Children in Ghana*, to name but a few. Scholars like Heidi Keller still take inspiration from the Whitings's work, as in her 2007 *Cultures of Infancy*.

BOX 3.4 CULTURAL VARIABILITY OF PERCEPTION

The late culture-and-personality school also revisited the earlier question of the cultural variability of perception. Two specific topics that were studied in this area were color perception and susceptibility to optical illusions. It had long been noticed that societies had extremely different vocabularies for color terms: some have as few as two terms (roughly black and white or dark and light), while others have names for dozens of colors. The obvious question is whether cultures and languages with fewer color terms actually *see* fewer colors or more generally whether the terminology of color affects the experience of color. Brent Berlin and Paul Kay published an epic study on "basic color terms" in 1969, in which they argued that there are semantic universals and evolutionary regularities in color systems across cultures, known as UE (for universals and evolution) theory. The simplest color-sets, as just mentioned, distinguish light/white from dark/black. The next stage adds red; the third stage adds either green or yellow, and the fourth stage includes both green and yellow. Blue joins the vocabulary next, followed by brown, and then purple, pink, and orange. The claim then was that, however cultures differ in describing colors, there is a cross-cultural tendency to see and name colors in a consistent way. Marshall Segall, Donald Campbell, and Melville Herskovits returned to the topic of visual perception and optical illusion, particularly the Müller-Lyer illusion, checked by Rivers in his research a half-century before (see Chapter 1). Starting from the observation, also made by Rivers, that some premodern societies are less prone to the illusion than urban Europeans and Americans, they reasoned that the difference could be explained in relation to the "built environment" or the kinds of structures that the two types of societies inhabited. In what they called the Western "carpentered world" of rectangular buildings with sharp corners, people learned to interpret the visual cues of corners (suggested by the arrow-heads in the Müller-Lyer graphic) as perspective and distance; societies without carpentered homes were unaccustomed to corners and thus less likely to interpret corner-like shapes as distant and longer. Both of these topics have received experimental and ethnographic testing since, but the question of the cultural relativity of perception is still very much an open one.

Acculturation: psychological adjustment to cultural change

While generations of anthropologists and cross-cultural psychologists have kept a steady eye on children, an equally fascinating subject, and one that sheds a different kind of light on culture and personality concepts and theories, is culture change. If, as psychologically-oriented anthropologists assert, cultural conditions shape personality, then changing cultural conditions should produce empirically observable changes in personality. Sociologist Robert Park is widely credited with coining the phrase "marginal man" to refer to the individual who "finds himself striving to live in two diverse cultural groups. The effect is to produce an unstable character—a personality type with characteristic forms of behavior" (1928: 881).

Of course, anthropologists have known almost from the beginning of the discipline that "natives" or "primitives" were largely if not always marginal people, affected by conquest, colonialism, and missionization long before the scholars arrived. We commonly call this process of exposure to two or more cultures *acculturation*, and anthropologists recognized its importance even before the rise of late culture-and-personality theory. Richard Thurnwald was already in a position to ponder "The Psychology of Acculturation" in a 1932 article in *American Anthropologist*, in which he likened learning a second and foreign culture to any other occasion "of accepting a new contrivance for one's own daily use" (1932: 558). In other words, acculturation was just a special kind of learning, one with identifiable processes and outcomes. By 1936, the matter was sufficiently pressing for three famous anthropologists—Robert Redfield, Ralph Linton, and Melville Herskovits—to proffer their "Memorandum for the Study of Acculturation," a precursor of Whiting's field manual for the study of socialization. In their short research guide, they defined acculturation as "those phenomena which result when groups of individuals having different cultures come into continuous first-hand contact, with subsequent changes in the original cultural patterns of either or both groups" (1936: 149). They then organized lists of kinds of appropriate source materials and research techniques, of types of contact situations and acculturation processes (e.g. coercion and resistance), of psychological mechanisms (e.g. the role of the individual, personality types among accepters and rejecters of change, gender, psychic conflict, etc.), and of outcomes, whether acceptance, adaptation, or reaction. In his own "The Significance of the Study of Acculturation for Anthropology" (1937), Herskovits argued that attention to acculturation brought history back into what could be an otherwise static examination of culture—for our purposes, particularly personal history or biography as acculturation studies highlight the "power or impotence of the individual in the face of established tradition, the mechanisms that enable an individual to bring about cultural change or to enforce cultural stability," not to mention "the educative forces which condition an individual to the patterns of behavior sanctioned by his society" or imposed by an intruding society (1937: 262).

John Gillin put his finger on a major point in regard to acculturation by subsuming it under the general problem of learning and "secondary" or "acquired" drives. From Freud to the Whitings, a cornerstone of psychological anthropology or of cultural psychology was the plasticity of human behavior and of the drives and instincts with which humans are allegedly born. Thus, Gillin insisted that a theory of learning was crucial "for the explanation and prediction of the acquisition and performance of learned behavior of individuals" (1942: 545), culture being a primary condition of the transformation of innate drives into culture-specific personality:

> A change of conditions in any particular, however, may produce a situation in which performance of the old patterns is either no longer rewarding or actually becomes punishing. In psychological terms, the customary habits tend to extinguish; in anthropological terms, we may say that the old patterns are no longer followed, or that they tend to be lost.
>
> (546–7)

> All or any such changes in conditions may lead to the development of new acquired drives—secondary drives, desires, or wishes, if you prefer—in the members of the society undergoing acculturation. Insofar as such drives become common to the members of the group they become cultural drives, and new patterns of customary response for their satisfaction will tend to develop.
>
> (547)

But naturally it takes some time for new acquired drives or new personality formations to appear, propagate, and settle, resulting in "an inevitable period characterized by some confusion and lack of stability in behavior"—and many such dislocated peoples "seem to linger interminably in the period of readjustment with no appreciable approach toward stabilization" (548), troubled by new anxieties and overall "negativism" or depression.

In the late culture-and-personality era, acculturation became a more common and urgent subject, bringing with it advances in understanding. Fred Voget, for instance, realized that there was not a single acculturation style but many: documenting an Iroquois group living near Montreal, Quebec, he identified four different positions along the acculturation spectrum:

- "native" or "those individuals whose basic orientation was in terms of the unmodified aboriginal past" (essentially unacculturated)
- "native-modified" or individuals who "were nativist in orientation, but their formal education within the dominant society together with a limited participation in segments of American culture had led them to support modifications of native institutions and to inject new meanings into 'native' ceremonial forms"
- "American-modified" or those "who still thought of themselves as Indians and with some notable exceptions, maintained a limited social participation with the native-modified group, but their cultural integration basically was in terms of the dominant American society. Moreover, some members manifested strong tendencies to participate in white society on the basis of equality, and their efforts in this wise led them into exploitative activities vis-à-vis the dominant society and the subordinate groups"

- "American-marginal" who were "distinguished from the remainder by full identification with the dominant society and culture. The group apparently comprised mixed-bloods who had cut themselves off completely from social contacts with the other three groups. Their marginality derived in part from their own activities and from local discrimination by whites familiar with their ancestry."

(1951: 221)

Another eager scholar of acculturation, also working with a Native American population, was Alfred (A.) Irving Hallowell (see the following for his use of "projective tests" in personality research). In fact, several chapters of his 1955 *Culture and Experience* dealt with acculturation among the Ojibwa (citing Gillin in the process). Noting different levels of acculturation in different Ojibwa communities, he also introduced three other assumptions. First, "A considerable degree of acculturation could occur without any radical change in [their] personality structure," decoupling social experience from personality in any simple causal way. Yet, second, "In the most highly acculturated group the readjustments demanded in the acculturation process produced stresses and strains that were leading to certain modifications in the modal personality." Third and most interestingly, "While some few individuals, more especially women, were making an excellent social and psychological adjustment, the men, on the whole, were much less successful" (1955: 335). In general, he judged that the trend in Ojibwa personality was acceleration in a "regressive direction. These people are being thrown back on their psychological heels as it were. They are compelled to function with a great paucity of inner resources. There is a kind of frustration of maturity" (352). He declared that the Ojibwa living at Lac du Flambeau were at a "psychological impasse" (364).

Soon thereafter, Stephen Boggs added a study of Ojibwa children under conditions of culture contact, asserting that child-rearing practices were changing profoundly and that "serious alteration in the process of personality formation has occurred in the group which has undergone cultural disintegration" (1958: 54). Meanwhile, George Spindler's *Sociocultural and Psychological Processes in Menomini Acculturation* (1955), crediting Hallowell's long-term work, applied personality tests to a Native American people in Wisconsin and to a control group of white men, several of them married to Menomini women. Like Gillin, he proposed a continuum of levels of acculturation, in this case five—native-oriented, Peyote cult members, traditional, lower status acculturated, and elite acculturated, the last predictably most similar in personality to whites. As two final examples out of many, Norman Chance's investigation of Eskimo acculturation showed the opposite effect as the Ojibwa, with women presenting "much higher *emotional disturbance scores*" presumably due to "the greater stress placed on them as a result of their loss of many traditional roles without adequate replacement and an accompanying loss of prestige" (1965: 381, emphasis in the original). Even so, Chance found a relative "lack of serious psychological impairment…among members of either sex…. [B]oth are adjusting to their rapidly changing social and cultural environment quite well" (387). On the other hand, late in the culture-and-personality era but also focusing on Alaska, Arthur Hippler contended that the Athabascans were not doing nearly as well. Opining that their "cold, harsh, non-nurturant environment" compelled them to "isolate themselves from each other," spawning child-rearing (especially mothering) practices that bred fearful and demon-haunted individuals who "were mutually suspicious of each other, warlike, and aggressive" (1973: 1530), he believed that traditional social institutions had evolved to deal with these character features. However, this culture-and-personality balancing act, "based on a fairly rigid personality type, could not endure serious changes in its structure without massive personal disorganization on the part of its members. Apparently, this has happened" (1537–8).

BOX 3.5 ANTHONY WALLACE: MAZEWAY AND CULTURE CHANGE

In groping for terminology to talk about traditional and modern personalities and the transition between them, scholars floated all sorts of terms from "mind" and "mentality" to "personality," "self," and "character." One other option, proposed by Anthony Wallace, was *mazeway*. In his 1961 synopsis *Culture and Personality* he formulated mazeway as "the entire set of cognitive maps of positive and negative goals, of self, others, and material objects, and of their possible dynamic interrelations in process, which an individual maintains at a given time" (1964: 15–6). Personality, in contrast, "covers the same territory, but on a higher level of abstraction, in which mazeway particulars are classified and grouped under various rubrics" (16). Stating that mazeway "is to the individual what *culture* is to the group" (16, emphasis in the original), he went on to explain, in a three-page outline, that mazeway consists of "values" (positive organic, positive symbolic, altruistic, and negative), "objects" (first and foremost self and self-image), "human environment," "nonhuman environment" (plants, animals, land), "supernatural environment," and "techniques" or "images of ways of manipulating objects in order to experience desired end-states or values" (19). Wallace's mazeway concept never caught on in anthropology, but he did employ it usefully in a classic analysis of culture change. In 1956, he wrote that in circumstances of disruptive culture contact, the preexisting cultural and psychological adaptations (what he called the "steady state") may begin to fail. This situation sets off a period of "increased individual stress," which "poses the threat of mazeway disintegration" and "cultural distortion" (1956: 269). As Hallowell commented, individuals revert to "regressive" behavior, until some inspired person offers a "mazeway reformulation"; very often, such a new model for personality and for culture first comes to an individual with an especially troubled personality (one who is prone to visions, hallucinations, and even near-death experiences) and appears in dreams and fantasies. This person, commonly recognized as a "prophet," promotes "a new mazeway *Gestalt*" (270) for personal and social transformation. Such a psychosocial event

> would seem to belong to a general clinical category of sudden and radical changes in personality, along with transformation occurring in psychotic breaks, spontaneous remissions, narcosynthesis, some occasions in psychotherapy, "brainwashing," and shock treatments…. Physical stress and exhaustion often seem to precede the vision-trance type of transformation, and it seems probably that chemical substances produced in the body under stress may be important in rendering a person capable of this type of experience.
>
> (271)

Whatever its psychological source and substrate, if the prophet begins to communicate it to others, and then to organize and institutionalize it (in the manner implied by Sapir in the previous chapter), it may develop into a "revitalization movement" and settle into a new steady state or "normal" culture.

What's on your mind? Projective tests in anthropological fieldwork

As we have indicated in this chapter and near the end of the last chapter, psychologically-oriented anthropologists frequently augmented their standard qualitative method of participant observation—watching, joining in, and trying to understand a culture from personal subjective experience—with formal quantitative psychological tests. Some of these were measures of intelligence, perception, and even reflexes and motor skills. In this battery of instruments, however, was a set of several "projective tests." Based on the Freudian concept of projection in which a person "projects" their inner thoughts, feelings, and motives out onto the external world (especially onto another person), projective tests theoretically permit a view into the test-taker's mind by giving them an ambiguous or incomplete stimulus and asking them to react to, explain, or complete it.

The projective test with which most people are probably familiar is the Rorschach or "ink-blot" test. Deployed at least as early as the 1940s in Cora Du Bois's study of Alorese personality (see Chapter 2), it is usually associated with Freudian psychoanalysis but was not designed by Freud himself. Rather, in 1921, in a book titled *Psycho-diagnostics*, Hermann Rorschach created ten cards with anomalous shapes in ink (half black-and-white, half with more or less color), which he claimed were valuable for diagnosing schizophrenia. The patient was asked to describe what s/he saw, and the answers were scored against an elaborate rubric featuring many categories such as movement, form, chromatic color, texture, shading, human, animal, blood, clothing, clouds, explosion, sex, and more. These results could purportedly identify deviant verbalization, inappropriate logic, perseveration, aggression, and morbid thoughts, among other psychopathologies (Figure 3.3).

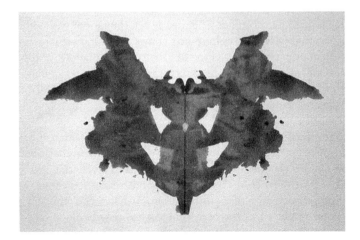

Figure 3.3 A Rorschach inkblot, designed to diagnose certain kinds of mental illness but also used extensively by psychological anthropologists to discover personality traits across cultures.

Despite the fact that the Rorschach test was not originally intended to be applied to normal individuals or to groups, many anthropologists seized upon it as a tool for comparative psychology. Du Bois, as just mentioned, took it to her field site, as did Spindler, the Whitings, Leighton and Kluckhohn, and the authors of *The Authoritarian Personality*; Mead and Métraux recommended it as part of their tool kit for studying culture at a distance. One of its most avid adopters was Hallowell, who wrote about it in his "The Rorschach Technique in the Study of Personality and Culture" (a paper also anthologized in his *Culture and Experience*). Conceding that it was "devised as a measure of individual variation in personality organization," he reasoned that "if an adequate sample of a population is secured the analysis of the group results should enable us to differentiate 'communal,' 'idiosyncratic,' and 'role' components of personality" (1945: 205).

If it is true that the Rorschach test can be re-tasked to analyze healthy individuals and entire societies, two serious questions remain: is the test cross-culturally valid, and if so, can it be applied to indigenous and/or nonliterate peoples, whose norms and values are so different? Happily, Hallowell judged in the affirmative:

> Responses in sufficient quantities for interpretation can be obtained from non-European or non-literate peoples provided that the test is administered with care. Thus anthropology is provided with a practical psychological tool that recommends itself because (a) the equipment needed is simple; (b) there is a minimum of verbal instructions to subjects; (c) the literacy of the subjects is not involved; (d) an interpreter can be used, if necessary; (e) the subjects can take their time without affecting the results, yet relative time of responses can be used diagnostically; (f) the subjects cannot tell each other the answers, because there are no right and wrong answers; (g) it can be used with all age groups, and (h) while certain standards in administration have to be met, these are not too rigid.
>
> (201–2)

He also announced that "basic principles of Rorschach interpretation can be applied to data secured from non-literate peoples" and even that "it is possible to make use of local norms and thus achieve greater precision in interpretation" (204)—although what the local norms of Rorschach interpretation might be is difficult to say. Confident of the appropriateness of the inkblots for societies like the Ojibwa, Hallowell used them to measure both traditional/precontact personality and personality under acculturation. To increase objectivity, some anthropologists performed the tests and collected the data but left it to a third party, a qualified psychologist, to interpret the data.

BOX 3.6 THOMAS GLADWIN: TRUK PERSONALITY

Another acclaimed application of Rorschach testing was a collaborative effort of an anthropologist, Thomas Gladwin, and a psychologist, Seymour Sarason. *Truk: Man in Paradise* (1953) discussed the people of an island in the western Pacific and not unexpectedly reflected the influence of Du Bois's work on Alor. Incorporating biography, dream analysis, and Rorschach and other projective testing with ethnographic observation, the authors concluded that this supposedly sexually free society (similar to Mead's alleged portrait of Samoans) harbored a fair amount of sexual tension and conflict. Uniquely, Gladwin and Sarason explicitly did not attempt to correlate specific elements of Trukese culture with resultant personality but only to identify "proximal" determinants of personality in the formative years of Trukese youths.

Despite this confidence and these checks on interpretation, a good number of anthropologists remained skeptical about the Rorschach and other projective tests. Several big names in the field gathered for a symposium, including Hallowell, Spindler, S. F. Nadel, Melford Spiro (see the following), and Jules Henry, the proceedings of which were published in *American Anthropologist* in 1955. Henry, the lead author of the article, expressed concern that "I would not know what I had once I had a batch of Rorschach responses" and further stipulated that he was "opposed to anything that places an instrument between me and a responding human being" (Henry et al. 1955: 245). "In about the same amount of time that is given to obtaining all the responses to the Rorschach Test," he contended, "one can obtain excellent material on personality in a culture outside the Euro-American tradition, if one takes the trouble to train one's self in *interviewing methods and theory*" (246, emphasis in the original). Nadel, a British social anthropologist, was still more sanguine, questioning the profit of projective testing, which, if it existed, was "neither an immediate one nor one easily gained. The projective techniques certainly do not provide anything in the nature of a shortcut" (247); he was not even sure of "the varying readiness of different groups to 'project' at all" (248), undermining the whole philosophy of such exercises. Worst of all, he was doubtful of the "consistency of personality" (249) in the first place.

Naturally, Spindler, Hallowell, and others were much more supportive of the Rorschach and related instruments. Melford Spiro called it "an important technique for either purpose" of understanding a particular culture or culture in general (256), while Spindler placed special value on the Rorschach for studying acculturation, and Hallowell reiterated his conviction that "the test is valid cross-culturally" (263) and that in fact "any discussion of projective techniques as instruments having a potential usefulness in anthropological field work should not be limited to the Rorschach" (264).

In their critique of the cross-cultural use of Rorschach images three years later, Cyril Adcock and James Ritchie used much more negative language than Henry or Nadel. Conducting their own analysis of scores taken from three categories of Maori (indigenous New Zealander) and one *pakeha* or white New Zealand population, they concluded vehemently that

1   The meaning of the stimulus material used in the Rorschach test cannot be assumed to be cross-culturally equivalent. The cards become part of the subject's culture as soon as he enters into the test situation and they then have his meaning, not that of the tester's culture.
2   Rorschach scoring symbols cease to convey the subjective meaning of the informant's culture since the symbols and their meaning derive from the tester's culture.
3   The meaning of such symbols must therefore be re-established for each culture before valid interpretation can be made.
4   Factor analysis facilitates this reinterpretation.
5   Ethnologists must be prepared to face the fact that the results of such factorial guidance may seriously limit the confidence which can be placed in the results of cross-cultural Rorschach research.

(1958: 891)

Whether or not they ameliorated the worries about the Rorschach inkblots, anthropologists also had other projective psychological tests at their disposal. A common one was the Thematic Apperception Test or TAT. Conceived by Christiana Morgan and Henry Murray in 1935 to access the fantasies of psychoanalytic patients, it was comprised of thirty-one cards, thirty black-and-white images of social interaction scenes, and one blank card asking the patient to imagine a picture and tell a related story (Figure 3.4).

Figure 3.4 A card from the Thematic Apperception Test, a projective test of personality. *Science History Images / Alamy Stock Photo.*

Anthropologists often used a subset of the TAT cards in conjunction with Rorschach images, and sometimes they modified or created cards to be culturally appropriate for the local society. For instance, granting that TAT pictures were not culture-neutral but rather that they were "based on the cultural pattern of Europe and America" (Chowdhury 1960: 245), Uma Chowdhury produced a set suitable for India. One of the most extensive revisions was manufactured for Robert Edgerton's (1971) comparative analysis of four East African societies. He commissioned African artists to draw scenes that conveyed native norms and values, making the testing more locally relevant but the results less cross-culturally comparable.

One more type of projective test solicited individuals to draw their own pictures. One of the first of these to be promulgated in psychology was Florence Goodenough's 1926 Draw-a-Man Test, which encouraged subjects to share their thoughts and feelings about themselves and/or other people. Karen Machover followed in 1948 with the Draw-a-Person Test, which has sometimes been expanded to drawing a person, a house, and a tree. In all these cases and others branching from them, drawers are presumed to project their inner attitudes onto pictures that can be quantified and interpreted. In still other instances, anthropologists like Bateson and Mead, and Mead's student Belo, collected the drawings of children and attempted to interpret those pictures themselves or submitted them to psychologists for interpretation.

Big data in culture and personality: cross-cultural surveys

One of the banes of culture-and-personality research, and indeed of all anthropology, has been the lack of standardized quantitative data to make cross-cultural comparisons. Of course, philosophically, all anthropology is comparative, even if an ethnography of a single culture implicitly only compares that culture to one's own. To a certain limited extent, some of the classic culture-and-personality texts had been comparative, holding up three (in the case of Benedict's *Patterns of Culture*) or six (in the case of Whiting's *Six Cultures*) societies against each other. However, the weakness of these works was the small sample size and the qualitative nature of the data, often collected by different ethnographers with different research interests.

Not long after the basic questions of psychological anthropology were put on the table, some anthropologists began to take an entirely different approach. Instead of direct observation and psychological testing in one or a few societies, they aspired to a large sample (known in statistics as a "large-n"), reaching to dozens if not hundreds of societies (recall that John Whiting originally dreamed of one hundred societies in his project). With such "big data," as it is called today, anthropologists could perform sophisticated statistical analyses and, perhaps most importantly of all they hoped, derive correlations or even cause-and-effect relations.

Any anthropologist can concatenate any set of studies that they like, but a major step forward occurred when scholars began to organize and categorize the available cultural information. George Peter Murdock (1897–1985) took the lead in presenting the first edition of the *Outline of Cultural Materials* in 1938. According to the introduction to the fourth edition published in 1961 and compiled by a team of experts including Murdock, Leo Simmons of *Sun Chief* fame, and John Whiting, among others, the original intent of the *Outline* was to be "a tool for the Cross-Cultural Survey, an organization established in 1937 by the Institute of Human Relations at Yale University as part of its program of interdisciplinary research in the social sciences," with a mission

> to organize in readily accessible form the available data on a statistically representative sample of all known cultures—primitive, historical, and contemporary—for the purpose of testing cross-cultural generalization, revealing deficiencies in the descriptive literature, and directing corrective field work.
>
> (Murdock et al. 1961: xiii)

By the early 1940s, this unprecedented database was mobilized to study alcohol use in "primitive" societies (Horton 1943) and human reproduction across cultures (Ford 1945). Inevitably the information was recruited for the war effort during World War II, yielding seven *Strategic Bulletins of Oceania* and nine *Military Government Handbooks* on various Pacific Islands for the U.S. Navy. After the war, to make the data more widely accessible, the project was converted into an interuniversity system known as the Human Relations Area Files or HRAF. For optimum usefulness, the thousands of pages of ethnographic material were photographed and coded—at the time of the 1961 *Outline* into seventy-nine major categories or divisions and 631 subcategories. The major divisions included methodology, geography, human biology, "behavior processes and personality," history and culture change (such as innovation and acculturation), language, several categories on food and food production, clothing, a number of categories on economic activity, arts, marriage/family/kinship, politics and the state, sex, religion, and dozens more. In 1957, Murdock published his own "World Ethnographic Sample" of 565 societies with fifteen columns of coded traits, which he and Douglas White followed in 1969 with their "Standard Cross-Cultural Sample" with a more targeted selection of 186 societies.

With the caveat that a database is only as good as the data that goes into it, an assortment of anthropologists turned to this resource, or found or made resources of their own, to do large-n comparisons, and not exclusively in the psychological realm. Whiting and Child incorporated an analysis of sixty-five societies from HRAF in their 1953 *Child Training and Personality* (see earlier) to test various psychoanalytic hypotheses. Irvin Child joined with Herbert Barry and Margaret Bacon a few years later to explore one of the perennial questions of culture-and-personality anthropology, namely, the relationship between child training and fundamental economic practices. They hypothesized that "the degree of accumulation of food resources is the underlying variable likely to be of special importance for the understanding of our results" (1959: 53) and checked the claim against a sample of 104 societies drawn from Murdock's material and earlier work by Bacon and Barry. Not unreasonably, they believed that if "economic role and general personality tend to be appropriate for the type of subsistence economy, we may expect the training of children to foreshadow these adaptations" (53), and accordingly they considered six variables—obedience training, responsibility training, nurturance training, self-reliance training, and general independence training. Instead of finding a direct link between these factors and the economy, their main discovery was that a more general variable, which they called "pressure toward compliance vs. assertion" (58), was in play. They also reported interesting connections between compliance/assertion and social institutions, such as settlement size, degree of political integration, social stratification, polygyny, unilineal descent, and fixed versus shifting residence.

Cross-cultural surveys were also put to more specialized purposes. R. W. Shirley and A. Kimball Romney (1962) queried the relationship between love-magic practices and socialization anxiety, while Beatrice Whiting (1950) included a statistical analysis of the association between sorcery and the presence or absence of "superordinate justice" or political institutions to punish behavior in her ethnography on Paiute sorcery. In fact, religion became a prime subject for cross-cultural correlations, as in John Whiting's research, in tandem with Richard Kluckhohn and Albert Anthony, on male initiation rites and child-rearing practices. They hypothesized that societies

> which have sleeping arrangements in which the mother and baby share the same bed for at least a year to the exclusion of the father and societies which have a taboo restricting the mother's sexual behavior for at least a year after childbirth will be more likely to have a ceremony of transition from boyhood to manhood than those societies where these conditions do not occur (or occur for briefer periods).
>
> (Whiting, Kluckhohn, and Anthony 1958: 364)

Charles Harrington (1968) turned the method on the question of male genital operations, William Stephens (1961) on menstrual taboos, and Judith Brown (1963) on female initiation rites. Finally, on topics that we will meet again later in this book, Roy D'Andrade (1961) took a sample of sixty-four societies from HRAF to study dreams, and Erika Bourguignon (1973) put a sample of 488 societies to work to identify geographic and other correlations with trance behavior (see Chapter 8).

Evaluating cross-cultural surveys as early as 1970, Raoul Naroll determined that the method was in wide use for studies of child-rearing and adult behavior as well as of kinship and arts. He concluded that the greatest success of the survey method was in studying groups and cultures but that as "a tool for investigating variation among individual human beings it is clumsy and dull and so far has not proved rewarding" (1970: 1127). He also cautioned practitioners of cross-cultural surveys to beware of problems in sampling, defining the social unit under investigation, classification and coding of cultural behaviors, deviant cases, and the general phenomenon of finding random correlations in any large body of data.

BOX 3.7 MELFORD SPIRO: FALSE DICHOTOMY OF CULTURE AND PERSONALITY

In 1951, when the late phase of culture-and-personality had barely gotten off the ground, Melford Spiro issued something of a manifesto in his article "Culture and Personality: The Natural History of a False Dichotomy." Appropriately enough published in the journal *Psychiatry*, Spiro used the essay to state his position

> that the concepts of personality and of culture cannot be separated empirically, and that the dichotomy that is held to obtain between them is a consequences of Western intellectual history, on the one hand, and of contemporary fallacies of thinking about them, on the other.
>
> (1951: 19)

He began by tracing the history of the culture concept from Tylor to the mid-twentieth century, during which culture increasingly became a distinct "thing" to study; worse yet, culture became explanatory, that is, people "behave that way *because* of their culture" (22, emphasis in the original). Further, it was unclear whether culture referred to behavior or something that preceded and caused behavior: "In other words is culture to be located outside of behavior or is its locus *in* behavior?" (22, emphasis in the original). Frankly, the same question could be asked of personality. He accused Boas of trying to have it both ways—of expanding culture to embrace cultural norms and institutions as well as behavior and the products of behavior. Following David Bidney, and anticipating Clifford Geertz (see Chapter 5), Spiro stipulated that human culture would be impossible without "a minimal human nature to account for man's ability to create culture in the first place" (26)—and we might add, to transmit and acquire culture—but "man's phylogenetic behavioral storehouse is meager indeed," so much so that "the invention of culture—learned ways of behaving—was not a luxury but a dire necessity" for our early ancestors (27). In other words, culture is, as Geertz would later put it, "ingredient" to humans, not a mere superficial coating on a complete pre-cultural being. In Spiro's more challenging language, his assertion was

> (a) that an extracultural human nature is a necessary condition for the phylogenetic invention of culture and for the ontogenetic acquisition of the *cultural heritage*; and (b) that the ontogenetic acquisition of culture assumes the existence of a cultural heritage which can be acquired to form the personal culture. If these two propositions are valid, one may conclude (c) that *the development of personality and the acquisition of culture are one and the same process.*
>
> (30–1, emphasis added)

Phrased otherwise, as a child learns culture, those "teachings—beliefs, cognitions, attitudes, emotions, behavior—do not remain outside himself. They are incorporated within himself to become *his* beliefs, *his* cognitions, *his* attitudes, *his* emotions, *his* behaviors" (36, emphasis in the original). To grasp his argument, it is imperative to understand his concept of "cultural heritage." Cultural heritage was for Spiro what culture is for most anthropologists: it is all the external, public knowledge that an individual *might* acquire as a member of society. But he also insisted that cultural heritage "is not homogeneous for all members of the society" (37): there is not a single cultural heritage in the way that most observers assume there is a single culture. The child is not and cannot be "exposed to the society as a whole":

> he is exposed only to the members of his own family. *His* cultural heritage is what the members of his family wish to teach him, and what they teach him is a function of what *they* believe, what *they* know, what *they* do, and what *they* feel.... Thus social inheritance is much more like biological inheritance than we have been prepared to admit.
>
> (38, emphasis in the original)

We might realistically liken cultural heritage to a library, housing all of the knowledge of a society. But any particular individual only reads or gets to read part of it, which is *her* cultural heritage. More, an individual may have access to the cultural heritage of more than one society, whether by being personally bicultural (the offspring of members of two different cultures) or taking an interest in another culture's heritage. Finally, whatever source(s) an individual draws from, the learning and internalization process will "distort" the heritage(s), giving it or them new interpretations and meanings. Therefore, the standard failure of anthropology is the inability to see that a typical ethnography "is a description of the cultural heritage of a society"—which may be the actual culture *of no member at all*—and consequent inability "to distinguish between the cultural heritage of society and the culture an individual" (41). Spiro's two ultimate claims were these: first,

> Personality and culture, then, are not different or mutually exclusive entities; they are part and parcel of the same process of interaction. Both personality and culture reside in the individual or, to put it differently, they are the individual as modified by learning,
>
> (43)

and second,

> the culture of any society is not the sum of the individual cultural heredities, nor is it the direct manifestation of the total cultural heritage; it is, rather, the product of the interaction of all the individuals in the society.
>
> (41)

Summary: achievements and shortcomings

In a number of ways and quite intentionally, anthropologists between the mid-1940s and the early 1970s perpetuated and perfected concepts and theories born during the early years of the culture-and-personality school. These advances included:

- the study of large, complex, modern societies and countries, in addition to anthropology's traditional focus on small, premodern groups

- the effort to be more systematic and quantitative in the observation of childhood and child-rearing, sometimes literally taking the form of manuals and field guides
- the introduction of new concepts, such as national character, acculturation, mazeway, and cultural heritage
- experimentation with new methods for data collection and analysis, such as photography, projective testing, and large-n cross-cultural surveys
- more ambitious cross-cultural comparison to check hypotheses and assumptions, with a central database of ethnographic knowledge.

All the same, as we will see in the next chapter, by the end of the era, some anthropologists were ready to rethink culture-and-personality research or abandon it altogether. Among their complaints with the first fifty years of anthropological effort, critics charged that:

- entire societies and nations were summed up with a few or even one personality trait or child-rearing practice, most absurdly Russian national character and swaddling
- the results of culture-and-personality research were inconclusive at best and disappointing at worst
- psychological tests, designed specifically for Western cultures, were spuriously applied to other cultures
- during this period in history, anthropological methods and findings were becoming too politicized and militarized
- models in psychological anthropology seemed to have little to do with what was actually going on inside the minds of people.

Anthropology would subsequently take some dramatic turns in reaction, as the next two chapters, and indeed the rest of the book, will attest.

Chapter 4

The cognitive turn in anthropology

Ethnoscience and structuralism

Key figures:
Alfred L. Kroeber (1876–1960)
Leslie White (1900–1975)
Claude Lévi-Strauss (1908–2009)
Ward Goodenough (1919–2013)
Stephen Tyler (1932–present)
Charles Frake (1930–present)

Key texts:
"The Superorganic" (1917)
"Componential Analysis and the Study of Meaning" (1956)
Structural Anthropology (1958)
"The Concept of Culture" (1959)
The Savage Mind (originally published as *La Pensée sauvage*, 1962)
Cognitive Anthropology (1969)

Even as the culture-and-personality school of anthropology was renewing itself in the 1950s, a revolt was gathering within the discipline against the older generations' psychological anthropology and against anthropology-as-usual. This insurrection was influenced by advances in allied disciplines—psychology and linguistics, especially—and by dissatisfaction not only with the results of previous psychological anthropology but also with broader anthropological concepts and methods. The very concept of "culture" itself was subjected to revision, and the fundamental questions that anthropology should be asking, and the kinds of answers it should be seeking, were rethought.

Out of this ferment arose two quite distinct and yet surprisingly related anthropological approaches. One we will call, among its many suggested names, *ethnoscience,* and the other we will call *structuralism,* although, as we will see shortly, both demonstrated an interest in "structure," which each conceived in a different way. Despite their differences, they had certain features in common:

1   a desire to make anthropology more rigorous and scientific, particularly in reaction to some of the perceived flabbiness of culture-and-personality work
2   a shift away from "personality" toward "mind" or mental processes
3   a comparative disinterest in childhood and culture acquisition

4   a central preoccupation with kinship and kinship terminologies
5   the adoption of language as the central paradigm for understanding culture and mind.

Equally fundamental to both the ethnoscientists and the structuralists was *classification*. The mind was viewed as a classifying device, and culture as we find it—the ideas, actions, and utterances of people—was the product or manifestation of such classification systems (or, in the case of structuralism, the one universal classification system). This emphasis on classification was not new. The father of modern sociology, Émile Durkheim, had put classification at the core of his analysis of religion and society in his crucially important 1912 book *The Elementary Forms of Religious Life*. Using ethnographic data, particularly on Australian Aboriginal societies, he pondered what the absolute most primitive or minimal form of religion might be, and his answer was totemism (a subject that also preoccupied turn-of-the-century anthropologists [see Chapter 1] and that would reappear in Claude Lévi-Strauss's construction of structuralism [see the following]). Durkheim reasoned that humans found themselves born into a social world that was already categorized and organized, into families and lineages and clans and such, and that this classification scheme was then imposed or projected onto the natural world. The natural world, such as plant and animal species, was divided up and assigned to already-existing and socially real human groups in the form of totems as a symbolic reflection of the social world. The idea of religion itself, Durkheim concluded, depended on the compulsory quality of society: "the god of the clan, the totemic principle, can therefore be nothing else than the clan itself, personified and represented to the imagination under the visible form of the animal or vegetable which serves as totem" (1965: 236)—notwithstanding the fact that a totem is hardly a "god."

The schools of ethnoscience and structuralism were not the only ones in anthropology or in social science to take a cue from Durkheim's emphasis on classification nor did they always acknowledge their debt to him. Further, as indicated earlier, both new anthropological approaches placed more value on language than Durkheim did. Nevertheless, the dual stress on classification and language led some anthropologists down very different paths than their immediate predecessors.

What do natives know: ethnoscience

A number of anthropologists who were children during the days of Margaret Mead's *Coming of Age in Samoa* and Ruth Benedict's *Patterns of Culture* rejected the methods and concepts of their elders, judging those earlier ideas and practices to lack rigor and sophistication, and to essentially misrepresent both culture and psychological processes. Instead of fretting about toilet training and swaddling, this next generation of anthropologists insisted that their discipline should concentrate on what members of a society have in their heads and what a fieldworker needs to get into her head in order to understand and participate in that society.

The perspective that they advocated was known by various names—componential analysis, ethnosemantics, the new ethnography, cognitive anthropology, and so on—but we choose here to adopt the label "ethnoscience" both for convenience and because (a) that term conveys both the "ethno-" or local cultural element of knowledge and the "science" quality of native thinking and this aspirational new anthropology alike, and (b) the term "cognitive anthropology" acquired different connotations in ensuing years (see Chapter 10).

In his edited volume of ethnoscience literature, Stephen A. Tyler proclaimed that the new field, which he called cognitive anthropology, constitutes a new theoretical orientation. It focuses on discovering how different peoples organize and use their cultures. This is not so much a search for some generalized unit of behavioral analysis as it is an attempt to *understand the organizing principles underlying behavior.* It is assumed that each people has a unique system for perceiving and organizing material phenomena—things, events, behavior, and emotions. The object of study is not these material phenomena themselves, but *the way they are organized in the minds of men.* Cultures then are not material phenomena; *they are cognitive organizations of material phenomena.* Consequently, cultures are neither described by mere arbitrary lists of anatomical traits and institutions such as house type, family type, kinship type, economic type, and personality type, nor are they necessarily equated with some overall integrative pattern of these phenomena. Such descriptions may tell us something about the way an anthropologist thinks about a culture, but there is little, if any, reason to believe that they tell us anything of how the people of some culture think about their culture.

(1969: 3, emphasis added)

The mission of this new anthropology was

to provide answers to the questions: How would the people of some other culture expect me to behave if I were a member of their culture; and *what are the rules of appropriate behavior in their culture?* Answers to these questions are provided by *an adequate description of the rules used by the people in that culture.* Consequently, this description itself constitutes the "theory" for that culture, for it represents the conceptual model of organization used by its members. Such a theory is validated by our ability to predict how these people would expect us to behave if we were members of their culture.

(5, emphasis added)

Thus, as Tyler implied, the goal was not a single universal "theory of culture" but rather the discovery and explication of the multitudinous local theories of culture, that is, a particular society's categorization of its own lived world.

In a word, then, "the anthropologist's problem is to discover how other people create order out of what appears to him to be utter chaos" (6), and this order is accomplished through classification:

We classify because life in a world where nothing was the same would be intolerable.... There is nothing in the external world which demands that certain things go together and others do not. It is our perception of similarities and differences together with a set of hierarchical cues that determine which things go together.... Thus we subjectively group the phenomena of our perceptual world into named classes.

(7)

This clarifies the proposed role for anthropology in the investigation of culture and of mind: our discipline should not seek

a description of events or an account of change. The cultural anthropologist is only concerned with those events which are expressions of underlying thoughts. His aim is to penetrate beyond mere material representation to the logical nexus of underlying concepts.

(14)

The birth of ethnoscience is commonly traced to two articles published in 1956 in the same issue of the journal *Language*. Floyd Lounsbury applied linguistic concepts to Pawnee (Native North American) kinship terminology, comparing the components of language to the components of kinship. On the premise that "[a]ll responses of an organism are classificatory: they effect classifications of stimuli" (1956: 190), he literally proposed that phonology or the sounds of language could be approached in the same way as kinship semantics or the meanings of kin terms. In phonology, the unit is the phone, whereas in kinship, the unit is the individual. "Phone type" designates a category of phones or sounds that are "the same" for the linguist and the speaker of the language; "kin type" similarly specifies a category of kinsmen who stand in the same relationship for the anthropologist and the member of the society. Finally, "phoneme" is a "class of nonconstrastive phone types which share a distinctive bundle of phonetic features," just as a "kin class" is a "class of kin types which are not contrasted terminologically and which share some distinctive bundle of semantic features" (191). Through this arcane phraseology, Lounsbury asserted that kinship terminology "is but a special area of vocabulary, and its structure is a special case of semantic structure" (191).

In the article immediately following Lounsbury's, Ward Goodenough introduced his foundational "Componential Analysis and the Study of Meaning." Positing that "the methods of componential analysis as they have been developed for analyzing linguistic forms are applicable in principle for analyzing other types of cultural forms" (1956: 195), he offered a similar inquiry into Truk (Pacific Island) kinship terminology. In a very technical presentation, he recommended the method of collecting every word or "lexeme" that pertains to the matter of kinship to explore how they can be grouped according to their referents: for example, gender (in English kinship terms, for example, "mother" versus "father" or "brother" versus "sister"). He further opined that such a technique could be applied to other areas of culture, such as color terms.

To make a long story short, both Lounsbury and Goodenough directed anthropology's attention to the *semantic* dimension of culture, that is, to the fact that culture consists of words (and other signs) that have a meaning and that can and should be studied and organized in the same way that linguists study language. But by this time, there was also a revolution in linguistics underway, located in the work of such thinkers as Ferdinand de Saussure and Noam Chomsky. The structuralism of Claude Lévi-Strauss (see the following) would exploit the grammatical side of this new linguistics, but the semantic side which was the obsession of ethnoscience—hence sometimes also called ethnosemantics—shared many of the same traits. Top among them were (a) the isolation of the basic or minimal units of language/culture and (b) the identification of the rules for combination of those units. These rules were thought to be unconscious to speakers of the language and members of the society (although, of course, individuals could become conscious of them) and to be the "principles that underlie behavior" (Blount 2011: 12), whether that behavior is speech or social action. As Ben Blount, in his recent summary of cognitive anthropology, puts it, the central contention was "that observable behavioral phenomena are recognized as expressions of more basic and fundamental underlying organizational order and principles" (12)—or, in the words of anthropologists then and since, of underlying *structure*.

It should be obvious that this new agenda for anthropology was premised on a new concept of culture, one which was not committed to older notions of institution or even of behavior or artifacts and certainly not of child-rearing. In another essay, Goodenough defined culture from an ethnoscience or componential analysis point of view as "whatever one has to know or believe in order to operate in a manner acceptable to its members, and do so in any role that they accept for any one of themselves" (1957: 167). Culture thus was regarded as *knowledge*—as knowledge that members actually had in their heads, as knowledge that anthropologists needed to acquire to understand and participate in the society, and as knowledge that we must report in our ethnographic writings. This is why the movement was also known as "the new ethnography."

Not only was culture essentially knowledge, but it was also predominantly linguistic and propositional knowledge, i.e. words and sentences. The duty of anthropologists was to extract and reconstruct native knowledge, the local ethnoscience, where, as William Sturtevant wrote in a 1964 issue of *American Anthropologist* devoted to "Transcultural Studies in Cognition," science means specifically "classification" (1964: 99). Culture, Sturtevant added, "amounts to the sum of a given society's folk classifications, all of that society's ethnoscience, its particular ways of classifying its material and social universe" (100). This diverges dramatically from the goals of Mead, Benedict, Whiting, and the other prior and contemporary psychologically oriented anthropology fieldworkers, who, Sturtevant and his colleagues complained, had fostered and perpetuated an "underdeveloped condition of ethnographic method" (100). Accordingly, he called for "the improvement of ethnographic method, to make cultural descriptions replicable and accurate, so that we know what we are comparing. *Ethnoscience shows promise as the New Ethnography required to advance the whole of cultural anthropology*" (101, emphasis added).

Of what did this new method consist, and how was it related to ethnoscience claims about language, knowledge, and mind? With a view to exposing what locals have in their heads, the fundamental methodological strategy was called "elicitation," that is, providing situations and exercises to evoke, elicit, or draw out mental (again, often unconscious) knowledge in spoken form. First, the fieldworker had to decide what domain of knowledge to investigate—kin terminology, colors, religion, medicine, food, or what have you. The intention was to encourage the informant to utter the words that pertain to that particular domain and then analyze how each word is used (i.e. what it "means" or when one would say it) and how each is related to the others, specifically which ones "go with" which others or how they are organized or classified. The researcher could engage the informant in a number of activities, such as "free listing, frame elicitation, triad tests, pile sorts, paired comparisons, rank order, true and false tests, and cultural consensus tasks" (Simova, Robertson, and Beasley 2009). Another tactic was sentence completion of the sort, "You said that _____ and ___ are ways to treat malaria. What other ways are there for treating malaria?" (Weller and Romney 1988: 12).

As a trivial but illustrative example, imagine that an anthropologist from a society without pigs landed in the United States, whose people eat a variety of pig meats. First, the researcher might hear an American use the word "pig" and inquire into the word's meaning, or the researcher might see the animal, point to it, and inquire as to its name. She could then ask, "What kind of meat comes from a pig?" to which the answer might be "pork." She might then encounter a thin round slice of pig meat, call it "pork," and be corrected: "No, that is ham." Next, she might see long, straight, thin pieces of pig meat, call it "pork," and be corrected again: "No, that is bacon"—only to call round thin pieces of meat "bacon" and be informed that that is "Canadian bacon." The anthropologist would begin to organize this information into a system of local knowledge, highlighting one or both of two features:

1   a taxonomy or tree, a kind of outline, with "Meat" at the top level, branching down to "Pig-based meat" and then splitting into "Pork," "Ham," and "Bacon" (perhaps with a further split between "Bacon" and "Canadian Bacon") (Figure 4.1)

    Eventually too, we would learn that there are other meats (e.g. beef), which also come in many different subtypes (sirloin steak, round steak, ground round, etc.), further filling up our chart of ethno-meat-knowledge.

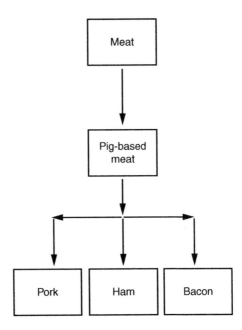

Figure 4.1 Taxonomy of "Meat".

Figure 4.2 Butcher diagram: cuts of pork.

2   a set of criteria or membership conditions for each item in our ethno-meat system. These could consist of "definition" (e.g. bacon, according to the U.S. Dairy Association, is "the cured belly of a pig carcass") or of a number of variables that, in combination, distinguish one meat from another, such as the location from which it is cut, how it is prepared, and so forth (Figure 4.2).

More importantly, presumably, the knowledge that we produce in our ethnographic description can be attributed to the members of that society: they know the terms, can perceive the differences, and can accurately and consistently apply the appropriate label to the item. This same procedure, then, could be replicated in every area of cultural life.

BOX 4.1 CHARLES FRAKE: SUBANUN ETHNOMEDICAL KNOWLEDGE

Charles Frake put the ideas of ethnoscience into practice in his fieldwork among the Subanun of Mindanao (the Philippines). In one of his most informative papers, he explored the decidedly nontrivial arena of medical knowledge or how the Subanan go about diagnosing disease. In researching the ethnomedical knowledge of such a society, Frake explained that we start to

> note the kinds of questions the Subanun ask about these cases, we record the alternative (or contrasting) replies to each kind of question, and then we seek to differentiate the factors by which a Subanun decides one reply, rather than an alternative, applies in a particular situation.
>
> (1961: 115)

The "fundamental unit of Subanun diagnosis," he asserted, "is the *diagnostic category* (or 'disease') labelled by a 'disease name'…which classifies particular illnesses, symptomatic or pathogenic components of illnesses, or stages of illnesses" (115, emphasis in the original). The Subanun word for "disease name" was *ŋalan mesait en*, and when they asked questions about their own or others' afflictions, a particular *ŋalan mesait en* was the suitable response, and "a Subanun must select one disease name out of a set of contrasting alternatives as appropriately categorizing a given set of symptoms" (116) in the same way that our hypothetical American notes contrasts between different cuts of pig meat and attaches the correct label. To narrow the discussion, Frake selected skin diseases for further analysis. First, he described how they distinguished *nuka* (skin disease) from *samad* (wound); then, under the heading *nuka*, he discovered *meŋebag* (inflammation), *buni* (ringworm), and *beldut* (sore, which was further subdivided into *telemaw* or distal ulcer and *baga'* or proximal ulcer). A *samad* could also become a *meŋebag* if the relevant symptoms appeared, and a *pugu* (rash) could turn into a *nuka*. Thus, we can think of a "disease name" as

> a minimal, congruent (i.e., meaningful) answer to the question, 'What kind of illness is that?' (*dita? gleruun ai run ma iin*)' Alternatively, it is a congruent insertion in the frame, 'The name of (his) disease is _____. (*ŋalan en ig mesait en _____.*)',
>
> (122)

explaining two different ways to elicit the information. Thus, most fully elaborating the methodology of ethnoscience and how it works in relation to Subanun ethnomedicine, Frake stated,

> A classification of Subanun diagnostic criteria follows from (1) the questions which elicit them and (2) the status of the answers as diagnostic labels.

1 By eliciting question
    1.1 Pathogenic criteria [i.e., agent or mechanism that produces illness]
    1.2 Prodromal criteria [i.e., prior conditions]
    1.3 Symptomatic criteria.
    1.4 Etiological criteria [i.e., why a particular person develops a particular illness]
2 By status of the answer as a diagnostic label
    2.1 Elementary criteria.
    2.2 Complex criteria.

(125)

Once more, ostensibly, all of this is knowledge that the Subanun actually have and use, even if unconsciously.

In an essay titled "*The Ethnographic Study of Cognitive Systems*" (originally published in 1962 but anthologized in Tyler's 1969 reader in cognitive anthropology), Charles Frake added some nuance to the conceptual arsenal of ethnoscience. The first key concept was *segregate*, defined as "a terminologically distinguished array of objects" (1969: 31); a segregate is a category, like "sandwich," that contains one or more specific types, arranged into a *contrast set* (for instance, hamburger versus peanut butter and jelly sandwich). Each particular item or category possesses its *attributes* that make it an instance of that item/category (for instance, bun versus bread). Segregates were organized at a higher level into *semantic domains*, which Tyler earlier in the book defined as "a class of objects all of which share at least one feature in common which differentiates them from other semantic domains" (1969: 8), as in the case of "food." All of the semantic domains in a language and culture comprised the *folk taxonomy* or local cultural model of reality, by means of which members could make statements about, judgments about, and responses to their world.

As we can see, the ethnoscientific approach so far discussed favors a "trait list" attitude toward linguistic labels and cultural knowledge, that is, without being too flippant, that a "Big Mac" can be distinguished from other burgers and sandwiches by listing its ingredients (two all-beef patties, special sauce, etc.). Another suggestion was to think—and that members of a society do think—in terms not of trait lists but of *prototypes*, bundles of characteristics that most closely fit and most potently represent a type. A good example is the type "bird," the prototype of which might be a robin or sparrow; other "birds" diverge from the ideal to a lesser (for instance, ostrich) or greater (for instance, penguin) extent. "Individuals appear to use a focal representative, a prototype, to define a category and to identify other members of the category according to the degree of similarity to the prototype" (Blount 2011: 19), and, invoking once more the Gestalt school of psychology, Roy D'Andrade contended that "it is as if the human cognitive system were a structure seeking device ... [finding] ... which attributes of a class of instances are most strongly correlated and creates generic or basic-level objects by forming a gestalt configuration of these attributes" (1995: 120).

Ethnoscientists had to face two profound related challenges to their conception of their "new ethnography" as an uncovering of unconscious folk knowledge of a society. The first was the problem of the *psychological reality* of their descriptions: ethnoscientists had criticized previous anthropological practices for building an abstraction of culture that only existed in the mind of the researcher but not in the members themselves. The complicated componential structures that ethnoscientists offered as their finished product seemed unlikely as literal accounts of what people had in their heads, and the fact that much of this putative knowledge was unconscious meant that it could not be checked against the natives' own avowals of their knowledge. Connected to this objection was the second problem of *whose* knowledge in particular it was claimed to be. Hypothetically, as we noted earlier, ethnoscience should clarify what *any* member of the society needs to know in order to function as a mature adult, but there were serious questions about the distribution and variation of knowledge. In a study of the ethno-knowledge of birds among the Dené of Canada, Peter Gardner realized that, when asked for a local term to embrace all twenty-six species of birds included in the study, several of the people considered the question unreasonable; they were

definite that there was no term for "all these": /besi x*ulle/, "Their name is nothing." Yet others gave a head term that we could gloss as "bird" immediately, with great certainty (often voluntarily), and, in some cases, with approximations of an actual, fairly appropriate definition:

"They got wings" [said in English].
"They fly."
"They all fly."

(1976: 449)

Among the other locals to whom the question was posed,

Four used the term solely for a particular species (among them, they so labeled three different species). Five used it solely for what might be called a genus (with two, two, four, five or eight member species, as elicited). Five used it solely for what might be called a family, or order (with four, seven, eight, nine, or an unspecified number of species out of the set used). Two used it for both a species and a family. Five used it for both a genus and a family. Eight used it for both a genus and the Class Aves. Two used it for both a family and the Class Aves. Three used it for all three of the following-a species, a family, and the Class Aves. Five used it for all three of these—a genus, a family, and the Class Aves.

(452)

This dizzying and disturbing disagreement led Gardner to conclude that knowledge is diverse and distributed "in a way that makes it unproductive and perhaps even unreasonable in this particular instance to define the culture in terms of an average, the shared, the sum, or a mean around which there is variance" (459). Or, in one devastating sentence, "Actual informants do not know everything; they manifest cognitive variability in many ways" (464).

Such discoveries raise the more intriguing question of whether human classification and labeling is entirely culturally relative or whether it is guided if not determined by the differences that are really out there in the world. If humans are only noticing and naming real objective distinctions, then the cultural and psychological sides of classification are not very compelling. If, on the other hand, the external world is what it is *but is not obligating to our perceptions and labels*, then we can and must consider how much innate psychological tendencies and learned cultural diversity shape these folk taxonomies. This was one question that comparative ethnoscience could potentially address.

Yet, as Penelope Brown said in her 2006 synopsis of early cognitive anthropology, the approach "lost its impact on mainstream anthropology in the early 1970s, due in part to the contrast between the hubris of its sweeping goals and the limited nature of the studies (lexical semantics of particular domains, predominantly kinship, biological, and color terminologies), and partly to the impoverished view of cultural knowledge" (2006: 99). Indeed, I cannot think of one attempt at, let alone one successful accomplishment of, an ethnoscientific ethnography of an entire culture; considering that it took Frake an article just to detail skin diseases, it would probably take a thick tome to cover all Subanun ethnomedicine and an extensive set of volumes to treat all the other domains of their culture. And when it was done, we would still not be sure if we had captured "what the Subanun know." Accordingly, 1950s and 1960s ethnoscience progressed into twenty-first-century cognitive anthropology with an eye on "cultural models" and "schemas" along with neuroscience and evolutionary psychology, as we will see in the final chapter.

BOX 4.2 PAUL SILLITOE: WOLA ANIMAL CLASSIFICATION

Although ethnoscience no longer exists in its original form, and "cognitive anthropology" means something different today than it did a half-century ago, anthropologists have hardly lost their interest in documenting local knowledge or classification systems and in relating those findings to other aspects of culture and society. In fact, if we give up the assumption that knowledge is shared evenly throughout a society, then the subject acquires new importance. In 2002, Paul Sillitoe published an article on zoological classification among the Wola of Papua New Guinea, whose naming of animals tends "to challenge hierarchy, obfuscate boundaries, and think in terms of 'fuzzy sets,' confounding the assumption of agreed classes and threatening intellectual anarchy" (2002: 1162). For starters, Sillitoe maintained that the Wola do not have a term that quite translates to "animal" in general; the closest equivalent is *acha* meaning "game" and applying only to edible animals. Worse, they "further contradict the tenets of scientific classification by giving the same name to two or more animals, which, although similar, they acknowledge are not identical" (1164). They had no names at all for some of the invertebrates in their environment, calling them simply *imbiy na wiy*, "nameless." Finally, not surprisingly, Wola individuals disagreed with each other on how to name and classify animals. The unwary observer might consider this madness or at least cultural confusion, but Sillitoe argued that, in a sort of Durkheimian fashion, the classification of animals reflected the structure and ethos of society. Wola society itself was "acephalous," that is, it had no paramount leader or formal political hierarchy, and so fuzzy boundaries and idiosyncratic understandings were normal for them. Equally significantly, because there were no political elites or scientific experts, "there is by definition no authority to arbitrate when persons disagree, whether their dispute is over some serious wrongdoing or merely a difference over the identification of some wild animal" (1166). Ultimately, there may be less need to explain *their* lack of agreement over animal classification than *our* hard-won agreement (if and when it is achieved!) on the matter.

Local culture, universal mind: structuralism

At the same moment that ethnoscientists and cognitive anthropologists were mounting their attack on conventional anthropological concepts and methods, an alternative challenge was arising in France. It was also inspired by developments in linguistics and cut its teeth on kinship studies, and its chief proponent in anthropology was Claude Lévi-Strauss (1908–2009), by many reckonings the most influential anthropologist of the mid-twentieth century.

To fully grasp the thinking of Lévi-Strauss, we must digress for a moment to the structural linguistics of Ferdinand de Saussure, whose *Course in General Linguistics*—actually a posthumous compilation of his lectures—was published in 1916. In a statement that stands as a preemptive criticism of ethnoscience, Saussure wrote, "Some people regard language, when reduced to its elements, as a naming-process only—a list of words, each corresponding to the thing that it names" (1959: 5). Granting that words are not names for things but *signs* or symbols for concepts, which can vary between cultures and over time (and even between individuals), Saussure moved on to the crucial distinction between *langue* and *parole*. *Parole* in his interpretation was actual speech, the things that people say. Of much greater import to linguistics, he declared, underneath or behind *parole* was *langue* or "language," by which he meant the rules that make speech possible. What people said, which was subjective, variable, even messy and error ridden, was less interesting than the rules of language, which were objective, collective, and constant. A more immediate influence on Lévi-Strauss was the linguist Roman Jakobson, whom he met in 1941 and whose interpretation and critique of Saussure "proposed that underlying the diversity of languages and phonological components there was a small set of basic distinctions (binary oppositions) which generated the diversities. Lévi-Strauss seized upon this concept" (Voss 1977: 23).

Like Lounsbury and Goodenough and seven years ahead of their seminal papers launching ethnoscience or componential analysis, Lévi-Strauss began with kinship. In his *The Elementary Structures of Kinship*, first published in 1949, he took up a topic that had vexed anthropologists and other theorists for decades—the incest taboo. Recall that Freud in *Totem and Taboo* had placed the Oedipal desire to possess the mother at the heart of the incest taboo, which itself was at the heart of all orderly society (see Chapter 1). Lévi-Strauss proposed a very different solution, in which "kinship nomenclatures and marriage rules are complementary aspects of a system of exchanges whereby reciprocity is established and maintained between the constituent units of the group" (1969: xlii)—and the incest taboo is the rule that guarantees this reciprocity.

However humans first came to the realization, they determined that social groups like families could form peaceful and enduring bonds through gift exchange or reciprocity, including "material objects, social values and *women*" (62, emphasis added). After hundreds of pages of cross-cultural evidence, he concluded that the outlawing of incest "is less a rule prohibiting marriage with the mother, sister or daughter, than a rule obliging the mother, sister or daughter to be given to others. It is the supreme rule of the gift" (481). Beyond a novel alternative to Freud's prehistoric psychodrama, the relevance of this idea for psychological anthropology is twofold. First, it conceives of society as a great communication system in which women (and other valuable things) are "words" or "bits" in a sort of language or conversation. In Saussurian fashion, it is not specific women, or even the incest taboo itself, that are important but the rules that make social life possible. Second, anticipating where Lévi-Strauss's thinking would eventually go, he maintained that incest prohibitions and marriage rules tended to divide society into *two* woman-exchanging, inter-marrying or "exogamous" (and never intra-marrying or "endogamous") halves. He called this "dual organization," and anthropologists know it better today as the moiety system. The promise to exchange the women of one moiety with men of the other moiety instead of keeping those women for themselves was, he believed, the basis for *alliances* between groups and the integration of society.

BOX 4.3 CLAUDE LÉVI-STRAUSS: PRIMITIVE AND MODERN MENTALITY

It is consequential that, in the middle of his treatise on marriage exchanges and alliances, Lévi-Strauss injected a chapter on "the archaic illusion," the common and condescending assumption of "the relationship between primitive and infant thought" (87). The line, he insisted, should be drawn between *children's* thought and *adults'* thought, not between "primitive" and "modern." Across all cultures, the thinking of children is unsophisticated and not fully socialized, tending toward mistakes like magical thought and failed cause-and-effect relations. "In all societies the level of child thought is equally remote from the adult level of thinking" (92), because of differences both in mental maturity and in cultural experience. Thus, Lévi-Strauss contended, child minds are consistent across cultures, while adult minds vary more or less extensively, because "the mental schemata of the adult diverge in accordance with the culture and period to which he belongs" (93). What too many observers have seen as "primitive mentality," as "an absence of differentiation" in the thoughts of indigenous peoples is nothing more than "a different system of differentiation" (94), as ethnoscientists would certainly agree. In the end, "Primitive thought is as completely and systematically socialized as our own"; what is noteworthy and singular is the thought of the child and of the mentally ill, "which have a relative and individual independence which, of course, has a different explanation in each case" (97). In other words, the thinking of the child and the neurotic or psychotic is "abnormal" precisely because it does not follow cultural norms (see Chapter 9).

Presciently, Lévi-Strauss ended his book with a comment about language that would be reflected in his later work. Praising linguistics as the only social science to have reached a perfection that "allows the reconstitution of the origin of systems and their synthesis," he suggested that anthropology and sociology should follow its lead of identifying elementary units (like sounds and words) and the rules of combination between them. In the case of marriage and kinship, there are

> only three possible elementary kinship structures; these three structures are constructed by means of two forms of exchange; and these two forms of exchange themselves depend upon a single differential characteristic.... Ultimately, the whole imposing apparatus of prescriptions and prohibitions could be reconstructed *a priori* from one question, and one alone: in the society concerned, what is the relationship between the rule of residence and the rule of descent?
>
> (493)

Lévi-Strauss's thinking would become more fixed on this notion of a few or even one simple rule or principle behind complex cultural phenomena, culminating in his theory of structuralism or structural anthropology. In fact, some of his key papers from 1944 to 1957 were collected into a volume titled *Structural Anthropology*, first released in 1958. In that publication he confidently stated that in the study of social life, "anthropology proceeds by examining its unconscious foundations" (1963: 18), where the underlying rules and structures—the *langue* of culture, if you will—are located, rather than the hurly-burly of behavior and cultural products, the *parole* of culture. He went on to congratulate linguistics for "by far the greatest progress" in social analysis, as the only social science "which can truly claim to be a science" (31), its rigorous methods already yielding fruit for anthropology in the explication of kinship. The precise value of linguistics, he opined, was in redirecting effort "from the study of *conscious* linguistic phenomena to study of their *unconscious* infrastructure"; consequently, linguistics "does not treat *terms* as independent entities, taking instead as its basis of analysis the *relations* between terms," encouraging investigators to search for the "system" underneath culture and social life and therefore "discovering *general laws*" across cultures (33).

The program of Lévi-Strauss became yet more clear when he instructed social scientists to reach "beyond the superficial conscious and historical expression of…phenomena to attain fundamental and objective realities consisting of systems of relations which are the products of unconscious thought processes" (58). Hence, he could and must ask whether all cultural phenomena, from kinship to religion and beyond, "consist of systems of behavior that represent the projection, on the level of conscious and socialized thought, of universal laws which regulate the unconscious activities of the mind?" (59). As argued in his aforementioned analysis of kinship and marriage, he proposed that we imagine all of culture and society as a language, as a system of communication, in which words, goods, and women are the bits that circulate between individuals and groups (61).

As with ethnoscience, the power of a theory like structuralism lies not only or mostly in its concepts and programmatic statements as in its methodological potential: how can we apply it, and how does it allow us to study culture differently and produce new results? Perhaps the most famous methodological recommendations of Lévi-Strauss came in the chapter titled "The Structural Study of Myth." Along with kinship, many anthropologists considered the study of religion to be in disarray if not at a dead-end in the 1950s. The problem, he conceded, was that at first glance religious thought and behavior seemed to display "no logic, no continuity"—"anything is likely to happen" in myths and rituals (208). But again, that is the superficial *parole* of religion, behind which we can and must find the consistent and simple *langue*.

> (1) If there is a meaning to be found in mythology, it cannot reside in the isolated elements which enter into the composition of a myth, but only in the way those elements are combined. (2) Although myth belongs to the same category as language, being, as a matter of fact, only part of it, language in myth exhibits specific properties. (3) Those properties are only to be found *above* the ordinary linguistic level, that is, they exhibit more complex features than those which are to be found in any other kind of linguistic expression.
>
> (210)

The way to get at the underlying or overarching principle beneath myth was essentially to "diagram" the myth, literally "breaking down its story into the shortest possible sentences, and writing each sentence on an index card bearing a number corresponding to the unfolding of the story" (211). These bits, these "mythemes" or building blocks of the myth, could then be scoured for relations—and not just "isolated relations but *bundles of such relations*" (211, emphasis in the original), which are both the meaning of the myth and the evidence of unconscious principles are work. He wickedly selected the original ancient Greek story of Oedipus to demonstrate his technique, chopping the narrative into plot elements to expose binary pairs that were allegedly the meaning of the myth, such as the overrating/underrating of blood relations or the autochthonous/ the denial of the autochthonous origin of mankind. Felicitously (but probably if not certainly spuriously) dismissing the problems of translation and disparate versions, since the same themes or principles shine through regardless, he affirmed that actual performance of a myth (mere *parole*) and variants were irrelevant; only the mental *langue* of myth commanded our concern, and *langue* or principle was sufficient "to provide a logical model capable of overcoming a contradiction (an impossible achievement if, as it happens, the contradiction is real)" (229). In the process, multiple tellings or performances may proliferate, "each slightly different from the others. Thus, myth grows spiral-wise until the intellectual impulse which has produced it is exhausted. Its *growth* is a continuous process, whereas its *structure* remains discontinuous" (229, emphasis in the original).

BOX 4.4 NOAM CHOMSKY: LANGUAGE ACQUISITION DEVICE

Although Lévi-Strauss did not yet have it to call upon, the linguistic theory of Noam Chomsky would add support and additional concepts for the structural approach. Totally obliterating the behaviorist account of language learning in his 1959 review of B. F. Skinner's *Verbal Behavior*, which held that children acquire language by sheer imitation and reward, Chomsky went on to make two crucial points. First, neither actual speech nor semantics (the study of words and meanings) was of import to linguists, only the rules of combination of words or *grammar*; moreover, this grammar was largely unconscious to the average speaker. Second, it seemed to him that the individual acquisition of language, and the species capability to acquire language at all, must depend on a mind/brain function specialized for that purpose, which he called a "language acquisition device" or LAD. In these terms, while ethnoscientists pursued "structure" in terms of semantics and knowledge, Chomsky envisioned "structure" as grammar and rules.

Lévi-Strauss attacked the problem of mentality (primitive and otherwise) directly in his 1962 *The Savage Mind*. In that work, where he averred that anthropology was basically psychology (see the first sentence of Chapter 1), he commenced from the position that classification was the main function or activity of mind and is a virtue in its own right: "Any classification is superior to chaos, and even a classification at the level of sensible properties is a step towards rational ordering" (1968: 15). But, suggesting along the way that science and magic "require the same sort of mental operations" (13)—since doubtless there *was* only one sort of mental operation—he submitted that the untutored mind, savage or civilized, was no scientist but rather what he called a *bricoleur*. From the French *bricolage* for the craftman's talent to make heterogeneous, even infinite products from a limited set of tools or resources, a *bricoleur*, a tinkerer rather than a more systematic engineer, operates in a universe where

> the rules of his game are always to make do with 'whatever is at hand,' that is to say with a set of tools and materials which is always finite and is also heterogeneous because what it contains bears no relation to the current project, or indeed to any particular project.
>
> (17)

"Mythical thought is therefore a kind of intellectual 'bricolage'" (17).

Having established to his satisfaction that mythical thinking (and perhaps most thinking) is a do-the-best-with-what-you-have affair, he condemned the appeal to "primitive mentality" in previous generations of anthropologists as a failure to appreciate that other societies had their own "complex and consistent conscious systems" of classification (40) and that the mental practices of the average citizen of "civilization" were not so far from those of the unschooled savages. As he had demonstrated in his 1949 book, kinship and totemism were "in fact only a particular case of the general problem of classification" (62). Then he returned to the question of grammar or "transformation"—and specifically to the topic of totemism—to state that any structure (linguistic, cultural, or otherwise) consisted of *oppositions*, in the simplest form *binary pairs*, which comprised a "system of difference"; consequently, two systems of difference—say, kinship groups and natural species—could be inter-translated or superimposed by analogy or homology.

These ideas of binary pairs, opposition, and the (ultimately unsuccessful) resolution of opposition or contradiction crystalized in Lévi-Strauss's ensuing writing. His four-volume *Mythologiques*, published between 1964 and 1971 and featuring such titles as *The Raw and the Cooked* and *The Naked Man*, continued the analysis of myths and manners with an eye to the mental logic that energizes them. Recurrent binary pairs included, as the title of the first volume suggested, raw/cooked as well as male/female, nature/culture, dead/alive, and so forth. Obviously, there is no way to eliminate or resolve such oppositions; all the *bricoleur*-mind can do is play with them, confront and express them, again and again. But what was finally important in culture was not the culture-specific details of myth or any other public product but the ostensibly innate, universal structure of thought itself that made humans this kind of classifying creature.

BOX 4.5 LÉVI-STRAUSS'S STRUCTURALISM

Lévi-Strauss's version of structuralism can be seen as a variation on LeVine's model of $P \rightarrow C$, where "personality" is understood narrowly as the innate structure of mind.

This, then, is the definitive difference between the "structure" of ethnoscience and that of Lévi-Straussian structuralism. Ethnoscientists, from Goodenough to Tyler and Frake, were intently interested in the content, in the words, in the semantics of culture. As mentioned earlier in the discussion of Chomsky, they were in search of "local knowledge" and the relationships (unconscious mental lists, outlines, and flow charts) between elements of knowledge. They were *not* particularly or overtly interested in, or at least explicit about, the *mind* in which such knowledge dwelt. Lévi-Strauss was exactly the reverse: anything approaching "knowledge," like myth, was only evidence of mind itself. The knowledge as knowledge was incidental, even an obstruction (just as actual speech was an obstruction to Chomsky in his excavation of mental transformational grammars), on the way to the structure not of words, things, or acts but *underneath* or *behind* those public expressions.

Structural analyses like those modeled by Lévi-Strauss became all the rage for a time, including among anthropologists who had made a name for themselves with their own pre-structuralist works. One prime example is Edmund Leach's "Genesis as Myth" (1969), in which he subjected the first book of the Judeo-Christian scriptures to a structuralist treatment, complete with a graphic presentation of the binary oppositions at work in that story, such as life/death, moving world/static world, west/east, animal/plant, and herdsman/gardener. Lévi-Straussian structuralism proved most productive in mythology studies and was employed noticeably less in other areas of culture. Also, it could be asked what else, after the identification of this binary mental process supposedly driving all myth and culture, could be gained from such exercises: once we know the mind is a binary-classification machine, what else is there to learn? Lastly, the same objection of "psychological reality" lodged against ethnoscience could be made against structuralism: are the systems built by the structuralist analyst really ones that members have in their heads—or would even recognize or accept?

BOX 4.6 MARY DOUGLAS: CATEGORIES, POLLUTION, AND DANGER

Mary Douglas does not properly belong to either school of cognitive anthropology, yet her seminal thinking shows a certain affinity for their penchant for classification. Conspicuously a "neo-Durkheimian," her landmark book *Purity and Danger*, first published in 1966, concurred that classification was the essence of mental activity and social life. In addition, she asked two other previously neglected questions: what happens when categorial boundaries are crossed, and why do cultural category systems often have a *moral* component? It might be noticed that early cognitive theories of culture posited a human person who is basically a rational knower (ethnoscience) or a playful thinker (structuralism). Douglas maintained that cultural classification is frequently if not ordinarily an emotional matter and one of deadly seriousness. For people who are committed to a particular classificatory order, it is not merely, as Lévi-Strauss opined, that classification is better than chaos; threats to or violations of order are experienced as painful, even dangerous. Disorder is labeled, and felt, as *pollution*, to which humans react with dismay and potentially disgust. This sense of pollution, she wrote, "is the reaction which condemns any object or idea likely to confuse or contradict cherished classifications" (1988: 36). "Dirt," in a word, "is essentially disorder" (2): few things are dirty in themselves but only in relation to cultural concepts of orderliness and propriety. But "dirt" is the price that you pay for order: dirt "is never a unique, isolated event. Where there is dirt there is a system" (35), and where there is a system there is dirt. The classic manifestation of dirt and danger is Durkheim's notion of the "profane," which threatens and endangers the "sacred" (the greatest of all binaries). Douglas noticed that cultures around the world perceive hazard and risk in all sorts of violations of prized order—breaking the rules, to be sure, but also ambiguity and anomaly, "transitional states" (i.e. when individuals or groups are undergoing changes), margins and borders, and the comparatively unstructured domains of life. She illustrated her point by analyzing one particular ritual system of order, the dietary laws in the biblical book of Leviticus. Various animals are explicitly named as not only unfit for consumption but as "abomination," hateful and disgusting, such as those that "chew the cud" but do not "have the cloven hoof" or, vice versa, that do not "chew the cud" but do "have the cloven hoof." Shellfish are also forbidden and "impure." In an almost ethnoscientific way, Douglas reasoned that the category "animal" or, even more, "clean animal," had certain features—both "chew the cud" and "have the cloven hoof": "Cloven-hoofed, cud-chewing ungulates are the model of the proper kind of food for a pastoralist. If they eat wild game, they can eat wild game that shares these distinctive characters and is therefore of the same general species" (54). Any animal that deviated from these features was anomalous, unclassifiable, and hateful. Likewise with seafood: a "fish" has scales and fins. Therefore, any marine life, like shrimp or lobster, that lacks scales and/or fins is out of order, an anomaly and a violation, and unholy.

Culture without mind—and without individuals?

In anthropology as in physics, it seems that for every action there is an equal and opposite reaction. The two postwar cognitive anthropologies just reviewed were palpable reactions to the earlier culture-and-personality school of anthropology. In turn, cognitive anthropologies and the entire psychological project in anthropology spawned its own reaction against personality, mind, and psychology as a whole. An anti-psychology, anti-cognitive streak in anthropology and social science was not entirely novel in the 1950s. Karl Marx's materialist theory of society and history, dating back to the mid-1800s, was fairly indifferent to individuals and to personality processes. For him, groups, specifically *classes*, were the key actors in society and history, and individuals were basically products of their historical era and their class position. Subsequent Marxist theorists tended to downplay the role of the individual and the significance of psychology.

Within anthropology, resistance to psychological/cognitive thinking originated in an unlikely place, from one of Boas's star students, Alfred Kroeber (1876–1960). In an early, controversial, and sometimes misunderstood essay, he appeared to assert that culture was information and that human beings were no more than "carriers" of this information: "tradition, what is 'given through,' handed along, from one to another, is only a message. It must of course be carried; but the messenger after all is extrinsic to the news" (1917: 178). Granting that culture (or, in his words, civilization) "in a sense exists only in the mind" and that all cultural facts "can have existence only through mentality," he proceeded to announce that culture "is not mental action itself; it is carried by men, without being in them" (189)—the precise opposite of what others like Spiro would say (see Chapter 3).

In perhaps his strongest statement, Kroeber wrote:

> The reason why mental heredity has nothing to do with civilization, is that *civilization is not mental action but a body or stream of products of mental exercise.* Mental activity, as biologists have dealt with it, being organic, any demonstration concerning it consequently proves nothing whatever as to social events. *Mentality relates to the individual. The social or cultural, on the other hand, is in its very essence non-individual.* Civilization, as such, *begins only where the individual ends;* and whoever does not in some measure perceive this fact, though as a brute and rootless one, can find no meaning in civilization, and history for him must be only a wearying jumble, or an opportunity for the exercise of art.
>
> (192–3, emphasis added)

Arguing against the "great man" theory of history and the role of individual "genius" in cultural change, he believed that "the content of the invention or discovery springs in no way from the make-up of the great man, or that of his ancestors, but is a product purely of the civilization into which he with millions of others is born as a meaningless and regularly recurring event" (196). It was as if culture, and the appearance of new ideas, inventions, and discoveries, happened without any input from individuals: when a society was "prepared and hungry" for change, "the enunciation seems to have been destined to come almost precisely when it did come" (197).

In the final analysis, Kroeber did not so much deny the reality of individuals and of psychological processes as rule them out from social science. Social science, he affirmed, should "refuse to deal with either individuality or the individual. And it bases this refusal solely on its denial of the validity of either factor for the achievement of its proper aims" (206). Getting to the title of his essay, he explained that both bodies and minds were "organic" but that culture and society were "superorganic," different from, above, and independent of bodies and minds:

> The mind and the body are but facets of the same organic material or activity; the social substance—or unsubstantial fabric, if one prefers the phrase—the existence that we call civilization, transcends them utterly for all its being forever rooted in life.
>
> (212)

Again, bodies and minds merely "carry" culture, which is conceptually and factually separate from them.

Although this attitude sparked an immediate debate—in the very next issue of *American Anthropologist* Edward Sapir responded that culture or civilization cannot do anything by itself, that "it is always the individual that really thinks and acts and dreams and revolts" (1917: 442) and that between "the psychic and the social there is no chasm in [Kroeber's] sense at all" (444)—Kroeber bolstered his position with a study of the cycles of fashion, which appeared to run as if autonomous of human thought or choice. Inspecting women's fashion over a long period of time, he deemed that there was

> reasonable evidence of an underlying pulsation in the width of civilized women's skirts...; of an analogous rhythm in skirt length...; some indication that the position of the waist line may completely alter, also following a "normal" curve, in a seventy-year period; and a possibility that the width of shoulder exposure varies in the same manner, but the longest rhythm of all.
>
> (1919: 257–8)

The message was that the regularity and timescale of fashion trends "dwarfs the influence which any individual can possibly have exerted in an alteration of costume" (260).

In the prime of ethnoscience and structuralism, the most adamant advocate of culture's ontological independence from psychology and the individual was Leslie White (1900–75). Proffering a rejuvenated kind of cultural evolutionism in an article, "The Concept of Culture," and a book, *The Evolution of Culture* (both in 1959), he made two strenuous claims—first, that culture is the proper subject matter for anthropology, and second, that culture is *not* behavior and most definitely not *mental behavior*. Accordingly, he proposed to redefine anthropology as, if not replace anthropology with, *culturology*, distinguishing "between psychology, the scientific study of behavior on the one hand, and culturology, the scientific study of culture, on the other" (1959a: 229).

Notwithstanding that psychology is not in fact concerned only with behavior but also or more so with mental phenomena, for White, the critical feature of culture was that it involved symbols, and even more essentially, the capacity to create symbols and infuse them with meaning (see Chapter 5). He called this ability "symboling," the bestowal of "meaning upon a thing or an act, or grasping and appreciating meanings thus bestowed" (231), adding a new dimension to human experience. Now,

> When things and events dependent upon symboling are considered and interpreted in terms of their relationship to human organisms, i.e., in a somatic context, they may properly be called *human behavior*, and the science, *psychology*. When things and events dependent upon symboling are considered and interpreted in an extrasomatic context, i.e., in terms of their relationships to one another rather than to human organisms, we may call them *culture*, and the science, *culturology*.
>
> (231, emphasis in the original)

This stress on symboling and its effects led him to a new definition of culture as "a class of things and events, dependent upon symboling, considered in an extrasomatic [outside the body] context"; he believed that such an approach

> rescues cultural anthropology from intangible, imperceptible, and ontologically unreal abstractions and provides it with a real, substantial, observable, subject matter. And it distinguishes sharply between behavior—behaving organisms—and culture; between the science of psychology and the science of culture.
>
> (234)

Although he did not dispute that the "locus" of culture (that is, where we find it) is "within human organisms" as well as "within processes of social interaction between human beings" and "within material objects" (235) and therefore that ideas and attitudes are also culture, he all the same insisted that culture, including "its variations in time and place, and its processes of change *are to be explained in terms of culture itself*" (239, emphasis added). In other words, we cannot explain culture in terms of psychology, let alone biology, and we cannot reduce culture to psychological or mental phenomena and processes. He even invoked the difference between *langue* and *parole* to make his point:

> Our distinction between human behavior and culture, between psychology and culturology, is precisely like the one that has been in use for decades between speech and language, between the psychology of speech and the science of linguistics. If it is valid for the one it is valid for the other.
>
> (247)

BOX 4.7 LESLIE WHITE AND ALFRED KROEBER AS ANTI-PERSONALITY

White, and to a lesser extent Kroeber, is the epitome of LeVine's anti-personality model, C → P, in which personality or the individual is a product of culture—or is altogether irrelevant to the study of culture and outside the domain of anthropology (**C without P**).

Summary: achievements and shortcomings

The postwar cognitive turn in anthropology marked a new era and a generational shift in the discipline, a critical response to the first decades of psychologically oriented anthropology and a fresh school of thought that could claim some significant advances:

- It promised to make anthropology more scientific and rigorous
- It showed the crucial role of classification in culture and in the thinking that produces and reproduces culture
- It envisioned a new concept (or several rival concepts) of culture as well as original methodology for field research and for ethnographic writing
- It believed that it was discovering what members of society actually had in their heads as opposed to interpretations and abstractions only true and relevant for anthropologists themselves
- It brought language to the fore as a central way of thinking about culture and as a paradigm for culture
- It offered the potential to solve problems that had long plagued anthropology, such as the meaning of kinship systems and the interpretation of myths.

For all of its promise and its apparent rigor, however, both practitioners and critics of the incipient cognitive turn pointed out a number of inadequacies and frustrations:

- The methods and ethnographic writing-practices were tedious and cumbersome: no one ever successfully conducted an ethnoscientific or structural study of an entire culture, focusing instead on very small bites of culture.
- The two different approaches (ethnoscience and structuralism) spawned competing and incompatible views of culture and of mind.
- It did not resolve the problem of psychological reality, that is, troubling questions remained as to whether researchers were discovering what/how natives really thought or whether they were merely replacing one abstraction with another, more elegant one.
- Its results were rather sterile: it is not greatly interesting to read an ethnoscientific account, and once structuralism established that the mind works on the principle of binary oppositions, it is not clear what else it has to offer; it also had little to say about actual events or practices—which were for structuralism mere epiphenomena and for ethnoscience no more than "speech" compared to the reality of "language."
- It ignored some of the central concerns of preceding research, especially child-rearing, social systems, and learning, which were and are legitimate if not essential anthropological topics.
- It helped spawn a counter-movement that was prepared to chuck the entire psychological perspective altogether.

Chapter 5

Mind in symbols, body, and practice

Psychological anthropology since the 1970s

Key figures:
Mary Douglas (1921–2007)
Clifford Geertz (1926–2006)
Pierre Bourdieu (1930–2002)
Dan Sperber (1942–present)
Thomas Csordas (1952–present)

Key texts:
Natural Symbols (1970)
The Interpretation of Cultures (1973)
Rethinking Symbolism (1974)
Outline of a Theory of Practice (1977)
"Anthropology and Psychology: Towards an Epidemiology of Representations" (1985)
"Embodiment as a Paradigm for Anthropology" (1990)

"In the next generation, indeed, we may expect to see graduate students in cultural anthropology who are aware that every human being has, in addition to his culture and his personality, both a body and a brain" (1964: 200), Anthony Wallace prophesied in the final sentence of his 1961 *Culture and Personality*. Actually, the body had been present if not central in the culture-and-personality school, as in Freudian theory, with its focus on visceral experiences, such as sleeping arrangements, weaning, toilet training, and physical discipline. The body had curiously disappeared in cognitive anthropology, which replaced personality or character with the narrower concept of mind or cognition; cognition itself was perceived as mental structure, as classifying and theorizing, to the exclusion of affective and embodied behavior.

Each for their own reasons, many anthropologists had become dissatisfied with the various schools of psychology by the 1960s. John Honigmann, in a 1959 review of "psychocultural" research, went so far as to pronounce that "culture and personality, in America at least, is supposed to be dead, presumably having lost its popularity in the fifties" (1959: 67), although he saw a glimmer of life in such areas of study as ethnic identity and mental illness. But the exhaustion of the first half-century of psychological anthropology was just one part of a general crisis in the discipline, reflected by ruminations like Edmund Leach's 1961 *Rethinking Anthropology* and Dell Hymes's 1969 *Reinventing Anthropology*. At the very least, no self-respecting anthropologist or other social scientist could again use terms like "primitive" or "savage," and there was brutal criticism of anthropology (from inside and outside) as colonial, stuck in the past and obsessed with "traditional" societies while ignoring contemporary social forces, and losing sight of its original mission if not fading into irrelevance altogether.

Troubled but also energized by this self-critique, influenced by new developments in allied fields such as linguistics and philosophy, and asking new questions while approaching old questions in new ways, another wave of anthropological thought pushed the discipline in exciting and more sophisticated directions. Not all of the contributors to this new perspective necessarily saw themselves as psychological anthropologists, but their work yielded insights for psychological anthropology that also reverberated through other domains of the discipline and showed the potential to bring all of those domains into closer conversation, including the physical or biological branch. At the center of these diverse but entangled movements were the concepts of the symbol—hardly a completely new idea—and of the human body as a social construction and a site of cultural knowledge and action.

Public thought, embodied culture: Clifford Geertz

In a barely veiled attack on ethnoscience and Lévi-Straussian structuralism, Clifford Geertz castigated certain anthropological theories for promoting the notion that "we need not attend, save cursorily, to behavior at all":

> Culture is most effectively treated, the argument goes, purely as a symbolic system (the catch phrase is, "in its own terms"), by isolating its elements, specifying the internal relationships among those elements, and then characterizing the whole system in some general way—according to the core symbols around which it is organized, the underlying structures of which it is a surface expression, or the ideological principles upon which it is based. Though a distinct improvement over "learned behavior" and "mental phenomena" notions of what culture is, and the source of some of the most powerful theoretical ideas in contemporary anthropology, this hermetical approach to things seems to me to run the danger (and increasingly to have been overtaken by it) of locking cultural analysis away from its proper object, the informal logic of actual life.
>
> (1973: 17)

"Nothing has done more, I think, to discredit cultural analysis," he pronounced, "than the construction of impeccable depictions of formal order in whose actual existence nobody can quite believe"; a good anthropological account of culture should be rich—"thick" was the term he used, borrowed from the philosopher Gilbert Ryle (see the following)—and when it is not

> but leads us instead somewhere else—into an admiration of its own elegance, of its author's cleverness, or of the beauties of Euclidean order—it may have its intrinsic charms; but it is something else than what the task at hand…calls for.
>
> (18)

Clifford Geertz (1926–2006), probably the most important American anthropologist of the late twentieth century, made this assessment in his 1973 *The Interpretation of Cultures*, a volume of his essays mostly written in the 1960s, which has been required reading for anthropologists ever since. Overtly drawing inspiration from two philosophers—Ryle and Suzanne Langer—he helped move symbols to the fore in anthropology and to rehabilitate them from the meanings assigned to them by Lévi-Strauss and White (see Chapter 4). In a classic essay on religion, he defined a symbol as "any object, act, event, quality, or relation which serves as a vehicle for a conception—the conception is the symbol's 'meaning'" (91). That assertion is more or less standard (although Dan Sperber will beg to differ; see the following), but its profound implication for Geertz soon became apparent: since symbols are generally and even necessarily external, visible, public signs of meaning, "they are tangible formulations of notions, abstractions from experience fixed in perceptible forms, concrete embodiments of ideas, attitudes, judgments, longings, or beliefs" (91).

"Culture is public because meaning is" (12)—this is the logical conclusion. But Geertz took the radical step from there to contend that, since the conceptions of thought conveyed by symbols are public, thought itself is. Indeed, his starting assumption was

> that human thought is basically social and public.... Thinking consists not of "happenings in the head" (though happenings there and elsewhere are necessary for it to occur) but of a traffic in what have been called...significant symbols—words for the most part but also gestures, drawings, musical sounds, mechanical devices like clocks, or natural objects like jewels. (45)

Accordingly, he defined culture as "an historically transmitted pattern of meanings, a system of inherited conceptions expressed in symbolic forms by means of which men communicate, perpetuate, and develop their knowledge about and attitudes toward life" (89).

BOX 5.1 PHILOSOPHY AND ANTHROPOLOGY

Anthropology has had a relationship with philosophy that is as long and productive as its association with psychology. In fact, one of the first scholars to write about anthropology was the philosopher Immanuel Kant in his 1798 *Anthropology from a Pragmatic Point of View*, in which he opined that humans were both physiological or natural beings and "pragmatic" (practical and acting) ones; anthropology was thus equally hybrid, at once "the investigation of what *nature* makes of the human being" and "what *he* as a free-acting being makes of himself, or can and should make of himself" (2006: 3, emphasis in the original). The more direct influences on Geertz, and trailblazers in a philosophical revolution, were Gilbert Ryle and Suzanne Langer. Ryle's 1949 *The Concept of Mind* had a powerful impact on Geertz's anthropology. In that treatise, Ryle took exception to the Cartesian dualism of mind and body (the first chapter is called "Descartes' Myth"). His retort was that "when we describe people as exercising qualities of mind, we are not referring to occult episodes of which their overt acts and utterances are effects; we are referring to those overt acts and utterances themselves" (1970: 26). In other words, as Geertz appropriated him, Ryle held that "mind" was public action. Starting with the observation that much of our "knowledge" is practical or pragmatic (knowing *how*, like being able to ride a bicycle) rather than factual or propositional (knowing *that*, like being able to explain the physics of riding a bicycle), Ryle argued that mind is not a "shadowy operation" (49) behind behavior but is immanent in behavior. "Overt intelligent performances are not clues to the workings of minds; they are those workings" (57). One last time, "when we characterize people by mental predicates"—such as "thinking," "believing," or "symboling"—"we are not making untestable inferences to any ghostly processes occurring in streams of consciousness which we are debarred from visiting; we are describing the ways in which those people conduct parts of their predominantly public behavior" (50). A few years before Ryle, Suzanne Langer proudly declared that she was in the vanguard of a "new key" in philosophy, one that put symbolism at the crux of not only religion and art but of all culture and thought. All experience, including perception, is "primarily symbolic" (1942: 16), she argued; symbolization, the process of making and using symbols, is "the starting point of all intellection in the human sense, and is more general than thinking, fancying, or taking action" (33). Truly, thinking itself commences with concepts, not raw percepts, and all concepts are symbolic in that they refer to "types" or "classes," not to individual things. Her greater challenge to conventional analyses of thought—especially ones that, like ethnoscience and structuralism, privilege language—was that meaning was not strictly linguistic and that language was not the only or model form of meaning. She distinguished language or "discursive" meaning from nonlinguistic, nondiscursive, and *symbolic* meaning. Language, she reasoned, has a vocabulary and grammar, while nonlinguistic symbolism does not; a painting, for instance, cannot be broken down into meaningful bits or morphemes (i.e. it is not as if each color or brush stroke has a specific meaning). Therefore, it is possible to assemble a dictionary of language signs but not of symbols (i.e. we could never arrive at a final list of "definitions" or meanings of nonlinguistic symbols). Finally, one language can be translated (although not always perfectly) into another language, but one symbol or symbol-system cannot be translated faithfully into another (i.e. it would be nonsensical to translate a symphony into a poem or Christian symbolism into Hindu symbolism, for that matter). The key to Langer's new key of philosophy was *metaphor*: metaphor, she believed, is a brand of thinking, although it is not "rational" or fact-based; instead, much of symbolism is image based and image driven, and images quickly pile onto images, forging links in a metaphorical or associative chain. "Metaphor is the growth of every semantic" (119), producing a tangled and virtually impenetrable forest of meaning and metaphor, which she called "vegetative thought," where "the very use of language exhibits a rampant confusion of metaphorical meanings clinging to every symbol, sometimes to the complete obscurance of any reasonable literal meaning" (120–1). In saying this, she anticipated Lévi-Strauss's portrayal of the mind as a *bricoleur*.

From the perspective of any particular member of a society, "such symbols are largely given" (Geertz 1973: 45), along with their conceptions or the thoughts that members are expected to have. But cultural symbols have much more cognitive force than that: taking a cue from the emerging field of computer technology and cybernetics, Geertz insisted that culture functions "as a set of control mechanisms—plans recipes, rules, instructions (*what computer engineers call 'programs'*)—for governing behavior" (44, emphasis added). Or in more detail, cultural symbols

> are extrinsic sources of information in terms of which human life can be patterned—extrapersonal mechanisms for the perception, understanding, judgment, and manipulation of the world. Culture patterns—religious, philosophical, aesthetic, scientific, ideological—are "programs"; they provide a template or blueprint for the organization of social and psychological processes, much as genetic systems provide such a template for the organization of organic processes.

(216)

Culture in this view is the "software" that runs the "hardware" of the biological human being.

Unlike some understandings of computers that see hardware as separate from and unaffected by software—or, more immediately germane to our purposes, contrary to the likes of Kroeber and White, who envisioned culture as a mere accoutrement carried by biological and psychological units—Geertz described culture as integral to the human individual. This provided the opening for him to unify the organic or physical aspect of humans with the cultural aspect, the key being the evolutionary history of the species (see Chapter 10).

In two prescient chapters of his book—his 1962 essay "The Growth of Culture and the Evolution of Mind" and his 1966 paper "The Impact of the Concept of Culture on the Concept of Man"—Geertz made his case. Dismissing the "stratigraphic" model of humankind and culture (in which the chemical, biological, psychological, and cultural "layers" are built on top of each other and hardly interact), he countered that the various dimensions of humankind thoroughly interpenetrated such that there is no precultural "organic" human over whom a veneer of culture is laid. A baby is born with few instincts and little cognitive content—s/he is literally quite "unfinished" or incomplete as a being—and matures in the presence of culture. "What this means," Geertz maintained, "is that culture, rather than being added on, so to speak, to a finished or virtually finished animal, was ingredient, and centrally ingredient, in the production of that animal itself" (47). He was quite sure that "there is no such thing as a human nature independent of culture"; human infants denied access to culture "would be unworkable monstrosities with very few useful instincts, fewer recognizable sentiments, and no intellect" (49). "We are, in sum, incomplete or unfinished animals who complete or finish ourselves through culture—and not through culture in general but through highly particular forms of it" (49).

And as is the individual, so is the species. Indeed, humans are born so woefully incomplete because evolutionary history left us this way. When, millions of years ago, the ancestors of modern humans had much smaller brains, they had little or no culture. As the human body developed its modern form—including the brain but also the eyes, the hands, and every part of the body—it did so in the increasingly dense context of culture (first, stone tools, then fire, shelters, and eventually language and art). Consequently, culture became ingrained in the body, just as the body became culturized, but no organ of the body more so than the brain:

> As our central nervous system—and most particularly its crowning curse and glory, the neocortex—grew up in part in interaction with culture, it is incapable of directing our behavior or organizing our experience without the guidance provided by systems of significant symbols.
>
> (49)

"Tools, hunting, family organization, and later, art, religion, and 'science' molded man somatically; and they are, therefore, necessary not merely to his survival but to his existential realization" (83). In short, culture became a required constituent—one at first external to the individual's body and gradually internal to it—of our very humanness. Human "mind," then, is nothing more than "a class of skills, propensities, capacities, tendencies, habits" largely acquired from and practiced in public, and "as such, it is neither an action nor a thing, but an organized system of dispositions which finds its manifestations in some actions and some things" (58)—which he called symbols (Figure 5.1).

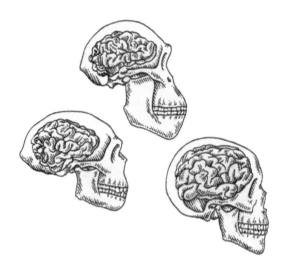

Figure 5.1 Comparative brain volume of *Australopithecus, Homo erectus,* and *modern Homo sapiens.*

BOX 5.2 MARY DOUGLAS: BODY AS NATURAL SYMBOL

The human body is not only suspended in a web of symbols, and a construction of those symbols, but it is, according to Mary Douglas, itself the ultimate symbol. Close on the heels of her *Purity and Danger* (see Chapter 4), she published her seminal 1970 *Natural Symbols*, in which she argued that "the image of the body is used in different ways to reflect and enhance each person's experience in society" (1996: xxxvi). Fretting that modern societies had lost the sense of shared symbols and meanings, she insisted that in all cultures, including our own, not only is the human body the locus of experience—we experience the world "from inside" and "through" our body—but we also experience our own and others' bodies as symbolically meaningful. What we put into our body (as in dietary restrictions, like the laws of Leviticus) is laden with cultural significance. Far beyond such rules, we dress, color, draw on, cut, scar, and otherwise modify the body in a complex communication system; different bodily presentations signal messages of gender, age, class, ethnicity, and so on. More importantly for Douglas, we map features of the "body social" onto the body personal:

> The physical experience of the body, always modified by the social categories through which it is known, sustains a particular view of society. There is a continual exchange of meanings between the two kinds of bodily experience so that each reinforces the categories of the other. As a result of this interaction the body itself is a highly restricted medium of expression. The forms it adopts in movement and repose express social pressures in manifold ways. The care that is given to it,

in grooming, feeding and therapy, the theories about what it needs in the way of sleep and exercise, about the stages it should go through, the pains it can stand, its span of life, all the cultural categories in which it is perceived, must correlate closely with the categories in which society is seen in so far as these also draw upon the same culturally processed idea of the body.

(1996: 69)

It goes without saying that there are culturally specific ways of walking, standing, sitting, sleeping, etc. The contribution of Douglas was that the body social (society) and the body personal could be equally analyzed on a graph representing two variables, which she called "group" and "grid." Put simply, "group" (think of it as the vertical axis of the graph) designates the strength of the bonds between members of a society and the strength of the boundaries of the society vis-à-vis other societies, whereas "grid" (picture it as the horizontal axis of the graph) indicates the amount of differentiation within society in terms of its social roles and statuses. A "high-group" society is extremely collectivized and protective of its boundaries, while a "low-group" society is individualized and more porous at its boundaries; a "high-grid" society is internally hierarchical, while a "low-grid" society is egalitarian, allowing individuals more freedom to determine and change their social position. Douglas claimed that as goes the society, so goes the individual and her body—or what she called, more technically, "consonance." The person's social experience and personal/bodily experience normally coincide: if the society is concerned about its boundaries, the individual will be concerned about his body, namely, what touches or crosses his skin or penetrates his orifices. A society that worries less about its borders produces individuals who are less obsessive about theirs. Likewise, if society makes rigid social distinctions, the individual will be rigid about her body, how it is groomed and dressed and such, but if society is more relaxed about its internal differentiations, persons will be more relaxed in their bodily comportment. Of course, and significantly, Douglas noted that there may be nonconformists in a high-group/grid society, "abnormals" who reject its inflexible norms, and we can spot them by how they inhabit their bodies—whether these are shamans with their "wild" and "unkempt" appearance or "hippies" with their indifference to standards of dress and hygiene, both putting foreign substances like drugs into their bodies.

Symbolic mechanism and catchy ideas: Dan Sperber

Geertz followed in the tradition of semiology (the study of meaning) blazed by Saussure and pursued by Lévi-Strauss in his own way by taking a symbol as a sign or a token of a meaning—as he put it earlier, as a vehicle for a conception. But what if symbols are not signs and do not "have meaning" in the normal sense? That was a question posed by Dan Sperber in *Rethinking Symbolism*, originally published in 1974, the year after Geertz's *The Interpretation of Cultures*. Sperber launched from the extraordinarily important and at the time novel (but since widely accepted) suggestion that "the most interesting cultural knowledge is tacit knowledge—that is to say, that which is not made explicit" (1979: x) or, as Langer would have said, which is at least so far not discursive or formulated in words and which may not be formulable in words at all. Sperber further distinguished different types of knowledge:

> When those who have this [tacit] knowledge are able to make it explicit, I shall speak of *implicit knowledge*. When they are incapable of this, I shall speak of *unconscious knowledge*. *Explicit and expressly-imparted knowledge* may in principle be learned by rote, and it is therefore only direct evidence of the quantitative limits of human learning ability. Conversely, tacit knowledge may in no case be acquired by rote; it must be reconstructed by each individual.
>
> (x, emphasis added)

For anthropologists examining tacit knowledge, he opined that "the basic data are intuitions, they are the judgments that the members of a cultural group systematically express without elaborating on the underlying argument" (xi).

This attention to tacit, unspoken (and sometimes unspeakable) knowledge and the intuitions that inform it is key to Sperber's theory of symbolism since he claimed that "its explicit forms are unintelligible by themselves and their study has always presupposed the existence of an underlying tacit knowledge" (xi). In this, he meant that observers assume that members of a society who use a symbol have, as Geertz posited, some conception of what that symbol means, and the job of the observer is to "decode" the symbol and determine what it is a sign of. The project of what Geertz called "the interpretation of cultures," in other words, is semiological—to discover the meaning of cultural symbols.

Sperber vehemently disagreed. Asserting that "symbolic interpretation is not a matter of decoding, but an improvisation that rests on implicit knowledge and obeys unconscious rules," he made the drastic move of rejecting the semiological approach (also taken by Freud, who believed that symbols such as hysterical symptoms or even everyday behavior had decodable meanings) and declaring that symbolism was a cognitive matter. In fact, he went so far as to assert that symbolism rests on "a cognitive mechanism," an "autonomous mechanism that, alongside the perceptual and conceptual mechanisms, participates in the construction of knowledge and in the functioning of memory"; like Lévi-Strauss but toward very different ends, his position was the symbolism was "part of the innate mental equipment that makes experience possible" (xi–xii).

Asking the unprecedented question of *why* we consider something a symbol in the first place, he responded that the typical outsider to a society labels an object, a gesture, etc. a symbol "because it is false" (not literally or propositionally true) as far as that outsider is concerned (3). It does not even help to query the member who is using the symbol for its meaning, because, Sperber was convinced, the answer given by the member is "exegesis" (a term used in literature and religious studies for explanation or commentary of a text) and "exegesis is not an interpretation but rather an extension of the symbol and must itself be interpreted" (34), that is, any member's explanation of a symbol is *more symbol*. But Sperber's understanding of symbolism is more corrosive to the common conception that we have yet appreciated. Since we call something "symbolic" when we mean *it could not possibly be true, but I am too polite to say so*, then what do we do when members of the society think it *is* true? For instance, fieldworkers are quick to call shamanic healing "symbolic," but presumably members of the society think that it works; nobody goes to a shaman (or a medical doctor) for symbolism but rather for effective treatment. If, therefore, "symbolic" is a label, and one that depends on judgments relative to cultural knowledge, then "the notion of a symbol is not universal but cultural, present or absent, differing from culture to culture, or even within a given culture"—which is why he made the sweeping proposal that "the notion of the symbol, at least provisionally, be removed from the vocabulary of the theory of symbolism, and be described only as a native notion" (50).

To make a long and complex story short, after a thorough critique of the symbol-theories of Lévi-Strauss, Freud, and others, Sperber professed that symbols "are not signs. They are not paired with interpretations in a code structure. Their interpretations are not meanings" (85). More, the analogy between symbolism and language has only limited application; as Langer also argued, (nondiscursive) symbolism actually differs from language fairly profoundly. The only recourse for Sperber was to identify a symbolic mechanism in the mind, akin to Chomsky's language-acquisition device. First, he made the additional distinction between "semantic knowledge" (which is about categories and classification) and "encyclopedic knowledge" (which we could call empirical and/or cultural knowledge about the world), the difference conveyed in the semantic sentence "A lion is an animal" versus the encyclopedic sentence "A lion is a dangerous animal" (91–2). Symbols, he claimed, are more like encyclopedic or empirical knowledge than semantic knowledge since they seem to be about the world and are often culturally specific, but they diverge from ordinary encyclopedic knowledge in being apparently irrational or incomprehensible. An example of mild symbolism might be "A lion is the king of the jungle," whereas a case of strong symbolism would be "A lion is a person" or "A lion can cure cancer."

Essentially, then, Sperber's position is that when a statement or object or gesture, etc. has the look of an encyclopedic or empirical fact but makes no factual sense, the mind kicks it to a secondary mental processing system, the symbolic mechanism. "The symbolic mechanism tries to establish by its own means the relevance of the defective conceptual representation" (113). Reworking Lévi-Strauss, Sperber held that

> the symbolic mechanism is the *bricoleur* of the mind. It starts from the principle that waste-products of the conceptual industry deserve to be saved because something can always be made of them. But the symbolic mechanism does not try to decode the information it processes. It is precisely because this information has partly escaped the conceptual code, the most powerful of the codes available to humans, that it is, in the final analysis, submitted to it. It is therefore not a question of discovering the meaning of symbolic representations but, on the contrary, of inventing a relevance and a place in memory for them despite the failure in this respect of the conceptual categories of meaning. A representation is symbolic precisely to the extent that it is not entirely explicable, that is to say, expressible by semantic means.
>
> (113)

Sperber described the operation of this symbolic mechanism in terms of two steps or "aspects"—"one, a displacement of attention, or *focalization*; and the other, a search in memory, or *evocation*" (119). In effect, the symbolic mechanism puts the alleged symbol in quotation marks—"They say, 'A lion is the king of the jungle'"—then refocuses the symbol and calls up an "evocational field" consisting of all the memories and knowledge that might help render the symbol intelligible. His concept of evocational field is noteworthy, because such fields (constellations of empirical and cultural knowledge) "differ greatly from one society to another, diverge depending on the particular point of view adopted in one society, and vary when that society changes" (139). Consequently, there cannot be universal cross-cultural meaning for a symbol and hardly ever universal meaning *within* a society across individuals, groups, and situations. Whether dealing with myth or other symbols, there is perhaps a universal focalization—away from literal signification toward something else—and then "a cultural evocational field, and an individual evocation" (140).

BOX 5.3 GANANATH OBEYESEKERE: PERSONAL SYMBOLS

If a symbol is a vehicle for meaning in the Geertzian sense, and if this meaning is public rather than inside the heads of individuals, then the implication is that there should be a single semiotic meaning for any particular cultural symbol, making it possible to "interpret" cultures or to read them like a text, which was Geertz's ultimate suggestion. Sperber, to the contrary, denies the possibility, or at least stresses the unlikelihood, that different members of a society, with their specific personal knowledge, experiences, and memories, will share the same "meaning" for a symbol. We all have encountered occasions when people seem to understand and react differently toward the same symbol, be it a national flag or a religious icon. Certainly, the expert and the layperson may have divergent and incompatible interpretations of symbols, but even among regular folk, meaning may vary. Gananath Obeyesekere suggested that symbols are *potential* vehicles for meaning, and perhaps intended vehicles for "conventional" or "official" meaning, but they are not actually meaning*ful* until they are taken up by an individual and refracted through actual personal, biographical experience. In his presentation, he discussed hair as an important Hindu symbol, whether it is wearing hair long or shaving it off. He showed through the lives of specific people how the dialectical process—cultural symbols shaping the experience of persons and the actions of persons reproducing the symbols—works. In the first turn, "the Hindu's experiences are articulated in terms of traditional symbols" (1981: 21); in other words, the symbol precedes the individual and makes certain experiences possible and typical. Thus, "the Hindu's consciousness is already influenced by his culture, facilitating the expression of intrapsychic conflict in a cultural idiom" (21). However, through selection among available public symbols and application to the individual's life and unique biographical experience, the symbol is appropriated and "reloaded," if you will, as a "personal symbol." A personal symbol for Obeyesekere is one of the public social symbols "whose primary significance and meaning lie in the personal life and experience of individuals. And individuals are also cultural beings or persons" (44). Thus, humans are produced by but also produce symbols. Public symbols á la Geertz are the set of local symbols in which a person can communicate and even organize his or her experience, but individuals can "say" different things with that language depending on what they see, think, and feel. Then, as Edward Sapir taught us (see Chapter 2), a symbol that has been personalized can be redeployed as a new or newly meaningful public form, allowing for change in symbols and meanings. Finally, that the "language" of Hinduism includes hair simply reinforces Mary Douglas's idea that the body is a potent medium and metaphor for experience and extrapersonal reality. Long or tonsured hair as a public and personal symbol involves "wearing" the body in a symbolic way, just as tattooers or body piercers or for that matter Freudian neurotics do.

For all his effort, Sperber conceded that he had "certainly not established the existence of a separate symbolic mechanism" (147), and while it does encourage us to think anew about symbols, not all anthropologists have adopted his specific alternative to customary methodologies of symbolic interpretation. Much more catching within the discipline was his later article, ironically, on how cultural ideas catch on in a society. In his 1985 "Anthropology and Psychology," he characterized culture—or "cultural things"—as "distributions of representations in a human population, ecological patterns of psychological things" (1985: 73). If this is so, then we can and should, he reasoned, take an "epidemiological" approach to cultural items or ideas, which, as can be seen, he dubbed *representations*. That is, just as a bacterium or virus spreads through a population because of specifiable qualities of the infection and of the infected groups, so a cultural representation spreads through a society, "infecting" the minds of individuals. If this analogy feels odd or uncomfortable, it was precisely the one developed by Sperber: "The human mind is susceptible to cultural representations, in the same way the human organism is susceptible to diseases" (74).

To realize the productivity of this viewpoint, we begin with his account of a representation, which "involves a relationship between three terms: an object is a representation *of* something, *for* some information processing device"; then "there are representations internal to the information processing device"—in this case, the brain—"i.e. *mental representations*; and there are representations external to the device which the device can process as inputs, i.e. *public representations*" (77, emphasis in the original). Any particular public representation, like any particular disease, can be more or less widely distributed within a human population; some are rare, some are endemic. "Widely distributed, long-lasting representations are what we are primarily referring to when we talk of culture"; significantly and accurately, though, there is "no threshold, no boundary with cultural representations on one side, and individual ones on the other" (74). Just as a disease is a disease whether a few or a lot of people have it, so culture is culture whether shared by a few, a lot, or all members of a society.

The important question, obviously, is "why are some representations more successful in a human population, more contagious, more 'catching' than others?" (74). This suggests, indeed demands, an investigation into the traits of easily caught and widely shared cultural things, and hence the "epidemiology of representations is a study of the causal chains in which these mental and public representations are involved" (77). We are then encouraged to consider at least three bundles of variables—first, the features of specific representations (analogous to the biochemistry of a virus); second, the qualities of the human mind, which will play host to the representations; third, the traits of society and social organization, which facilitate or inhibit the spread of any particular representation. Sperber offered the lesson that what "makes some representations harder to internalize, remember or externalize than others, what makes them, therefore more complex for humans, is the organization of human cognitive and communicative abilities" (80), and that is surely part of the story.

Yet, as just noted, there are other forces at play, including the nature of the representations and the organization of social relations and institutions. For instance, Sperber proposed what he called a "Law of the Epidemiology of Representations," to wit, "In an oral tradition, all cultural representations are easily remembered ones; hard to remember representations are forgotten, or transformed into more easily remembered ones, before reaching a cultural level of distribution" (86). That may well be, but it raises two pertinent questions. For one, *why* are some representations more easily remembered? What is it about the cultural thing—or about the way that the cultural thing is presented—that makes it memorable? That is not entirely a mental question. For another, what about non-oral societies, societies with writing, television, and the internet? How do those media affect the transmissibility of cultural representations? And for that matter, how do institutions like the family, the school system, religion, government, and so on affect which representations are widely circulated and which ones stick? (Think of catechisms and spelling workbooks.)

Fittingly, Sperber's introduction of the concept of epidemiology and of how and why certain cultural things stick has stuck securely in anthropology, especially in the study of religion, from Pascal Boyer's analysis of religious ideas to Harvey Whitehouse's modes of religiosity (see Chapter 10). It has proved highly pregnant for suggesting research questions and agendas and for developing a holistic approach to culture that integrates particular cultural items, individual minds, and social structures.

BOX 5.4 MEDIA VIRUSES

The mark of an effective idea is how many different practical uses it can be put to. While Sperber perhaps cannot take all the credit, the epidemiological view of culture has been absorbed in many corners of society, from business to the internet itself. "Going viral" is a catch-phrase of our time (one that is highly catchy on its own), and people try consciously to make their ideas or products catchy. Douglas Rushkoff, as in his *Media Virus!: Hidden Agendas in Popular Culture* (1994), also heralded the dark side of cultural contagion and manipulation. Many commentators and would-be gurus have run with the notion of "what sticks," applying it to every dimension of life from business to religion. Kara Powell and Chap Clark (2011) offer tips for "sticky faith" or how parents can make their children more dependably religious (guidebook sold separately). Jeremy Miller (2015) teaches techniques for "sticky branding" to "stand out, attract customers, and grow an incredible brand," while Larry Osborne (2010) combines these two purposes to create "sticky teams" particularly in ministry. Most Sperberian of all is Chip Heath and Dan Heath's (2007) *Made to Stick: Why Some Ideas Survive and Others Die*, with equally sticky tips for how to generate viral ideas: make them simple, unexpected, concrete, credible, and emotional and put them into stories. It seems that today, whether we know it or not, we live in a Sperberian world.

Behavior without knowledge: Pierre Bourdieu

Maybe no term has lodged itself in the contemporary anthropological psyche as thoroughly as "habitus," brought to scholarly attention by Pierre Bourdieu in his 1972 *Outline of a Theory of Practice* (originally in French, translated into English in 1977) and reprised in his 1980 *The Logic of Practice* (published in English in 1990). The idea and word, however, were actually introduced forty years earlier by Marcel Mauss, collaborator and nephew of Durkheim, in his 1934 lecture "Techniques of the Body." Commenting that different societies had different ways of standing, walking, running, marching, and even placing their hands—and anticipating both Bourdieu and Douglas—Mauss surmised that in such instances,

> we are dealing with *techniques of the body*. The body is man's first and most natural instrument. Or more accurately, not to speak of instruments, man's first and most natural technical object, and at the same time technical means, in his body.
>
> (1992: 461, emphasis in the original)

Starting from the observation that how we inhabit and move our body varies according to gender and age, he specified a number of areas of bodily techniques, some highly germane to the original project of psychological anthropology and the culture-and-personality school—techniques of birth and of infancy (including "rearing and feeding the child" [466]); of sleeping, waking, and resting; of walking, climbing, jumping, running, dancing, swimming, holding, throwing, etc.; of caring for the body, including washing; eating and drinking; and of sexuality. Some of these bodily ways of dwelling are formally taught and learned, while others are picked up casually if not unconsciously from social interaction. To encompass these and other such skills, he adopted the Latin word *habitus*.

Bourdieu borrowed the term to solve a specific problem, namely, to rescue human behavior, the concept of culture, and anthropology itself from the dichotomy of social structure (the external or public) versus personality or mind (the internal or psychological/mental, often today referred to as "agency")—or in his own terms, "objectivism" and "subjectivism." External structures do not compel or necessarily predict behavior, but behavior is certainly not free of them; internal psychological processes are not independent of public institutions and symbols but are not determined by them either. More simply, behavior is not the sheer enactment of cultural rules, but neither is it absolute free will. Bourdieu's answer was to resuscitate the *habitus* concept.

The resolution of a false dilemma, Bourdieu defined *habitus* as

> systems of durable, transposable *dispositions*, structured structures predisposed to function structuring structures, that is, as principles of the generation and structuring of practices and representations which can be objectively "regulated" and "regular" without in any way being the product of obedience to rules, objectively adapted to their goals without presupposing a conscious aiming at ends or an express mastery of the operations necessary to attain them and, being all this, collectively orchestrated without being the product of the orchestrating action of a conductor.
>
> (1977: 72, emphasis in the original)

A few pages later, he explained that *habitus*, as

> the durably installed *generative principle of regulated improvisations*, produces practices which tend to reproduce the regularities immanent in the objective conditions of the production of their generative principle, while adjusting to the demands inscribed as objective potentialities in the situation, as defined by the cognitive and motivating structures making up the habitus.
>
> (78, emphasis added)

In these rather convoluted statements, he was arguing that we must "abandon all theories which explicitly or implicitly treat practice as a mechanical reaction, directly determined by the antecedent conditions"—including cultural rules and social institutions—"which one would, moreover, have to postulate in infinite number" but at the same time must resist the inclination to credit behavior to "some creative free will" and "the conscious and deliberate intentions of their authors" (73).

The fact is, Bourdieu reckoned along with Mauss and others, individual humans are often *not* conscious of the reasons and meanings of their behavior—and need not be. Illustrating his point with discussions of honor and of gift giving, he contended that much of our behavior is based on practical reason, calling it therefore "practice," which practical reason was built up from a life-history of social experience. The *habitus* that makes possible such practice is unconscious, but he believed that "the 'unconscious' is never anything other than the forgetting of history which history itself produces by incorporating the objective structures it produces in the second natures of habitus" (78–9). "Genesis amnesia" (79) was his phrase for this phenomenon of forgetting how our own dispositions toward thought and action were acquired.

In his second stab at elucidating *habitus*, he said that it is

> a product of history, [one that] produces individual and collective practices—more history—in accordance with the schemes generated by history. It ensures the active presence of past experiences, which, deposited in each organism in the form of schemes of perception, thought, and action, tend to guarantee the "correctness" of practices and their constancy over time, more reliably than all formal rules and explicit norms. This system of dispositions…is the principle of the continuity and regularity which objectivism sees in social practices without being able to account for it; and also of the regulated transformations that cannot be explained either by the extrinsic, instantaneous determinisms of mechanistic sociology or by the purely internal but equally instantaneous determinism of spontaneist subjectivism.
>
> (1990: 54)

The key to understanding Bourdieu's thinking, and of its sway on anthropology and the other social sciences, is the purported *productivity* of *habitus*. As designers of artificial intelligence have discovered to their dismay, it is ungainly if not impossible to program every rule to deal with every conceivable contingency of real life. Instead, they have equipped robots and computers with strategies for dealing with new situations and capacities for improvising behavior and, in the process, acquiring knowledge and skill that can be applied to subsequent situations. In a word, these machines are programmed with a simple *habitus* which can thereafter continue to build up that *habitus*, converting its experiences (history) into increasing and improving practices.

BOX 5.5 JEAN PIAGET AND MAURICE MERLEAU-PONTY: PSYCHOLOGY AND PHILOSOPHY OF EMBODIED KNOWLEDGE

It may be recognized by this point that Bourdieu is the heir to two other psychological and philosophical traditions, not fully integrated by previous anthropologists. The psychological tradition is that of Jean Piaget (1896–1980), whose lifelong observations of children led to his theory of *genetic epistemology* or the gradual accretion of knowledge. Granting that there is a mental maturation component to knowledge, Piaget's work often focused on "skills" rather than propositional knowledge—skills that were embodied and that were, like Bourdieu's *habitus*, applicable and applied to subsequent situations. Some of these behavioral or practical "schemas," in Piaget's terminology, were innate, as during the earliest stage of development, the sensorimotor. However, more interesting ones were acquired through bodily interaction with objects, such as the discovery that objects that disappear out of sight (such as a ball rolling under a couch) continue to exist or that liquid poured from one vessel to another retains its volume regardless of the shape of the vessel (Piaget's famous law of conservation). These schemas are perfect examples of experience/history transformed into practical knowledge and then forgotten *as* history and held as strategies or dispositions—a sort of second nature—that can produce future practices which, in turn, tend to perpetuate those dispositions … but can always modify them too. The philosophical tradition most relevant to Bourdieu's theories is that of Maurice Merleau-Ponty (1908–61), especially his 1945 *Phenomenology of Perception*. Merleau-Ponty also attacked a tired dichotomy in Western thought—mind/body dualism—arguing instead that our experience, indeed our knowledge and our mind, is embodied. Mind and body are not, in his analysis, two separate dimensions or substances; rather, mind is embodied, and body is mindful. One example he offered to clarify his position was the blind person with a cane: whereas (we tend to assume), a sighted person's body ends at the surface of their skin, the blind person's perceptive organs *include* the cane. The cane becomes *an extension of the body*, through which perception occurs and knowledge is gained. Likewise, a woman wearing a hat, after having it knocked off a few times walking through doorways, learns to adapt her practice by ducking her head *as if the hat were part of her body*. For one last example, a pianist or guitarist may learn to interact with, to inhabit, their musical instrument as if it were an extension of their body. The deeper repercussion, of course, is that our body with or without a cane or hat is the locus of our experience and knowledge, that we learn about the world and about what we can do in and to that world with our arms and legs, our fingers and toes, our eyes and ears. With different bodies (senses, appendages, and so on) we would know the world differently and develop different strategies or schemas for occupying it. Phenomenology, the philosophical study of experience, has since become an essential strain in anthropology as well.

Returning to humans, Bourdieu concluded that *habitus* "makes possible the free production of all the thoughts, perceptions, and actions inherent in the particular conditions of its production"; it is or has "an infinite capacity for generating products—thoughts, perceptions, expressions and actions—whose limits are set by the historically and socially situated conditions of its production" (1990: 55). He added that,

> being the product of a particular class of objective regularities, the *habitus* tends to generate all the "reasonable," "common-sense," behaviors (and only these) which are possible within the limits of these regularities, and which are likely to be positively sanctioned because they are objectively adjusted to the logic characteristic of a particular field, whose objective future they anticipate.
>
> (55–6)

A specific element of the *habitus* is what Bourdieu called "body *hexis*" or what Mauss seemed to mean by his use of *habitus*: for Bourdieu, "the motor function" and "pattern of postures" included but were hardly limited to "a way of walking, a tilt of the head, facial expressions, ways of sitting and of using implements, always associated with a tone of voice, a style of speech, and (how could it be otherwise?) a certain subjective experience" (1977: 87).

Habitus for Bourdieu is a product of past experience which "anticipates" and presumes a future that is consistent with that past. However, no doubt he would allow that one's *habitus* can change in the encounter with new experience. Like Piaget's child, the first response to novel circumstances is to apply one's preexisting dispositions and schemas, but when those fail, the *habitus* can incorporate new skills and dispositions, which we call "learning." Naturally, a *habitus* long established is not necessarily easily surrendered, and adults frequently demonstrate an insistence on maintaining old and inadequate skills in the face of new information and experiences. Bourdieu referred to the "practical belief" in one's own knowledge and abilities as *doxa*, "the sense of the probable outcome that is given by practical mastery of the specific regularities that constitute the economy of a field [which] is the basis of 'sensible' practices" (1990: 66). Doxa, often translated as "belief" (e.g. orthodoxy or heterodoxy) is not belief in the conscious and propositional sense but closer to confidence in the "relationship of immediate adherence" of one's *habitus* and the world in which it was made.

Bourdieu sometimes seemed to exaggerate the stability and stubbornness of *habitus*, underestimating its adaptive capacity. But if we think of acculturation or of Anthony Wallace's revitalization movements again (see Chapter 3), then we can reinterpret these change processes as clashes between a *habitus* forged in one social milieu and the practical realities of a more or less dramatically altered milieu. Individuals may cling to their old *habitus*, even unto extinction, or they may absorb items from their new experience into an adapted *habitus* (i.e. acculturation); an enterprising individual may eventually propose minor or major adjustments to the *habitus* (or what Wallace called the "mazeway") and to the society and experience that enables it, resulting in a revitalization movement and cultural change.

Bourdieu has also been knocked for inflating the unconscious quality of *habitus*. He sometimes described it as not just out of our conscious awareness but as "unthinkable" and "unnameable." At the worst, bringing it to consciousness threatened to destroy it. Certainly, practice without conscious knowledge is quite possible and common, but techniques of the body and mind and the practices that flow from them can be identified, elaborated, and formalized—whether they are learning in the academy or marching in the military—without being any the less powerful and productive. We might go so far as to say that the mission of higher education and modernity is to make the unconscious *habitus* more conscious and amenable to management, if not to governance.

BOX 5.6 FRITS STAAL: RITUALS WITHOUT MEANING

Consistent with Bourdieu's conception of practice without explicit knowledge, Frits Staal analyzed Vedic rituals in Hinduism as essentially "meaningless." He was not claiming that rituals are vain or vacuous but rather that—true to Sperber's insistence on symbols without semantic content—it is wrong to assume that ritual "consists in symbolic activities which refer to something else" (1979: 3). There "are no symbolic meanings going through [performers'] minds when they are engaged in performing ritual"; instead, "they concentrate on correctness of act, recitation, and chant" (3), that is, on the *practice* of the ritual more than its *meaning*. Accordingly, when the anthropologist queries the priest as to why the ritual is conducted, the answers include

> we do it because our ancestors did it; because we are eligible to do it; because it is good for society; because it is good; because it is our duty; because it is said to lead to immortality; because it leads to immortality.

> (3)

In Sperberian fashion, these are not so much meanings of their symbolic acts as *part of their symbolic acts, "more symbol."* Ritual then, Staal reasoned, "is primarily activity. It is an activity governed by explicit rules. The important thing is what you do, not what you think, believe or say" (4)—in other words, *practice*. To be sure, ritual acts may be meaningful (in the sense of significant or subjectively powerful) to participants and observers alike, as the kind of "personal symbol" identified by Obeyesekere, and they may regard ritual acts as efficacious, that is as achieving particular ends. But Staal insisted that at bottom ritual "is pure activity, without meaning or goal" (9); the key point is that *ritual is symbolic practice that is performed because it must be performed. It is action for its own sake.* This is not to say that ritual has no positive social "side effects," such as integrating society, raising mood and morale, or preserving or enhancing the power and prestige of the ritual-performing class. Ritual, in the end and in Bourdieu's language, is a product of the *habitus* of the priests and the audiences, built up from witnessing and performing past rituals and leaving a precipitate of ritual dispositions (in Geertz's words, "moods and motivations") or structured structures that function as structuring structures, spinning out future ritual practices. And like honor or gift giving, we do it because it is what we do; we can offer "meanings" or interpretations for our practices if pressed to, but the practice would and does go on without those meanings and interpretations.

Embodiment as an anthropological paradigm: Thomas Csordas

Many anthropologists answered the call to take the body, tacit knowledge or no "knowledge" in the cognitive or propositional sense at all, and embodied practice seriously, and not only by those directly interested in psychological questions. Indeed, embodiment and practice became watchwords in other disciplines too, posing an overdue corrective to two millennia of Western tradition of segregating body from mind and denigrating body in comparison to mind; a prime example of the same challenge is George Lakoff and Mark Johnson's 1999 *Philosophy in the Flesh: The Embodied Mind and Its Challenge to Western Thought.* No anthropologist rose to the task more than Thomas Csordas. In the same year that Bourdieu's second book on *habitus* and practice was released in English translation, Csordas (1990) published his essay "Embodiment as a Paradigm for Anthropology." He followed this article in 1993 with "Somatic Modes of Attention" and then a book in 2002 containing both of those papers along with several others.

The thrust of his earliest writing was that, although embodiment was already in the air in anthropological thinking, it could be expounded and adopted as a paradigm "for the study of culture and the self," based on the postulate "that the body is not an *object* to be studied in relation to culture, but is to be considered as the *subject* of culture, or in other words as the existential ground of culture" (1990: 5, emphasis in the original). Discussing Mauss, Merleau-Ponty, and Bourdieu at some length, Csordas also marshaled ethnographic accounts of charismatic Christianity in North America to illustrate that, even in a "spiritual" and "otherworldly" cultural tradition, the body is a center of interest, experience, and practice. For instance, demons are very much believed to present a threat to the bodies of church members, ever violating the bodily integrity of humans (crossing our defended boundaries, as Mary Douglas would say) through attacks and possession. At the same time, God is believed to intervene in the body, whether through penetration by the Holy Spirit and gifts like speaking in tongues or through healing. The body is also definitely a site of spiritual concern, in regard to how it is dressed and groomed and how it moves (whether rejecting secular body-techniques like dancing or valuing spiritual ones like enthusiastic religious services).

"If embodiment is to attain the status of a paradigm," Csordas concluded,

> it should make possible the reinterpretation of data and problems already analyzed from other perspectives; and if this is to be in a strong sense, it should be possible even to construct an embodied account of language, typically the domain of linguistic, semiotic, and textual analyses,
>
> (23)

as he did in his treatment of Pentecostal glossolalia (speaking in tongues). Here is a case of speech without meaning par excellence since members seldom if ever avow understanding the words that they or others utter. We might dismiss nonsense syllables as meaningless, as lacking all semantic content, but that is not the position taken by Pentecostals:

> The stripping away of the semantic dimension in glossolalia is not an absence, but rather the drawing back of a discursive curtain to reveal the grounding of language in natural life, as a bodily act. Glossolalia reveals language as incarnate, and this existential fact is homologous with the religious significance of the Word made Flesh, the unity of human and divine.
>
> (25)

And Csordas identified speaking in tongues as only one of the Pentecostal techniques of the body in which members learn to detect being "overcome by the power of the Holy Spirit" (78) with their body as medium. Likewise, learning to prophesy—which members would explain as acquiring the gift of prophecy—is a case of acquiring a new *habitus* including ways to understand one's own experiences, knowledge, and embodied feelings.

Glossolalia, prophesying, or other verbal practice—indeed, any and all religious practice—"asserts the unity of body and mind, establishes a shared human world, and expresses transcendence…. Thought is not independent of utterance" (31) nor are thought and language independent from the body and embodied practice. The paradigm of embodiment collapses the bankrupt duality of mind and body which even, Csordas complained, pervaded much of psychological anthropology (36). In opposition to tendencies in earlier theories of anthropology and psychology, and in more than two thousand years of Western civilization, he declared that "the body is a productive starting point for analyzing culture and self" (39)—we might even assert, along with other anthropologists and related social scientists, *the* starting point for analyses that promise to (re)unite mind and body, knowledge and emotion, and person and society.

Csordas himself moved the paradigm forward in his second essay, suggesting that, compared to the model of culture as semantics (ethnoscience), grammar (structuralism), or text (Geertzian interpretation), "the paradigm of embodiment means not that cultures have the same structure as bodily experience, but that embodied experience is the starting point for analyzing human participation in a cultural world" (1993: 135). He added the concept of "somatic modes of attention" to highlight "culturally elaborated ways of attending to and with one's body in surroundings that include the embodied presence of others" (138). He was emphasizing both "paying attention *to* the body," as his charismatic Christians did when they had a sensation that they interpreted as a divine presence, and "paying attention *with* the body," in fact *thinking* with the body or *thinking bodily*, which contrasts drastically from our tendency to view thinking "as a cognitive function rather than as a bodily engagement" (138).

Finally, not only is cognition bodily and the body cognitive, but the social is cognitively embodied and cognitive embodiment is social:

> Because we are not isolated subjectivities trapped within our bodies, but share an intersubjective milieu with others, we must also specify that a somatic mode of attention means not only attention to and with one's own body, but includes attention to the bodies of others. Our concern is the cultural elaboration of sensory engagement, not preoccupation with one's own body as an isolated phenomenon. Thus, we must include, for example, the cultural elaboration of an erotic sensibility that accompanies attention to attractiveness and the elaboration of interactive, moral, and aesthetic sensibilities surrounding attention to "fatness." These examples of attention to the bodily form of others also include attending with one's own body—there is certainly a visceral element of erotic attention, and there can be a visceral component to attending to other aspects of others' bodily forms. Attending to others' bodily movements is even more clear-cut in cases of dancing, making love, playing team sports, and in the uncanny sense of a presence over one's shoulder. In all of these, there is a somatic mode of attention to the position and movement of others' bodies.
>
> (139)

BOX 5.7 LEARNING BY APPRENTICESHIP

"If you really want to know what the fishing industry is all about, you must go fishing," the ship's captain told the anthropologist (Pálsson, 1994: 905). A good Icelandic skipper guides his ship and crew to success by "skill," which means his "dexterity and alertness to the tasks at hand"; he certainly uses his technology and gadgets, but these tools are "an extension of his person" (910) as he executes the complex and dangerous work of finding a fishing spot, setting nets, drawing in nets, removing fish, and sailing home. Becoming a skipper "demands several years of training, both formal and informal. A prospective skipper, usually a fisherman's son, began his career as a deck-hand" while still a teenager (915). To earn an official skipper's license, he "has to receive formal training in a specialized institution, the Marine Academy," the two-year classroom program of which entitles him to the status, rights, and duties of "skipper," but "you learn even more by simply taking part, by living the life at sea" (915). Preparation for the contingencies and dangers of the real world depended on the elusive quality of experience, which often was not or could not be put into words. Indeed, although they valued "attentiveness," skippers

> rarely mentioned how they actually make decisions. One reason is that they are guided more by practical results than by an interest in theoretical advancement. Often they "simply" notice that a particular strategy seems to work, without worrying about why that is the case.... What fishermen label as hunches and

fishing mood is particularly difficult to verbalize; some important decisions are "out of the blue".... Decision-making, then, is based less on detached calculation or "mental" reflection than on practical involvement.

(919)

Cases like the Icelander skipper redirect our analysis away from "knowledge" in the sense of discourse or language or propositions to embodied skills and encourage us to imagine cultural learning as a kind of *enskilment*, commonly taking the form of "apprenticeship." According to Michael Coy in a 1989 volume dedicated to the anthropology of apprenticeship—or to apprenticeship at the heart of culture—apprenticeship

is the means of imparting specialized knowledge to a new generation of practitioners. It is the rite of passage that transforms novices into experts. It is a means of learning things that cannot be easily communicated by conventional means. Apprenticeship is employed where there is implicit knowledge to be acquired through long-term observation and experience. This knowledge relates not only to the physical skills associated with a craft, but also to the means of structuring economic and social relationships between oneself and other practitioners, between oneself and one's clients.

(1989b: xi–xii)

The characteristic and consequent feature of apprenticeship is that it is "personal, hands-on, and experiential. Apprenticeship training is utilized where there is more to performing the role at hand than reading a description of its content can communicate" (1989a: 1–2). It is normal in fields like arts and crafts, where mental and manual skills must be combined in ways that, frankly, cannot quite be conveyed in words and propositional knowledge but require embodied understanding of raw materials and tools; however, to an extent, it is part of all learning processes since there is always much "knowledge" that is not spoken and may even be, as Bourdieu surmised, unspeakable. Therefore, Coy urged that studying apprenticeship is "an excellent way to *learn about learning*" (2, emphasis in the original). Among the ethnographic cases in the volume was John Singleton's study of Japanese pottery, where the *minarai* or apprentice (literally, one who learns by observation) is "subject to demands for long, repetitive practice of standard wheel-thrown forms" and "must patiently endure tacit 'spiritual' or character testing" (Singleton 1989: 13). The *minarai* literally spent the first year in the stage of *shitabataraki* ("hackwork"), silently and unobtrusively watching the master and performing unskilled labor like cleaning; during this time, the apprentice's *habitus* was slowly being built as he learned "to anticipate accurately the master's and household's need to which the apprentice can contribute" (19). In the next phase, he made his first attempts at using the pottery wheel, acquiring a sense of and feel for the wheel, the kiln, the clays, and the shapes that he and they could make in interaction. The apprenticeship could last from three to ten years, during which little formal instruction took place; instead, "Rote practice of standard forms, like a professional musician's practice with a standard repertoire" (20) is the nature of learning and of working throughout one's career—much the way the aforesaid musician learns by playing scales over and over again and then practicing a set of songs until perfecting them. Predictably, this apprenticeship perspective has been especially productive in anthropological studies of music, dance, and other embodied and tacit knowledge/ skills but is applicable to virtually every walk of life.

Summary: achievements and shortcomings

The 1970s marked a dramatic turn and advance in anthropological thinking about mind, knowledge, and meaning. Among its primary contributions were

- a serious rethinking of the fundamental questions and concepts of psychological anthropology
- the integration of new insights and intellectual traditions from psychology and philosophy
- a more sophisticated and critical approach to symbols and their cultural meaning
- a recognition of much of cultural knowledge as tacit, unconscious, and even nondiscursive— ordinarily not put into words and sometimes impossible to put into words
- a crucial stress on the body as essential to learning and to experience—that "mind" is not separate or separable from the body but that much if not all knowledge is embodied, just as the body is produced by cultural knowledge and practice.

Despite these breakthroughs, which continue to reverberate in the discipline to this day, critics raised a number of critiques and debates, which help to define contemporary anthropology:

- the new breed of psychological anthropologists lost sight of the original questions of the subdiscipline, regarding childhood experience and the relationship between child-rearing, social institutions, and personality
- in the case of Geertz, his theory of culture was still too linguistic ("culture-as-text") and his theory of symbols too "muscular" (as one of my graduate professors used to say), that is, symbols were given too much power and agency of their own
- in the case of Sperber, his proposal of a symbolic mechanism merely shifted the problem and took the facile road of positing yet another "mental device" to explain a mysterious phenomenon
- in the case of Bourdieu, his concept of *habitus* was too unconscious, too class-specific, and too rigid—and more devastatingly, was not much more than "personality" in fancy new language (another of my graduate professors waved away Bourdieu as a "johnny-come-lately" who was merely repackaging insights from his own generation)

There is little arguing with the fact, though, that anthropology today exists in a post-Geertz, post-Sperber, and post-Bourdieu state and that embodiment truly has become a central paradigm, as the chapters in the second half of this book will attest.

Part II

Contemporary issues in psychological anthropology

Chapter 6

Self and personhood

Key questions:
Does the concept of self vary across cultures, and if so, how?
   Is there a difference between a culture's normative concept of self and the self-experience or self-representation of actual individuals?
   Is the Western individualistic self unique among the world's cultures?
   Does the concept of person vary across cultures, and if so, how?
   Is a person always and only an "individual," or can personhood be divisible, partible, and/or permeable or porous?
   Do cultures recognize other-than-human persons, and if so, what kinds, and how do humans interact with them?

Two of the most basic yet most elusive concepts in psychology, and therefore in psychologically oriented anthropology, are "self" and "person." Surprisingly then, neither term figured prominently in the first decades of anthropology, when it was more common to speak of personality, character, or mind. Self or person may also seem self-evident: surely all individuals in all societies possess a sense of self and personhood, and it is perhaps difficult for some people to imagine that such a sense could differ much. However, consistent with anthropology's empirical awareness of and theoretical commitment to diversity and the cultural construction of even the most fundamental notions, Melford Spiro asserted in 1993 that

> it can be reliably presumed that conceptions of the self are also cross-culturally variable. And, it might be added, not only *conceptions* of the self, but also the self *itself*, for if the self varies across individuals within one and the same society, then it surely can be presumed that it varies across societies.
>
> (1993: 107–8)

An additional obstacle to the comparative study of self and personhood is what Spiro called the "conflation and confusion" of related and overlapping but nonsynonymous terms, such as self, person, personality, character, identity, individual, consciousness, ego, and so on. As we will see later, investigators often use one or more of these terms without clear definition and/or switch between them such that "it is often difficult to apprehend the entity to which this term refers" (143). And a further obstacle is the tendency, of which Spiro was highly critical, to conflate and confuse cultural ideals or normative statements about self and person (that is, what the society values or believes to be true) with people's actual experience and understanding.

That societies have ideals or norms about self and person—or, as Spiro put it earlier, conceptions of the self—is a signal of an important issue that will reappear throughout this and following chapters. Namely, while anthropology (and academic psychology) may bring certain analytical categories to the cross-cultural study of psychological questions, *those cultures often if not always have their own categories and terminology for talking and thinking about personality.* These local self/person concepts are part of local psychologies or "ethnopsychologies," defined by Catherine Lutz in her examination of emotion among the Ifaluk (see Chapter 7) as

> the way people conceptualize, monitor, and discuss their own and others' mental processes. All ethnotheories explain some aspect of variability in the world; ethnopsychologies explain inter- and intrapersonal variations, and they both construct and derive from people's observations of changes in consciousness, action, and relationships.
>
> (1998: 83)

Other cultures' ethnopsychologies are worth knowing in their own right and often if not always diverge from familiar academic psychology. At the extreme, some critics have disparaged academic psychology as nothing more than Western ethnopsychology.

The anthropology of self

That the self is a subject that should be studied and can be studied sociologically and anthropologically is a fairly recent revelation. It was only in 1902 that Charles Cooley suggested the term "looking glass self" to convey how an individual's self develops through social interactions and, more specifically, through a comprehension of how others perceive one's self. In his 1934 *Mind, Self, and Society*, sociologist George Herbert Mead elaborated the argument that the self

> is something which has a development; it is not initially there, at birth, but arises in the process of social experience and activity, that is, develops in the given individual as a result of his relations to that process as a whole and to other individuals within that process.
>
> (1934: 135)

Through noticing the reactions of "significant others" and learning to take their perspective—to see oneself from the outside, as it were—a sense of self is gradually acquired.

A few years later, Marcel Mauss, who also gave us valuable insights about techniques of the body and *habitus* (see Chapter 5), explored two topics concerning the self—first, how the concept is related to and distinguished from others, like person, and, second, how it evolved over time. In a statement originally issued in 1938, Mauss attempted to show

> how recent is the world 'self' (*moi*), used philosophically; how recent 'the category of "self"' (*moi*), 'the cult of the "self"' (*moi*) (its aberration); how recent even 'the respect of "self"' (*moi*), in particular the respect of others (its normal state).
>
> (1985: 3)

Note that he used the French word *moi* (me) for "self." As others have since commented, the term "person" derives from the Latin *persona* (literally per-sona, "to sound through"), which initially designated "a mask, a tragic mask, a ritual mask, and the ancestral mask" (13), that is, more a role to play or a "public face" than one's "authentic self." Mauss claimed that gradually, "person" became a legal concept but not one applicable to all individuals: "the slave is excluded from it… He has no 'personality'…. He does not own his body, nor has he ancestors, name, cognomen, or personal belongings" (17). From there, "person" became a moral category, "persons" having moral weight and moral obligations (notice, for instance, that arguments against abortion often hinge on the "personhood" of the fetus), given its final push by Christianity: "It is Christians who have made a metaphysical entity of the 'moral person,' after they became aware of its religious power. Our own notion of the human person is still basically the Christian one" (19). Only lately, "person" became a psychological concept, illustrating the point that "the category of 'self'…continues here slowly, and almost right up to our own time, to be built upon, to be made clearer and more specific, becoming identified with self-knowledge and the psychological consciousness" (20).

While Mauss thought that it was becoming clearer, we can see that he too shifted between "self" and "person" in his presentation. Accordingly, twenty years thereafter, Spiro accused scholars of operating with multiple jumbled concepts of self, one pointing to "the psychobiological organism—that which is bounded by the skin"—(i.e. the total individual), another to "the individual's mental representation of his own person (i.e. his 'self-representation')," and yet a third to "some psychological entity (an ego, a soul, an 'I') within the person" (1993: 109–10). In other words, "self" could mean the complete individual, the individual's mind, a part of the individual's mind, or the individual's sense and knowledge of her body and/or mind. Actually, it was worse since Spiro isolated seven different usages of the term "self":

1   The person, or the individual, including the package of biological, psychological, social, and cultural characteristics he or she is constituted.
2   The cultural conception of the person or individual.
3   The cultural conception of some psychic entity or structure within the person, variously designated as "pure ego," "transcendental ego," "soul," and the like.
4   The person's construal of such an entity as the center or locus of his or her initiative, sensations, perceptions, emotions, and the like.
5   The personality or the configuration of cognitive orientations, perceptual sets, and motivational dispositions that are uniquely characteristic of each person.
6   The sense of self or the person's awareness that he or she is both separate and different from other persons. The former is often referred to as "self-other differentiation," the latter as "personal individuation."
7   The self-representation or the mental representation of the attributes of one's own person as they are known, both consciously and unconsciously, to the person himself or herself.

(114)

Most germane for us here is the second point, cultural concepts of what a self or person is, which entails socialization and enculturation processes to inculcate those ideas as well as social rewards and punishments for obtaining or failing to obtain the correct kind of self.

BOX 6.1 MICHEL FOUCAULT: TECHNOLOGIES OF THE SELF

Probably no one since the mid-twentieth century from outside of anthropology has had more impact on the discipline, and on all the social sciences, than Michel Foucault (1926–84). An intellect of unusual range, his life's work could be simplistically viewed as an exposition of the history of institutions like the mental hospital, the clinic, the prison, and the government or state. His chief insight was that such phenomena, and more pervasive social facts, such as sexuality, *have* a history that explains their transformations over time and their current status. In books like his 1961 *History of Madness in the Classical Age*, his 1963 *The Birth of the Clinic*, and his 1974 *Discipline and Punish*, he practiced what he came to call an "archaeological," and later a "genealogical," method, unearthing layers of development. But his thoughts went much further, eventually positing that mankind itself—the human—is a historical achievement. Notably, the institutions on which he focused were, in his estimation, sites of knowledge as well as of power and control, all impinging directly on the human body; certainly, it is easy to appreciate how incarceration in a prison or mental institution involves bodily restraint and chastisement. Discipline or "biopower" was a central concept for Foucault which was embedded in two social formations aimed at regulating the behavior of individuals. One of these sources was language or, as he called it, discourse or a discursive regime; this included ways of talking, and thus ways of thinking, that rendered some behaviors more conceivable and permissible than others. For instance, in psychiatry, all of the terminology of diagnosis and treatment would constitute its discourse. The discursive regime also took the form of, or could be and was translated into, practices up to and including medicating, locking up, and restraining (as with a straitjacket), along with more subtle tools, like monitoring and documenting—what some scholars have come to call the "audit culture." The other source, which also could be deployed through language, was "technologies of the self" by means of which the individual was made to know himself, monitor himself, and regulate himself. In an essay titled "Technologies of the Self," Foucault characterized these as socially specific knowledge and habits or strategies that

> permit individuals to effect, by their own means or with the help of others, a certain number of operations on their own bodies and souls, thoughts, conduct, and way of being, so as to transform themselves in order to attain a certain state of happiness, purity, wisdom, perfection, or immortality.
>
> (1988: 18)

Among the early technologies of the self identified by Foucault was the Christian tradition of confession. Clearly, these technologies and the knowledge that they produced—for the individual and for the governing elites who increasingly collected, archived, studied, and used that knowledge—were and are a kind of power. They are power over the individual, including power to induce the individual to exercise power over herself in accordance with official desires, but they are also power to summon "the individual," "the self," into being in the first place. Hence, Foucault could declare that the modern individual or self was an invention of these very technologies of the self.

The cross-cultural study of self

Although "self" was not the core concept in early psychological anthropology, there were direct explorations of it by mid-century. In 1959, Dorothy Lee described the self of the Wintu (Native American) as expressed in their language; she found that the Wintu did not share the Western notion of "an established separate self" but that "a Wintu self is identical with the parts of his body and is not related to them as 'other' so long as they are physically part of him" (1959: 135). Furthermore, the self was not nearly as significant for them as for Westerners: "with the Wintu the universe is not centered in the self" (138).

It was A. Irving Hallowell who most tirelessly pursued the self in this early period. A 1954 article titled "The Self and Its Behavioral Environment" (anthologized in *Culture and Experience*) examined the self generally and with special consideration of the Ojibwa. Reasoning first that "self-awareness" (which may or may not be equivalent to "self" or "having a self") is a generic human trait, he nevertheless held that it is "the focus of complex, and functionally dependent, sets of linguistic and cultural variables that enter into the personal adjustment of human beings as members of particular societies" (1955: 75)—in short, that it "is a culturally identifiable variable" (76). Mentioning Cooley, Mead, and Lee, and struggling with the terminological morass of "self," "ego," "personality," etc. before settling on self as self-awareness or the reflexive knowledge that one has an "object to himself" (80), Hallowell postulated a number of orientations-of-self-to-world provided by the individual's "behavioral environment." Among these orientations were object orientation, spatiotemporal orientation, motivational orientation, normative orientation, and of course self-orientation. As for the Ojibwa self, it

> is not oriented to a behavioral environment in which a distinction between human beings and supernatural beings is stressed. The fundamental differentiation of primary concern to the self is how other selves rank in order of *power*.... The power ranking of different classes of entities is so important because events only become intelligible in terms of their activities. All the effective agents throughout the entire behavioral environment of the Ojibwa are selves—my own self or other selves. *Impersonal* forces are never the causes of events. *Somebody* is always responsible.
>
> (181, emphasis in the original)

We will return to this matter of nonhuman selves or persons later.

BOX 6.2 CHIMPANZEE SELF-AWARENESS

There is experimental evidence that humans are not the only species capable of a sense of self. In 1970, the psychologist Gordon Gallup conducted experiments to determine if a chimpanzee knows who s/he is. He set chimps in front of a mirror, and eventually, they discovered that the image in the glass was "themselves." They related their motions to the motions in the mirror, and they even began to examine themselves for the first time, looking at parts of themselves that they had never seen before, like their ears and the inside of their mouths. Going a step further, once the animals had become familiar with themselves, Gallup made subtle changes in their appearance, like putting a spot of paint on their foreheads. Back in front of the mirror, they quickly realized that "they" were different and explored the spot, touching it and sniffing their fingers to figure out what was going on. Chimps that had never seen a mirror before did not react to the spot at all; they had not yet acquired a sense of self. Other experiments have suggested that chimps may also have *intersubjectivity*, that is, an awareness that other beings have minds and even what may be in those minds. Chimps that are shown the secret hiding place of a key to locked-up food, and then shown humans who behave as if they do not know where the key is, will guide the humans to the key with facial and hand gestures, indicating that they know what the humans do not know and that the humans need to know it.

There is little doubt that cultures speak differently about the self. In fact, many societies lack a word for "self" at all or, if they have a word, they use it less often or in different ways than Western societies do. At an extreme, doctrinal Buddhism denies the reality of the self altogether, if by self, we mean some enduring essence of the individual (something like the Christian concept of soul). The principle of *anatta* or "no self" is a corollary or outcome of the more general doctrine of *pratityasamutpada* or "dependent origination," which teaches that everything is impermanent or interdependent and comes into being in each moment in relation to other things and states. (Of course, this is a great simplification, and not all schools of Buddhism share exactly the same interpretation.) In her recent ethnography of a Thai village, Julia Cassaniti reports that laypeople have absorbed this concept of official Buddhism, which affects their self and conduct; indeed, like talk about the self in the United States, talk about or in terms of nonself is omnipresent in the Thai community. Although people often professed ignorance of it—saying that it was the business of monks and scholars—the more Cassaniti learned about and looked for the notion, "the more I found evidence of teachings about it" (2015: 19). One informant named Goy "talked about it so passionately and articulately" (23–4) that it was clearly familiar and important to ordinary folks, and it colored their emotional experience and everyday lives. People spoke often of—and put into practice—*tham jai* or "making the heart," which Casssaniti associates with "Buddhist ideas about the importance of being aware of change (in the sense of the Pali word *anicca*, or impermanence)" (2–3). The ideal condition of the self is a "cool heart" or calm (*jai yen*), itself an effect of the Thai Buddhist virtue of *tong ploy* or letting go (Figure 6.1). Compared to the agitation of the Western self, her Thai hosts

> didn't seem to get angry, or sad, or full of joy, or excited, as far as I could tell. I didn't encounter these or any of the other emotion that, as I had been taught in psychology classes, were universal and cross-culturally basic to human experience.
>
> (41)

Figure 6.1 Thai Buddhism teaches detachment from the self and encourages a "cool heart".

Although these Thai Buddhists appear to embrace the high doctrines of their religion and culture, one of the most pernicious problems in the anthropological examination of self is, as Spiro opined and Douglas Hollan concurred, presuming that people actually believe and practice reigning public or official concepts. Spiro warned that most often, anthropologists are not collecting "the individual's conception of his self (the self-representation), but the cultural conception of the person" (1993: 117), and Hollan likewise cautioned that "cultural models and conceptions of the self should not be conflated with the experiential self. Self-concepts may also be derived from one's own personal and social experience" (1992: 286). For instance, in contrast to Cassaniti's Thai Buddhists, Spiro's Burmese Buddhists did "not internalize the doctrine of *Anatta*":

> Instead, they strongly believe in the very ego or soul that this doctrine denies. They do so on two accounts, experiential and pragmatic. First, because they themselves experience a subjective sense of a self, the culturally normative concept of an ego-less person does not correspond to their personal experience. Second, and perhaps more important, they find the doctrine of a selfless person not congenial to their soteriological aspirations.
>
> (1992: 119)

Similarly, Unni Wikan urged care in assuming that culturally normative discourses about the self in Bali represented how Balinese people really understood, experienced, and felt about the self, stressing that there is a "fundamental difference between the outer forms of conduct and the inner life of experience" (1987: 355). Rather than lacking a self and being all social mask, Wikan contended that "behind a surface aestheticism, grace, and gaiety" lurked a self characterized by "social uneasiness, great concern with the individual thoughts and intentions of others, and ubiquitous fear" (338).

Research on the self in other cultures reveals other remarkable lessons. Revisiting Hallowell's work on the Ojibwa, Thomas Hay maintained that members of that society "hold at least two self-concepts and these two are inconsistent"—and he suggested that this was widely true across cultures (1977: 74). One self-concept, more easily put into words, was the "conscious" self-concept; the other was "unconscious":

> The central characteristics (for present purposes) that the Ojibwa attribute to themselves *in the conscious self-concept* are, first, a complete *lack* of any abilities or "powers," either natural or magical, second, a nearly complete lack of the capacity for anger. The characteristics that they unconsciously attribute to themselves are, first, great magical power, especially when angry, such that any expression of anger may result in the illness or death of the object of the anger, and second, a tendency to become enraged on slight provocation. In these two self-concepts the Ojibwa ascribe opposite characteristics to themselves.
>
> (74–5, emphasis in the original)

Further, Hay judged that part of the conscious self-concept was "complementary" to their concept of the environment—specifically, that other beings in the world, known collectively as *pawiganak* or "dream visitors" (what Westerners might call spiritual beings), possessed the powers that people denied in themselves. In a fashion, we could think of the *pawiganak* as the alter or projection of the Ojibwa self, if not as an externalized component of the self.

One implication or extension of the notion of self as culturally constructed is that it takes work to create and perpetuate a self. Contemporary psychology has embraced and promoted the idea of "self-work" to exercise the self and whip it into an ideal form; Foucault meant something comparable when he wrote of technologies of the self, only with a more ominous tone. Dorinne Kondo accompanied participants to a Japanese ethics training seminar at which attendees intentionally worked on their selves. She found that a "striking feature of the ethics ideology was its comprehensive attempt to place selves within a larger, integrated frame of reference. Selves were seen as embedded in the contexts of family and, especially, work" (1987: 242). Even prior to the seminar, the owner of the factory whose workers were recruited for the meeting distributed pamphlets and articles encouraging his employees to cultivate certain self skills and held noontime gatherings to read and chant slogans like "Let's cooperate on the job" (242). Acknowledging the Japanese terms *tatemae* and *hone* for "what is done to smooth social relations and 'real' feeling" (245), respectively, Kondo argued that in Japan, "a human being is always and inevitably involved in a multiplicity of social relationships. Boundaries between self and other are fluid and constantly changing," and the cultural ideal "is an accommodation of the social and emotional selves, where powerful emotionality creates a self sensitive to others not by social fiat, but out of caring and love" (245–6). The seminar then was an arena for self-fashioning *in line with cultural and workplace expectations*, with verbal and physical exercises to strengthen these habits of self, from cleaning the meeting space to shouting sentences together. Every utterance was intended to

> foster cheerfulness and positiveness through the energy it generated by shouting. It would deepen our ideas about filial piety through giving thanks to our parents and, in the case of company seminars, heighten the feeling of being part of a company.
>
> (254)

BOX 6.3 MUSLIM NEOLIBERAL SELF

Such formal self-work is hardly unique to Japan; quite possibly, all readers of this book have been subjected to some similar experience and/or have actively engaged in self-work on their own initiative. One other example, which combines the unlikely ingredients of modern corporate life and religion, is described by Daromir Rudnyckyj in his analysis of "spiritual economy" and "neoliberal Islam." Following the teachings of scholars like Imaduddin Abdulrahmin who wrote *The Spirit of Tawhid and Work Motivation* (*tawhid* meaning monotheism, the oneness of God), organizations in Indonesia like Emotional and Spiritual Quotient (ESQ) or Management of the Heart sponsored training sessions aimed to promote Muslim principles and to produce a new kind of modern neoliberal Muslim self that was compatible with modern work. Both of these programs sought to construct a corporate Muslim self, one who was rational and efficient, hard-working, self-disciplined, and personally responsible, attentive to time, clean, and moral. In this view, "faith itself became an object of development" (2010: 126)—and of the very same kind of neoliberal development found elsewhere, in which "governmentality" shifts from the formal institutions of government to other institutions like the corporation and the religion and ultimately to the self. As in all equivalent efforts to reshape the self for economic purposes, one of the primary goals was "inculcating ethics of individual accountability that are deemed commensurable with norms of transparency, productivity, and rationalization for purposes of profit" (132). And central to that project, as in Japan and Thai Buddhism, was the crafting of emotion; what Rudnyckyj calls "governing through affect" involves personal transformation, such as "opening the heart," "the circulation of tears," and ultimately "management of the heart" (158).

To make one final point, anthropologists among other social scientists have come to emphasize the role of "narration" or talking and telling stories about the self as a crucial resource for constructing a self. As Elinor Ochs and Lisa Capps summarized in a review of self-narration, narrative activity

> provides tellers with an opportunity to impose order on otherwise disconnected events, and to create continuity between past, present, and imagined worlds. Narrative also interfaces self and society, constituting a crucial resource for socializing emotions, attitudes, and identities, developing interpersonal relationships, and constituting membership in a community.
>
> (1996: 19)

Michaela Schäuble (2014) demonstrates how telling and performing history in biographies and rituals contributes to the formation and propagation of a sense of individual and collective victimhood in present-day Croatia. Two last cases, from a volume appropriately enough titled *Fluent Selves*, will have to suffice. Peter Gow describes how the Piro people of the Peruvian Amazon have a specialized language genre for "exemplary personal experience narratives that deal with very unusual and emotionally charged life events"; connected to a particular individual—in the kind of society that is often assumed to lack a concept of individuality (see the following)—and owned and told by that person, these stories "focus attention on the uniqueness of individual experience, and on its multiplication through the act of telling the story to others" (2014: 69). This case supports the claim of Ochs and Capp that "narrative and self are inseparable," where self is understood "to be an unfolding reflective awareness of being-in-the-world, including a sense of one's past and future" (1992: 20–1). The second case shows how the self that unfolds over a lifetime must, in some cultures, be folded back up after death. Among the Mapuche of Chile, the self is always a work-in-progress during life—"constituted by a multiplicity of relationships, as necessarily contingent, multiple, fluid, and, as Mapuche people themselves say, 'unfinished'" (Course 2014: 144). The self-building process terminates upon death, at which time, the former work-in-progress self is close or "finished": just as the Mapuche self in life is created and sustained through social relationships and exchanges, so "these relationships must be severed before the 'spirit' of the deceased can move on to the unspecified realm of the dead," which is accomplished "through an incredibly detailed and thorough biography of the deceased known as *nütramtun*: every place he ever went, every person he ever met, every achievement" (153). In effect, just as stories make the self, stories unmake the self.

Is the Western Individualistic Self Peculiar among the World's Culture—or Even Real?

If one thing seems certain to the average American or European, it is that s/he has a self and that this self is distinctly and uniquely his or hers. Clifford Geertz colorfully expounded the standard Western conception of self as

> a bounded, unique, more or less integrated motivational and cognitive universe; a dynamic center of awareness, emotion, judgment, and action organized into a distinctive whole and set contrastively both against other such wholes [i.e., other people] and against a social and natural background.
>
> (1974: 29)

He further stipulated that such a notion of self is "a rather peculiar idea within the context of the world's cultures" (1974: 29). This raises two serious questions: is the Western self actually so perfectly individual, and is such an individualistic self rare across cultures?

The alleged contrast between the Western self and all the other self-concepts in the world is usually cast in terms of individualism versus collectivism or sociocentrism or, in the words of India scholar Louis Dumont, "wholism" in which "the stress is placed on the society as a whole, as a collective Man" and the individual is minimized or ignored (1970: 8). Spiro voiced what seems to be the anthropological consensus, however, that "these bipolar types of self—a Western and a non-Western—are wildly overdrawn" (1993: 116). As already mentioned, he discovered an individualized self among the supposedly collectivist, if not selfless, Burmese Buddhists. A year before, Douglas Hollan compared the American self with the self among the Toraja, an indigenous group from Sulawesi, Indonesia. Despite the fact that the Toraja are "a strongly 'sociocentric' people," he documented instances of Torajans displaying "a sense of their own autonomy [and] protest[ing] vigorously when that autonomy is challenged" (1992: 292). More, even when acting in a collectivist or sociocentric way, Hollan argued that they did so as a matter of individual choice.

As another example, a cross-cultural study of Turkish, Mexican American, and white American students by Sandra Carpenter and Zahide Karakitapoglu-Aygün did report that the former two groups ranked their social and collective identities more highly than did the white Americans. Yet all three samples

> emphasized the personal identity the most, followed by social and collective identity orientations. This finding implies that one's personal thoughts, ideas, values, sense of uniqueness, and feelings of being distinct from others seem to be the most important aspect of the self regardless of culture.
>
> (2005: 312)

Adrie Suzanne Kusserow, one of the most tireless critics of the simplistic dualism of West-versus-the-rest selves, stressed a number of errors, beginning with the assumption that individualism and sociocentrism are mutually exclusive; instead, as seems sensible, any individual or society can be more-or-less individualistic and sociocentric at the same time. Next, "the West" too often means the United States specifically, with American concepts and attitudes taken to represent Western society. Third, she complained that sociocentrism, devalued in American/Western societies, tends to be ascribed to women and the lower class (and perhaps to ethnic minorities) as a way of marginalizing and othering them. Finally, and worst of all, she counseled against "the homogenization of Western individualism" (1999: 541), that is, the presumption that all Westerners hold the same concept of the individualistic self and *that it is the only concept they hold and the only experience or self-representation they possess.* To wit, her own research on child-rearing in New York City exposed three different kinds of American individualism:

1 "hard defensive," characterized by values of "perseverance, self-pride, and independence" and significantly associated with the lower working class
2 "hard offensive," promoting values of "independence, self-confidence, self-determination, and perseverance" and associated with the upper working class
3 "soft offensive," featuring values of "uniqueness, individuality, self-esteem, and self-confidence" and associated with the upper-middle class.

"Sociocentric emphases and practices do not impede the child's development of hard individualism" in the two working classes, she concluded; instead, "Parents engage in frequent nonchalant switching between individualist mode and sociocentric mode in child-rearing practices, talk to and about child." Among the upper-middle class, she found talk "about importance of sociocentric qualities quite prevalent, but parents worried a great deal that this might be threatening the development of the soft individualism" (555).

Paralleling Kusserow's point about homogenization of the self but nine years earlier, Katherine Ewing advised against what she called the "illusion of wholeness." In the best anthropological tradition, she posited that

> in all cultures people can be observed to project multiple, inconsistent self-representations that are context-dependent and may shift rapidly. At any particular moment a person usually experiences his or her articulated self as a symbolic, timeless whole, but this self may quickly be displaced by another, quite different, "self," which is based on a different definition of the situation.
>
> (1990: 251)

She linked this insight to the growing anthropological discovery of diversity and even inconsistency within culture, which too often suffered from its own illusion of homogeneity and wholeness. Instead, individuals can hold a variety or sequence of self-concepts and self-representations, just as they commonly hold disparate and incompatible beliefs or values at the same time, and shift between them almost imperceptibly without any loss of a sense of integral self. Varieties of self-experience are most noticeable during the life span, but she also stressed how they can occur from moment to moment and from situation to situation; additionally, she bound revitalization movements (see Chapter 3) to the process of attempting to manage inconsistencies and cobble together a coherent self and social experience. In the end,

> Self-representations are embedded in a particular frame of reference, are culturally shaped, and are highly contextual. Contexts themselves rapidly shift, as actors negotiate status and seek to achieve specific goals, implicitly redefining themselves and each other during the course of the interaction. They assimilate ongoing experience to established representations of self and other, by a process related to the psychoanalytic phenomenon of transference. When existing self-representations are rendered inadequate by explicit conflict that requires resolution, the individual may draw on a range of rhetorical strategies, either regressive and defensive, or integrating and creative, in an effort to adapt to the new situation.
>
> (273–4)

In other words, Americans and Westerners are not quite as individualistic as we usually think—and they are not quite as *in-dividual*, as unitary and indivisible, as we think, which will be explored further later.

The anthropology of personhood

The concept of person is arguably more important for anthropology than the concept of self and has received more anthropological attention. The cause of its significance, as Mauss recognized in his early treatment of the term, is its legal and moral connotations. In Western parlance, a "person" has legal rights and responsibilities that a nonperson (such as a plant or an animal) does not; more, a "person" is entitled to moral consideration in a way that a nonperson is not. Note, as mentioned earlier, that much of the debate about abortion in the United States is conducted in the language of personhood: abortion foes insist that—and sometimes press for legislation enshrining that—a fetus is a "person" (not a "self," which it most likely is not) and therefore has a legal right to life. Indeed, historically minded social scientists from Mauss to Foucault have proposed that the Western category of person arose for legal and religious purposes, to hold the individual accountable for his or her crimes and sins and to assign guilt and therefore punishment to the culpable person.

Since the concept of person, as much as or more so than the concept of self, has a cultural history, we should suspect that its history and status in other cultures will diverge. At stake are (a) how a "person" is understood to be constituted (i.e. what makes someone a "person") and what a person is constituted of, (b) what freedoms and obligations pertain to a person (i.e. how may or must we treat or interact with a person), (c) by what standards a person is judged (i.e. who is a good or moral person and why), and (d) who or what qualifies as a person, including *but not necessarily limited to human beings*.

BOX 6.4 MEYER FORTES: TALLENSI PERSONHOOD

One of the earliest and most penetrating analyses of personhood in another culture was Meyer Fortes's description of Tallensi (West African) person. First presented at a 1971 seminar and then reprinted in his 1987 *Religion, Morality and the Person: Essays on Tallensi Religion*, the psychologically trained Fortes began with the observation that, at least in certain circumstances, the Tallensi regarded a crocodile as a person, though not a human (1987: 254). The local word for person was *nit* (plural *niriba*), while the term for human was *nisaal*. *Nisaal* and the synonym *nin-voo* (person-alive) were contrasted to other living things (*bon-vor*, thing-alive) although humans and other beings were composed of the same basic substances of flesh, blood, and bone. Fortes inferred (since the Tallensi were not very explicit about it) that the key difference between humans and animals was that "animals have no genealogies.... [They] do not have descent and kinship credentials. They do not have social organization with the implications of moral and jural rules. They have no ritual practices, no ancestors," although they do have "life and individuality" (255). More critically, humans themselves were not endowed with full personhood at birth. Personhood was gradually acquired or achieved, starting with the conditions of birth itself: "To become a person one must be properly and normally born and this, ideally, means singly born, head first, of parents licitly permitted to procreate" (261). But that was only the minimal qualification to commence the personhood process. Over a lifetime a man—and less so a woman—gained or accreted personhood such that

> the ideal of a complete person is an adult male who has reach old age and lineage eldership, who has male descendants in the patrilineal line and who is qualified by a proper death to become their worshipped ancestor. Nevertheless women are not wholly debarred from attaining a degree of personhood corresponding, in their sphere of life, to that of any man
>
> (264)

Indeed, Fortes maintained that a man could not reach personhood until his father died, placing him at the head of his family, and that his quest for personhood was "not finally proven to have succeeded until it is confirmed in the funeral divination at the time of his death" (271). In other words, a man was only recognized as a full person postmortem. As for crocodile persons, Fortes concluded that if

> society is the source of personhood, it follows that society can confer it on any object it chooses, human or non-human, the living or the dead, animate or inanimate, materially tangible or imagined, above all, both on singular and on collective objects.
>
> (253)

Depending upon the society, anthropologists find that personhood may be determined by group membership, material and symbolic possessions (like names), and other variables. Describing the Tchambuli, who were featured in Margaret Mead's famous study of gender and personality (see Chapter 2), Deborah Gewertz stated that

> To be a person among the Tchambuli is, first of all, to be a member of a patriclan, a land-owning, residential, and ceremonial group. Tchambuli describe a patriclan as "the people with the same totems," a phrase that indicates that members of the clan hold common ownership of numerous totemic names—names referring to the ancestors who once held them and to the territories and resources owned and lived in by these ancestors.… Each individual also inherits several totemic names from his or her father's affines.
>   Thus, Tchambuli become repositories of both their patrilineal and matrilateral relationships through their possession of certain names. To be a person among them is to embody these relationships.
>
> (1984: 619)

The next year, Simon Harrison portrayed the Avatip, also of New Guinea, as operating with "a dualistic conception of personhood, according to which distinct facets of the 'person' express themselves in ritual and secular contexts" (1985: 115). He explained that every individual regardless of age or gender was thought to consist of two "basic dimensions of selfhood," namely, *mawul* and *kaiyik*. *Mawul* could be translated as "understanding," the part of a person that makes her "aware of social conventions and apprehends them as having moral force"; *kaiyik* is closer to "spirit," that is, "the individual's life-force, an *élan vital* conceived as the source of growth and health, of self-assertion and self-will and, in time, of mystical powers over others" (117). He continued:

> The *mawul* is the seat of thought, knowledge and affective response. It is thought of as the quintessentially "moral" or "social" aspect of the personality, the hallmark of full socialization. To have a *mawul* is to be rational, to have all one's appropriate adult skills and knowledge, and to be conscious of one's obligations. But more than this it involves an empathic disposition toward others....
>
> *Kaiyik* ("Spirit"), the counterpart of *mawul*, means an "image" of something: a shadow or reflection, a carving or painted design, or nowadays also a photograph.... The *kaiyik* is the source of vitality and its display in spontaneous action. It can wax and wane in strength; and it can be removed by sorcery and spirit attack, causing lassitude, illness and eventually death unless magical measures are taken to retrieve it. Out of the body, it usually appears as the individual's "double," though it can also impersonate others. A *kaiyik* on the loose is a public nuisance, playing irresponsible and frightening tricks: scaring travelers in the bush, ruining the luck of hunters or capsizing canoes. Detached from the *mawul* it is amoral and mischievous, being the pure animating energy of human individuality temporarily disincarnated and unconstrained.
>
> (118–19)

The Avatip person was clearly then a composite being, in need of both of its main components. Interestingly, *mawul* was believed to develop naturally with maturity, but *kaiyik* had to be fostered with ritual and magical activity. More profoundly, *kaiyik*, held to be fundamentally male, began as an internal force or substance but was thought and hoped "gradually to project itself out of him into the form of a mystical guardian or alter ego, a conscious agency in its own right" (123)—in other words, to become an external and relatively separate aspect of his personhood.

Across cultures, the individual's body is commonly if not always entailed in personhood, although, as in the Avatip case, the person is not always equivalent to or constrained by the body. For the Cashinahua (also spelled Kashinawa) of Brazil and Peru, the body was the locus of personhood but also of health and of knowledge—or what we might call, in tribute to Foucault, health/knowledge. Cecilia McCallum stated that among the Cashinahua "a healthy body is one that constantly learns through the senses and expresses the accumulated knowledge in social action and speech"; "An ill body is one that no longer knows. Curing, therefore, acts to restore a person's capacity to know" (McCallum 1996: 347). Indeed, the Cashinahua body was a nexus and product of a person's spirits (in the plural) and "physical, mental, and emotional capacities," including speech (348). Spirit and body were not opposed; they were hardly distinguished. Nor in their ethnopsychology was a person's mind separate from body: the Cashinahua did not even assign knowledge to the brain, and they had no word for "mind" in contrast to body. They attributed no special role to the brain, rather conceiving knowledge to be distributed throughout the body. Each organ—"skin, hands, ears, genitals, liver, and eyes"—is "linked to a specific process of acquiring knowledge and of putting it to use in physical action" (355–6). "Thus the body integrates different kinds of knowledge acquired in a varied manner, in different body parts" (356). Not surprisingly, changes in spirit were experienced in the body as "medical" symptoms like fainting and dizziness. Illness and ultimately death were understood as loss of knowledge, specifically of closing off connections with other people, and illness was treated with various kinds of *dau* or medicine, which is any substance "used to transform the body's capacity to know" (363).

BOX 6.5 PERSONHOOD, SUBSTANCE, AND SPEECH IN MUINANE CULTURE

Speaking of substances and transformations of the body and person, in all times and places the bodies and persons of human beings are penetrated by materials from the outside, which affect both bodily health and personhood. The Muinane of the Colombian Amazon assert that humans are "intrinsically moral" persons (Londono Sulkin 2012: 48), tending toward "loving care, a sense of purpose, coolness or calm equanimity, respect, and good humor" (30). Muinane moral personhood is fundamentally about body and more generally about substance; people are "alive, aware, articulate, and capable of competent, moral, and sociable action in part because of 'speeches' and 'breaths' that constituted their bodies and resonated inside them" (31). The moral person or body is built by these multiple speeches and breaths from interaction, including interaction with the physical world. Each plant, animal, and other substance has its own speech and breath. Tobacco is perhaps the most moral of substances, giving humans "proper thoughts/emotions and the capacity to learn, remember, and discern" (96). Both male and female bodies consist of tobacco juice, but only men can trade and share tobacco. Coca is only consumed by adult men and is closely associated with morality in its cultivation, preparation, and consumption. Women's bodies and morality, by contrast, are associated with and composed of manioc, chilies, and cool herbs. The connection between bodies, substances, and morality in Muinane culture can be traced to two ideas. First, different people have different substances—even different tobaccos—that breed different behaviors in them. Second, animals are said to be essentially immoral, ignoring the social and sexual norms of humans. Animal species have their own speeches and breaths, even their own tobaccos, but if an animal speech, breath, tobacco invades a human, immoral behavior results. Thus, "it was not rare for people to claim that a man who misbehaved had a jaguar inside, or that he spoke the speech of a jaguar" (55). In short, the Muinane assert that "hot speeches or breaths ensuing from animals' tobaccos and other substances altered people's sensibilities so much that they did not perceive or act as real people" (50), that is, as moral people.

The cases just discussed emphasize the social and interactional quality of personhood, but the person can also be practiced and perfected in solitude and silence. Donal Carbaugh, Michael Berry, and Marjatta Nurmikari-Berry accentuated the value of "being alone in a good way" in Finland. Quietude (*hiljaisuus*) was considered to be natural and beneficial to the person and to others, allowing the Finnish person *olla omissa oloissaan* ("being undisturbed in one's thoughts") and *mietiskellä* ("being contemplative and thoughtful") (2006: 208). Being alone in a good way, they said,

> is a social achievement and a matter of social tact, as one exercises a proper propensity for silence, or, from another angle, a proper verbal reserve. In doing so, one honors one's own and others' privacy. In the process, meaningful Finnish action is linked to a proper care of self and others, thereby protecting all social actors from unwanted intrusions.
>
> (211)

The dividual or partible person

One corollary of the professed collectivist or sociocentric self (see earlier) is that the person is not quite free of or from other individuals and relations in society. In fact, in investigating the Hindu caste system, Louis Dumont reasoned that hierarchy was more important than individuality in India and that the individual did not really exist or at least was not socially significant. What was relevant was the caste position and role. A few years later, two other studies—one on India (Marriott and Inden 1977), the other on Melanesia (Leenhardt 1979)—encouraged anthropologists to consider at least some non-Western persons as not individuals but *dividuals*, that is, not as unified and indivisible ("individual" derives from the roots for not-divide) but as fundamentally multiple, composite, and divisible. In the words of Maurice Leenhardt, writing on Melanesia where much of this perspective has focused, the Melanesian person

> knows himself only by the relationships he maintains with others. He exists only insofar as he acts his role in the course of his relationships. He is situated only with respect to them. If we try to draw this, we cannot use a dot marked "self" (*ego*), but must make a number of lines to mark relationships ... The empty space is him, and this is what is named.
>
> (1979: 153)

Soon thereafter Marilyn Strathern popularized the term "dividual" in her ethnography of Melanesia, claiming that the Melanesian was a "multiple person produced as the object of multiple relationships" (1988: 185). Such a person was his or her social relationships incarnate, "plural and composite." Or to be fair, she insisted that the Melanesian person was and was not an individual: "Melanesian persons are as dividually as they are individually conceived" (13). As noted earlier, Magnus Course (2011, 2014) discerned something similar among the Mapuche of Chile, where the personhood is less an individual essence than a social status achieved by possession of a human body and "the capacity for productive sociality" (2014: 25). Mapuche personhood, as among the Tallensi, is a lifelong process of building and nurturing social relationships through ritual and reciprocity, and only at death is this process ended or "finished" (Figure 6.2).

Figure 6.2 Melanesian cultures have provided some of the strongest anthropological evidence for the "dividual" or "partible person".

In his fittingly titled *Encompassing Others*, Edward LiPuma summarized the dividual as having the following traits:

Persons are the compound and the plural site of the relations that bring them together. Collective sociality/life is defined as an essential unity. Singular person is a composite. The social and the individual are parallel, homologous, and equivalent.

There is no explicit ideology of persons, only contextually situated images.

Persons grow transactionally as the beneficiary of other people's actions.

Persons depend on others for knowledge about themselves, and they are not the authors of this knowledge.

(2000: 132–3)

Other fieldworkers have refined the notion of the dividual, suggesting, for instance, "partible person" as an alternative or clarification; one powerful implication of the partibility of persons is that not only does the person have parts but that these parts might be able to detach from the person, resulting in a noncontiguous person, that is, personhood that does not stop at limits of his or her body. Returning to India, Cecilia Busby opined that the Indian person is not so much partible as *permeable*: "persons are not internally divided" and "there are no disposable parts," but

the person is not rigidly contained.… The boundary of the body is considered permeable, so that substance can flow between persons, and connections can be made. The Indian person is not partible, but rather could be called "permeable," having "fluid boundaries".

(1997: 274–5)

Karl Smith (2012) offers the term *porosity* as a substitute for both partibility and permeability, underscoring the fact that a human person—Melanesian, Indian, and Western alike—is constructed by letting the external (whether that is substances, ideas/representations, relationships, or features of other persons) in and letting the internal out.

BOX 6.6 ALFRED GELL: DISTRIBUTED PERSONHOOD

In the unlikely context of the anthropology of art, Alfred Gell shed crucial light on the process of partibility and porosity with his concept of *distributed personhood*. It is not correct, he asserted, to look at each object or piece of art as a separate thing or at the object/piece as separate from its maker (and potentially its user). First, objects may be among the class of "other-than-human persons" (see the following) with a life and mind of their own. But much more, "a person" need not be restricted to just one place or body; that is, "persons may be 'distributed,' i.e. all their 'parts' are not physically attached, but are distributed around the ambience" (1998: 106). Gell also reckoned that "religious" practices like magic were based on the same premise: a magic spell can be worked on a piece of the target's clothing or hair or fingernail because "as the body grows, it sheds its parts, and these become distributed" (108) such that bits of the person are spread around the environment—bits which retain a connection, a "oneness," with the person. Of course, each distributed bit of a person or object can have its own "micro-history," but they still maintain a unity. Therefore,

> a person and a person's mind are not confined to particular spatiotemporal coordinates, but consist of a spread of biographical events and memories of events, and a dispersed category of material objects, traces, and leaving, which can be attributed to a person and which, in aggregate, testify to agency and patienthood during a biographical career which may, indeed, prolong itself long after biological death. The person is thus understood as the sum total of the indexes which testify, in life and subsequently, to the biographical existence of this or that individual.
>
> (222–3)

In a word, things can be persons in their own right, or they can be distributed parts of the person who made them and presumably of every person who has owned or interacted with the object during its "career."

Humans and other persons

Hallowell noticed that the Ojibwa language puts stones in the grammatical category of animate beings; when he asked if all stones are alive, an old man answered, "No! But some are" (1976: 362). Language was Hallowell's first clue that the Ojibwa did not conceive of persons in the same way that Western cultures do. Things that Westerners believe are inanimate and impersonal, like trees, stones, the sun or moon, thunder, and material objects like pots and pipes, were regarded as animate, as *persons*, in Ojibwa. For instance, people reported seeing stones move or hearing them speak, and people spoke to such objects in turn. They also referred to important objects in kin terms, especially as "grandfathers," and these "other-than-human grandfathers are sources of power to human beings through the 'blessings' they bestow, i.e., a sharing of their power which enhances the 'power' of human beings" (360). Finally, their sacred stories or myths (*âtíso'kanak*) reflected a personal and social relationship between humans and other beings who "behave like people" (365). Thus, Hallowell concluded that much if not all of what we consider inanimate and impersonal, like the sun, was for the Ojibwa "not a natural object in our sense at all. ... [T]he sun is a 'person' of the other-than-human class" (366). Ultimately, "any concept of impersonal 'natural' forces is totally foreign to Ojibwa thought" (367) since everything was personal and social; indeed, the Ojibwa had no notion "of impersonal forces as major determinants of events" (382) as all events including thunder and lightning were the actions of persons, and the Ojibwa were puzzled that white people thought otherwise. For the Ojibwa the world was a great social system of human persons and other-than-human persons, in which one set of social principles applied to all.

The irresistible implication of Gell's observation that parts of humans as well as material objects can share in a human's personhood is that nonhuman species, things, and forces or phenomena can have personhood in their own right. Truly, anthropologists have realized that personhood of the nonhuman world is one of the most pervasive notions across cultures. Commonly dubbed "animism," it was highlighted as the elementary form of religion in E. B. Tylor's epochal *Primitive Culture*, identifying the presence of mind or will, or what we more frequently today call "agency" or "intentionality," in nature. A rehabilitation of animism as a key cultural concept has recently been underway, commencing with Nurit

Bird-David's 1999 essay on personhood, environment, and relational epistemology among the Nayaka of south India. Tracing the analysis of personhood from Tylor through Hallowell to Marriott and Strathern, Bird-David depicted the Nayaka *devaru* "spirits" as "superpersons" and as "dividual persons" (1999: S68), objectifications of the sharing relationships in the society and means of making such relationships visible and knowable. In trance, Nayaka men commune with and "bring to life" various *devaru*, distinguishing each being

> by its dividuated personality: by how it idiosyncratically interrelates with Nayaka (how it laughs, with, talks with, gets angry at, responds to Nayaka, etc.)... Conversation with the *devaru* is highly personal, informal, and friendly, including joking, teasing, bargaining, etc.... With numerous repetitions or minor variations on a theme, Nayaka and *devaru* nag and tease, praise and flatter, blame and cajole each other, expressing and demanding care and concern.
>
> (S76)

The essence of animism—or more rightly, the essence of personhood, whether ascribed to humans or other-than-humans—is relationship. As Graham Harvey put it in his passionate *Animism: Respecting the Living World*, animism means that

> the world is full of persons, only some of whom are human, and... life is always lived in relationships with others.... Persons are beings, rather than objects, who are animated and social toward others (even if they are not always sociable).
>
> (2006: xi)

When humans understand this fact, it becomes incumbent upon us to know and acknowledge who or what is a person since it is not always obvious, but it can be crucial.

Once we start looking for it, we find other-than-human personhood everywhere. The Ainu of northern Japan, for instance, insisted that plants, animals, and even man-made objects were "spirit-owning" or "spirit-bearing" beings who had to be treated respectfully. In life, there were restrictions on how humans could interact with them, and even (and perhaps mainly) in death, these restrictions held; for instance, people had to maintain a separate location for the disposal of each type of spirit-owning being, called *keyohniusi*, and negligence of their duties toward these beings could bring sickness or worse (Ohnuki-Tierney 1974). The Huron (Native American) spoke of plant, animal, and even inanimate objects having spirits, which were the same size and shape as their physical bodies. The Dani of New Guinea, like many peoples of the world, experienced the spirits of or in natural objects or places like hills, rocks, ponds, and whirlpools. The Anutans (Pacific Islands) made claims about a type of spirits called *tupua penua* or land/totemic spirits, associated either with species like the shark, octopus, or sea turtle or with natural features and sites. These spirits were god-like in some ways—with names, individual personalities, and power, who are bound to locations, prayed to, and invoked in song and story—yet also amoral, egotistical, and dangerous. Finally, among infinite examples, Catherine Allerton describes how the Manggarai of Indonesia confer personhood on spaces and places. Rooms in houses are permeable persons, absorbing some of the qualities of residents and "addressed as unseen persons in rituals" (2013: 41). Houses have their own composite personhood as do paths and the physical environment as a whole: Allerton refers to it as an "animate landscape" (97) that is filled with spiritual persons and is itself an agent or person.

BOX 6.7 CHALK SAINTS AND GODDESS STATUES AS OTHER-THAN-HUMAN PERSONS

Other-than-human personhood is not found only in premodern societies. The Catholics of Apaio in southern Chile revere their San Antonio de Padua, seeking his blessings and fearing his anger. The only thing is, San Antonio is a 15-cm (6-in.) painted chalk statue, not even, according to Giovanna Bacchiddu, particularly well crafted. Nor is he among the official saint-statues housed in the local church. Rather, he is owned by a poor woman who gladly sends him to visit people in need of his services. Pilgrims take him to their home for ten days on average, where they perform a ritual or novena, and while he is with them, he "brings corporeal manifestation of the sacred into everyday life" (Bacchiddu 2011: 28). San Antonio is known to be powerful but also complicated, like any person. He "expects a return" (29), and devotees negotiate with him as if he is human, "formulating a question and waiting for an answer, making an offer and thereby agreeing on an exchange, or otherwise offering an apology and expecting the apology to be accepted" (31–2). Of course, he "is treated like a guest, welcomed in the house and offered a special treatment" (33). And people have the same emotional reaction and attachment to him that they would to any honored guest. One woman "talks about the saint as if he were a person of flesh and bone. She calls him affectionately Chuco or Anchuquito, giving him not one but two nicknames, a practice in use among close acquaintances or relatives"; further, she "depicts him as someone that listens, delivers, warns, guides people's actions by giving the right weather at the right time to have them act in one way rather than in another" (31). Overall, believers enter into a "social relation" with the little saint that "is necessarily indistinguishable from a physical relation," one that "is made visible and activated through the body, through physical interaction with the saint, because for each spiritual address, such as asking something to the saint, a physical counterpart is needed to complete the circle" (37). The chalk statue is a person, and the "same code of conduct is valid" in dealing with him as with any member of society since he is "an individual, like a fellow human being" (38).

Meanwhile in contemporary England, "The Goddess is alive in Glastonbury, visible for all to see in the shapes of the sacred landscape," declares the Glastonbury Goddess Temple (www.goddesstemple.co.uk). Tracing its spiritual history to King Arthur, the magical island of Avalon, and pre-Christian British religion, the Goddess Temple is the abode of deities in the form of "willow wickerwork statues who are venerated, spoken with, petitioned, and said… to 'embody' the Goddess" (Whitehead 2013: 76). While acolytes of the Goddess may say that the figures represent her, they also say that she is "present in" them and in the surrounding land. Like the Goddess, the Nine Morgens are materialized in wicker statues and possess healing powers. Even more, followers assert that they "sometimes move, that their facial expressions change, and that 'things' occur around them" (77). The Goddess statue is routinely dressed and decorated "to display colors corresponding with one of the eight points in the ritual year" (78), but she is present not only in that wicker body but in other objects and images too: one female artist (the Goddess' worshippers are predominantly women) painted a picture of the Goddess and asserted that "it took roughly three days after the painting was finished for the Goddess to 'settle in' (her words) to the image," after which the image was seen "as containing and embodying the Goddess" (81). The Goddess is also taken in procession (see www.youtube.com/watch?v=msxgiUwFvtA for a video of the 2013 event), as Christian icons and statues often are, and when she returns to her temple home, women place items like earrings, stone, seashells, and pictures on or near her, kissing their own fingers and transferring the kiss to the figure. In the temple, the Goddess also receives offerings from devotees "in times of hardship or need, in thanks, or simple celebration of her" (86). And in these actions and the round of rituals, "intimate, day-to-day relationships with the Goddess figure and the Nine Morgens can take on 'real' interactions" (88). Believers claim that each statue has its own personality and changing mood—"sometimes they look pissy or serious, and sometimes they look happy and pleased"—and ultimately, they are more than symbols of the divine persons: "the statues are the Morgens" (88) (Figure 6.3).

Figure 6.3 Goddess conference in Glastonbury.

Another more specialized kind of other-than-human personhood reigns in the Amazonian region, according to Eduardo Vivieros de Castro. In a seminal 1998 article, he introduced the concept of "perspectivism" to label this unique way of being in the world. Among Amazonian societies, "animals are people, or see themselves as persons," which is not extraordinary; what is extraordinary is that

> *animals and spirits see themselves as humans*: they perceive themselves as (or become) anthropomorphic beings when they are in their own houses or villages and they experience their own habits and characteristics in the form of culture—they see their food as human food (jaguars see blood as manioc beer, vultures see the maggots in rotting meat as grilled fish, etc.), they see their bodily attributes (fur, feathers, claws, beaks etc.) as body decorations or cultural instruments, they see their social system as organized in the same way as human institutions are.
>
> (1998: 470, emphasis added)

In other words, animals experience their personhood as human personhood and accordingly experience humans as either predators or prey, that is, *who is the person* depends on perspective (human or animal).

The difference between animals and humans in such societies is not their "culture" or their "mind" or personality since both share human culture and mentality from their own point of view. The difference is their *bodies*. Consistent with but beyond Mary Douglas, Pierre Bourdieu, or Thomas Csordas (see Chapter 5), it is a human body that gives humans a human experience and perspective, a jaguar body that gives jaguars a jaguar experience and perspective, a peccary body that gives peccaries a peccary experience and perspective, and so on. And, in accordance with Londono Sulkin, human or animal bodies "are not thought of as given but rather as made" through ingesting and sharing substances (480). Therefore, it is an even-present possibility—and danger—that a human can transform into an animal and vice versa. Only the shaman has the inclination and strength to assume the identity and perspective—the personhood—of other species:

> To put on mask-clothing is not so much to conceal a human essence beneath an animal appearance, but rather *to activate the powers of a different body*. The animal clothes that shamans use to travel the cosmos are not fantasies but *instruments*: they are akin to diving equipment, or space suits, and not to carnival masks.
>
> (482, emphasis in the original)

Last but hardly least, this talk of instruments and the personhood and social agency of substances and objects is taken to the highest level by Bruno Latour, whose "actor-network theory" recognized and included nonhuman and even inanimate things in the field of social action. Following from his study of scientists and engineers (Latour 1987), he reckoned that humans and their technological devices and the materials they work with or on (animals, microbes, DNA, etc.) interact in a complex network of relationships. Humans do not merely act on inert things but are acted on, in turn, by those things, which is why he included humans and nonhumans alike in the category of "actants." Anthropologists have since taken an interest in the "social life of things" (e.g. Appadurai 1986), from museum objects to ordinary commodities, and lately in the "social life of materials" (e.g. Drazin and Küchler 2015) or the substances that objects are made of, like gold or oil or cloth. This all makes for a very thick web of personhoods and relationships in the social life of humans.

Findings and results

The anthropological study of self and personhood has revealed aspects of culture and of human experience not plumbed by the first decades of psychological anthropology. Among its discoveries are:

- the concept of self is culturally diverse, and the individual's sense of sense is socially constructed through practice and interaction
- an individual's experience or representation of self may or may not perfectly reflect cultural concepts and norms
- an individual may not have a single homogeneous self; the self may vary over time and between situations

- the individualistic nature of the Western self is exaggerated as is the collectivist or soci-ocentric self of non-Western societies
- personhood is a jural and moral concept with a distinct history in Western societies and a different history and practice in other societies
- personhood can be linked to multiple social variables, including age, family group, name, place, and of course the body
- not all societies conceive of the person as an indivisible whole, an "individual," but rather as internally plural and externally distributed
- many (if not all) societies attribute at least some aspects of personhood to nonhumans, including animals, plants, objects, process and phenomena, instruments, and materials.

Chapter 7

Emotions

Key questions:
How can emotions be studied cross-culturally—if studied scientifically at all?

Are there basic or universal emotions?

Can English- or Western-language emotion terms be applied cross-culturally? If not, how do other cultures understand and discuss emotions?

Must emotions be individual and original to be genuine, that is, are emotionality and conventionality mutually exclusive?

Do people in all cultures display emotions equally? Do they even believe that it is possible to know another person's inner feelings and thoughts?

What are the social and political consequences of experiencing and expressing certain emotions?

How are specific emotions, such as anger, fear, and love, culturally diverse and culturally constructed?

For the longest time, scholars largely acted as if emotions were beyond the reach of scientific investigation. Either emotions were understood as too ethereal, too "spiritual" for scientific description and analysis, or they were viewed as purely natural and physiological—just bodily states, like racing heart or red face—and therefore perhaps a subject for biologists but not for social scientists. Anthropologists, however, have questioned both of these, and other Western assumptions, although writing as late as 2005, Charles Lindholm opined that "until quite recently anthropology has had very little to say about how emotions are interpreted, how they differ cross-culturally, or whether emotions have any universal character" (2005: 30). The veracity of that statement, of course, depends on how one defines "recently" since Margaret Mead and Ruth Benedict in their own ways were querying emotion cross-culturally in the 1930s. But there is no doubt that significant advances have come in the last few decades.

According to Catherine Lutz, as in the case of self and personhood, the United States and other Western societies operate with a culturally specific concept of emotions that tends to limit our ability to see their cultural qualities and effects. Not only, as just mentioned, are they viewed as natural and/or ineffable, but they tend to be discussed—and dismissed—as at best private, mental, and psychological and as at worst irrational, thoughtless, and an actual impediment to thought. In binary Western philosophy, emotions are associated with the body, which is distinct from (and inferior to) the mind. "To be emotional," Lutz chastised

Western civilization for believing, "is to fail to process information rationally and hence to undermine the possibilities for sensible, or intelligent, action" (1988: 60). Presumed to be irrational, emotions are often deemed to be uncontrolled, involuntary, verging on wild, excessive, and painful (a synonym for emotion—passion—derives from the Latin root for "suffer"): we "fall" in love or "explode" in anger. This is why Lutz added that emotions are commonly judged as dangerous, as making us weak and vulnerable, and associated with and more appropriate for (putatively) weaker types, like women, children, neurotics, and "primitive" peoples (74). Of course, some emotions may be suitable for adult males (perhaps anger), but that goes to show that there is a cultural politics of emotion.

As we will explore later, not all societies share these assessments of emotion nor do they label, evaluate, or practice emotions in the same way. These facts make it odd that such an illustrious anthropologist as Edmund Leach would have asserted, in a critique of a book by Clifford Geertz, that the idea of an anthropology of emotions is "complete rubbish. I can make no sense of a line of thought which claims that 'passions' are culturally defined" (1981: 32). I think in the early twenty-first century that nearly all anthropologists would disagree with him and that the following pages will prove him wrong.

Toward an anthropology of emotions

Years before Geertz declared that culture was public because meaning is and behavior definitely is (see Chapter 5), anthropologists were curious about emotions in different cultures. Recall that Margaret Mead claimed that the emotions or "temperament" assigned to each gender varied across cultures, from the effeminate men of Tchambuli to the masculine women of the Mundugumor. In her classic *Patterns of Culture*, Ruth Benedict surmised that all humans share the same fundamental "arc of possibilities" or range of emotions but that specific societies emphasized specific emotions; entire societies could be summarized with one or a few emotion-words, and societies were distinguished by the type and degree of their key emotions, such as the exuberance of the Kwakiutl. Indeed, we might say that much of Freudian psychology, so influential on early anthropology, was centered on emotions (sometimes construed as drives or instincts) and their permutations and pathologies.

Emotion was admittedly not the primary focus of more cognitivist (ethnoscientific and structuralist; see Chapter 4) approaches to culture for the very reason that it is typically seen as separate from, if not opposed to, cognition. Geertz made emotion a critical aspect of his analysis of Balinese culture, which he concluded experienced or suffered from an extreme case of "stage fright" (it was precisely his comments on the political nature of Balinese emotions that drew Leach's condemnation). In an essay on Balinese personhood first published in 1965 but anthologized in his legendary *The Interpretation of Cultures*, Geertz contended that the extreme formality and "ceremoniousness" of Balinese social life led to "a thoroughgoing attempt to block the more creatural aspects of the human condition—individuality, spontaneity, perishability, emotionality, vulnerability—from sight" (1973: 399). This effort to disguise all personal feelings was not totally successful, he believed, but it was highly normative and "wished for"; failing at the expectation of controlling one's affect and letting one's true self show through resulted in the feeling of *lek*, sometimes translated as "shame" but more accurately recognized, Geertz said, as stage fright, "a diffuse, usually mild, though in certain situations virtually paralyzing, nervousness before the prospect (and the fact) of social interaction, a chronic, mostly low-grade worry that one will not be able to bring it off with the required finesse" (402).

If there is a first clue here for the anthropology of emotions, it is, as John Leavitt phrased it, that "Much of what we identify as emotional experience in the West and elsewhere, while experienced by the individual subject, appears to be highly stereotypical in nature" (1996: 527). In short, emotion is not entirely internal or private and would not be comprehensible if it was since part of the point of emotion is its expression (or suppression). But while almost all anthropologists would concur that emotion is to an extent cultural, there has been considerable debate about the exact way in which to represent that relationship. One camp takes a cognitivist, even linguistic, approach to emotion; Lindholm claimed that Catherine Lutz and Lila Abu-Lughod (who will be discussed later) held the position "that emotion can best be understood as a form of cognitive assessment that arouses the body as well as the mind" (2005: 40). Michelle Rosaldo allegedly epitomized this viewpoint when she offered that emotions "are thoughts somehow 'felt' in flushes, pulses, 'movements' of our livers, minds, hearts, stomachs, skin. *They are embodied thoughts*, thoughts steeped with the apprehension that 'I am involved'" (1984: 143, emphasis added).

Margot Lyon regarded this cognitivist approach as an element of a cultural constructionist perspective on emotion, in which "our categories of thought (and thus the ideas we have), how we talk (and thus what we say), and our experiences and feelings, and what we express and do are primarily determined by the culture in which we live" (1995: 244). She and others, though, have been critical of a strictly constructionist view of emotion that emotion is *all* culture; rather, one

> must go beyond constructionism if one aims, for example, to understand the role of contemporary institutional contexts in the generation and development of cultural difference. This holds as well for the generation, experience, and expression of emotion. By going beyond purely cultural accounts, one may more directly address the problematic relationship between private meaning and public symbol (or action).
>
> (245)

In particular, and consistent with the direction of anthropology since the 1970s, Lyon urged that we transcend a mainly cognitive or semantic stance (here, again, associated with Lutz and Rosaldo) and attend to the embodied quality of culturally informed emotions:

> The study of emotion can provide an expanded understanding of the place of the body in society through a consideration of the agency of the body. Emotion has a central role in bodily agency, for by its very nature it links the somatic and the communicative aspects of being and thus encompasses bodily as well as social and cultural domains.
>
> (256)

Reminding us of the phenomenology of Maurice Merleau-Ponty, which inspired anthropologists like Bourdieu, Sperber, and Csordas, Leavitt added that to define "emotions as words or concepts or models of emotion is to lose the feeling side of the phenomenon and reduce emotion to a kind of meaning" (1996: 522). Thus, while we surely want to take local terminologies of emotion seriously, we do not want to take them as exhaustive or indicative of actual experienced emotion any more than we want to take cultural discourses about the self as exhaustive or indicative of an individual's actual self-experiences and self-representations (see Chapter 6).

As a way out of the impasse, Lindholm suggested a dialectical approach to emotion and culture, accepting cultural variation, embodiment, and individual experience. "The view of the emotions as active elements motivating an individual's relationship with culture," he proposed, "makes better sense of ethnographic data than does the notion that emotions are really a form of cognition, wholly socially and linguistically constituted" (2005: 41). It is then possible to say "that the psychological substrate out of which mixtures" of cultural terms for emotions and embodied emotional experiences "come is universal, though the specific colorations and intensities will differ across cultures and individuals. Each culture will produce its own blend of basic feeling states, since these states do not have hard and fast boundaries and can be mingled in specific ways" (42). In short,

> an adequate psychological anthropology ought not to try to prove that every culture is emotionally unique (this is both obvious and fruitless), but that differences are cultur- ally, structurally, and historically motivated variations resting upon a common psychic ground. The real task is the double one of seeking to discover what that ground may be and of finding what factors determine the alternative paths taken in the repression, expression, and interpretation of emotion.
>
> (43)

One concrete proposition for comprehending the cultural organization of emotions was that the same emotion may be *hypercognized* or *hypocognized*. Lindholm taught that Ifaluk, Ilongot, and Samoan societies hypercognize anger: they possess "a large vocabulary for discussing it" and talk about it often, if not always positively, since hypercognition does not mean approval (42). On the other hand, they hypocognize sadness, with fewer words for it and less time and attention devoted to it. In fact, we might think of hyper- or hypocognition of emotions as one instance of Thomas Csordas's notion of "somatic modes of attention," learning to pay attention or not to emotional and physical feelings.

BOX 7.1 HYPOCOGNITION OF EMOTIONS

The idea of hyper-/hypocognition of emotions was introduced by Robert Levy in his study of Tahitians. While cutting across the standard categories of culture and per- sonality to identify the "public" and "private" factors that shape Tahitian society and behavior, Levy contended that some emotions were more culturally articulated than others; some were easily and commonly talked about via an extensive vocabulary, while others were characterized "by cultural invisibility or at least by difficulty of access to communication" (1973: 324), that is, "hypocognated." Guilt was one such emotion:

> the feeling of guilt is *culturally* played down to the point of conceptual invisibil- ity. The Tahitian language has no word which signifies anything like a sense of guilt.... The ordinary Tahitian way of expressing what would seem to a western observer to be the context of 'guilt feelings' is the nonspecific term *pe'ape'a*, which indicates 'trouble,' either as an internal sensation or as an aspect of a social or interpersonal situation.
>
> (342, emphasis added)

Potentially, emotions in general were hypocognated on the island as Levy asserted that there "is no Tahitian term for either 'feelings' or 'emotions'" (271).

On emotional universals and "basic emotions"

One obvious question that follows from these considerations is whether or not some emotions are universal and "basic" in the same way that Berlin and Kay concluded that there are basic color terms and therefore supposedly universal ways of experiencing or organizing color perceptions (see Chapter 3). On this question too, there is lively debate. Marie-Odile Junker and Louise Blacksmith (the latter a member of the Cree Nation) examined Eastern Cree language and culture for emotional universals, specifically testing a set of hypotheses from Anna Wierzbicka (1999), such as that

- all languages feature a word for "feel"
- all languages evaluate some feelings as good or bad
- all languages have words like "cry" or "smile"
- all cultures connect certain feelings with particular facial expressions or gestures
- all languages have terms for emotions
- all languages associate feeling with areas of the body and particular sensations or "symptoms" of those areas.

They found that Cree had three words for "feel"—and remarkably, no infinitive verb form for "to feel"—and, worse, that the verb *iteyimu* could mean "s/he feels" as well as "s/he thinks," while *mushihu* designated physical sensation exclusively (Junker and Blacksmith 2006: 281–2). For these and other reasons, they concluded that Cree casts doubt on the universal language of feeling and on the link between emotions and body sensations; informants did not identify any examples of Cree expressions in which they connect emotional feelings with "events and processes taking place inside the body" (297).

Zhengdao Ye tested another assumption about emotional universals: namely, how emotions are expressed on the face. For sure, individuals in all societies convey emotions with facial (and other) gestures, but Ye reported a folk model of emotions and facial expressions that was unique to China. Immediately, Ye asserted that Chinese people "do not generally correlate facial expressions with a discrete emotion category" (2004: 198). Thirty-seven different phrases referred to facial movement in relation to emotion, like *mei fei se wu* ("eyebrows fly, facial expression dances"), which corresponds to "a good feeling which is a response to a desirable event" (207). Most interestingly,

> the lower part of the Chinese face is where most of the facial movements occur for Chinese people. This is in stark contrast to most Western cultures, where the expressivity of the face is registered in the upper part of the face.
>
> (209)

All said,

> the simplistic assumption that there is a set of basic emotions based on the English language, and that complex facial expressions can be easily translated into those categories, loses its ground in the face of the evidence derived from the Chinese data.
>
> (211)

Summing up the current scene, Robert Solomon, a philosopher steeped in psychology and anthropology, lodged a set of objections to the idea of basic emotions. First, there is no agreement on how many such emotions exist (six? ten? more?). Second, it is unclear what "basic" means in this context: one possibility is that such emotions are natural and biological, while another is that they are like building blocks, assembled to form less basic, derived, or secondary emotions. Third, even if some emotions are basic in one sense or another, cultures still have "display rules" for how and when—and by whom—an emotion should be expressed: "Many cultures have very different rules depending on one's age and social status" (2002: 119), not to mention gender. Fourth, Solomon insisted that every emotion, including the basic ones, has multiple dimensions—behavioral, physiological, phenomenological (how it is experienced), cognitive (how it is understood and appraised), and social contextual (131–2). Ultimately, he posited that what counts as a basic emotion may vary across cultures: "What if basic emotions are those *considered to be important in some particular society?*" (139, emphasis in the original), important not necessarily meaning common or valued but highly cognized, as discussed earlier—leaving "basic" still to be culturally diverse.

BOX 7.2 ANNA WIERZBICKA: TOWARD A CULTURE-INDEPENDENT SEMANTIC METALANGUAGE OF EMOTIONS

It might be noticed that, in our presentation and in the Anglophone research on emotions, English emotion-words have tended to be the yardstick by which scholars measure emotion cross-culturally. But Anna Wierzbicka argued strenuously that "English terms of emotion constitute a folk taxonomy"—an ethnopsychology—"not an objective, culture-free analytical framework, so obviously we cannot assume that English words such as *disgust, fear,* or *shame*"—often credited among the basic emotions—"are clues to human concepts, or to basic psychological realities" (1986: 584). In other words, what are the odds that English happened to carve up and label emotions in the natural or real, let alone only, way? For instance, Wierzbicka taught that "Polish does not have a word corresponding exactly to the English word *disgust*," while the "Australian Aboriginal language Gidjingali does not seem to distinguish lexically 'fear' from 'shame'" (584). In a series of books and articles, she insisted that what was therefore lacking and desperately needed in anthropology was "a culture-independent semantic metalanguage" (584) for emotions (and, by the way, probably for all other cultural phenomena, especially religion), a procedure for defining emotions that did not fall into one or another folk taxonomy. She demonstrated the process and its virtues with a deconstruction of the Polish verb *tęsknić,* which might be translated as "to miss" or "to pine for" or "to feel homesick" but is not quite equivalent to any of those translations. Polish usage of the emotion verb works as follows:

X *tęskni* do [sic] Y ("X feels '*tęsknota*' to Y") =
    X is far away from Y
    X thinks of Y
    X feels something good toward Y
    X wants to be together with Y
    X knows he or she cannot be together with Y
    X feels something bad because of that.

(586)

To establish the difference between *tęsknić* and its English alternatives, Wierzbicka explained that

> if a teenage daughter leaves the family home and goes to study in a distant city, her Polish parents would usually *tęsknić*, but one could not say that they were *homesick* for the daughter, that they felt *nostalgia* for her, and one would hardly say that they were *pining* for her. One would say that they *missed* her, but *miss* implies much less than *tęsknić*.
>
> (586, emphasis in the original)

By contrast, she showed what a meta-analysis of some related English emotions would entail:

X is homesick =
    X is far away from his or her home
    X thinks of his or her home
    X feels something good toward his or her home
    X wants to be there
    X knows he or she cannot be there at that time
    X feels something bad because of that.
X is pining after Y =
    X is away from Y
    X thinks of Y
    X feels something good toward Y
    X wants to be with Y
    X knows that he or she cannot be with Y
    X feels something bad because of that
    X can't think of anything else because of that.

(586–7)

It can be seen that the Polish and English words—and indeed the two different English words—share certain similarities but also diverge in more or less subtle ways. When considering even more diverse languages and cultures, it simply cannot be assumed that the emotion vocabulary of one language is appropriate to another. Thus, as to the question of basic or universal emotions, "whether emotion terms available in different languages truly converge in different languages is a problem that cannot be resolved without rigorous semantic analysis, and without a language-independent semantic metalanguage" (593).

An ethnopsychology of emotion: the Ifaluk

In the previous chapter, we introduced the notion of ethnopsychology, of other cultures' own psychological terms, models, and theories. As mentioned at that time, one of the chief proponents of the study of ethnopsychologies has been Catherine Lutz, whose work on Ifaluk in the Caroline Islands (western Pacific) explored local conceptions of personhood and emotion, and supported Wierzbicka's call for an examination of indigenous emotions without forcing them into English terms and categories. The first crucial thing that Lutz reported was that the people of Ifaluk did not separate emotion from thought; instead, the native word *nunuwan* referred "to mental events ranging from what we term thought to what we term emotion" (1998: 92). There was also a moral dimension to *nunuwan*, associated with proper and mature behavior; interestingly too, an adult should have more than one *nunuwan*, while children and the mentally ill typically possessed only one.

Rather than distinguishing emotion from rational thought, the Ifaluk distinguished *nunuwan* from *tip-*, the latter signifying will or desire, implying "preference and personal choice" (93), and clearly connected to norms of social behavior and to social hierarchies. For instance, if a person of lower status and power asked a senior or superordinate for permission to do something and

> the elder knows of no rule or has no preference to the contrary, he or she will say, "*Ye shag tipum*," which is literally, "It's just your will," or, in other words, "[In the absence of external constraints] it's up to you." Where social rules or values are not at stake, the person's *tip-* is granted free reign.
>
> (93)

Turning to specific emotion-words, Lutz identified what might be considered some basic Ifaluk emotions. First among these was *fago*, which she interpreted as "compassion/love/sadness" in relation to the needs and nurturance of others (119). With this key word and feeling,

> people on Ifaluk communicate a central part of their view of human relationships; they impart their sense of the place of suffering in their lives, of the naturalness of interpersonal kindness in the face of their pain, and of their feeling that maturity consists, above all else, in the ability to nurture others. *Fago* speaks to the sense that life is fragile, that connections to others both are precious and may be severed through death or travel, that love may equal loss.
>
> (119)

That is, the "primary contexts in which *fago* occurs are those in which the person confronts another who is somehow *in need*" (121, emphasis in the original) such that we might also associate it with sympathy or empathy. In fact, the Ifaluk term for the needy or poor was *gafago* which included the

> sick or dying; those who must leave the island and their families for some period; those who lack the ability to procure their own food, such as children, the aged, and the infirm; and those who lack the mental abilities or social status that would enable them to make decisions and move as autonomous agents in the world. Thus, the needy are the foodless, the landless, the kinless … the unhealthy and the socially subordinate.
>
> (122)

Fago was not only a key (and socially complex) emotion but also a morally exemplary one. A good Ifaluk person felt *fago* and acted accordingly. "The ability to experience *fago* is seen as one of the central characteristics of the mature person"; moreover, display of *fago* was an essential element of rank and prestige: "God, chiefs, parents, and elders all maintain the position and respect they command through their exercise of this emotion" (139–40).

Lutz also compared and contrasted *fago* with English/Western concepts of love. Like love, *fago* was a powerful and empowering thing, praiseworthy and offered as praise. However, *fago* did not have romantic connotations; romantic love was actually regarded with suspicion by the Ifaluk. Further, Western love implies equality, but *fago* implied dependence and social inequality. Finally, *fago* was tinged with sadness but "cannot be used to talk about a sense of general hopelessness or global loss, as sadness can"; "Overall, *fago* connotes or propels activity much more than does sadness, which most American emotion analysts have classified as a passive emotion" (148–9).

Lutz dealt with two other Ifaluk emotions with similar social consequences. One was *song*, which she classified as anger but more importantly *justifiable anger*. Commonly invoked in everyday speech, *song* was just one term in a rich vocabulary of ire, including

> the irritability that often accompanies sickness (*tipmochmoch*), the anger that builds up slowly in the face of a succession of minor but unwanted events (*lingeringer*), the annoyance that occurs when relatives fail to live up to their obligations (*nguch*), and, finally, there is the anger that occurs in the face of personal misfortunes and slights which one is helpless to redress (*tang*).
>
> (157)

But she continued that "each of these emotions is sharply distinguished from the anger which is righteous indignation, or justifiable anger (*song*)" (157). All manifestations of anger in Ifaluk (and potentially every other society) were political in the sense that they reacted to and commented on relations and circumstances, and often as not cried out for an end to certain conditions. But *song* was the most political type of Ifaluk anger:

> The scene that the term *song* paints is one in which (1) there is a rule or value violation, (2) it is pointed out by someone, (3) who simultaneously calls for the condemnation of the act, and (4) the perpetrator reacts in fear to that anger, (5) amending his or her ways.
>
> (157)

Predictably, some individuals were entitled to *song*, especially chiefs but also parents and elders; subordinates like commoners, youths, and children were not granted the right to be *song* at their betters.

The third key Ifaluk emotion was *metagu*, which Lutz rendered as fear or anxiety alongside its counterpart *rus* or panic/fright/surprise. Both were experiences of the dangers of society and reality, although

> *metagu* is much more often used to talk about the response to strange situations and to another's justifiable anger, while *rus* is more often used to talk about events which are seen as posing an immediate physical threat to oneself or another, such as meeting a drunk on the path or a shark while spearfishing, or realizing that one's child is about to die.
>
> (186)

Strangers were an object of fear, as were the spirits, who were uniquely dangerous for "their lack of *fago*" (195). *Rus* was a more intense sensation, akin to panic and also more associated with physiological symptoms of terror; *metagu* by comparison was "a less dramatic emotion. Although it involves an assessment of danger and of the need for avoidance, *metagu* is described as involving ideas more than bodily changes" (187). As mentioned, *metagu* was an appropriate response to a superior's *song*, making it to a political emotion: "To the Ifaluk way of thinking, fear is what keeps people good" (201).

Conventional emotions: the Egyptian Bedouins

In Western thinking, emotions are only real and only "count" when they are deeply felt, personal, and "authentic." Expressions of emotions that are obligatory or cliché are often condemned and rejected as insincere, as not how the person really feels. Yet in Western societies there are conventional ways of showing emotion, including stock phrases, such as "You poor thing" or "You have my deepest sympathies," and many people share their sentiments via third-party media like cards, poetry, and songs.

Among the Bedouins studied by Lila Abu-Lughod, a genre of poetry called *ghinnawa* ("little song") served "as a vehicle for personal expression and confidential communication" (1986: 26); "They usually described a sentiment and were perceived by others as personal statements about interpersonal situations" (27). The *ghinnawa*, she concluded, "can be considered the poetry of personal life: individuals recite poetry in specific social contexts, for the most part private, articulating in it sentiments about their personal situations and closest relationships" (31).

The problem for the Bedouins as Abu-Lughod saw it was their strong code of honor (*sharaf*, especially for men, while women's honor was sometimes known as *ird*) and modesty (*hasham*). Men in particular were loath to show weakness or to do or display anything that would threaten their individual freedom or autonomy. The emotions normally conveyed in poetry were precisely the ones that tended to "suggest a self that is vulnerable or weak, a self moved by deep feelings of love and longing," such as intense hurt at losing a loved one; in a society where men did not avow or express affection, even for their wives, and where a woman's show of love or sexual desire was seen as immodest, the emotions embedded in poems "are not at first glance the sentiments of proud and autonomous individuals, nor are they the sentiments of chaste individuals" (34) (Figure 7.1).

Figure 7.1 Egyptian Bedouin men live by a strict code of honor that defines how they may display emotions.
Simon Balson / Alamy Stock Photo.

To put it simply, "Only certain sentiments would be appropriate to self-presentation in terms of these ideals" of honor and modesty (205), and *ghinnawas* were the acceptable medium for forbidden sentiments—which Abu-Lughod cleverly called *veiled* sentiments. Among the most common feelings expressed through poetry were love, loss, and longing, fit neither for a proud man or a modest woman. Nor were the verses sung between men and women; rather, they were performed ordinarily in same-sex company. A few examples from the repertoire reported in the book include:

> They always left me
> stuffed with false promises.
>
> My tears rushed down like a flood on a hill
> flowing over the match of the rich man
>
> Despair of them, dear one, made you
> a stray who wanders between watering places.

(231)

But while Westerners might be inclined to dismiss such conventional performances as unreflective of actual personal feeling at best, or as fake at worst, Abu-Lughod was right in insisting that the recitation of poetry is not a social mask "hiding spontaneous inner feelings" (238)—or worse, substituting for the lack of inner feelings (i.e. that Bedouin people are all mask and no inner emotion). Instead, when people have powerful but culturally problematic feelings, they "reach for ready-made forms to give voice to those personal sentiments that seem to violate the cultural ideals" (238). A genre like *ghinnawa* "cloaks statements in the veils of formula, convention, and tradition, thus suiting it to the task of carrying messages about the self that contravene the official cultural ideals" (239). Nor should we be too quick to dismiss the invocation of conventional words to express intense personal feelings: what is more romantic in English-speaking cultures than reciting Shakespeare to one's lover? After all, there probably are no truly original emotions to be had.

BOX 7.3 OPACITY OF OTHER MINDS IN PACIFIC-REGION SOCIETIES

Egyptian Bedouins may veil certain emotions in poetic quotations, but the peoples of the Pacific region are legendary for building impenetrable walls around their emotions. Joel Robbins and Alan Rumsey coined the phrase "the opacity of other minds" to name the widespread attitude that "it is impossible or at least extremely difficult to know what other people think or feel" and explained that throughout the area "people are often expected to refrain from speculating (at least publicly) about what others may be thinking, and penalties for gossip about other people's intentions are often very high" (2008: 407–8). Not all societies across the Pacific stress the opacity of emotions equally, and they have different reasons for holding this position. Some do not trust avowals of inner psychological states, while others consider thoughts and feelings to be almost private property upon which others should not trespass. At the far end of the spectrum are the

Bosavi of Papua New Guinea, where children are taught "explicitly … not to verbally guess at or express others' unvoiced intentions and unclear meanings" (Schieffelin 2008: 433). In verbal interactions, adults do not elaborate on children's sentences or attempt to interpret them; rather they encourage the youngsters to explain their own feelings. For instance, if a child cries or misbehaves, adults do not ask, "Are you hungry?" or "Are you sick?" but instead, "Ge oba?" or "What's with you?" And although people are enculturated to express sympathy, speakers do not give reasons for their sympathetic words: "Everyone gets the point, without verbally speculating about another's desires, internal states or intentions" (435). The Bosavi treat personal thoughts and feelings as matters of ownership. It is important to learn "who things belong to, and whether or not one has a right to just take those things," and another person's "unexpressed or inarticulate thoughts and desires" are considered that person's property; "Just as one does not take and use things that are not theirs to take, one does not speak others' thoughts, ones that they have not themselves articulated. Thoughts and desires are one's own" (435). The Bosavi are an extreme case but not an exceptional one. When faced with the question of others' ideas and emotions, the people of Vanatinai island say that "We cannot know their *renuanga*," the local word for an "interior, active, although covert, state of desire or feeling" (Lepowsky 2011: 44–5), and Samoans likewise hold that the *loto*, "the inner depths of the self … is a pool of darkness that one cannot fathom" (Mageo 2011: 76). The Asabano people of Papua New Guinea believe that "the inner states of others cannot be known with certainty" (Lohmann 2011: 98), and on the island of Yap "[n]ot sharing, not expressing, and not acting upon one's 'true' feelings, opinions, or thoughts … is indeed one of the core cultural values" (Throop 2011: 121) along with "privacy, secrecy, and concealment" (136). Significantly, although psychological opacity is prominent in Oceania, it is not unique there: Kevin Groark (2008) reports a similar phenomenon among the Tzotzil Maya of Chiapas, Mexico.

The cross-cultural study of specific emotions

Anthropology has made valuable contributions to the description and analysis of particular emotions across cultures. The remainder of the chapter will explore a sampling of emotions, including three that are generally considered universal or basic emotions—anger, fear, and love—yet we find significant variation in how they are cognized, elaborated, expressed, and valued. There are certainly other emotions that deserve, and have received, anthropological attention, and other examples of the three selected emotions, but to examine all or many of those emotions is beyond the scope of the chapter, and the emotions featured here convey the achievements of an anthropological perspective on this central psychological matter.

One caveat before proceeding: admittedly, we are using orthodox English emotion-words to organize this section. However, it will become immediately clear how limiting our Anglophone ethnopsychology is and how other ethnopsychologies erode familiar categories.

Anger

All around the world, humans experience anger, but *when* they experience it, how they show it, and what social effects they expect it to have vary substantially. Recall, for instance, that justifiable anger or *song* among the Ifaluk was the prerogative of superiors like chiefs, parents, and elders. On the island of Tonga, according to Andrea Bender et al., displays of anger are comparatively rare, partly because "socially disruptive feelings are evaluated negatively" (2007: 196), while other societies nurture certain specific kinds of anger for certain specific kinds of persons.

Among the Kaluli of Papua New Guinea, anger "is an important emotion and expressive form," especially for men, and forms a recognizable complex of emotions along with grief and shame (Schieffelin 1983: 182). What Edward Schieffelin called "assertive energy" demonstrates "the productive vitality of male essence and supports the favored Kaluli ethos of exuberant vigor and personal dynamism"; thus,

> A man's temper, or "tendency to get angry," is an important feature by which Kaluli judge his character and assess the degree to which he is a force to be reckoned with. It represents the vigor with which he will stand up for or pursue his interest vis-à-vis others, and the likelihood that he will retaliate for wrong or injury. Anger is an affect both feared and admired.
>
> (183)

Equally importantly, he ascertained that "nearly every reason to be angry, any loss, wrong, injury, insult, or disappointment, is interpreted in terms of the scheme of reciprocity" (186)— or perhaps more accurately, the failure of reciprocity, that is, when a man feels that he has not been reciprocated (Figure 7.2). An angry man

> is in some sense owed something: he has a legitimate (if often hopeless) expectation that he is due redress ... and a display of anger is frequently meant to be a forceful plea for support. When a man has suffered wrong or loss (and where the culprit has made himself scarce), he may stamp furiously up and down the outside yard or inside hall of the longhouse yelling the particulars of his injury for everyone to hear in order to arouse their sympathetic attention and inspire their backing for redress.
>
> (186)

Figure 7.2   Among Kaluli men, anger and grief are highly culturally shaped.
Hemis / Alamy Stock Photo.

Other examples suggest the intimate connection between anger and masculinity. In her account of the Ilongot of the Philippines, renowned as headhunters, Michelle Rosaldo (1980) discovered that men were regarded as possessing more *beya* (knowledge) than women but also more *liget* (passion). Both *beya* and *liget* were central components in Ilongot ethnopsychology and self-understanding; neither was viewed as inherent in the gender but a result of men's more extensive traveling and their more strenuous and dangerous tasks. *Liget* was thought to reside in the heart and referred, as among the Kaluli, to energy, movement, enthusiasm, anger, and the capacity for violence. To have *liget* meant to be ready to take action, to be forceful, quick-moving, even a little stubborn, and to overcome shyness, fear, and reservation. It was accordingly seen in a generally positive light. Born from insults, slights, and other insinuations of inequality or envy, *liget* made the heart withdraw from social interaction and oppose other people, and was thereby also associated with separation, social confusion, and chaos. Potentially disruptive, "good *liget*" was harnessed with *beya* and was not upsetting but intense and beautiful, related to productive work, strength and courage, sexuality—and killing. The Ilongot said that a young man's *liget* outweighed his *beya*, and at its peak—assisted and organized by older men—Ilongot youths would go on headhunting expeditions in a frenzy of wild and passionate *liget*, which many men described as virility in its fullest. Indeed, the indigenous term for men on the hunt for heads was not "hunters" but "anxious seekers" (*gelasaget*)—anxious for a head but also for masculinity and eventually for marriage. Successfully taking one head was normally sufficient to cool the ardor of *liget*.

For the Gisu of Uganda, manly anger or *lirima* was held as a trait of violent emotion, a force that "catches" a man or "boils over" in him, spurring his attitudes and actions (Heald 1986). It was linked to jealousy, hatred, and resentment and associated with physiological changes like a lump in the throat or a rush of adrenaline. But *lirima* was not a wild uncontrolled emotion; having *lirima* implied control, strength of character, courage, and determination. Most curiously, it was not viewed as entirely natural in men; rather, it had to be cultivated and instilled. During their circumcision ritual (which occurred between the ages of eighteen and twenty-five), the initiates were compelled to stand in the compound of their fathers and to display no fear or pain; upon successful completion of the ordeal, candidates were granted the status, and the implements, of manhood. Ironically, although the Gisu recognized themselves as undesirably angry and bellicose, they continued to inculcate those values and emotions in their men.

BOX 7.4 ETHNOSEMANTICS OF ANGER AMONG THE YANKUNNYTJATJARA

Cliff Goddard performed an analysis of terms for anger among the Yankunnytjatjara of Aboriginal Australia in the style of Wierzbicka's semantic metalanguage (see earlier). In their language, he found three words that could be translated as anger or used in the sentence "He got angry at me." The first, *pikaringanyi*, "involves little more than the urge or readiness to fight or inflict pain…. Accordingly, we often find that English words such as 'hostile, aggressive, feisty, combative, mad at' provide more appropriate translation equivalents than 'angry'" (1991: 269)

X pikaringanyi (Z-ku) =
    a   something is happening to X
    b   X wants to fight/cause pain (to Z)."

(1991: 269)

He further noted that even babies and animals were capable of *pikaringanyi*, indicating that "judgment or appraisal is not a necessary component" of its meaning or experience" (271). The second term, *mirpanarinyi*, was closer to the English word "angry."

X mirpanarinyi (Z-ku) =
    a   something is happening inside X
    b   the kind of thing that happens to people
    c   when they think:
        this (Z) is bad
    d   and because of that
        they don't want to do anything good (for Z)
        they want to do something bad (to Z).

(272)

Finally, *kuyaringanyi* (from the root *kuya* for bad or useless) denoted "a negative appraisal of someone or something, leading to a disinclination to offer assistance, but stopping short of the active hostility of *mirpanarinyi*. Appropriate translation equivalents include 'resent, go off someone, be pissed off with'" (274).

X kuyaringanyi (Z-ku) =
    a   something is happening to X
    b   the kind of thing that happens to people
    c   when they think:
        this (Z) is bad
    d   and because of that
        they don't want to do anything good (for Z).

(274)

Despite its ubiquity, there is evidence that anger is not a totally universal emotion, at least in cultural discourse. In fact, Jean Briggs (1970) titled her celebrated study of Utku (northeast Canada) society and affect *Never in Anger* precisely because that group claimed that not only did they never express anger but that *they never experienced anger*. In their society, despite (or perhaps because of) a forbidding natural environment and unusually close quarters, the Utku valued a mild and even temper above all other personal qualities. The social ideal was a person who was kind and concerned, helpful and generous, and sociable but not resentful or angry. In fact, they actually feared and distrusted people who did not overtly display goodwill and happiness—unhappiness was interpreted as hostility—and generally they did not like individuals to exhibit too much emotion at all. The three most disliked personality traits were bad temper, selfishness, and refusal to help others. Young children were expected to be easily angered or frightened since they lacked *ihuma* (sense or reason), but as they matured they were required to check such feelings. By Western standards, parents were even a bit cruel in suppressing the emotionality of children, ignoring them, teasing them, and transmitting the message that violent emotions (and actual violence) are not good and that an Utku person must learn to inhibit such feelings. Finally, although animosity and hateful feelings were to be downplayed within the family, they were given some free expression toward nonkin. Distant relatives or nonrelatives could be the brunt of hostile talk, gossip, and name-calling, branded with epithets like greedy, lazy, and unhelpful and even accused of stealing or other anti-social behavior.

As mentioned previously, Tongan society restricted the display of anger, a restriction that was—as among the Ifaluk—connected to social hierarchy. In a word, anger was a right granted to superordinates but not to underlings:

> Not being treated with respect or in a way appropriate to one's relative rank causes anger in Tonga. Being involved in an interaction with a person of higher rank mitigates at least anger expression and probably even anger elicitation. If expressed at all, anger is rather expressed toward equally ranked (or lower-ranking) people.
>
> (Bender et al. 2007: 226)

This equation goes a long way to explaining why anger is more often sanctioned among men than women cross-culturally: too often ranked below men, women are often confined to the emotional displays of subordinates. Whether or not they feel anger equally and in the same way as men, women are frequently less free to show it, sometimes presenting as dissociated mental states recognized as "spirit possession" (see Chapter 8). As one example among many, L. A. Rebhun found that women in northeast Brazil realized that they bore the burden "of suppressing anger, hatred, or irritation and of putting up with unfair treatment silently" (1994: 360), which they called "swallowing frogs." Inevitably, those feelings came out, in too-Freudian fashion, as bodily ailments, "such as evil-eye sickness (*mal olhado*), 'nerves' (*nervos*), shock sickness (*susto*), open chest (*peito aberto*), and blood-boiling bruises" (360).

Fear

In an era of global terrorism, there is arguably no more salient emotion, none more in need of an anthropological perspective, than fear. Likewise, while there is definitely a politics of anger, fear has unprecedented potential for organization and mobilization, for institutionalization, both to perpetrate fear and to combat it (there is, after all, no international "war on anger").

At least as much as, if not more than, other emotions, fear has a cognitive or epistemological dimension; that is, what an individual or society fears depends on specific knowledge and belief about dangers. For instance, the Yanomamo of Brazil and Venezuela were afraid of attack by *hekura* spirits, but people who have never heard of these beings lack any dread of them. Similarly, the Piaroa of Venezuela felt threatened by every morsel they ate since they learned that when a person kills and eats an animal, that animal's spirit could enter the person's body and begin to consume her from the inside; indeed, in a sense, all eating constituted cannibalism since animals (and plants too) were formerly persons (see Chapter 6), so humans consuming animals and animals consuming humans was mutual cannibalism (Overing 1986).

Every society inhabits its own world of fear, as Alexander Leighton and Dorothea Leighton's (1942) study of types and sources of "uneasiness and fear" among the Navajo illustrated. Much more recently, Yasmine Musharbash and Gier Henning Presterudstuen explored the question of local fear in *Monster Anthropology in Australasia and Beyond*: "No matter whether monsters are evil, mischievous, protective, or lasciviously seductive, their actions (as much as their bodies) are culturally specific," writes Musharbash in the introduction, "and they *target* and make sense only in particular societies" (2014: 11, emphasis in the original). To choose just one example from the collected essays, Joanne Thurman tells that the Mak Mak Marranunggu of northern Australia believe they share their country with three kinds of dangerous entities—Nugabig or big hairy black cave men, Minmin or paranormal lights, and Latharr-ghun the underground dragon. As scary as these creatures are, Thurman contends that their primary cultural function is "in identifying those who do not belong" (2014: 31), those who are strangers to the land and have no right to be there. Although they can attack anyone, members of the society attain some level of safety by "identifying themselves to country through traditional rituals" (35).

There are, of course, many things to fear besides monsters, demons, and such, but whatever the source, fear like politics is local. In fact, David Leheny (2006) explored this very relationship in his study of Japanese fears and anxieties titled *Think Global, Fear Local*. While "fear" might not quite be the right word for both cases, the two circumstances on which he focused were international terrorism and sexually precocious schoolgirls. Although wildly unequal in threat level, both sparked a kind of social panic and spawned heavy social and political reactions. Japanese, whose (justified) nightmares have given the world irradiated monsters like Godzilla, continue to channel traditional and modern frights into new genres, including horror-based video games, such as "Resident Evil" (Pruett 2010).

The productive capacity of fear, though not pleasant, is potent. No society has been shaped (perhaps scarred) by fear more than the Semai of southern Malaysia. Renowned for their nonviolence, most readers find Semai peacefulness sweet until they realize the high price paid for it. Clayton Robarchek, one of the main ethnographers of the Semai, stated that two key "psychocultural themes" in the society were "dependence and danger" (1986: 177). As he explained, "nearly every entity and activity, no matter how apparently benign, carries with it the potential for bringing injury, illness and death" (178), especially but not only interactions with strangers and of course *mara'*, malicious spirits that caused accidents and illness. But interaction with kin was also fraught with peril, captured in the local term *punan* or *pehunan*, defined as "a state of extreme danger caused by failure to have one's wants, especially food and other 'oral' wants (tobacco, water) satisfied"; a person whose desires were frustrated by others— as well as the person who frustrated those desires—was exposed to the threat of "accidents, illness and death" (182). Naturally, as he detailed in an earlier essay, Semai individuals had to learn to fear, and Semai socialization carried an overt message of fear to children.

> Courage, independence, and self-reliance are not paramount Semai virtues. The child's distress is, rather, encouraged and reinforced by adults who actively teach him to fear strangers.... At the appearance of an unfamiliar face in the hamlet, the Semai mother clutches her infant tightly, buries his face against her breast, and turns away crying "afraid, afraid!"
>
> (1979: 559)

In an unconventional ethnography of the Semai, Robert Knox Dentan made it clear where this unusual emotional attitude comes from. Subjected for generations to violence in the form of war, slavery, and child abduction at the hands of Malays, British, and Japanese, the Semai adapted to menace by extreme passivity, "surrender," and what psychologists call learned helplessness; maybe responding at first with resistance, they soon retreated to "defeat, powerlessness, and internalized terror" (2008: 14). Strangers, their god (described as a "vicious ludicrous monster [74] and a "stupid, incontinent, violent dupe" [84]), and even each other are all sources of dread, and parents encourage this anxiety in their children:

> Semai tell horror stories to their children, stories about people who steal children to enslave them or gouge out their eyes to sell to the rich, stories of the Lord. They want to scare the children, continue telling the stories, smiling even when the kids are wailing

or in tears. Children need to learn that the world hates children, will hurt them if it can: steal them, enslave them, mutilate them. It's the same lesson American parents increasingly teach their own children, with a good deal less historical justification: *stranger danger, beware attractive people who are not what they seem, trust no one.* Fear, both peoples believe, is good for kids. Teach your children fear because you love them, not because you enjoy their fear, their clinging to you, or your power to make them fear and cling.

(81, emphasis in the original)

In other words, the precious nonviolence of the Semai "isn't about being pacifist or 'good'" nor is it "free" (142); rather, it has come at a frightful cost.

The Semai case swings anthropological attention away from the individual experience of fear to the social construction and efficacy of fear. At least since Michael Taussig's (1986) *Shamanism, Colonialism, and the Wild Man: A Study in Terror and Healing,* anthropology has taken a very different view of fear. Taussig recounted the story of extraordinary, though likely not exceptional, colonial brutality in the Putumayo region of Colombia, where fear bred more fear. Specifically, he argued that native peoples figured as "wild men" in the imaginations of settlers—terrible, primitive, and treacherous—who reacted out of their own fright by terrorizing those peoples in the most cruel and disproportionate ways. Subsequently, anthropological studies of fear have emphasized its political, indeed its intentional and orchestrated, quality. Gastón Gordillo, for instance, cited Taussig in his analysis of violence and terror in Argentina, where the Toba people recruited into sugar plantations were subjected to "appalling working conditions, high mortality rates linked to rampant diseases, and political repression" (2002: 34). Not only did they interpret their plight as affliction by the myriad devils that resided in the hills, but they believed that the plantation owners made pacts with these devils to torment them. One particular evil creature, *el Familiar,* allegedly lived in the basement of a factory, and "the fear of the Familiar was often encouraged by members of the plantation administration" (44) as a means to keep workers in line.

This case, and others that we will discuss later, highlight one other point about fear that anthropologists have noted, namely, its temporal nature. That is, people may fear what they know or see in the present, but they can also bear wounds from horrors of the past while they anticipate with trepidation real or imagined hazards from the future. A powerful account of such fear across time and its debilitating personal and social effects comes from Linda Green, who documented violence and fear in Guatemala in a 1994 essay and a 1999 book, both titled "Fear as a Way of Life." During the wars of the twentieth century, the Mayan people of Guatemala suffered profoundly, and although the worst of the fighting may have subsided, the effects of fear

are pervasive and insidious in Guatemala. Fear destabilizes social relations by driving a wedge of distrust within families, between neighbors, among friends. Fear divides communities through suspicion and apprehension not only of strangers but of each other. Fear thrives on ambiguities. Denunciations, gossip, innuendos, and rumors of death lists create a climate of suspicion. No one can be sure who is who. The spectacle of torture and death and of massacres and disappearances in the recent past have become more deeply inscribed in individual bodies and the collective imagination through a constant sense of threat.

(1994: 227)

This chronic and routine or normalized fear led to "doubting one's own perceptions of reality" and "shreds the social fabric" (230). It taught people, especially the widows and other kin who survived it, "the dual lessons of silence and secrecy" (238) and manifested in bodily symptoms like "headaches, gastritis, ulcers, weakness, diarrhea, irritability, inability to sleep, weak blood—disorders usually clustered under the syndrome of posttraumatic distress—and...'folk' illnesses such as *nervios* (nerves), *susto* (fright), and *penas* (pain, sorrow, grief)" (247).

Carole McGranahan found something similar in Tibet, where members of the former resistance to Chinese invasion dared not speak of their memories or their hopes. She called this position of suspended animation "historical arrest" or "the apprehension and detaining of particular pasts in anticipation of their eventual release. As such, arrested histories are not so much erased or forgotten as they are postponed and archived for future use" (2005: 571). Fear, not surprisingly, "is part of the production of arrested histories and a response to it, processes through which certain political projects are made true" (590).

But to be sure, violence and fear are not just matters of history and memory. As Jane Margold asserted, in too many places today "state power is based on the intimidation of civilians" for the purpose of "disciplining particular categories of people" (1999: 63), especially those who stand in the way of state projects, whether development and extraction of resources or merely the power and survival of the regime. Margold wrote about Mindanao in the Philippines, where authorities cowed citizens with "heavy deployment of government troops, economic blockades against small-scale local miners, and displacement of tribal peoples," not to mention "bombing of rural villages," "the extra-judicial killings of political leaders representing peasant and urban poor groups," and "the violent eviction of thousands of poor families" (66). A most egregious case of "state terrorism" is contemporary Myanmar, where the "military State constructs fear and vulnerability among its citizenry through the strategic use of political violence" (Skidmore 2003: 5). "The sheer weight of fear imposed on Burmese," Monique Skidmore opined, "leads them to respond outwardly with inertia" (8)—presenting "a blank exterior persona: listless eyes in wooden bodies" (10) that observers have called the "Burmese daze." Through constant surveillance, propaganda, and punishment, "the military confuses, distorts, and controls time with the aim of stopping Burmese people from imagining futures other than the one mandating their incorporation into a totalitarian State" (10), and Skidmore concluded that "the State deliberately constructs affect" (11) by running a steady stream of fear through society, engendering a stunned population "of individuals unable and unwilling to trust each other" (15).

We could easily multiply examples and add the dominant current form of intimidation through fear—global religious terrorism—but one more point will have to suffice. In a series of publications, Setha Low has described how everyday fear in the United States, including fear of minority races and lower classes, has driven Americans to retreat into gated and guarded communities. Inscribing the country's anxieties on its space and producing "a literal landscape of fear" (1997: 53) and a "fortress city," she maintained that, as in the previous cases, fear frayed the social fabric, people "trading a sense of community for security" and "moving away from community and retreating from their community responsibilities" (66–7). But walls and gates have not been able to contain the sense of risk to income and employment that attends globalization, resulting in a pervasive feeling of "precarity" (the noun form of precarious) that rips apart communities, silences workers, and leaves many people queasy and nervous.

BOX 7.5 SADNESS AMONG THE KALULI

No anthropological study of emotions would be complete without some mention of Steven Feld's remarkable work on sadness among the Kaluli. First published in 1982 and building on the prior research of Edward Schieffelin, Feld discovered a fascinating connection between human emotion and ambient sounds, especially bird sounds—in a word, that "sound modes become expressive embodiments of basic Kaluli concepts of sentiment and appeal" (2012: 24). Like many highly social peoples, the Kaluli valued "fellowship, comradery, and companionship," and "their deepest fears are those of loneliness" (29). Unlike some societies detailed earlier, the Kaluli were a highly emotionally demonstrative people, and the "absence of a friend or kinsmen at a gathering can set off a great burst of nostalgia and sentimentality" (29), which, reminiscent of the Bedouins, could be expressed in weeping songs or sung laments. Also, as with the Bedouins, such emotional displays were gendered: men expressed brief intense emotion, while women "start their weeping in the very fast hysterical manner and maintain a level of great intensity for a sustained time"; "it is generally women who add text and only women who turn the sung weeping into wept song" (33–4). Perhaps only a scholar fluent in music could discern that the melody of Kaluli weeping songs follows the call of a local bird, the muni, and that in general the Kaluli heard emotions expressed in bird sounds. "Bird sounds metaphorize Kaluli feelings and sentiments because of their intimate connection with the transition from visible to invisible in death, and invisible back to visible in spirit reflection" of dead ancestors (84). Different birds certainly sang different messages: some "say their names," while seven species "speak Bosavi language," and others "weep," but the muni bird sings the Kaluli's *gisalo* song (82). Among the many song-forms in the society, *sa-yelema* "is the most melodically and textually elaborate form of weeping, and it is also the most moving human sound expression in Bosavi because it is the closest sound to 'being a bird.' *Sa-yelema* is a melodic-sung-texted weeping" (92). "Moving from spontaneous and improvised to compositionally crafted weeping creates an aesthetic tension demanding the response that, like the deceased, the weeper, too, has become a bird" (129).

Love

TEVYE: "Do you love me?"

GOLDE: "Do I love him?

For twenty-five years I lived with him, fought with him, starved with him,
Twenty-five years my bed is his—if that's not love, what is?"

TEVYE: "Then you love me?"

GOLDE: "I suppose I do."

TEVYE: "And I suppose I love you too."

TEVYE AND GOLDE TOGETHER: "It doesn't change a thing, but even so,
After twenty-five years, it's nice to know."

This classic exchange between husband and wife in the musical play and film *Fiddler on the Roof* nicely exhibits the fact that love may or may not be part of a marriage and that the presence or absence of love may or may not be important or even ideal.

As with the concept of the individualistic self (see Chapter 6), a perennial question in anthropology has been whether love is a uniquely Western phenomenon or whether it occurs in all societies. It was perhaps historian and cultural theorist Denis de Rougemont who first put the question on the agenda in his 1940 book *Love in the Western World*, where he proposed that love was a very recent product of European culture, specifically the medieval tradition of courtship, troubadour songs, and knightly chivalry. Since then, parallel to the Western individual self, a widely-held assumption has been that only the modern West experiences love. Anthropology, which is perfectly placed to adjudicate the matter, was unfortunately mostly silent on love, according to Charles Lindholm as late as 2006, who bluntly castigated the discipline for preferring the study of "cannibalism and incest" over "'soft' and 'feminine' topics like love" and for the culture-and-personality school's "over-emphasis on the importance of early childhood training (tellingly derided as diaperology) and its use of untrustworthy personality tests for the discovery of the emotions characteristic of other cultures" (2006: 7).

In the past decade, anthropology has committed many more resources to the cross-cultural investigation of love, with admirable results. Yet the examination of love has been hobbled by a focus on *romantic* love or the love between man and woman or husband and wife, to the exclusion of other forms (including romantic same-sex love). To be clear, in English, the word "love" is quite polysemous: one might say that s/he loves their spouse, their child, their sibling, their country, or their favorite sports team *and mean quite different things* (presumably and hopefully, only one of those relationships involves sexual attraction). Further, the debate has often been framed in terms of whether or not romantic love exists in a society, which is not entirely the point; instead, to quote Emmanuel Obiechina from his research on African literature, "The question is not whether love and sexual attraction as normal human traits exist within Western and African"—and any and all other—"societies, but how they are woven into the fabric of life" (1973: 34). That is, as with anger, fear, and every other emotion, how is it cognized and elaborated, valued, and practiced in a given society?

Until a robust anthropology of filial and sibling love, along with other versions like patriotic love, has been developed, we cannot say that we possess a complete anthropology of love. For now, we have little choice but to concentrate on romantic love. In contemplating love in many non-Western and past societies, Lindholm decided that the "most obvious and surprising difference is that in every one of these cultures love and marriage were at odds with one another.... In fact, in most of the complex societies for which we have records of romantic passion, conjugal love between husband and wife was considered absurd and impossible"; consequently, when love could be identified in a society, it was "directed toward individuals one could not marry" (2006: 11). He offered the example of the Marri Baluch of Iran, among whom "romantic relationships are idealized, and a love affair 'is a thing of surpassing beauty and value,' implying absolute trust, mutuality, and loyalty; such a love is to be pursued at all costs" (13). At the same time,

> Unlike Western love relationships, *romance among the Marri stands absolutely opposed to marriage, which is never for love. It is, in fact, shameful even to show affection for one's spouse*. True romance has to be secret, and with a married woman of a distant camp. This is a dangerous matter, since other camps are hostile, and meeting with unguarded women is punishable by death.
>
> (13, emphasis added)

Among the Egyptian Bedouins too, Abu-Lughod found that love-matches "are actively dis-
couraged, and thwarted when discovered" (1986: 149) and that even married couples should
not demonstrate inordinate attachment to each other, which would signal dependence in the
man and immodesty in the woman.

The rejection of love as a basis for marriage does not mean—obviously, in the case
of the Marri Baluch—that love does not exist; it *does* mean that we cannot take for
granted the American and Western association of love, marriage, and sexuality. Nonetheless, the Marri Baluch also contradict the assumption of the singularity of love to
Western societies, and anthropologists like William Jankowiak, one of the premier anthropological scholars of love, have been among the firmest advocates for the cross-
cultural reality of love. Back in 1992, he and Edward Fischer turned to George Murdock's
Standard Cross-Cultural Sample (see Chapter 3) to approach the subject by the method
of large-scale cross-cultural survey. Defining romantic love as "any intense attraction
that involves the idealization of the other, within an erotic context, with the expectation of enduring for some time into the future"—and contrasting it to companionship
or companionate love or "the growth of a more peaceful, comfortable, and fulfilling relationship" or "strong and enduring affection built upon long term association" (1992:
150)—they determined that romantic love was present around the world although une-
venly distributed across cultural areas:

- circum-Mediterranean: 95.7 percent
- sub-Saharan Africa: 76.9 percent
- East Eurasia: 94.1 percent
- Insular Pacific: 93.1 percent
- North America: 82.8 percent
- South and Central America: 84.6 percent

(152)

In other words, they surmised that romantic love was "a near-universal" (154), although they
conceded that not every individual necessarily experiences such love and that it "may in fact
be muted, though never entirely repressed, by other cultural variables" (153).

It is true that love may be and commonly is "muted" by culture, but the more important
issue, recognized by sociologist William Goode in 1959, is how and why love is *controlled*
by culture. He reasoned that "the stratification and lineage patterns would be weakened
greatly if love's potentially disruptive effects were not kept in check" (1959: 42). This is
why marriages were conventionally arranged in most societies, with or without the expectation of eventual love, and why love was often downplayed even in marriages. And
the control of love entailed a number of other institutional adaptations, such as marrying
children off at a young age, isolating the sexes from each other, highly valuing female
chastity and virginity, and most definitely discouraging elopement and such escapes from
social regulation.

Accepting then that love may well exist widely across cultures, anthropology proceeds to
the investigation of the diversity of concepts of love and to its cultural and political practice.
Helen Harris, for instance, reported that Mangaia of the Cook Islands used the term *inangaro*
as "a multipurpose word translating broadly as 'wanting, needing, liking, or loving'" (1995:
106) but that for them love

is not a cultivated or even anticipated psychological experience; it is conceived as an emotional state that arises involuntarily, sometimes intensely—and often unfortunately—as it overturns the plans of parents and disturbs the web of relationships that binds individuals to their family and community.

(109)

In Papua New Guinea, where some of the most ambivalent gender relations have been observed, Huli men and women spent little time together, gardening, cooking, and sleeping separately; this segregation, though, did not prevent a tradition of romantic love as represented in a genre of love or courtship songs called *dawe* celebrating "feelings of desire, attachment, and loss, particularly in relation to a man's first true love" (Wardlow 2006: 58). Those last words are key to *dawe* and Huli notions of love as the songs were sung exclusively by men in the presence of other men and never to or for women (officially, women did not even know about the songs). For men performing and hearing them,

> love is always positioned as an object of nostalgia. *Dawe* songs are about the loss of a man's first true love, but they are only sung by men who are already long married, and the assumption is that one never marries one's first true love. Love is never what one has … and always what one has had to give up.

(59)

The Fulbe of northern Cameroon were still more hesitant about love. According to Helen Regis, "the culture does not recognize it as an ideal. It has no legitimate place in the social life of the community. The Fulbe therefore have a tremendous incentive *not* to fall in love" (1995: 141). People who conspicuously fell in love were subjected to criticism; even married couples denied having affection for their spouses. In fact, since emotional reserve was prized in the society, the "Fulbe lover is constantly on guard, lest he or she reveal authentic feelings in an inappropriate context and expose him or herself to public opprobrium" (141). Likewise, in northeast Brazil (see the following), "marriage is not necessarily an outcome of sexual love nor love a part of marriage" (Rebhun 1995: 241). One elderly man told the anthropologist that there were three kinds of marriage—economic, intelligent, and sentimental—and "it's the third that is the worst of all because sentiment, it stays diminishing and diminishing until it goes away and there is no more reason to stay together" (239). This may explain the fact that, while marriage was a public institution, "passionate love was clandestine: a transcendent, irrational, tragic, and glorious ardor" (243). Among the Lahu of southwest China, a tradition of courtship songs and love-suicide songs coincided with the attitude that spousal love was best revealed in harmonious teamwork "rather than in the private emotional attachment between the husband and wife" (Du 2008: 101). In a Western society like Lithuania, conceptions of love were jaded compared to American romanticization: love was conceived as an important bond of honesty, trust, and happiness but also as a fantasy—temporary, impractical, and dubious—and not equivalent to "real love," which was more temperate and less intense (de Munck 2008: 77). For the Makassar of Indonesia, love Western-style was simply "viewed as an illness" (Röttger-Rössler 2008: 156).

An especially telling case of the politics of love emerged in Wynne Maggi's study of the Kalasha of Pakistan. The non-Muslim Kalasha were surrounded by Muslims, and one of the ways in which they declared their difference from their neighbors was their endorsement of love-marriages as opposed to the arranged marriages customary among Pakistani Muslims. Indeed, although many Kalasha marriages too were arranged, at least initially, the "cultural right that young Kalasha people claim to translate love and longing into marriage, unique in this very conservative region, is a central marker of Kalasha ethnicity" (2006: 82). It was not the only marker, however: the Kalasha themselves asserted that "our women are free," and they expressed this freedom by dressing brightly, dancing and singing in public, even drinking wine and showing their faces without a veil (86). This female freedom extended into marriage, where women could decide to leave a marriage, and husbands "are well aware that they have a few short years to win their 'little wife's' affection and loyalty" (84). Therefore, the husband and his kin plied the wife with gifts, from food treats to consumer goods. Because they respected their children's choices, parents often submitted to their children's love-preferences even when a marriage arrangement had been negotiated, and when the parents did not, the young lovers had the cultural option to elope. But young people had one other weapon they could use against intransigent parents—the threat of conversion to Islam:

> By converting, the couple would escape the authority of their parents and of Kalasha traditions. They would be married by a mullah and bound in a new moral community. Converting to Islam is a desperate act, because it is irrevocable—but for this very reason it is an effective threat that gives young lovers powerful leverage in these emotionally charged situations.
>
> (87–8)

Thus, unhappy parents were likely to capitulate to their children's wishes for a love-match, rather than lose them altogether to a foreign religion (Figure 7.3).

Figure 7.3 Kalasha women enjoy unique freedoms in dress and in love.
PAUL GROVER / Alamy Stock Photo.

Finally, while the claim of Western exclusivity in love is no longer defensible, it remains that romantic love for many individuals and societies in the world today is a mark of modernity. Wardlow was explicit that the Huli regarded romantic love and companionate marriage as "associated with being a modern person" (2006: 62), which the older generation did not quite share or understand. From Aboriginal Australia to China, Western magazines, movies, and missionaries have circulated images and norms of love, passion, and monogamy—usually bundled into one modern complex—transnationally. For instance, Pamela Stern and Richard Condon described the changes in Copper Inuit (central Arctic Canada) relationships, where emotional restraint and casual marriage (and reportedly wife-exchange) were replaced with Western-style overt acts of affection: "Couples, both young and old, were observed walking hand in hand, hugging at the community hall, and kissing one another goodbye at the start of the workday" (1995: 213). According to Deborah Shamoon (2012), early twentieth-century Japanese schoolgirls were given the license to show romantic affection *to each other*, modeled on youth magazines, in the interests of modernity and on the assumption that such relationships were age-appropriate substitutes and preparations for eventual heterosexual bonds.

BOX 7.6 NANCY SCHEPER-HUGHES: THE PROBLEM OF MATERNAL LOVE IN NORTHEAST BRAZIL

Whatever the status of romantic/passionate/sexual love, surely most people would agree that a mother's love for her child is natural and universal. Alas, Nancy Scheper-Hughes's research in northeast Brazil questioned even this assumption. In this very poor region, overworked and underfed laborers and single mothers often struggled with weakness and sickness, which was roundly blamed on their racial inferiority rather than their social plight. Their frailty extended inevitably to their babies, who were often born prematurely and severely underweight: babies of starving mothers were born starving too. Some infants were too weak even to eat, which was attributed not to the mother's poverty but to the child's spiritual condition: "Our babies [are] born already *wanting to die*," one mother stated (1992: 315). Scheper-Hughes used the phrase "doomed baby syndrome" to explain the practice of mothers allowing their babies to starve to death because that is what the mothers believed the babies desired. "It is better to let the weak ones die," one mother proclaimed, because the "little angels" came into the world for the sole purpose of dying (368). How can a mother impassively watch her child die, Scheper-Hughes wondered. It was not a lack of "maternal instinct," she reasoned since children who survived were loved and cared for. Instead, in a world where on average five of her nine pregnancies ended in fatality, a woman reserved her affection until the baby proved its will to live. "Motherlove," Scheper-Hughes concluded, was not absent nor was it automatic but rather "grows slowly, tentatively, and fearfully" (359) in reaction to bitter experience.

Findings and results

Breaking through the alleged barriers against the scientific study of emotions, anthropology has uncovered a rich social and political construction, meaning, and use of emotions across cultures. Some of the key realizations include:

- it is uncertain whether there are basic or universal emotions, and even if there are, culture can still modify their expression and value
- emotions are not purely natural and physical nor are they purely culturally constructed, and they are not entirely cognitive or language-based
- a culture may hypercognize or hypcognize particular emotions
- English or any other folk emotion terms cannot be unproblematically deployed as a neutral cross-cultural classification of emotions; an independent metalanguage may be necessary
- emotions have not only social but political significance and consequences
- authentic individual emotions may be genuinely expressed in conventional forms like poetry or song
- not all societies teach that it is desirable—if possible—to know the inner thoughts and feelings of other people
- anger, fear, and love, among other emotions, are labeled, felt, displayed, and judged diversely across cultures
- emotions are never completely internal or private but are inherently public and political.

Chapter 8

Dreaming and altered states of consciousness

Key questions:
Are altered states of consciousness common or even universal across cultures, and how are they understood and used in various cultures?

How are dreams, ostensibly the most private of mental experiences, shaped by culture? And how, in different societies, is culture shaped by dreams?

What do dream beliefs and indigenous dream-interpretation systems tell us about notions of self and personhood?

What is trance, and how is it related to the characteristics of particular societies?

What is possession (spirit possession, possession trance), and how is it understood and practiced across cultures?

How is shamanism related to altered states of consciousness, and how is the shaman's personality or consciousness different from an ordinary person's?

One of the perennial and most elusive topics in psychology (and philosophy) is consciousness. Humans are sure they possess it and overwhelmingly proud of it—many have been certain that *only* humans possess it—yet there is little comprehension of or consensus on what consciousness is, how it operates, or how it is possible at all. It is not, for instance, synonymous with personality or self since, as Freud authoritatively established, there is much mental activity that is unconscious or subconscious—and therefore, significantly, which is un-linguistic or sub-linguistic.

In 1992, Imants Baruss, writing in the journal *Anthropology of Consciousness*, asked what academics and professionals mean by the term. He reported that nearly two-thirds agreed that consciousness was equivalent to "awareness," a kind of reflexiveness of thought or experience in which the individual knows that s/he is having thoughts and experiences; the same number accepted the proposition that consciousness "is a stream of thoughts, feelings, and sensations, some of which are more directly the focus of attention than others" and "the explicit knowledge of one's situation, mental states or actions as opposed to lack of such awareness" (1992: 29). However, Baruss also identified three different kinds or levels of consciousness. What he called consciousness1 was "a normal waking state" as opposed to being "in a stupor or coma" and therefore "not identical with awareness" nor excluding "animals, machines or martians" (29). Closer to awareness or self-knowledge was consciousness2, which entailed a person's or organism's "representation of itself that it can utilize in goal-directed behavior"; Baruss further distinguished between *behavioral consciousness2* and *subjective consciousness2*. Finally, consciousness3 was defined nebulously as "the sense of existence of the subject of mental acts" and "consciousness without an object" (29).

Whatever we may make of this particular analysis, it suggests that consciousness is more diverse than we first realize, that is, it is appropriate to speak of *consciousnesses* rather than a single consciousness. Further, various states of consciousness or mind are possible, and an individual may move through these states during an ordinary day—from normal waking consciousness (whatever that means) to daydream and reverie to dreams, visions, hypnosis, hallucinations, intoxication, "peak experiences," out-of-body experiences, etc. Sometimes, all of the non-normal conditions are bundled under the rubric of *altered states of consciousness*, defined by Arnold Ludwig in Charles Tart's influential volume as

> any mental state(s), induced by various physiological, psychological, or pharmacological maneuvers or agents, which can be recognized subjectively by the individual himself (or by an objective observer of the individual) as representing a sufficient deviation in subjective experience or psychological functioning from certain general norms for that individual during alert, waking consciousness.
>
> (1990: 18)

Several of the features of this definition indicate the salience of an anthropological perspective, including the fact that an altered state of consciousness is assessed relative to norms that may be more or less culturally determined and culturally diverse, that it may depend on the judgment of self or outside observer, and that it may be intentionally induced. Indeed, societies engage in a wide array of mind-altering practices, from ingestion of psychoactive substances (alcohol, marijuana, LSD, ayahuasca, and many more) to meditation, chanting, drumming, dancing and spinning, sleep and food deprivation, isolation, and such. As Ludwig pointed out, such practices can be employed for purposes from brainwashing to religious conversion, healing, spirit possession, shamanism, and prophetic or ecstatic trance. They are also obviously valued differently in different societies and social contexts; what may be a highly undesirable state of mind at one time and place may be a desirable or prized one in another.

In this chapter, we will focus on three altered states of consciousness and their cultural construction, interpretation, valuation, and use—dreams, trance, and shamanism. Before proceeding, it is worth noting, along with Chris Hables Gray, that the study of altered states of consciousness or of consciousness in the first place is not a perfectly innocent undertaking. Also in the pages of *Anthropology of Consciousness*, he argues that consciousness studies is more than purely academic but "is an industry as well with active research programs in medicine, business, and the military" (2007: 3). Applications of this research, which could affect and perhaps should alarm all of us, range from the investigation of mind-altering drugs to scientific mind reading techniques (which he likens to spying on our thoughts) to neuromarketing (using consciousness science to encourage buying); human enhancement technologies (to make us smarter, require less sleep, and so on); and "neurosecurity" or legal-military monitoring and manipulation of the minds of suspected or potential criminals, combatants, and terrorists.

The anthropology of dreams

Dreams have been of interest to anthropologists since the rise of psychological anthropology; early practitioners of the culture-and-personality school, like Cora Du Bois and Géza Róheim, influenced by Freudian psychoanalysis, considered dreams to be valuable data on individual and collective mental processes. In 1935, Jackson Steward Lincoln published what may be the first text specifically on dreams in "primitive" cultures, in which he sought to solve the problem of using personal, inner mental experiences as cultural information. He opined that the dreams of "primitive" peoples (and probably not just them) "always fall into two distinct classes, the unsought, or spontaneous dreams occurring in sleep, here called 'individual' dreams, and the sought or induced 'culture pattern' dreams of special tribal significance. The latter are sometimes called traditional dreams" (1935: 22). Along with the enduring concept of the culture pattern dream, he also insisted, intervening in the "primitive mentality" debate, that the

> psychological structure of primitive dreams appears to be identical with that of non-primitive ones.... Wish-fulfillment and conflict are as evident in primitive dreams as elsewhere and the manifest content shows dramatization, symbolization, condensation, displacement, and secondary elaboration, or rationalization, of the latent wishes and conflicts.
>
> (26)

He further added, anticipating Lévi-Strauss, that the "same structure has also been found to hold for myths" (26).

Soon, studies of the dreams of specific societies appeared. Dorothy Eggan analyzed a collection of dreams of the Hopi chief Don Talayesva (the figure documented in Leo Simmons's *Sun Chief*; see Chapter 2). She concluded that the Hopi lacked

> a well-developed, culturally interpreted, body of dream lore which has been transmitted from generation to generation. Even where a dream referent seems to be invested with an almost universal Hopi definition, an informant most frequently explains such an element in his own dreams in terms of personal viewpoint and considers the dream "good" or "bad" in accordance with his emotional and physical state upon awakening.
>
> (1949: 178)

The absence of culturally elaborated dream symbolism did not mean that dreams were irrelevant to Hopi society. Rather, dreams exerted "a varying but considerable influence in the lives of these people, and they have definite rules for the treatment of them"; for instance, "in order to negate the effects of a bad dream it must be told immediately on awakening, even though a reluctant listener must be aroused in the middle of the night" (196). The upshot, according to Eggan, was that while there may be an "unsocialized residue of the personality" legible in dreams, those nighttime experiences were also informative of "where a culture has succeeded in applying the most effective control and support" to the individual mind (197).

A few years later, George Devereux made the important connection between dreams and learning, with special reference to shamanism (see the following). It goes without saying, despite the fact that dreams are subjective phenomena, that dreams are molded by cultural learning; that is why modern urban people dream of cars, computers, and office jobs, while Australian Aboriginals dreamt of kangaroos and ancestral places. But it is not just that everyday cultural knowledge and experience enters dreams; dream content also enters cultural knowledge and experience. Devereux explained that for the Mohave (southwest North America), "magical powers, and the knowledge of the myths, skills, and songs pertaining to them, were supposed to be acquired in dream"; granting that people gain information while awake, they maintained nonetheless "that this knowledge remains barren, i.e. ineffective, unless it is also 'dreamed'" (1957: 1036). Like others before and since, Devereux contended that dreams and myths were closely associated, and both were sources or forms of power:

> Although Mohave shamans and singers are supposed to acquire their knowledge in dream, they actually learn it in waking life and then have dreams which condense or allude to this body of knowledge.... The power of the songs is not inherent in their letter-perfect wording and reproduction; it is due to the fact that they are accepted as condensed equivalents of the myth. Where songs are forgotten, the prose version of the myth is used therapeutically. Power dreams and the songs which actualize power are both condensations of the myth.
>
> (1044)

Dreams and The Dreaming in Australian Aboriginal Societies

Writing on dream interpretation in Haiti (see the following), Erika Bourguignon made the point that "cultures differ greatly in the importance they place on dreams" (1954: 262). Probably no peoples on earth have hypercognized dreams and raised them to such cultural prominence as Australian Aboriginals, who are renowned for their cultural-religious concept of The Dreaming. Although Aboriginal cultures varied to a considerable degree, across the continent, dreams were not only given great weight but were elevated to a pivotal ontological and cosmological status. Among the Warlpiri of central Australia, the same term—*jukurrpa*—refers to individual nighttime dreams and to a supernatural notion that William Stanner in 1953 called "a sacred, heroic time long ago when man and nature came to be as they are; but neither 'time' nor 'history' as we understand them is involved in this meaning" (57). This was because, Stanner tried to convey, The Dreaming (called by some The Dream, The Eternal Dream, or simply Dreaming) "is also, in a sense, still part of the present" (58). As an epoch at the beginning of time, The Dreaming is

> a cosmogony, an account of the begetting of the universe, a study about creation. It is also a cosmology, an account or theory of how what was created became an ordered system. To be more precise, how the universe became a moral system.
>
> (60–1)

During that original Dreaming, the ancestral beings emerged from the ground of an already-existing earth and had adventures, giving the landscape, and ultimately human beings and human cultures, their form. The Dreaming was the source and subject of myth, song, ritual, and design (Figure 8.1).

Figure 8.1 The Dreamtime or Dreaming and its characters, as depicted here in rock paintings, are central to Australian Aboriginal art, culture, and consciousness.

But The Dreaming, as Stanner implied, is not in the past; it is, in his words, *everywhen*, including today. It is (re)experienced during rituals and is embodied in trees, mountains, waterholes, and cultural artifacts; Warlpiri individuals would point at specific trees, etc. and tell me that those were *jukurrpa*, while other trees of the same species were merely trees. And of course, The Dreaming erupts into everyday experience through dreams, which, as for Devereux's Mohave shamans, can be a fountain of new cultural and ritual knowledge. Individuals may dream songs, designs, or entire ritual sequences, although such individuals would never claim them as personal inventions or as innovations since that knowledge is eternal but not previously revealed to humans. Elders evaluate the dream materials, determine if they are true (*junga* in Warlpiri, "really true," as opposed to *yijardu* or only factually true), assign ownership and control over them, and integrate them into the corpus of cultural-ritual knowledge.

BOX 8.1 DREAMS AMONG THE BARDI

The Bardi from the northwest Kimberley area of Western Australia exemplify these points well. Katie Glaskin told that they understood their dreams "as coming from a source external to the dreamer: through the medium of dreams, spirits of the deceased, spirit beings, and ancestral figures are said to communicate with the dreamer and 'reveal' to him or her certain things" (2005: 299). Curiously, unlike with the Warlpiri *jukurrpa*, she said that there was no single settled term for dreaming as a cosmogonic Genesis moment: the Bardi might use the word for nighttime dreams (*buwarra* or *buwarrang*) or *milamilonjun* ("from a long, long time ago"), *inamunonjun* ("supernatural beings"), or simply "The Law." When discussing dreams, Bardi people also mentioned *raya* or *rayi*, meaning "largely invisible pre-existing beings of both sexes, commonly referred to in English as 'kids,' 'small kids,' or 'spirit kids'" (302); all human babies were incarnations of these spirit beings, dormant in the land. In addition, a human had a *jarlng* or *jarlnga* (a totem species) and a *nimangaar* (shadow), and these components were "intrinsic to Bardi conceptualizations of personhood, to the 'processes of pro-creation, fertility and augmenting, of life itself'" (303). Finally, dreams were central to the role of *jarlngungurr* ("doctor," "clever man," colloquially "shaman"). Endowed with supernatural abilities of "healing, divination, sorcery, to transform themselves into animal form, travel in dreams, and to communicate with ancestral spirits and other spiritual entities," much of their power originated in dreams (303). As mentioned, one of the *jarlngungurr*'s key capabilities was to travel in dreams in order to effect a cure or seek more knowledge. Not surprisingly, they were believed to have more frequent and more potent dreams.

It should be obvious that dreams were and are productive for Aboriginal peoples. Dreams produced knowledge; they also produced spiritual power. They even produced life: dreams were key to fertility, and I was told by Aboriginals that in olden times, people dreamed of kangaroos, and there were many kangaroos, but today, people dream of cars, and there are many cars. Most profoundly, as suggested by Glaskin but also noted by generations of anthropologists, from the late nineteenth-century team of Spencer and Gillen to the emi-nent A. P. Elkin, Aboriginal peoples commonly believed that humans conceived children by dreaming them (which does not necessarily mean that they misunderstood or denied the biological aspects of reproduction): often, the father would "find" a spirit-child in a dream, and the mother's womb would nurture that spirit-being into human form. Since the spirit-child resided in a particular place before conception, there was a lifelong link between each human, specific sites, and eternal dreams.

The dreaming self: dreams and personhood across cultures

Freud memorably declared that dreams were the royal road to the unconscious. For anthro-pologists, dreams lead to much more complete discoveries about a society's concepts of self and person. The fundamental question is what exactly is happening during dreaming? A common denominator across cultures is the belief that dreams are real experiences had by some part—often a spiritual part—of a person, which teaches us what various cultures think about the components and properties of a person.

Thomas Gregor's ethnography of Mehinaku (Brazil) dreaming neatly illustrated the point. According to Gregor, the key to their understanding of dreams was a belief that every person had multiple souls, including the shadow soul, the sweat soul, and the eye soul. The eye soul was particularly able to travel apart from the body, both after death when it departed for the sky village and during sleep when it wandered on the earth—"an event that is subjectively experienced as a dream" (1981: 710). In other words, dreams were a person's memory of the actual voyages of the eye soul, which met and interacted with the souls of other people during the night (an eye soul could only interact with another person who was also asleep). This means that, in a serious way, "a dream is as much the soul's experience as the dream-er's, who receives it only from afar" (711); it might also be accurate to say that a dream was *more* the soul's experience than the person's since "the Mehinaku appear to separate them-selves from their dreams" and to perceive them from a position of "passive spectatorship" of what their eye soul did (712). This attitude speaks to deeper ideas and values in the society, which Gregor characterized as "individual-centered" (in contradiction of the stereotype that only Western societies are individualistic; see Chapter 6) and "a relative lack of well-defined groups" (719). For this reason, Mehinaku were described as intensely concerned about personal boundaries, placing dreams at the boundary and "the frontier of self and not-self" (717). Finally, just as emotions have social and political effects and consequences (see Chapter 7), so did Mehinaku dreams: "Dreams define the individual's relationships with spirits, launch the career of the would-be shaman, and start rituals that may eventually include most of the members of the tribe" (719).

In societies where personhood is extended to nonhumans, we should expect that other beings also have mental experiences like dreams. Indeed, among the Runa (Ecuadoran Amazon), dogs dream too since they, like humans, "possess souls because of their abilities to 'become aware of' those beings that stand in relation to them as predator or prey" (Kohn 2007: 8). Moreover, like humans, their consciousness can grow by consuming other animals and incorporating—literally, adding to their body—the consciousness of those species. For the Runa as for the Mehinaku, dreams are not imaginings or symbols but real events in the world, "a product of the ambulations of the soul" (12), both human souls and dog souls. Further, humans can understand the dreams of dogs but only if dogs are endowed with the gift of human language. Fascinatingly, "if people want dogs to understand them, they must give the dogs hallucinogenic drugs. That is, the Runa *must make their dogs into shamans so that they can traverse the ontological boundaries that separate them from humans*" (13, emphasis added).

The Tzotzil Maya share with the Mehinaku a notion of a multipart self, comprised of the waking self, the "essential soul" (*ch'ulel*), and the "animal companion" (*chon, vayijel*). The third of these resides outside the body, "on the sacred mountain of Tzontevitz,"

> and its identity is thought to determine social dominance and power, serving to naturalize the unequal distribution of skills among supposed equals. Powerful people are said to have large carnivores (jaguars, coyotes, etc.) as animal companions, while humble or "poor" people have smaller animals such as rabbits, squirrels, opossums, or skunks as companions.
>
> (Groark 2010: 106)

The essential soul is the locus of dreams; leaving the body at night to have its own adventures, the *ch'ulel* "is characterized by an unpredictable willfulness of its own, an oneiric volitional potential that often takes the dreamer by surprise" (106). But therein lies the political power of this semiautonomous self-fragment: Groark reasons that in a society that devalues self-assertion and authority over others, acts of willfulness can be deflected onto dreams, which are viewed as the acts of an "other," a nonself, and in extreme cases, the acts of deities who communicate with and authorize the person in a dream.

As one final example, Douglas Hollan also described how dreamers in Toraja (Sulawesi, Indonesia) could "externalize and project 'internal' conflict and concerns that manifest themselves in dreams" (1989: 167). Villagers distinguished three kinds of dreams—first, "a form of nocturnal cogitation in which the mind continues to mull over the day's events and activities" that does not quite qualify as a dream; second, *tauan* or fitful nightmares, including spirit attacks; and third, *tindo* or proper dreams which, once again, "are thought to be 'real' experiences in which the dreamer's soul communicates with the wandering souls of other sleeping humans or with the spirits, gods, and departed ancestors" (168–70). Some *tindo* were prophetic, but others were not; the interesting thing, according to Hollan, was the capacity of dreams and the interpretation of dreams to work as "a type of culturally constituted defense mechanism" against the manifest content of dreams—which may be hostile or antisocial—and against "shameful, threatening thoughts and emotions" in waking life (182).

Ethnopsychologies of dream interpretation

Freudian theory, and the psychology and anthropology that followed it, made much of dream interpretation; in fact, Freud's first important statement of psychoanalysis was his 1900 *The Interpretation of Dreams*, and even the general public knows the stock meanings of many alleged Freudian dream symbols (which are stereotypically sexual in nature). Other cultures have had their own interpretive systems for dreams as part of their ethnopsychology, including the Toraja just mentioned, who possessed a set of "dreambook" interpretations: receiving gold in a dream meant a forthcoming good rice harvest, standing on a mountaintop signaled becoming a leader, and nakedness was an augur of illness, to name but a few (Hollan 1989: 171).

In Haiti, as in many areas of the world, dreams were considered to be messages from the ancestors or the gods, who might "not only communicate a generalized demand for the fulfillment of religious obligations, but may actually specify details of religious procedure to be followed" (Bourguignon 1954: 268), much as we saw in Aboriginal Australia. When the meaning was not self-evident, a member of a *vodun* cult might consult a priest, but Bourguignon made the significant point that the mere telling of a dream to an expert or layperson was already an act of interpretation as it was unavoidably "made to conform to the dreamer's culturally styled notions as to what dreams are all about" (266).

The Mae Enga (New Guinea) were keen to anticipate the future, and dreams could be useful clues. Some dreams were obvious, whether "ominous" or "trivial," but others were "not immediately intelligible" (Meggitt 1962: 219). For the latter, some interpretive work was in order. To start, Meggitt noted that the gender and social status of the dreamer impacted the dream's importance. Dreams of women and children had the least import; the weightiest dreams came to "big men," male diviners, female mediums, and mature married women (often wives of big men). Meggitt recorded twenty-eight specific dream symbols and their local meanings, including:

- The dreamer sees or touches gourds growing on a vine: he will experience good fortune.
- The dreamer discovers in the forest a pool containing clean water: he will receive wealth.
- The dreamer gives pork or valuables to his betrothed: the betrothal will be broken off.

(224)

The Quiché Maya had some of the most formalized dream interpretation, including a formal office of initiated dream interpreters called *ajk'ij* (day-/sun/time keeper); in fact, at the town of Momostenango, Guatemala, Barbara Tedlock counted almost ten thousand daykeepers in a population of forty-five thousand. A daykeeper was initially identified "through birth, illness, and dreams—followed by marriage to a spirit spouse at initiation" (1981: 315) and then received extensive training, including by deities, who taught the novice how to read dreams. One interpretive lesson that they learned was that separate dreams could be part of one total dream: "All dreams dreamed on the same night by the same dreamer are regarded as completing each other, no matter how dissimilar the content might appear to be" (326). Indeed, a daykeeper might bundle together dreams from multiple dreamers on a given night.

BOX 8.2 DREAMS IN ISLAM

It is not only indigenous or premodern societies that value and interpret dreams. "Islam is the largest night dream culture in the world today," writes Iain Edgar;

> In Islam, the night dream is thought to offer a way to metaphysical and divinatory knowledge, to be a practical, alternative, and potentially accessible source of imaginative inspiration and guidance and to offer ethical clarity concerning action in the world.
>
> (2011: 1)

Since the prophet Muhammad received his first revelations in dream (*al-ruya*), dreams have been held in esteem, although not all dreams are necessarily divine communications. Hence, a lively tradition of dream interpretation developed, separating "true" dreams from "false," evil, or merely mundane ones and determining their meanings. A particularly interesting element of Islamic dream culture is *istikhara*, dream "incubation" or summoning. To seek or request a dream "involves reciting special ritual prayers before going to bed and meditation upon life choices before sleeping" (45). The continuing salience of dreams for Muslims is evidenced, Edgar reminds us ominously, by the role that they play in contemporary terrorism and jihadist Islam. He recounts dreams of Mullah Omar, head of the Taliban when it ruled Afghanistan, Osama bin Laden, and attempted terrorists like Zacarias Moussaoui and Richard Reid (the infamous "shoe bomber"), all of whom credited dreams for some of their inspiration and instruction.

The anthropology of trance

One of the most extraordinary things about the human mind is its proneness to dissociative states; for all of its other wonders, it is a fragile system that easily literally loses touch with reality and itself. Western psychology and psychiatry recognize dissociation as a phenomenon—and as a pathology or disorder, labeled dissociative identity disorder in the fifth edition of the *Diagnostic and Statistical Manual* (see Chapter 9). In that document, dissociative identity disorder is characterized by

> A. Disruption of identity characterized by two or more distinct personality states, *which may be described in some cultures as an experience of possession.* The disruption of marked discontinuity in sense of self and sense of agency, accompanied by related alterations in affect, behavior, consciousness, memory, perception, cognition, and/or sensory-motor functioning. These signs and symptoms may be observed by others or reported by the individual.
> B. Recurrent gaps in the recall of everyday events, important personal information, and/or traumatic events that are inconsistent with ordinary forgetting.
> C. The symptoms cause clinically significant distress or impairment in social, occupational, or other important areas of functioning.

D. *The disturbance is not a normal part of a broadly accepted cultural or religious practice.*
Note: In children, the symptoms are not better explained by imaginary playmates or
other fantasy play.
E. The symptoms are not attributable to the physiological effects of a substance (e.g.,
blackouts or chaotic behavior during alcohol intoxication) or another medical condition
(e.g., complex partial seizures).

(American Psychiatric Association 2013: 292, emphasis added)

Noting the two references to culture in the material, the key to the psychological understanding of dissociation is "discontinuity in a person's sense of agency," which means "not
feeling in control of, or as if you don't 'own' your feelings, thoughts, or actions. For example,
experiencing thoughts, feelings or actions that seem as if they are 'not mine' or belong to
someone else" (298), hence the loss of self and the sense of different "personality states" or
alters or other selves.

Among the many dissociative states is trance, recognized explicitly (but as "dissociative
trance disorder") in the fourth edition of the *Diagnostic and Statistical Manual*, defined
as "single or episodic disturbances in the state of consciousness, identity, or memory that
are indigenous to particular locations and cultures" and involve "narrowing of awareness
of immediate surroundings or stereotyped behaviors or movements that are experienced as
being beyond one's control" (Spiegel et al. 2011: 841). Anthropologists have observed that
trance behavior occurs widely across cultures, sometimes viewed as a disorder or pathology
and sometimes not. Societies have specific ways not only of understanding trance but of
inducing it and employing it, not all of which conform to academic psychology's perspective.

As a more-than-occasionally culturally-prized state of consciousness, anthropologists approach trance as a skill that can be acquired and taught. In 1975 Gregory Bateson, whose
encounter with Bali stretched back more than thirty years (see Chapter 2), reflected on how
Balinese society actively if not deliberately instructed members to achieve trance states. They
used ritual dancing "as an entry into ecstasy and an ego-alien world"; "whether or not the
Balinese 'know' what they are doing and intend this outcome, they somehow sense and recognize…that their kinesthetic socialization prepares the individual for altered consciousness—for
a temporary escape from the ego-organized world" (1975: 152). Through such culturally-
defined movement, a Balinese person learned "to perceive the body as an autonomous, ego-
alien entity" (153), that is, to dissociate himself—or his self—from his own body.

A decade later, combining the insights of Ludwig (see earlier) with contemporary brain science, Michael Winkelman proposed "a psychophysiological model of trance states" (1986: 174),
adding an anthropological cross-cultural survey of trance-induction processes. Based on forty-
five societies chosen from the Standard Cross-Cultural Sample (see Chapter 3), he identified a
list of mechanisms for bringing on a trance experience, including alcohol and psychotropic substances (sometimes called "entheogens" in the literature because they seem among users to allow
contact with gods or spirits); sexual abstinence; social isolation; sleep deprivation; fasting; ascetic
exercises, like exposure to cold or pain; "compulsive motor behavior," such as "uncontrolled
flailing of limbs [and] compulsive running about"; "auditory driving" in the form of "chanting,
singing, or percussion"; and spontaneous illness (187). He also proposed a variety of trance types:

1   Soul Flight, or Vision Quest, involving active seeking of trance states with visions,
     but no possession or practitioner/spirit dialogue.

2   Trance State without Soul Flight, Vision Quest, Possession, or Practitioner/Spirit Dialogue.
3   Both Soul Flight or Vision Quest and Possession or Practitioner/Spirit Dialogue.
4   Possession or Practitioner/Spirit Dialogue but no Soul Flight or Vision Quest.

(193–4)

As a final introductory comment, Felicitas Goodman also supported the idea of different phenomena conflated under the concept of "trance." Measuring the neurophysiological changes associated with what she called ritual body posture and ecstatic trance as opposed to channeling, she uncovered sufficient differences to designate two different altered states of consciousness, reckoning that such states "are not single strands, but rather bundles, sets, or families" of brain and body activity (1999: 58).

Trance types and social variables

A leading figure in the anthropological study of trance was Erika Bourguignon, whose major 1973 edited volume *Religion, Altered States of Consciousness, and Social Change* reprised her earlier cross-cultural survey and featured several other authors examining trance in various settings. Launching from the position that altered states of consciousness are not merely pathology but "are institutionalized and culturally patterned and utilized in specific ways" (1973a: 3), she analyzed a sample of 488 societies, ninety percent of which exhibited at least one form of institutionalized altered state. First, she noted some divergence between regions: the incidence ranged from eighty percent in the circum-Mediterranean area to ninety-seven percent in North America, with East Eurasia and the Pacific Islands coming close at ninety-four percent; South American (eighty-five percent) and sub-Saharan Africa (eighty-two percent) completed the survey.

More importantly, she divided trance into two categories—trance and possession trance. Possession trance (see the following) was defined as "states interpreted by the societies in which they occur as due to possession by spirits" while trance was "a residual and diversified category" for "states not so interpreted." Speaking of trance, she continued:

> most typically it involves the experience of hallucinations or visions, interpreted in the particular societies as experiences of the (or, a) soul of the person, its temporary absence, its journeys and adventures, and so on. Trance (T) may involve the repetition of messages of spirits to an audience, the imitation of the actions of spirits, or the narration of the subject's spirit journey; or it may involve a private, isolated experience of the individual, as in the vision quest of North American Indians. The experience is remembered by the trancer, for the memory of the experience and often its report to others is of particular importance in many cultures.

(12)

Accordingly, she calculated the occurrence of types by geographic region, depending on whether they had trance alone, possession trance alone, both, or neither. Her results were as follows:

- Trance: North America 72%, South America 54%, Pacific Islands 29%, circum-Mediterranean 23%, East Eurasia 22%, sub-Saharan Africa 16%
- Possession trance: sub-Saharan Africa 46%, circum-Mediterranean 43%, East Eurasia 38%, Pacific Islands 34%, South America 8%, North America 4%

- Both: East Eurasia 34%, Pacific Islands 31%, South America 22%, North America 21%, sub-Saharan Africa 20%, circum-Mediterranean 14%
- Neither: circum-Mediterranean 20%, sub-Saharan Africa 18%, South America 15%, East Eurasia and Pacific Islands 6%, North America 3%.

(18)

Looking for further correlations between social variables and possession trance specifically (but unfortunately, not simple trance), she discerned some fascinating relationships. The presence of possession trance was positively correlated—sometimes quite strongly—with

1 the size of the society (the larger the population, the more common was possession trance)
2 sedentary society (ninety-one percent of societies practicing possession trance had permanent settlements)
3 agriculture
4 social hierarchy, as measured by the presence of social classes and multiple levels of political authority
5 male dominance, as measured by patrilocal residence and patrilineal descent
6 the payment of bride price or bride service
7 institutionalized slavery (eighty-six percent of societies with possession tranced also practiced slavery).

Summarizing her findings, she stated that societies with possession trance were the most socially complex, trance societies were the most socially simple, and societies with both forms fell in between.

Possession trance

As indicated by Bourguignon's research, of the forms of trance, possession trance has received by far the most attention. Interestingly, the *Diagnostic and Statistical Manual* (4th edition) recognized possession trance too as "replacement of the customary sense of personal identity by a new identity, attributed to the influence of a spirit, deity, or other person, and associated with stereotyped 'involuntary' movements or amnesia"; in fact, the *DSM* proposed that it was "perhaps the most common Dissociative Disorder in Asia" but "is not a normal part of a broadly accepted cultural or religious practice" (quoted in Spiegel et al. 2011: 841). As happy as we are to see psychology taking possession trance seriously, anthropology contradicts the psychological assessment in two ways: first, we do not necessarily consider it a disorder or pathology, and second, we find that it is indeed a normal part of the cultural or religious practice of many a society.

Bourguignon returned in 1976 with a book dedicated to possession, of which possession trance was one variety. Possession, she asserted, involves "spirits, powers, persons, 'viewed as superhuman' at least in some cases, which can take over the will or consciousness of man"; more, such possession could be the choice of the possessing being ("spontaneous" in her terminology) or could be purposely sought or invoked by the human ("voluntary") (1976: 6). Also, she stipulated that the symptoms, if you will, of possession might exist in any given society, but the label "possession" was a cultural one, that possession "is an idea, a concept, a belief, which serves to interpret behavior" (7) which might be interpreted or labeled otherwise—including as mental illness—in another (Figure 8.2).

Figure 8.2 Spirit possession in vodun or "voodoo".

The really crucial point made in her book was that, when possession was believed locally, more than one attitude might be taken toward it. In the most familiar case, as in Christian societies (except when it comes to possession by the Holy Spirit, as in Pentecostalism), possession is dreaded and "vigorous efforts are made to drive out the spirit supposed to be in residence (often with physical violence)"; surprisingly, in other instances, possession is "desired and intentionally induced," as for example by mediums. Most remarkably of all, there are societies and circumstances "where the initial spontaneous behavior is considered deviant and perhaps sick, and where a cure involved bringing about possession trance in a controlled setting" (9). In other words, possession may not always be an affliction *but may be the treatment of an affliction, or both.* In the case of what we might dub possession therapy, relief from the worst symptoms of possession "does not consist in stopping the possession trance but, as it were, in domesticating it, in developing a new personality and a new status in society" (9).

BOX 8.3 JANICE BODDY: WOMEN AND SPIRIT POSSESSION IN HOFRIYAT SOCIETY

A classic case of spirit possession as both cause and cure of illness came from the northern Sudanese village of Hofriyat, studied by Janice Boddy. In Hofriyat, possession was a condition associated predominantly with women—and not merely with women but with married women between the ages of thirty-five and fifty-five, that is, the prime age of wife and mother. Thus, an understanding of possession trance requires an understanding of gender, with men and women conceptualized in the village as "fundamentally different kinds of persons exhibiting complementary qualities, abilities, and dispositions" (1988: 5). Men were thought to acquire considerably more *'aqel* or reason and self-control than women, who in contrast "are wholly governed by their carnal natures and unable to exercise conscious restraint" (6). Furthermore, women were defined almost exclusively in terms of their roles as wife and mother, with much greater restrictions placed on their choices and mobility. Along then came the *zairan* (plural of *zar*), a kind of Arabic *jinn* spirit believed to be natural rather than supernatural but still "able to infiltrate humans and take possession of them at will" (10). A woman who was already suffering psychological symptoms (anxiety or depression) was a likely victim of *zar* attack, resulting in nausea, fatigue, pain, and miscarriage, stillbirth, and other complaints pertinent to women and "women's blood." *Zar* possession, Boddy learned, "is a lifelong, fundamentally incurable condition that is, however, manageable"; in fact, "it may be transformed out of all resemblance to what we might consider illness" (11). The treatment, if we may call it that, involved a ceremony in which the victim, through trance, entered a permanent relationship with the *zar*: "the patient ideally enters trance; now identified, the intruder manifests itself through her body and makes known its demands, in return for which it should agree to restore, and refrain from further jeopardizing, her well-being" (11). After the initial cure (and women were expected to attend *zar* ceremonies for the rest of their lives), some of the former patients actually spoke of themselves in the plural—as *nehha* (we) rather than *ana* (I)—suggesting that she had dissociated from her individual self and become, so to speak, a composite self of human and *zar*. Not only was she thus detached from her prior suffering self, but she achieved "distance from her cultural context, the source of her over-objectification" as nothing more than a Hofriyat wife and mother (21). In other words, through permanent possession by and melding with the *zar*, "women can step outside their everyday world and gain perspective on their lives" (22)—and also gained some license from their failure as or deviation from the feminine norm.

The case of Hofriyat women introduces two important considerations to the investigation of possession and trance. First, as Arnaud Halloy and Vlad Namescu contend, and as Bateson illustrated earlier in Bali, possession and trance can rightly be seen as not just a mental state (let alone a disorder) but as a social skill, a kind of "*cultural expertise*, which every possessed person must gain and master if she wants her state to be socially recognized" (2012: 165, emphasis in the original). That is, to a certain extent, possession and trance are learned, performed, and perfected. It is predictable, then, that individuals have the possession and trance experiences that their cultures expect them to have. Second, possession and trance are not the exclusive domain of women, but women are disproportionately represented as subjects of possession and trance in the anthropological literature. Bourguignon reasoned more generally that possession trance

> offers alternative roles, which satisfy certain individual needs, and it does so by providing an alibi that the behavior is that of spirits and not of the human beings themselves. And furthermore, in order for human beings to play such assertive roles, they must be totally passive, giving over their bodies to what are ego-alien forces. In a hierarchical society, demanding submission to those in authority, one acquires authority by identification with symbols of power, identification with which goes as far as the total assumption of other's identity, total loss of its own.
>
> (1976: 40)

As the subordinated gender in many societies, it is likely that women would resort to this alternative more often than men.

Examples abound, like the island of Mayotte between mainland Africa and Madagascar. Michael Lambek documented that victims of possession were women, whose personality or subjectivity was totally displaced by a spirit during the possession encounter. Since the sufferer alternates between self and other, possession "allows for the coexistence of mutually incompatible ideologies (concerning the status of women, for example), without thereby overtly violating either one" (1980: 322). And, as in Hofriyat, the response to spirit attack was not exorcism or the expulsion of the intruder but "the socialization of the spirit" (319), literally as a spouse of the woman (or man, in the fewer cases of male affliction). Human and spirit-spouse entered into a long-term relationship of rights and responsibilities. All the while, not only was the woman learning, but so was the spirit: "The spirit learns to listen to others and to speak its own thoughts so that the others will understand in turn. The spirit also becomes more open concerning the topics about which it is willing to converse" (322).

Ma'i aitu or "spirit sickness" was the local term for possession on Samoa, according to Jeannette Mageo, which tended to affect young women rather than wives and mothers, but nevertheless, it shed light on "the problematics of gender" in that society (1991: 352). Mageo described Samoa as a place where personality was more determined by social roles and relations than by individual dispositions and where *fa'aaloalo* or "respect for status" was a central value. The women of the family were especially associated with family's status and *mana* and were expected to be quiet, solemn, and virginal. A young girl who flouted these norms, particularly by taking a lover, was called *tautalaitiiti*, literally "to talk while still young." Such girls were sometimes diagnosed as possessed by a *Teine*, one of the spirit-girls who were regarded as "anything but virgins" (359). When a girl was said to be possessed by a *Teine*, her impulsive and extravagant behavior was likened to that of a spirit-girl, donning bright clothing and wearing her hair down in a libertine way. The threat of possession inhibited inappropriate behavior for most girls, but ironically it also partially excused it for others since "the possessed girl cannot be said to be *tautalaitiiti*, for it is not she who acts, but an *aitu*. The status of the *aitu* is so exalted that there is no one of higher status, in relation to whom it could be considered impudent" (364).

Women are not the sole victims of possession and trance nor is it always the case that possessed people can be called victims at all; in some situations, it would be better to call them beneficiaries. Certainly, the Samoan girl benefited in a way from possession by a *Teine*. Kalpana Ram (2013) maintains that women in Tamil Nadu (southern India) sometimes gain prestige and authority from possession, literally holding court as the personification or medium of a spirit or goddess to hear the grievances of their neighbors and adjudicate them in the mannerisms and speech patterns of a goddess. Meanwhile, even before Bourguignon's influential work, John and Irene Hamer observed that Sidamo (southwest Ethiopia) men might use possession strategically. In that society, a man was required to distinguish himself in some way—as a lion-killer, warrior, speaker, farmer, etc. However, for the man who otherwise lacked talent,

> spirit possession provides an alternative opportunity for achieving status. A person with a powerful spirit may accumulate wealth from gifts, and he has the potentiality of attracting large audiences when he undergoes possession, even if he is completely ignored in the assembly of elders.
>
> (1966: 399)

The fact that spirit possession could allegedly be inherited from a parent among the Sidamo highlights one last point, namely, that possession and trance are frequently not entirely private or internal/mental matters but can be substantially organized and routinized. For instance, Arnaud Halloy reinforces his comment about learning possession with an investigation of a possession cult in Brazil known as Xangô. In a discussion powerfully linking possession, the body, and emotions, he explains that Xangô members understand that possession must be learned—which they call "indoctrinating the body" (*doutrinar o corpo*)—and that "learning possession means in the first place to learn to identify and react to specific emotional states in accordance with cultural representations and expectations" (2012: 177). Judging the experience of possession as "gratifying" (*gratificante*), the Xangô cult elaborates a series of three stages of possession through which "novices are expected to learn how to dance, and to behave according to their *orixa's* [spirit/god] archetypal and aesthetic prerequisites" (181). Associating possession cults with deprivation and frustration, and mentioning the *zar* (spelled *sar* in his article) cult described by Boddy, I. M. Lewis proposed a spectrum of possession phenomena, from "largely institutionalized" individual "hysterical possession" to "regular, stereotyped, and thoroughly institutionalized mode of entry into a specifically shamanistic cult group, with an organized leadership and following" to

> true prophetic movements, where the possessing mediums and shamans not only answer recurring problems within their own cultural tradition, but in response to new stimuli and pressures, announce messianic revelations and inaugurate spiritually inspired religions with a new and wider appeal and a strong embodiment of moral teaching.
>
> (1966: 322–3)

Possession cults and practices can also be part of much bigger religious institutions, including Christian churches. Examining the Spiritual Baptists of St. Vincent (Caribbean island), Wallace Zane described a practice—which he preferred to call a "ritual state of conscious"—of "mourning,"

> which involves seclusion in a dark room for eleven to fourteen days, during which the believer communes with God and receives revelations through spirit journeys. Spirit journeys may also take place during the worship services or at home during sleep. Each new member must go through a three day baptismal mourning, but members may "go down to the low grounds of mourning" whenever they feel the call from the Spirit of God. Released during a night-time service, they announce their revelations to the congregation.
>
> (1995: 19)

In fact, ritual possession is a fairly common phenomenon in Pentecostal and charismatic forms of Christianity, such as the southern Appalachian Pentecostal Holiness churches investigated by Steven Kane. During their regular snake-handling services, worshippers entered ritual trance states, one form of "anointing" or "the belief that the Holy Ghost 'moves' upon the believer and takes possession of his faculties imparting to him supernatural gifts" (1974: 296) like immunity to venom. Once again, Kane insisted that this dissociative state was far from random or spontaneous but learned, patterned, and integrated into worship, happening, for example, only during the "musical portions of the ceremony"; nor can the practitioners be dismissed as insane since outside church, "serpent handlers behave in a perfectly 'normal' and socially acceptable manner, operating with a keen sense of their own ego boundaries and personal limitations" (302). Finally, if Pentecostal snake-handling seems too extreme and deviant, S. E. Ackerman reminded us that possession has long been a doctrine of the Catholic church. In Ackerman's study of Malaysian Catholics, he found a charismatic community where "the human body is conceived of as a permeable receptacle of spiritual forces, both demonic and divine. The penetration of a body by these forces results in either negative or positive possession states"; accordingly, the discourse of this and similar churches "is centrally concerned with the intake and expulsion of demonic and divine spiritual forces" (1981: 95).

The vision quest

Bourguignon's cross-cultural survey determined that North American indigenous societies had a particularly high incidence of trance without possession, and one of its most distinctive forms was the vision quest. In many Native American societies, an individual would seek a vision at least once, sometimes repeatedly, in a lifetime. The most famous account of a vision is undoubtedly Black Elk's prophecy, as narrated by John Niehardt in the classic *Black Elk Speaks*, first published in 1932. As David Martínez more recently asserted, having a vision (*hanbleceya*) was "a normal part of Lakota personal development. In fact, not only was having a vision normal, but also there were social expectations, or peer pressure, about having such an experience" (2004: 82). Nor was the quest for a vision left to chance or individual whim: the seeker was accompanied by a "holy man" (*wicasa wakan*) "who knows the proper way of conducting this ritual"; indeed, it was "the proper execution of each component of the overall ritual that generated a visionary experience"—from smoking the pipe to building the sweat lodge—which explains why "the highest degree of formalization of the vision quest is found" among peoples like the Lakota (87).

In one of her earliest publications, Ruth Benedict assembled available research on Plains Indians vision quests, starting with the observation that these societies demonstrated "an inordinate pursuit of the vision" (1922: 1). Nevertheless, considerable variation existed among Native Americans; most basically, east and west of the Plains, the vision quest was "definitely an affair of adolescence, a ritual at entrance to maturity," while among Plains peoples "it is mature men who characteristically seek the vision" (2). She mentioned three other features of the Plains vision quest complex. First, in some but certainly not all societies, self-torture was part of the experience; torture customs were not, though, part of the vision quest among the Blackfoot and Arapaho. Second, it was common for layperson and aspiring shaman alike to seek a vision, where every man desired or was required to receive one (although the Dakota allegedly "make a sharp break between the laity and the shamans" [10]). Third, the vision quest was widely connected with attaining a guardian spirit, often an animal spirit, although meeting a guardian spirit was not a universal element in the vision quest, and a seeker sometimes "received his power or commands directly, without specifically acquiring a guardian spirit" (12). One of the most exceptional aspects of the vision quest occurred among the Blackfoot, who believed that a man could buy another man's vision to add to his social standing.

Speaking of the Blackfoot, Shayne Dahl has done some insightful work on their vision quest. To a degree, their version of the vision quest is a familiar

> solitary rite whereby individuals retreat from their communities to a sacred location in the wilderness such as the top of a mountain or butte in order to pray for a vision. They remain there without shelter, food or water for typically four days, which leaves them at heightened risk of dehydration, hypothermia, heat stroke, and sleep deprivation. Throughout their hardship, they pray for the spirits to pity their suffering as well as to grant them a transformative and spiritually empowering vision.
>
> (2011: 1)

At a deeper level, the ritual should be understood "as a sacrifice of one's life and therefore self to the Creator" (2). For the ordinary person, this is usually a one-time experience, "a temporary submission of personal agency to agencies of spirits (good or bad), who may visit questers where they sit, take them on soul flight journeys, or even attack them in the night"; however, apprentice shamans (see the following) "submit so much of their personal agency to spirits through progressive self-sacrifice that they become like the spirits insofar as they are poised in a liminal state between life and death, humanity and Creator" (3). It is incumbent upon us to grasp that the "Creator" is not exactly a being and that "creation" was not a single Genesis-time event. Rather, the Blackfoot term *Ihtsipaitapiiyo'pa* means "source of life" or, more profoundly, "flux." All reality is flux, and the ascetic feats that attract a vision push a person into this state or process of flux. A human being who undertakes this effort repeatedly, like a shaman, "becomes 'near flux' for the remainder of their lifetime"; they become like a spirit and acquire the "ability to see, communicate with and become permeated or possessed by spirits"—which gives them great power but also shortened lives (7).

BOX 8.4 VISION QUEST AMONG THE DUNNE-ZA

For the Dunne-za (northern Alberta and British Columbia, Canada), the vision quest was also a transformative event, but not, according to Robin Ridington, one that so much transformed humans into spirits as transformed individual lives into cultural mythology. Traditionally, every Dunne-za person "experienced a series of childhood vision quests to which he or she referred in later life as a source of power and identity" (1982: 215). The memories and lessons of the visions were initially "private and secret," but over a lifetime they were told to and shared with the group. Thus, during "the span of a life between child and old person, the medicine stories of a child's experience alone in the bush become an old person's stories known by everyone in camp. The stories become real in the theater of their telling" (215). Shaping the group's knowledge and feelings, and ever-shaped by preexisting cultural knowledge as well as the visions of other members, as a person ages, "his or her identity becomes more myth-like until, as an old person, the events of the medicine story encountered as a child become public information," acting as "a bridge between subjectivity and the intersubjective realm of culture" (219). To a considerable extent, myth becomes personal as the person becomes mythical.

The anthropology of shamanism

If almost everyone is capable of having (and learning) dissociative states, there are those in society, as with any other skill, who are specialists in altered states of consciousness. One such specialist is known to anthropology as the shaman. In his famous treatment of shamanism, the great scholar of religion Mircea Eliade (1972) called it a "technique of ecstasy"—literally of standing-out-of (*ek-statis*, "out-place," also meaning entrancement, insanity, or displacement in Greek) oneself and thereby gaining the powers of soul flight, communicating with spirits, and curing (as well as causing) maladies.

Named after a specialist role in Siberian societies, and widely distributed with variation across foraging and simpler horticultural and pastoral societies—which Bourguignon associated with trance-without-possession—shamans typically used altered states of consciousness to enter the spirit world, inducing dissociation of self or soul from body via standard techniques like "drumming, singing, chanting, dancing, and in many cultures the use of psychoactive substances" (Winkelman 2013: 48). Michael Winkelman adds that they prepared for their performance "through austerities such as fasting and water deprivation, exposure to temperature extremes, extensive exercise, painful exercise, celibacy, sleep deprivation, dream incubation, and social isolation to enhance these experiences" (48). In fact, a future shaman was often identified by his or her exceptional personality, including a tendency toward visions and hallucinations and frequently a near-death experience, recovery from which demonstrated unique spiritual capacities (Figure 8.3).

For these reasons, many observers have concluded that shamans must be mentally ill, perhaps schizophrenic (or at best, clever charlatans), but as we appreciate by now, that diagnosis misses the point. Richard Noll strenuously rejected "psychopathological interpretations of shamans" (1983: 444), stressing as a key difference between shamanism and schizophrenia that "the shaman voluntarily enters and leaves his altered states of consciousness while the schizophrenic is the helpless victim of his" (450). Noll even recommended the term "shamanic state of consciousness" to distinguish it from mental illness and other altered states. For those intent on labeling shamanism as illness, Larry Peters promoted the concept of "creative illness" for the non-normal personality of the shaman that gives him or her the ability—like some of the possessed women detailed earlier—to cure the mental or physical

Figure 8.3 Shaman in the Peruvian Amazon.

illnesses of others. Researching shamanism among the Tamang (Nepal), Peters explained that, whatever his or her incipient mental state, the shaman trained, disciplined, and used his or her consciousness in culturally informed ways. Peters judged that the Tamang shaman did not "suffer from an 'impairment of reality-testing'" (1982: 24) but instead inhabited—and mastered—a culturally specific model of reality:

> The world of spirits, the dreams and visions of the shaman, may seem abnormal from our cultural perspective, but from the perspective of the Tamang, it is all part of reality which consensus populates with numerous spirits believed to possess individuals, cause illness, and exist in other demonstrable ways. Seen from a relativistic point of view, shamanism is not a pathological delusion.... The shaman's training is a set of psychotherapeutic techniques designed to channel and guide the chaotic feelings created during the calling into a culturally constituted pattern.
>
> (24–5)

From a psychological anthropology perspective, the most relevant aspect of shamanism is the nature of the shaman's self and personhood, which, with variation across cultures, is both less and more than human. The alteration of the shaman's subjectivity begins, as always, with the body. Among some Australian Aboriginal (hunter-gatherer) societies, the conversion of an ordinary person into a shaman involved symbolic (to our minds, at least) replacement of internal organs with other substances, such as crystals; significantly, healing also often involved removing intrusive objects like stones or feathers from the bodies of patients. In his training to become a shaman, an Eskimo or Inuit (hunter-gatherer) apprentice might be symbolically (again, to our minds) killed and therefore no longer entirely alive as a human (Figure 8.4).

Figure 8.4 Navajo shaman in, or giving the appearance of, an altered state of consciousness.

Shamanic power did not always entail modifying the body but instead mastering forces already present in the body. For the !Kung or Ju/hoansi (hunter-gatherer) people of the Kalahari Desert, a shaman was a *n/um kausi* or "master-owner of *n/um*," which was an energy dormant in the base of the spine. (The ! and / characters in Ju/hoansi words designate click sounds in their language.) According to Richard Katz (1982), nearly all men and most women attempted to become *n/um kausi*, and those who mastered the force would dance themselves into a state of *kia* or trance; causing the *n/um* to heat painfully and rise along the spine, the shaman would collapse to the ground as his/her soul left the body and journeyed to the spirit world. Still in trance, the shaman might rub sweat containing spiritual energy on the patient or pull sickness out of the patient.

Moving to the shaman's own experience, Nathan Porath links the subjectivity of the Orang Sakai (Sumatra) shaman known as *kemantat* to the theories of Eliade and Bourguignon. The *kemantat* cures, Porath posits, "by willfully ceasing to be fully aware of the human physical dimension. Instead, he or she becomes aware of the spirit dimension," using that shift of mental focus to travel to and with the spirits (2013: 12). The Sakai people speak of this shamanic mindset as *tak soda' la'i* or "not to be aware anymore"; instead, the shaman enters the state of *semanget*, also linked to dreams and other altered consciousness. "Spirits can interact with humans through *semanget* because they are of the same substance—*Semanget*. Experientially spirits are the sense of other in the altered state of consciousness interacting with *semanget*, the sense of self, in those same states" (14). Of course, the shaman is the master of such modifications of awareness, but fascinatingly treatment of spirit affliction involves the sufferer too learning "to willfully shift awareness from the physical dimension to the *Semanget* one" (19).

As Dahl proposed earlier, the unique position of the shaman might consist not only of being able to shift consciousness or awareness but of being *permanently in a liminal, flux, or chaotic state*. Western societies tend to think of order as the norm and of chaos, flux, or fluidity as the (threatening) exception. In other societies like Bugkalot (also known as Ilongot, northern Philippines), reality is "contingent, fragmentary, perpetually assuming a coherence and stability that swiftly dissolves" (Mikkelsen 2016: 189), in which the shaman or *agoy'en* plays a crucial role. Flux or chaos (*gongot*) is a constant trait of the *agoy'en*, which gives him access to the spirits and to magical powers. Through their actions, including telling stories, the specialists "seek to momentarily establish an order of their own with chaos" (201), limiting the ability of the shape-shifting spirits (*be'tang*) to penetrate human bodies and minds.

Morten Axel Pedersen describes something similar among the Darhad of Mongolia. There, he reasons, shamanism is not a religion or belief system so much as a worldview or ontology based on *transition*. The power of the Darhad shaman is to adopt and move between perspectives—worldly and spiritual—that is, to inhabit "fluid and multiple" positions (2011: 67), to perform transformations. The shamanic ontology or state of being is "perpetual metamorphosis, malleability, and fluidity expressed in the unpredictable movements of wild animals and the inchoate trajectories of the shamanic spirits" (164). Indeed, Pedersen urges that we think of spirits less as beings and more as pure movement or transition—processes more than persons. The shaman, then, is the human who is most like the spirits, able to change and transform, a talent that is expedited by artifacts and paraphernalia, the key of which is a robe. In their shamanic garments, a sort of second body, they can see and be seen by the spirits; more, "the gown protects the shaman by 'absorbing' (*shingeh*) the 'souls' (*süns*) of both people and spirits into its many 'layers' (*salbagar*), so that they do not 'pierce' (*tsooloh*) her body too deeply" (163). As such, the shaman can capture and "personify as many relations as possible" (165), literally achieving *multiple personhood*. In short, their clothing, objects, and training provide Darhad shamans "with nonhuman perspectives, which, by facilitating a momentary transformation of their bodily 'affects, dispositions, and capacities,' enables [them] to cross otherwise unpassable ontological divides and return unharmed afterwards" (178).

Finally, if the Darhad shaman is a temporary multiple person, the Yanomami shaman or *shapori* is a permanent one. Consequentially, the term *shapori* is related to the word *shapono*, referring to a dwelling, both human and supernatural: humans reside in a *shapono*, and *hekura* spirits inhabit one too. In shamanic initiation, the shaman calls various specifically named *hekura* into himself, inviting them "into the shapori's body"; in so doing, "he also transforms into a hekura or, to say it better, assumes the identity as a living hekura-in-flesh" (Jokic 2015: 72–3). In his remarkable account, Zeljko Jokic says that a full-fledged shaman "is a unified multiplicity of all of his embodied spirits and also one of the spirits. He is a total but divided being: a fractal multiple 'one'" (74). He is a "living ancestor," an embodied spirit—or many embodied spirits. At the same time, his individual body is remade into a "cosmic body—a microcosm of other hekura and a matrix for the full manifestation of the Yanomami macrocosm and any of its constitutive components" (135). Like the Blackfoot shaman described by Dahl, he is a spirit, or many spirits, his singular consciousness made home to plural consciousnesses.

BOX 8.5 DAVID LEWIS-WILLIAMS: ROCK ART AND ENTOPTIC IMAGES

In a series of publications, such as *The Mind in the Cave: Consciousness and the Origins of Art* (2002), David Lewis-Williams has contended that prehistoric (Upper Paleolithic) rock art gives us a clue to the early stages of human consciousness and of shamanism if not religion or culture itself. He claimed that the shapes depicted in rock art resemble "entoptic" images that humans perceive when they are dizzy, intoxicated, otherwise mind-altered, or merely rub their eyes. Beginning in 1988 in an article co-authored by T. A. Dowson, he asserted that these artworks were signs of altered states of consciousness, representations of what ancient shamans saw. Other images, for instance among the !Kung or Ju/hoansi (also known as and called San by Lewis-Williams), portrayed thin elongated human figures, which supposedly convey the physical shamanic experience of being stretched. The work of Lewis-Williams is one example of the growing field of cognitive archaeology, which aims to examine the evolution and functioning of mental processes in prehistoric times (see Chapter 10).

Findings and results

By examining non-ordinary mental processes or states of consciousness, anthropologists have reached important understandings of the reciprocal influence of culture on mind and of mind on culture. It may be true that members of all societies have roughly the same capacity for altered states of consciousness, but how societies encourage, inculcate, interpret, value, and perform those states varies widely. Today we recognize that

- altered states of consciousness are not entirely spontaneous phenomena but may be induced and honed by society
- altered states of consciousness are not viewed as necessarily pathological or even undesirable
- dreams are an important source of knowledge in many societies; cultural knowledge enters dreams, and dream knowledge may enter culture
- ethnopsychological ideas about dreams tell us a great deal about local notions of self and personhood, especially that the "self" or "soul" is plural and may detach from the body
- trance or dissociation of the personality is extremely common across cultures, but its occurrence and forms are related to social variables, such as size and complexity of society
- across cultures, women seem to be particularly prone to trance and possession trance
- trance and trance possession may represent a loss of subjectivity and awareness—but they may also represent a gain in power and authority
- visions from spirits, and even possession by spirits, are not always to be avoided in societies but is sometimes eagerly sought
- ordinary people may be capable of altered states of consciousness and awareness, but the shaman is the specialist and master of such experiences
- the shaman often transforms bodily and psychologically into a different kind of person—or into a spirit or multiple spirits and selves.

Chapter 9

Mental illness

Key questions:
Do all cultures have a concept of "mental illness," and if so, do they have the same concept?

What is the anthropological perspective on medicine generally and on medical psychiatry in particular?

How is a society's ethnopsychology of mental illness related to other aspects of culture—especially religion and local concepts of body and self?

How is Western psychiatry a cultural system, and is there a distinct culture of psychiatry?

What does anthropology make of official categories and terminologies of mental illness, as in the *Diagnostic and Statistical Manual*?

What has anthropology learned through cross-cultural research on mental illness?

What can anthropology contribute to the understanding of mental health care institutions, such as hospitals, clinics, shelters, and prisons?

How does physical illness alter and threaten the patient's experience of self and personhood?

In his 1851 article "Diseases and Peculiarities of the Negro Race," American physician Samuel Cartwright recommended a new mental disorder for the American medical catalog. Drapetomania—derived from the roots *drapetes* for runaway slave and *mania* for frenzy or madness—designated the pathology of African slaves who desired to escape slavery. Based on a biblical premise of natural slavery and the duty of slaves to submit to their lot, the symptoms of drapetomania included sulkiness and dissatisfaction "without cause," for which Dr. Cartwright prescribed "whipping the devil out of them." Even many of those Africans who were not full-blown drapetomaniacs suffered from the uniquely African condition of dysaesthesia Aethiopica (literally, Ethiopian/African bad feeling), which presented as "rascality."

From its inception, anthropology has been intimately allied not only to psychology but to psychiatry in particular, from the pervasive influence of psychoanalysis (a theory of human mind and culture born in Freud's clinical practice), notions of "primitive mentality," and the general inferiority of non-Western minds to speculation about the insanity of shamans (see Chapter 8). A number of early (and recent) anthropologists were actually trained in medicine and/or in psychoanalysis or psychiatry, and anthropologists and other scholars have long been aware of so-called "cultural-bound syndromes," which are typically psychological in nature. Even Western biomedicine recognizes the culture-bound syndrome, sometimes also called folk illness, as a culture-specific pattern of abnormal behavior or ideation, which may have no exact equivalent in psychiatric classification. In *The Culture-Bound Syndrome: Folk Illnesses of Psychiatric and Anthropological Interest*, Ronald Simons and Charles Hughes (1985) listed two hundred such ailments, including *amok* (Malaysia), *windigo* (Native America), and Arctic hysteria and *wiitiko* psychosis. In contemporary China, *koro* is a pathological fear that the penis will shrink or retract into the body; a similar anxiety has been noted in West Africa. (See https://www.slideshare.net/UtkarshModi2/culture-bound-syndromes-54846096 for a slideshow of culture-bound conditions.)

The anthropological study of mental illness today stands at the confluence of psychological anthropology and medical anthropology, the latter defined by the Society for Medical Anthropology (2017) as the branch of anthropology investigating

> those factors which influence health and well being (broadly defined), the experience and distribution of illness, the prevention and treatment of sickness, healing processes, the social relations of therapy management, and the cultural importance and utilization of pluralistic medical systems.

In a textbook intended for health professionals, Cecil Helman defines medical anthropology as the study of

> how people in different cultures and social groups explain the causes of ill health, the types of treatments they believe in, and to whom they turn if they do get ill. It is also the study of how these beliefs and practices relate to biological, psychological, and social changes in the human organism, in both health and disease; ... [it is] the study of human suffering etc.
>
> (2007: 1)

That a textbook for health professionals would discuss medical anthropology highlights the fact that medical anthropology is an especially practical subdiscipline, not merely investigating cultural concepts of health, illness, and treatment but contributing to public policy and reform and to the quality of care at various sites, such as hospitals, outpatient clinics, shelters, and prisons (see the following). Currently, anthropological studies of mental illness may be found in specialized anthropology journals but also in medical journals like *Culture, Medicine, and Psychiatry*; *Transcultural Psychiatry*; and *The American Journal of Psychiatry*.

Note: in this chapter we will use "psychiatry" as an umbrella term for modern scientific understanding and treatment of mental disorders, without referring exclusively to the medical profession of psychiatry and without neglecting other allied professions, such as clinical psychology.

Mental illness as a cultural system

The first and greatest anthropological issue in considering mental illness is that both "mental" and "illness" are cultural concepts. Franziska Herbst no doubt describes many societies when she comments that Giri people of Papua New Guinea "know no such indigenous category as 'mental illness' that can be contrasted with other illnesses":

> The concept of "mental illness" that has its roots in Cartesian mind/body dualism does not exist in Giri culture. Giri understandings of the person (involving the component parts of the person and the relations between them) differ dramatically from the Cartesian model. Giri people do not separate the person into purely mental and physical components.
>
> (2016: 71)

As we have seen repeatedly in previous chapters, many societies do not possess a concept of "mental" or "mind" that is discrete from the individual person or from social relationships; further, particularly as the discussion of trance, possession, and shamanism illustrates, not all non-ordinary states of mind are judged as "illness."

Nor, in all cultures, is mental illness or aberrant behavior entirely "medicalized," that is, even if a person is regarded as troubled or sick, the treatment of such conditions may not be handed over to a "medical" institution or practitioner. In his 1924 *Medicine, Magic, and Religion*, W. H. R. Rivers, an early ethnologist, medical doctor, and psychologist (see Chapter 1), recognized medicine itself as a cultural phenomenon and as inseparably entangled with the cultural domains of magic and religion. In his 1926 *Psychology and Ethnology*, he understood medicine to be a social institution like all others, characterized by personhood beliefs, culturally informed practices, institutional forms, and divisions of labor that "cannot be ignored by the historian of medicine" (1999: 61).

We have already learned that Edward Sapir in 1938—in the pages of the journal *Psychiatry*—opined that anthropology and psychiatry were close cousins because both examined variations of thought and behavior within a society (see Chapter 2), further stressing that individual differences and exceptions could become sources of cultural regularities over time. In a prior article published in *The Journal of Abnormal and Social Psychology* titled "Cultural Anthropology and Psychiatry," he argued that the two fields "must, at some point, join hands in a highly significant way" because both shared a concern for "the adjustment processes of given individuals" in their respective societies (1932: 233). Sapir viewed "adjustment" as comprised of "two distinct and even conflicting types of process"—"those accommodations to the behavior requirements of the group" but also "the effort to retain and make felt in the opinions and attitudes of others" the unique and sometimes nonconforming ideas, feelings, and values of the individual (240). In the final analysis, both anthropology and psychiatry were the offspring of social psychology, and the key concept for both was *normality*, which is inescapably a cultural and even statistical notion (see Chapter 2 for Cora Du Bois on modal personality). Therefore, Sapir concluded that cultural anthropology does and should have "the healthiest of all skepticisms about the validity of the concept 'normal behavior,'" which he grasped to be "an exceedingly elastic thing"; anthropology is unique and valuable precisely "because it is constantly rediscovering the normal" (235).

Ruth Benedict also made the concept of normality the crux of her argument in her classic 1934 article "Anthropology and the Abnormal," published in the *Journal of General Psychology*. Her question was the central one: to what extent is a concept like "mental illness" an absolute—that is, the same ideations and behaviors are classified as mental illness around the world—and to what extent is it culturally determined? Sensibly equating mental illness with a certain kind of abnormality (and not all abnormality is mental illness, even in Western societies), she offered examples of shamanism, divination, trance, and catalepsy to argue that "those whom we regard as abnormals may function adequately in other cultures" (1934: 64)—and more than adequately as there are "cultures where an abnormality of our culture is the cornerstone of their social structure" (1934: 268), as with the role of the shaman. Indeed, within Western societies too, there are situations and social roles where what would otherwise be called abnormal is expected, welcomed, and required. In short, Benedict concluded that "normality is culturally defined" (72). And she carried her case further, associating normality with goodness and morality as judged in a society: "The concept of the normal is properly a variant of the concept of the good. *It is that which society has approved*" (73, emphasis added). Morality itself, she asserted, is little more than "a convenient term for socially approved habits. Mankind has always preferred to say, 'It is a morally good,' rather than 'It is habitual'…. [although] historically the two phrases are synonymous" (73). Consequently, there are few if any thoughts or behaviors that are abnormal or insane *in themselves* but only when assessed by some cultural standard of normality.

Western psychiatry as a cultural system

It follows—if abnormality, insanity, mental illness, or whatever we choose to call it is a cultural judgment relative to some standard of normality—that Western concepts and practices regarding mental illness are at least in part cultural. Sociology made this point before anthropology, and one of the first (though controversial) breakthroughs appeared in Talcott Parsons's mammoth and seminal 1951 book *The Social System*. He insisted that medicine be approached as "a 'mechanism' in the social system" and analyzed in terms of the social organization of its rules and roles. It is easy to see the positions of doctors, nurses, psychiatrists, and other professionals as roles, but Parsons demanded that we see the patient as playing a "sick role." Sociologically, he maintained that sickness—especially mental illness but also physical illness—could be understood as a sort of deviance, and the sick person could be understood as a sort of deviant. But this was, in his estimation, a socially ordered deviance, with an "institutionalized expectation system relative to the sick role," consisting of four elements:

a   "exemption from normal social responsibilities"—at the very least the sick person is excused from work or school, and at the extreme they are not legally culpable for their actions (e.g. the "insanity" defense)
b   dependency—the sick person cannot be expected "to get well by an act of decision or will" and "is in a condition that must be 'taken care of'"
c   undesirability—it is disagreeable to be ill, and the sick person has an "obligation to want to 'get well'"
d   help-seeking—sick persons should seek competent care (however that is culturally defined) and to cooperate in getting well, which may place them in a position of passivity relative to healthcare specialists.

(436–7)

The fact that Western medicine, including psychiatry, is culturally constructed implies that it has a social history, which is self-evident. In physical illness, germ theory is remarkably recent, and the very idea of mental illness—and certainly of mental illness as a *medical* issue—is new indeed. Michel Foucault persuasively illustrated this point in his first major publication: his 1961 *Histoire de la Folie* (literally, "history of madness" but translated into

English as *Madness and Civilization*). His analysis only commenced in the late Middle Ages and only dealt with Europe, but even within that limited scope, it is apparent that conceptions and practices regarding deviant behavior changed dramatically. Foucault noted that during the Renaissance, it was not uncommon to load "fools" onto ships and sail them along coasts and rivers (hence the term "ship of fools"). In other instances, those deemed "mad" were run out of town and left free to wander the countryside. Foucault noticed, though, that by the late 1400s, madmen and fools became a problem for European society, indeed, that "from the fifteenth century on, the face of madness has haunted the imagination of Western man" (1965: 15). His argument was that, at the moment in European history when reason was rising to prominence, the insane represented a violation of, a threat to, a very mockery of reason. Insanity was humanity's inner monster shown to itself; one of the most distasteful qualities of madness to early modern Europeans was its association with subhumanness and animality: "Animality has escaped domestication by human symbols and values; and it is animality that reveals the dark rage, the sterile madness that lies in man's heart" (21). It should come as no surprise that the alleged animality of "primitive people" was one of the most objectionable features of non-Western societies. Foucault proceeded to document shifts in attitudes and practices, beginning with "the great confinement" of the insane in institutions like the Hôpital Général in Paris in 1656—which we cannot call a mental hospital despite its name since, according to Foucault, it "had nothing to do with any medical concept. It was an instance of order" (40). The goal was to gather up and isolate madmen, offering them various mixes of religious training, work, and physical restraint. It was only in the mid-1700s that the medicalization of insanity arose, but this was a response to new fears—"a fear formulated in medical terms but animated, basically, by a moral myth" (202) that marked the fool with "an imaginary stigma of disease, which added its powers of terror" (205).

BOX 9.1 R. D. LAING AND THOMAS SZASZ: PSYCHIATRISTS AGAINST PSYCHIATRY

Social science analyses of the cultural construction and relativity of mental illness sometimes turned into brutal critiques of psychiatry from inside the discipline. Two prime examples are *The Politics of Experience* by R. D. Laing and the more combatively titled *The Myth of Mental Illness* by Thomas Szasz. Jumping off from the valid point that we cannot know another's experience, only their behavior, Laing condemned how society deems some experience "normal" while discounting and vilifying others. "What we call 'normal,'" he wrote, "is a product of repression, denial, splitting, projection, introjection, and other forms of destructive action on experience" (1967: 27). "Society highly values its normal man. It educates children to lose themselves and to become absurd, and thus to be normal" (28). Consequently, he urged us to take seriously the experience of supposed psychotics like schizophrenics. Szasz more scathingly called mental illness a concept that was "scientifically worthless and socially harmful" (1961: ix). He placed the psychiatry of his day in the same company "as alchemy and astrology," branding it a "pseudo science" (1). Psychiatry purports to be the study and treatment of mental illness, but "suppose, for a moment, that there is no such thing as mental illness and health" (2). Instead, rather like the later Foucault, Szasz sought to reinvent psychiatry not as the medical (pseudo)science of mental illness but as "the study of personal conduct" (7), which is shaped and evaluated by society.

Since the early modern period, Western thinking on mental illness has continued to evolve, from Freud's experiments with hypnosis to his "talking cure" and later to increasingly physiological and chemical approaches to conditions from depression to schizophrenia (let us not forget the era of electroshock therapy and lobotomy). Mental illness in its myriad forms has become what renowned medical anthropologist Arthur Kleinman called an "explanatory model" in medical systems. In a 1978 article titled "Concepts and a Model for the Comparison of Medical Systems as Cultural Systems" (published in *Social Science & Medicine*) and then his 1980 book *Patients and Healers in the Context of Culture: An Exploration of the Borderland between Anthropology, Medicine, and Psychiatry*, Kleinman proposed the term "explanatory model" to identify "the notions about an episode of sickness and its treatment that are employed by all those engaged in the clinical process" (1980: 105) and thus serve as "the main vehicle for the clinical construction of reality" (110). Such a model consists of the words, practices, roles, institutions, and instruments related to the five variables in the sickness episode—etiology or cause, time and mode of onset of symptoms, pathology, course of sickness, and treatment. Kleinman further asserted that there were three "sectors" or "social arenas" in any society's medical system that collectively shaped diagnosis and treatment—the popular, the folk, and the professional (1978: 86). The popular arena "comprises principally the family context of sickness and care, but also includes social network and community activities"; not only does the vast majority of medical care happen in this sector, in non-Western and Western societies alike, but "most decisions regarding when to seek aid in the other arenas, whom to consult, and whether to comply, along with most lay evaluations of the efficacy of treatment, are made in the popular domain" (86). The professional sector or arena "consists of professional scientific ('Western' or 'cosmopolitan') medicine and professionalized indigenous healing traditions (e.g. Chinese, Ayurvedic, Yunani, and chiropractic)" (87). Finally, the folk sector/arena "consists of non-professional healing specialists" (86), which is an incredibly broad and unstable category as any healing tradition may professionalize. Kleinman concluded that the three sectors/arenas "organize particular subsystems of socially legitimated beliefs, expectations, roles, relationships, transaction settings, and the like. These socially legitimated contexts of sickness and care, I shall refer to as separate clinical realities" (87), which may nevertheless overlap and interact (Figure 9.1).

Figure 9.1 Western psychology and psychotherapy is a culturally specific form of medical intervention.
Eight Arts Photography / Alamy Stock Photo.

BOX 9.2 CULTURE OF PSYCHIATRY

Some scholars, including psychiatrists themselves, have asserted that there is a "culture of psychiatry." In her introduction to the discipline, Linda Gask devoted an entire chapter to the subject of this culture, discussing "how psychiatry is both experienced from within (professionals and patients or mental health service users) and critically observed from outside" (2004: 36). Of course, in a sense, this is patently obvious: like every other human undertaking, psychiatry is socially organized, with schools and training institutions, workplaces (hospitals but also local clinics, residential homes, and prisons; see the following), professional organizations and publications, and a body of knowledge and standards of practice. American psychiatry even has its "bible": the *Diagnostic and Statistical Manual* (see Chapter 8 and the following). Arthur Kleinman has been an advocate of thinking in terms of psychiatry's culture, although as early as 1979, with his co-author T. C. Manschreck, he opined that psychiatry actually consisted of several disconnected subcultures. "Psychiatry has several partial identities," they posited, "reflecting its biologic, psychoanalytic, and social subspecialties. It has, however, no encompassing professional identity" (Manschreck and Kleinman 1979: 166). In order to have a truly unified culture, they recommended that psychiatry's branches needed a common language, a shared means of incorporating and assessing knowledge, a core set of values, and explicit disciplinary goals. Sadeq Rahimi, holding a joint appointment in the departments of anthropology and psychiatry at the University of Saskatchewan and writing in the journal *Anthropology & Medicine*, has recently been more sanguine about the notion of the culture of psychiatry. Citing both Gask and Manshreck and Kleinman, Rahimi takes the very modern anthropological attitude that "culture" is too strong a word, implying more unity and agency within the discipline than really exists. Based on fieldwork in a mental health facility in Boston, he concluded that psychiatry faces "an absence of direction and coherence, manifested in a sense of anxiety that at once permeates the field and emanates from social forces external to it" (2014: 316). In place of the "culture" of psychiatry, he suggests thinking

> about the *function* of psychiatry at a given time and place, about the *significance* of psychiatry in a given meaning system, the *objectives* towards which psychiatry is directed, and the *methods* through which psychiatry is practiced in each given time and place.
>
> (322, emphasis in the original)

Anthropology and the DSM

As mentioned earlier and in the previous chapter, the *Diagnostic and Statistical Manual* is a repository of psychiatric knowledge and a guide to diagnosis. Written by humans, it should shock no one that it has been examined as a cultural document and an exercise in cultural classification. The shifting entries and organization from edition to edition, and the addition or removal of specific disorders—famously, homosexuality was deleted from the list of mental disorders in 1973—testify to its social construction. At the same time, authors and users of the document have become increasingly aware of culture, as with the inclusion of more culturally sensitive analysis of trance and possession. Interestingly, the latest (fifth) edition drops the category of "culture-bound syndrome," but, according to Dominic Murphy, "the DSM-5 is still prone to see Western psychology as the human norm" (2015: 97); in fact, he poignantly comments that "Westerners in fact may be the ones with the culture-bound syndromes," like depression (108).

From inside the effort to make the DSM and psychiatry more culturally informed, Neil Krishan Aggarwal, also one of the authors of *DSM-5 Handbook on the Cultural Formulation Interview*, sheds light on the protocol for learning about the patient's culture. First acknowledging that psychiatric classification "is a cultural system that distinguishes normal from abnormal behaviors in society" and "reflects the healing priorities, social values, and professional ideologies of a historical moment" (2013: 393), he describes the creation of a task force charged with "adding cultural and international experts to DSM-5 work and study groups, and convening a Gender and Cross-Cultural Study Group" (394). As Kenneth Sakauye reports, the introduction of the fifth edition makes the firm statement that mental disorders "are defined in relation to cultural, social, and familial norms and values. Culture provides interpretive frameworks that shape the experience and expression of the symptoms, signs, and behaviors that are criteria for diagnosis" (2015: 16).

The previous edition featured the Outline for Cultural Formulation (OCF); intended "to correct the physician's disproportionate focus on disease management rather than the patient's lived experience of illness" (shades of R. D. Laing), the procedure

> draws extensively from anthropological theories and divides the clinical encounter into four main domains: (1) cultural identity of the individual, (2) cultural explanations of illness, (3) cultural levels of psychosocial support and functioning, and (4) cultural elements of the patient-physician relationship. A fifth domain summarizes pertinent information influencing diagnosis and treatment.
>
> (Aggarwal 2014: 395)

Doctors were even encouraged to "conduct mini-ethnographies with patients through the OCF just as anthropologists conduct ethnographies with informants" (395).

For the DSM-5, the OCF was reworked into a more structured Cultural Formulation Interview (CFI), which Aggarwal, in conjunction with Ravi De Silva and Roberto Lewis-Fernández, describes as an "evidence-based tool … composed of a series of questionnaires that assist clinicians in making person-centered cultural assessments to inform diagnosis and treatment planning" (De Silva, Aggarwal, and Lewis-Fernández 2015). The CFI protocol consists of four domains of inquiry—cultural definitions of the problem (seeking "to incorporate the patient's own view and language of his illness experience"); cultural perceptions of cause, context, and support (which they liken to a Kleinman's explanatory model); cultural factors that affect coping and past help-seeking; and cultural factors that affect current help-seeking. Ideally, the CFI "facilitates the evocation of the patient's own narrative of illness."

BOX 9.3 ROLAND LITTLEWOOD: CULTURE AND MENTAL ILLNESS

Through more than three decades and numerous publications, Roland Littlewood has emphasized the relationship between culture and mental illness, bringing his expertise to bear on the DSM. Trained as a psychiatrist and an anthropologist, his first book, *Aliens and Alienists: Ethnic Minorities and Psychiatry*, co-authored with Maurice Lipsedge and released in 1982, referred to his work among immigrants (especially from the West Indies) in the United Kingdom. He discovered an extraordinarily high incidence of schizophrenia among this population, concluding that "racism goes a long way to explaining everyday distress and psychological difficulties" for such migrants; indeed, subsequently, he found that such syndromes of alienation occur elsewhere as well—"in Ireland, among Croatians on the Dalmatian Coast, among French-Canadians, among Native Americans, among Australian Aborigines, and among the Maori [of New Zealand]" (Ramsay 1999: 735). In 1992, he reported on his own experience with the drafting of the fourth edition of the DSM, asking the fundamental question "Is the Classification Internationally Valid?" The third edition, he explained, included some recognition of the limits of its applicability related to gender and ethnicity, urging caution when "evaluating a person from an ethnic or cultural group different from the clinician's" unless the use is "culturally valid," but he warned that it "was not clear what this meant, nor how any translation should 'provide equivalent meanings, not necessarily dictionary equivalence'" (1992: 257). As it did in the preparation of the fifth edition seen earlier, the American Psychiatric Association commissioned a task force and called a conference including "over 50 cultural psychiatrists and anthropologists who were already involved in the debate," although only two of those specialists came from outside North America (258). A number of concerns and changes were shared, for instance, in the areas of paraphilia (sexual attraction to unusual objects or persons) and culture-bound disorders. Paraphilias were considered at least potentially "as cultural, locally reinforced, possibilities" rather than illnesses or perversions; firmer positions were taken on culturally specific complaints, for instance, by Japanese psychiatrists on *laijin kyofushu* or "interpersonal phobia," a surprisingly common problem in Japan (260). Acknowledging the implications of such revisions for the mental health sector in non-Western societies, Littlewood concluded that the

> extent to which the anthropologists can back up their perspective with quantitative data remains to be seen—as does the readiness of the American Psychiatric Association either to down play the cross-cultural value of their manual or to radically transform it into a valid international instrument.
>
> (260)

Beyond the specifics of DSM-5 procedures, there is a growing appreciation in psychiatry—as in other human-service professions, such as social work, nursing, policing and criminal justice, and education—of *cultural competence*. In a document on "Cultural Competence in Mental Health" drafted by the University of Pennsylvania Collaborative on Community Integration, cultural competence is defined as

> the ability to relate effectively to individuals from various groups and backgrounds.... Within the behavioral health system (which addresses both mental illnesses and substance abuse), cultural competence must be a guiding principle, so that services are culturally sensitive and provide culturally appropriate prevention, outreach, assessment and intervention.

The April 2012 issue of *Transcultural Psychiatry* was dedicated to the theme of "rethinking cultural competence," and to promote such skills the American Psychiatric Association offers training modules and best-practices guidelines for working with diverse populations, from Native Americans and Native Hawaiians to African Americans, Latino/as, LGBTQ, and women. (Notice that white men remain the unmarked category, against which all others are considered "diverse populations.") The description of the course called "The Practicality of Cultural Psychiatry: Bridging the Gap Between Theory and Practice" states that culture

> affects every aspect of clinical care, for both patients and clinicians. As patients, culture impacts whether we identify our condition as mental illness, the care we seek, the symptoms we experience and the present to clinicians, and our treatment expectations. As clinicians, our own personal cultures and the culture of biomedicine influence our illness classifications, what we attend to most in patients' experiences, our communication styles, the priorities and procedures that structures our work settings, and our moral stance toward care.
> (https://www.psychiatry.org/psychiatrists/cultural-competency/curriculum)

Anthropologists could not say it better ourselves.

Much of the testing and adjusting of psychiatric categories and practices has aimed at minority groups and immigrants in Western societies, like Littlewood's work, but some researchers have conducted field studies of psychopathological concepts in other cultures. Marjolein van Dujil, Etzel Cardeña, and Joop de Jong, for instance, explicitly checked the applicability of DSM (fourth edition) categories of dissociative disorders in Uganda, where they found "only partial support for the validity of the DSM-IV classification" (2005: 219). They uncovered a fairly rich indigenous vocabulary for altered mental states, like *Okukangarana* for "having been shocked by a situation in such a way that later on the person cannot remember the situation," *Eibugane* or "being influenced by unidentified forces that cause unusual behavior," and *Okusharara* or "feeling as if there is no blood in specific parts of the body," as well as possession trance, speaking in tongues, and making sounds and movements like a chicken, monkey, or goat (227). Based on their observations, they concluded that it "cannot be assumed that the DSM-IV nosology [disease classification] is translatable wholesale to other cultures unless previous research shows its validity and reliability in that particular context" (237).

BOX 9.4 LÉVI-STRAUSS: COMPARING THE SHAMAN AND THE PSYCHOANALYST

More than a few observers have noticed the similarities between the psychotherapeutic encounter and anthropological fieldwork. In both cases, the professional enters the mental and social world of the Other, seeking to understand unfamiliar meanings and motivations. Both must build relationships by becoming a part of someone else's lived experience. In a classic essay included in his *Structural Anthropology* (see Chapter 4), Claude Lévi-Strauss went further, comparing the work of the psycho-analyst with that of the shaman. His case centered on a curing ritual among the Cuna (sometimes spelled Kuna) people of Panama, intended to relieve a troubled childbirth, which would appear to be a perfectly physical problem. The ritual specialist known as *nele*, by interacting with spirits, could aid the woman, who was believed to suffer from a spiritual rather than medical ailment—the loss of one of her spiritual components, which he retrieved from an offending spirit. As Lévi-Strauss stated, the shaman's cur-ing song "constitutes a purely psychological treatment, for the shaman does not touch the body of the sick woman and administers no remedy"; yet the ritual or symbolic action *worked*, because it functioned as "a psychological *manipulation* of the sick or-gan" (1963: 191–2). The pivotal observation of Lévi-Strauss was that the shaman by "calling upon myth" reintegrates the woman, also providing her "with a *language*, by means of which unexpressed and otherwise inexpressible, psychic states can be imme-diately expressed" (197). Here was where he located the parallel between shamanism and psychoanalysis.

> In both cases the purpose is to bring to a conscious level conflicts and resist-ances which have remained unconscious, owing either to their repression by other psychological forces or—in the case of childbirth—to their own specific nature, which is not psychic but organic or even simply mechanical. In both cases also, the conflicts and resistances are resolved, not because of the knowledge, real or alleged, which the sick woman progressively acquires of them, but because this knowledge makes possible a specific experience, in the course of which conflicts materialize in an order and on a level permitting their free development and lead-ing to their resolution.
>
> (198)

It is not surprising that Roland Littlewood (1998) characterized many such cross-cultural episodes of healing, both on the part of the patient and the healer, as "ritual theater." The key difference, Lévi-Strauss hypothesized, is the source of the efficacy of this healing performance. In psychoanalysis, "the patient constructs an individual myth with elements drawn from his past"; in shamanic cure, "the patient receives from the outside a social myth which does not correspond to a former personal state" (199). Either way, he insisted, sufferers are healed by the power of stories: in psychoanalysis "the healer performs the actions and the pa-tient produces his myth; in the shamanistic cure the healer supplies the myth and the patient performs the actions" (201). This conclusion supported Lévi-Strauss's general contention that the mind, especially the unconscious, operated on the principle of myths and symbols, and therefore that the content of healing stories and experiences was less important than their form; if Freud was correct that neu-rotics are plagued by painful memories (suffer from reminiscences, he said), then new healthy memories can be constructed from individual biography or collective mythology. Lévi-Strauss added that "any myth represents a quest for the remem-brance of things past" (204), and recall from the previous chapter how over his lifetime the Dunne-za dreamer and vision quester became increasingly "mythical" while myths became more personal.

Mental health and illness in cross-cultural perspective

Anthropologists have ventured out of the clinic and the mental hospital to investigate how mental health and illness are construed in other cultures. And the anthropological search for the culture of mental health and illness, as we will see later, has inevitably brought researchers back to the clinic and hospital to consider how psychiatric categories are applied and how psychiatric care is organized and practiced in institutional settings.

As we have stressed elsewhere, the crux of the issue is that fact that most if not all societies have their ethnopsychology, which includes not only understandings and expressions of emotions, dreams, and other altered states of consciousness but also local conceptions of mind, body, and spirit (or we might say mind-body-spirit when these dimensions are not entirely differentiated) and of the causes, symptoms, and treatments of mental illness—insofar as, which we must always be warned, "mental illness" is a relevant label at all.

In the 1960s, Robert Edgerton contrasted psychosis in four African societies, finding differences in notions of cause, presentation, and prognosis. Among the Sebei, "madness" presented as public nakedness, "shouting and screaming, talking nonsense, wandering, eating dirt and collecting trash"; violence was also associated with insanity (1966: 413). The Kamba emphasized assault and murder, while the Hehe stressed fear and "retreat from people to a solitary life in the bush" (413). Interestingly, no group mentioned hallucinations, the hallmark of psychosis in the West. The Kamba and the Hehe believed that madness could be cured, but the Sebei and Pokot doubted it. The Sebei and Pokot had no indigenous explanation for insanity, but the Kamba and Hehe attributed it to magic, witchcraft, or ancestor spirits. Kamba and Hehe treatment combined magical rituals with native drugs, but the Sebei lacked a specialist to handle mental illnesses, and Pokot had little confidence in their medical experts or interventions.

Remaining in Africa, two recent papers have studied classes of mental illness in Uganda. Elialilia Okello and Solvig Ekblad considered indigenous ideas about depression, which Baganda people attributed to thoughts more than to emotions, rendering depression an "illness of thoughts" (2006: 287). Further, as we have become accustomed to seeing, the Baganda did not detach mental phenomena from the body or from the spiritual realm: "Depression is seen as an illness of thoughts ... and, since it is believed that both the heart and the brain think, depression is referred to those bodily regions" (290–1). Analyzing several cases of depression, they found multiple causal factors, including (what we would call) psychological ones but which have immanently social aspects, like "thinking too much about problems such as bereavement, illness of a close relative, excessive reading" as well as "relationship problems, sexual problems, and sexual abuse"; socioeconomic ones, including "loss of income, unemployment, lack of money for school fees, lack of basic necessities for one's children, and so on"; spiritual ones originating from witchcraft of angry spirits; and biological ones stemming from brain damage, chronic illness like HIV-AIDS and cancer, plus substance abuse (298–300). Help-seeking also followed a predictable pattern:

> the afflicted person is expected to start by seeking lay help from both significant relatives and religious leaders. If the illness fails to respond to the lay help then one consults a traditional healer or modern doctor depending on one's suspicions about the causes of

the illness. In some cases help from both modern and traditional medicine was sought simultaneously.

(308)

Traditional healers were especially consulted if the illness was chronic, if the condition was believed to be a traditional *byekika* or "clan illness," and if alternate and modern forms of care were not locally available.

Joanna Teuton, Richard Bentall, and Chris Dowrick turned their attention to Ugandan psychosis, reporting diverse opinions within one society. They distinguished between indigenous healers "who draw on indigenous spiritual paradigms and practices" and religious healers "whose practice is based on Christianity and Islam" (2007: 85). Both types of specialists had terms for insanity, such as "*eddalu* (madness), *akazole* and *kalogojo* (milder forms of madness) and *kutabuka mutwe* (disorganized head)"; significantly, religious healers also used scientific psychiatry labels like depression, neurosis, psychosis, and phobia (86). They disagreed, though, on the etiology of psychological illnesses: indigenous healers tended to attribute mental disorder to "communication from the family spirits" and to "disharmony in the spiritual world" caused by failure to perform expected rituals, while Christian and Islamic healers "conceptualized madness as a manifestation of evil, or as a form of punishment" (87). For the former, mental illness was sometimes seen as possession and thus the spirit's behavior rather than the patient's; furthermore, "madness is seen as a collective rather than an individual problem," as madness might strike a member of the family other than the one who neglected her ritual obligations (91). For the latter, evil spirits and minions of Satan rather than ancestor spirits were often the culprits, although the process was much the same. Curing accordingly entailed a battle between good and evil, with the power of God invoked to combat the sinister influence.

Finally, for present purposes, in a recent volume on mental illness and psychiatry in Africa, Ursula Read, Victor Doku, and Ama De-Graft Aikins analyze schizophrenia in West Africa through the lens of contemporary culture and (post)colonialism. Naturally, the modern institution of the insane asylum or mental hospital was a product of colonialism, with the first such hospital, the Kissy Lunatic Asylum, opened in British West Africa in Sierra Leone in 1844 (2015: 76). Characteristically, the institution housed not only the mentally ill but "various 'undifferentiated dependents'—paupers, beggars, criminals, the physically disabled, and the mentally retarded" (76)—who apparently were all deemed lunatics. It was only a century later that such places "began to take on more of a medical and scientific role" (76). After independence and in the later twentieth century, some experts reason that social changes wrought by industrialization and Westernization, "with the concomitant breakdown of traditional tribal life, might present particular stresses for Africans, possibly leading to a steep increase in cases of mental illness—in particular, schizophrenia and other psychoses" (79). Interestingly, they argue that "despite the best efforts of psychiatrists to identify schizophrenia among West African patients, there remained a significant number of cases—perhaps the majority—that failed to conform to the typical schizophrenic syndrome" (82). This leads them to determine that local folks conceive of mental illness in very different terms: indeed, "the concept of schizophrenia remains largely unknown among the general population in West African countries" (96), who still maintain traditional and at least partly spiritual understandings of behavioral disorder.

BOX 9.5 PSYCHOLOGICAL TOLL OF VIOLENCE, WAR, AND TRAUMA

Speaking of the pressures of modernity, numerous anthropologists and other mental health researchers have concentrated on the toll that violence and trauma take on people around the world, including but hardly limited to Africa. A leader in such work is Devon Hinton, who has published extensively on trauma and panic among refugees from war and imprisonment. In one such study, he and his colleagues calculated that fifty percent of Vietnamese refugees seeking assistance at psychiatric clinics suffered from panic disorder and further mentioned that half of all American veterans "with a severe trauma history" suffer from panic (Hinton et al. 2001: 337). However, Vietnamese (and also Cambodian) panic manifested differently than American. Because of an ethnopsychology and overall ethnomedicine that focused on internal "wind," Southeast Asians were more likely to complain of dizziness and to believe that chills were a harbinger of severe or fatal symptoms. Meanwhile, Priscilla Schulz, Christian Huber, and Patricia Resick estimated that between one-quarter and three-quarters of Bosnian refugees from the 1990s Yugoslavian conflict experienced psychological disorders, which various scholars have called "extreme traumatization," "sequential traumatization," or "cultural bereavement" (2006: 310). (See also Chapter 7 on the anthropology of fear.) Few places have witnessed the violence of the small West African country of Liberia. Several hundred thousand people died in Liberia's two civil wars between 1989 and 2003, leaving the survivors scarred physically and psychologically. Sharon Abramowitz tells that a post-conflict report on Liberian mental health found that forty percent of the population suffered from depression, eleven percent from suicidal thoughts, and seven percent from substance abuse (with even higher numbers among ex-combatants). Concerned not only about the damage to its citizens but about slipping back into war, the country and the world mounted a mental health intervention to aid the "traumatized nation" (Abramowitz 2014: 65), including not only individual trauma but "collective trauma" or "the disarticulation of the subjective, embodied person from the collective norms, social mores, and moral conduct that constitutes social order" (66). Some of the signs of collective trauma were fighting in the streets, sexual violence, and a general sense of dread and foreboding. Various international organizations, such as Save the Children, the Center for Victims of Torture, the Lutheran World Federation/World Service, and *Médecins du Monde* (Doctors of the World), arrived with the task of "implementing trauma healing and psychosocial interventions, and through them, instilling post-conflict *peace subjectivities*" (6, emphasis in the original). In other words, the goal was not so much curing individual mental illness as managing the society and preventing a relapse into war; in fact, some organizations actually instructed their workers "to turn away anyone with a serious mental illness" (45). The patchwork of nongovernmental organizations and individual medical professionals converted the country into what Abramowitz dubs an "interventionscape," where "flows of resources, personnel, bureaucratic protocols, administrative practices, financial mechanisms, and ethical guidelines shape the space of mental health, trauma-healing, and psychosocial intervention in the unique Liberian post-conflict landscape" (36). In the process, the Liberian people "were transformed into beneficiaries of a massive, uncoordinated, and decentralized project of humanitarian social engineering" (25)—and not only beneficiaries since many Liberians were themselves trained as mental-health providers and as trainers of other providers, recruiting the whole society to do therapy on itself. "Trauma" became part of everyday speech, and barely trained workers swept through the country as what Abramowitz calls "a vast, informal constabulary of care" (175), offering questionable advice, blending modern medicine with folk medicine and medicine with morality.

A good deal of research has also been done in Latin America. In a paper from 1964, William Holland and Roland Tharp presented data on psychological ideas and practices among the Tzotzil of highland Chiapas (Mexico). As is so common, the Tzotzil people held that illness—mental and physical alike—was due to the disconnection of one's spirit from one's body that occurred during dreams (see Chapter 8). Not entirely differentiating bodily, mental, and spiritual illness, like Lévi-Strauss's Cuna, Holland and Tharp also echoed Lévi-Strauss in saying that in many ways Tzotzil ritual cures were "analogous to modern psychotherapeutic practices":

> The *diagnostic* techniques utilize the following psychiatric mechanisms: (1) the patient enjoys an emotional catharsis even though somewhat superficial; (2) the patient relates to the curer whom he respects and in whose knowledge he has confidence; (3) the curer provides the sufferer with reassurance.
>
> The *ceremonial* phase of Tzotzil curing has much in common with modern group and family psychotherapy. (1) It breaks the patient's preoccupation with his complaints as his attention is fixed on goals outside of himself. (2) Reassurance is given the patient by his kinsmen who gather around him and assist in the ceremony. (3) The patient becomes the center of group attention. (4) The group reasserts the importance of his continued participation. (5) A pattern is offered for the re-establishment of social contacts.
>
> (1964: 49–50, emphasis in the original)

In a word, "Tzotzil psychotherapy attempts to induce changes in the sufferer's emotional state, attitudes, and social behavior" (51).

Brazilian Spiritism has attracted its share of attention in regard to mental illness, obviously accentuating the role of spirits. Alexander Moreira-Almeida and Francisco Lotufo Neto informed us that the Spiritist

> model for mental disorders includes the negative influences of discarnated spirits (termed "obsession") or trauma experienced in previous lives. In addition to conventional medical and psychological therapeutics, spiritist séances for disobsession are recommended, as well as "passes," prayers, and efforts to live according to ethical principles.
>
> (2005: 570)

The founder of Spiritism, known as Allan Kardec, taught that there were three levels of spirit power over victims, ranging from "simple obsession" to "fascination" to full-blown "subjugation or possession" in which the person's will was overwhelmed by the spirit. Not surprisingly, when Spiritism first appeared in the late nineteenth century, it was accused of being a *cause* of madness, but it has since become a popular *treatment* for mental illness, with a professional Brazilian Association of Spiritist Psychologists and almost fifty Spiritist hospitals founded between the 1930s and the 1970s (572).

Stanley Krippner examined Spiritism specifically in terms of multiple personality disorder (MPD). Resisting the temptation to dub all trance, possession, and shamanistic experiences as MDP, Krippner recognized both good and bad or positive and negative personality dissociations and multiplications, from the local society's point of view. Psychiatric MPD, he maintained, "most closely resembles the spiritist description of 'involuntary possession' used to describe those unfortunate individuals whose aberrant behavior is said to be due to long-term habitation and control by malevolent or immature spirits" (1987: 274). Even so, he contended that spiritist healers—who might be "a local medium, a hospital psychiatrist, or a clinical psychologist"—had never heard of MPD; curiously, though, some contemporary followers of Kardec had absorbed the medical category into their beliefs and practices, adapting the two curing traditions to each other. The key point, as our discussion of altered states of consciousness in the last chapter illustrated, is that possessing (or being possessed by) more than one personality was not always a bad thing. An intruding spirit could be domesticated, even turned into a therapist for other victims, and integrated as one part or splinter of the individual's complex and plural personality. Krippner rightly concluded "that the human being is extremely malleable. People can create personalities as required to defend themselves against trauma, to conform to cultural pressures, or to meet the expectations of a psychotherapist, medium, or exorcist" (293).

India has received more than its share of attention by scholars of mental illness, perhaps because it has its own rich traditions of diagnosis and treatment. In some general comments, Vinay Kumar Srivastava first noted the tremendous cultural diversity of the subcontinent but explained that Indian society tends to think that mental disorders are temporary and thus fix themselves, making mental illness less urgent than physical disease. As for theorizing mental illness, one understanding again is that "malignant and nefarious supernatural entities" bring it on; another view is that "constitutionally weak persons are more vulnerable to mental illness," which includes women (2002: 531). Childlessness is a particular trigger for women, as are "divorce, alcoholic husband, domestic unhappiness, protracted illness, and stresses at the place of work" (531). Psychological problems can further be attributed to rapid social change (urbanization and industrialization) or to "a sudden shock—a failure in examination, loss in business, betrayal in love, death of a loved one," and so forth (531). Preventive measures against mental disorders include keeping negative emotions like anger and jealousy at bay, and for this purpose, children are socialized to achieve "mental equilibrium and poise" (532). It is also important to keep the mind "cool." To deal with manifest emotional or behavioral problems, culture features a wide variety of healing rituals and festivals and of healing specialists, such as "the herbalist, bonesetter, midwife, masseur, ethnosurgeon, and shaman and faith healer" (534). Finally, Srivastava mentioned the central medical anthropological concept of "therapy management group" or the team of specialists, kin, and other people who assemble around the patient to provide support and care.

Vieda Skultans illustrated many of these issues in an article about a Mahanubhav healing temple in Maharashtra. The Abbasai temple was one of three Mahanubhav centers in the town of Phaltan, focusing on mental illness. Here families brought disturbed individuals (or disturbed individuals occasionally brought themselves) for aid; the temple provided living spaces for kin who remained on site for an average of three or four months, tending to their troubled relatives. Significantly, women were both frequent patients and frequent members of impromptu therapy management groups, commonly traveling to look after a husband or son. In many cases, as has become more than familiar by now, women retreated to the temple "because of some major upheaval or conflict in family relationships"; they were almost universally "divorced, widowed, or childless" and arrived "feeling depressed and tired" (1987: 664). Piquantly, Skultans surmised that such women "come to the temple, not so much because their symptoms are intolerable, as because their social situation is intolerable" (664). In other instances, families took misbehaving relatives to the location, dubbing them "mad" although there was a noticeable absence of clarity about what madness was, beyond standard symptoms like "dirtiness, incoherent and inappropriate talk, fighting without reason, inability to work or execute orders, aloofness and having no structure to one's daily activities" (667). The most striking aspect of life in the temple was that the mentally ill individuals were largely passive and uninvolved; it was instead the kinfolk, particularly the women, who "throw themselves into a round of frenzied, ritual activity, [while] the patients remain detached and seemingly disinterested spectators" (667). This frenzied activity typically featured women going into trance, which they welcomed and intentionally pursued as a means of redirecting alleged spiritual attacks away from their male kin and onto themselves. In other words, "women cultivate trance as a sacrificial device to ensure the health and well-being of the rest of the family" (661). Skultans saw this practice as an indicator of the social burden that women bore for the health of their families and for the related notion that illness, mental or otherwise, was a collective and not merely an individual affliction.

Within the Hindu community of Réunion Island, a French territory east of Madagascar, madness "is considered to be the result of a rupture of genealogy through denial of the founder, and of psychic-somatic unity, which leads the afflicted person to develop a fantasy of immortality" (Govindama 2006: 488). This ethnopsychology allowed Yolande Govindama to explore Ayurvedic medicine, a "science of longevity," which theorizes "a permanent interaction" between mind and body based on notions of bodily humors, such as wind, bile, and phlegm (489). Ayurveda then

> recognizes three other types of diseases: (1) those in which mental symptoms which disturb the social adaptation of the subject predominate, including psychotic problems, obsessive, and impulsive neuroses; (2) illnesses linked to psychic conflicts but which are expressed through physical symbols (functional disorders) like epilepsy, hysteria (with conversion), diarrhea provoked by anxiety, insomnia, fever caused by pain and sexual desire; and (3) those illnesses which result from physical problems but are predominately expressed as mental disorders, or those linked to intoxication by alcohol or drugs.
>
> (490)

Further, imbalances in the three humors can be caused by "desire" (*kama*) or "revulsion" (*dvesha*), which spawn destructive emotions like "envy, jealousy, anger, violence, and repugnance, which show themselves by the avoidance of an object [and] are the cause of physical or mental suffering" (490). Govindama went on to describe two curing practices, both aimed at addressing the mind via the body—a firewalking ritual and piercing ritual.

Finally, as in many parts of the world, ethnographers have documented "medical pluralism" in India and surrounding countries. Marie Caroline Saglio-Yatzimirsky and Brigitte Sébastia present the case of a temple in the south Indian town of Gunaseelam that hosts a clinic associated with Sowmanasya Mental Hospital, whose psychiatrists visit several times a week to dispense counseling and pharmaceuticals. Patients, as the article's title

("Mixing Tīrttam and Tablets: A Healing Proposal for Mentally Ill Patients in Gunaseelam [South India]") indicates, are given both pills and *tīrttam* or "a ritual during which the priest energetically sprinkles holy water on the devotees' faces" (2015: 130). Although both kinds of intervention are offered, "the psychiatric and religious conceptions of care remain mutually exclusive: psychiatrists trust only antipsychotic drugs, whereas priests credit the *tīrttam* and god's instruments of healing with more power" (133). In other cases, indigenous and Western biomedical systems have merged, as in the case of "Ayurvedic psychiatry." As Claudia Lang and Eva Jansen chronicle, for purposes of treating the high incidence of depression in the Indian state of Kerala, Ayurvedic doctors have been actively rethinking their notions of *unmāda* (mental disorder) in light of modern medicine. The result is a translation of traditional *bhūt vidyā* (Ayurvedic psychology) into scientific terms. For example, the supernatural forces or persons known as *bhūta* "were interpreted as bacteria, viruses, and fungi, and *bhūt vidyā* was categorized as bacteriology in some textbooks and by some clinicians" (2013: 29). Likewise, other Ayurvedic terms have been correlated with psychiatric language, such as *kapha unmāda* with severe depression and *prēta graha* with catatonic depression.

> The overall aim of contemporary Ayurvedic psychiatry is to purify Ayurvedic psychiatry from its nonscientific and superstitious connotations and institutionalize it as a scientific approach to psychiatric disorders. *Bhūt vidyā* and dosa-based concepts of mental illness are therefore revitalized and translated by adopting biopsychiatric categories, giving them a claim to modernity and contemporaneity.
>
> (34)

Ethnography in institutional sites of mental health care delivery

As a final topic for the chapter, anthropologists (like sociologists) have applied their field methods to formal institutional settings where mental health services are delivered, to discover how those institutions function, what sorts of relationships obtain between professionals and patients, and how health care policies and ideals are actually implemented. The most obvious site for the psychiatric encounter is the mental hospital or clinic. Elizabeth Davis, for instance, interrogates therapy in Thrace, Greece in the context—not unique to Greece—of reforms "to shift psychiatric treatment from custodial hospitals to outpatient clinics, challenging patients to help care for themselves" (2012: 4). Beyond a "grave uncertainty in the practice of Greek psychiatry" consistent with the assessment of Manschreck and Kleinman and of Rahimi, Davis bemoans "a marked absence in local clinical settings of cultural beliefs and practices that might make illness and healing intelligible" to Thracian patients receiving modern psychiatric services; instead, she asserts that culture "often appeared to patients and therapists alike as a *cause* of mental pathologies and treatment failures" (4). Highlighting issues of truth, culture, and freedom—patients attempting to deceive doctors, the culture of rural minority patients interpreted by therapists as a source of pathology, and liberalization of mental health care creating and imposing freedoms and responsibilities for patients—she concludes that reformed psychiatry "appears as a universalizable technology of the state" based on the more general neoliberal assumptions of "rational individualism" and market consumerism (30). Further, she considers the diagnostic process to be "a truth game, not only on the level of institutionally legitimized power indicated in Foucault's definition, but also at the level of confrontation between parties to the diagnostic encounter—a confrontation between discrepant strategies of truth" (55)—a game that is shot through with moral judgments. In a word, the psychiatric hospital or clinic "is a site for the production and application of scientific knowledge; its field of power and desire is organized by this knowledge" which translates (she says "disguises") cultural and moral questions as scientific and medical ones.

According to Whitney Duncan, a large segment of the patients in mental institutions in Oaxaca, Mexico suffer from their own kind of cultural syndrome, labeled by some therapists as "transcultural psychosis" (2014: 30). Classified as one form of "transnational disorder" that is "structurally produced and personally experienced within the borders of more than one country" (24), the proximate cause of such mental and emotional distress is migration across the U.S./Mexico border, subjecting people to conditions of "solitude, discrimination, unremitting anxiety and stress, and drug and alcohol use in the United States" (28). Living in constant isolation from family and in poverty and fear of arrest and deportation (variables of Littlewood's "alienation," mentioned earlier), migrants develop depression, stress disorder, and obsessive-compulsive disorder.

Returning to India, Saiba Varma discusses how the seemingly benign Global Mental Health movement altered practices and spaces in that country's mental health system. As in Greece, the United States, and elsewhere, the noble goals of reform are "to make mental health care more scientific, 'evidence-based,' and accessible—that is, more modern" (2016: 786), which includes or is premised on the shift away from mental hospitals toward "community-based supported homes, general hospitals, or small mental health specialist centers" (784), changing mental asylums into sites for research and training (Figure 9.2). In the process of modifying and modernizing mental health facilities, though, a (hopefully unintentional) disconnect resulted: while money was invested in "improving the look and prestige" of the newly-renamed Institute for Mental Health and Neurosciences in Kashmir, for example, "funds were not directed towards improving patient care in any substantive way."

> The closed wards where long-term patients resided did not undergo any upgrades, and it was not clear how they would gain from these developments. While the hospital's "outsides" continued to change—the faculty and library block were the most visible spaces—the "insides," the closed wards and those who inhabited them, were increasingly out of view and neglected. While the rationale for modernization included a concern for human rights abuses within institutions, the emphasis on generating manpower overrode these concerns, with long-term patients seeing very little to no qualitative changes in their lives. Rather, the shift of psychiatry from treatment to research-based science depended on separating from, or leaving behind, the long-term, chronically ill.
>
> (791)

In fact, the presence of chronically insane patients also seemed to be an embarrassment to the psychiatric profession, and "the senior psychiatrists avoided visiting the closed wards altogether, letting the junior residents make occasional visits only when there was a medical emergency" (792).

As the Greek and Indian cases underscore, much of the contemporary philosophy of mental health care encourages patients to leave the hospital and assume responsibility for their daily lives, if not for their ongoing recovery. Karen Nakamura provides an interesting case of this policy in Japan, where today "Japanese psychiatrists now use either

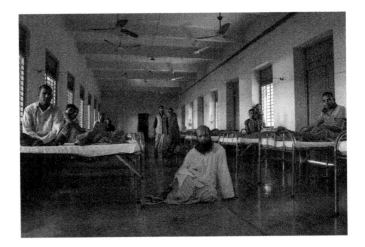

Figure 9.2 Patients at Pabna Mental Hospital in Bangladesh.
Khan Ronnie / Alamy Stock Photo.

the American DSM system of diagnosing and classifying mental illnesses or the more prevalent International Classification of Diseases (ICD) published by the World Health Organization" (2013: 37). As Japan embarked on its modernization phase after 1868, it incorporated German models of mental health; however, the mentally ill were legally confined to their homes until the Mental Hospital Law of 1919, which inaugurated the era of public mental hospitals. Subsequently, the 1950 Mental Hygiene Law expanded facilities for "people with psychiatric disabilities" (46) who were interned there and subjected to the standard practices of the time—mind-numbing drugs, brain operations, and general warehousing. Interestingly, Japanese psychiatry grew to differ from the Western variety in several ways: the vast majority of psychiatric hospitals are private rather than public, hospital stays are much longer (in 2007 averaging 318 days compared to seven days in the United States), patients are given multiple drugs together, and psychoanalytic-style "talk therapy" is almost unknown. When Dr. Toshiaki Kawamura settled at the Urakawa Red Cross Hospital in northern Japan in 1988, he brought a different vision—to shorten hospital stays and to empower patients to live independently. Central to this vision is Bethel House, a set of group homes and workplaces associated with the hospital, whose residents are mostly schizophrenics. Founded in 1984 in a church building, Bethel expanded to three group homes, three shared living facilities, and several other properties, where Nakamura did her fieldwork. What she documents is essentially a community of self-sufficient schizophrenics serving themselves with individual therapy, group therapy sessions, "social skills training" to help them function in the outside world, and "self-directed research" encouraging self-awareness through "concrete ways that you can help yourself or protect yourself and scenarios where you can practice them" (174). The expectation is not to be "cured" but to be functional; the hospital is open for return stays, but Bethel "provides a sense of community, belonging, and sanctuary for its members" (213). "Almost every aspect of Bethel focuses on the social—indeed, far from shying away from the problems of sociality, it welcomes them as a fundamental part of being humans in society" (210), and community members know that they are not along, that "when the end comes … they will die among friends" (214).

In the early twenty-first century, then, the psychiatric encounter and psychiatric work are no longer situated solely, perhaps even mainly, in traditional mental hospitals. Two other institutions that handle the mentally ill—whether or not by choice—are prisons and homeless shelters. Since many mental patients were "deinstitutionalized" in the United States, they have drifted into these other institutions. In fact, according to a 2006 Bureau of Justice Statistics report, more than half of American inmates brought a mental problem into jail, including, at the state prison level, thirty-three percent with mood or sadness disorders, thirty-eight percent with persistent anger, almost twelve percent with psychotic delusions, and eight percent with hallucinations (James and Glaze 2006: 2). Joseph Galanek for one describes how correctional officers have become major actors in the mental health system and "how a prison's context enables and structures relations between officers and inmates with severe psychiatric disorders" (2014: 117). Several years earlier Robert Desjarlais looked at a shelter for the homeless mentally ill in Boston through the lens of selfhood and person-hood. Naturally, both the homeless and the mentally ill are commonly seen as possessing a diminished self and personhood, as not entirely responsible for their actions and occasionally as somewhat less than human. As human beings nonetheless, residents understandably "tried at times to portray themselves in ways that effect some change in their life situation" and not merely passive or subhuman beings (1999: 470). Drawing on the work of philosopher Amelie Rorty, who invoked literary notions of "character" and "figure" among others to account for people's complex performances of self and person, Desjarlais analyzed the performances of the mentally ill homeless. Sometimes rejecting and fighting against characterizations as insane, the residents also "understood that they had to remain 'crazy' in order to hold onto their beds" (474) and so at times played the role of the mad character. In short, residents portrayed many different selves and personhoods in the ritual theater (á la Littlewood) of moment-to-moment interactions; they "shape-shifted in this untidy, institutional world of conversational pitches and counterpitches" (477).

BOX 9.6 SOCIAL AND PSYCHOLOGICAL IMPACT OF MENTAL AND PHYSICAL ILLNESS

In recent decades, Western biomedical psychiatry has begun to catch up to tradi-tional and indigenous notions of the integration of mind, body, and society. Freud recognized a century ago that the mind could make the body sick and that the body could make the mind sick. In her introduction to psychiatry mentioned earlier, Linda Gask noted with approval the medical community's move toward a "biopsy-chosocial approach" which comprehends that "mental disorders, like other types of medical problems, emerge within individuals who are part of a whole [sociocultural] system" (2004: 52). We have come to realize that humans are *psychosomatic* beings, with enmeshed minds and bodies or mind/bodies. This means too that physical ailments work effects on the mind, self, and personality; as the homeless mentally ill of Boston demonstrate, selfhood or personhood is not a permanent secure achieve-ment but can be reconstructed or deconstructed by bodily changes, from disease to simple old age. The experiences of survivors of colorectal cancer studied by Michelle

Ramirez et al. make the point. Dramatic alteration of the body due to colostomy, an operation in which part of the large intestine is removed and defecation subsequently occurs through an incision in the side, "often provokes a painful identity crisis due to the loss of body parts and changed bodily functioning" (2014: 244), namely, "unpredictable and at times publicly noticeable bowel output" (242). Patients must acquire, as the authors put it in Bourdieu's terms (see Chapter 5), a new "fecal habitus" entailing attention to the content and timing of meals, expertise with medical equipment, and practice of maintenance techniques like cleaning and irrigation. Above all, patients can and must develop new ways to think of themselves, new narratives of self, to combat the "assault [on] the body-self-society nexus of personhood" (247). An especially poignant example was anthropologist Robert Murphy, who reported the decline of his own health with the sober objectivity of a scholar. In *The Body Silent* he recounted his diagnosis of spinal tumor that led to progressive weakness and dependence, putting his situation in dialogue with the health concepts and practices of an indigenous people, the Mundurucu of the Amazon rainforest. His first experience of illness was as a "breach of order, an assault upon both flesh and thought"; his tumor "infringed upon both symbolic coherence and real systems of motor control" (1990: 33). After the awareness of the breach of the order of his personal and social life came the sense of losing a part of his self. A critical aspect of the deviance of illness is the attenuation of the self, resulting in a reduced or "damaged self." Murphy the sick person, the wheelchair-ridden person, the dependent person, could not do what Murphy the healthy person formerly did. Especially as a man, Murphy found this threatening to "the cultural values of masculinity: strength, activeness, speed, virility, stamina, and fortitude" (94–5). Worse yet, he discovered that illness carried a stigma, a judgment of inferiority. Wellness, he said, is "an unmarked category" (103), largely taken for granted, while sickness or disability is a negative mark, a kind of "embattled identity" similar to all other undervalued categories. His social relationships changed, too. He felt resented by healthy people, as if he were a traitor to the ideal of true humanity—and perhaps a reminder to healthy people of their own mortality. Old friends did not know how to talk to him; some stopped talking at all, and he replaced them with new friends in the disabled community. He also found himself asked (and forced) to submit to the handling of doctors, nurses, and physical therapists and to make their lives easier by not showing too much emotion and by being passively obedient (that is, to play the sick role). Finally, he felt his effect on his wife and family, who now had to rearrange their lives to accommodate his. "Such shifts within the family structure often create strains so deep that it self-destructs. … When [marriages] are additionally freighted with the problems of the handicapped, they frequently dissolve" (207).

Findings and results

Medical anthropology, including the study of personality disorder and mental illness across cultures, is one of the richest and most rewarding facets of the discipline. It also underscores many of the discoveries made elsewhere in regard to self, personhood, emotions, and altered states of consciousness. Among the most relevant and practical outcomes of the anthropological study of mental illness are:

- mental illness is not a universal cultural concept as neither "mental" nor "illness" is a culture-neutral term
- cultures construct their own standards of normality and judge abnormal behavior against those standards
- modern Western medical notions of mental illness have a cultural history and are socially organized
- objective-sounding classifications like the *Diagnostic and Statistical Manual* are cultural and historical products, always open to revision and only questionably appropriate for other cultures
- other cultures have their own ethnopsychologies of mental illness, or ethnopsychiatries, featuring local understandings of the causes, symptoms, and treatments for disorders; beliefs about spirits, the body, and social relationships are often intimately connected with individual mental states
- formal institutions for the delivery of mental health care have their own social histories and social organization, which often deviate from official policies and ideals and which expose fault lines of power and of cultural difference
- individuals diagnosed or labeled as mentally ill commonly suffer affronts to their self and personhood, and bodily illnesses can also corrode one's self, personality, and social relationships.

Chapter 10

Cognition, schemas, and neuroanthropology

Key questions:
What is the current state of cognitive anthropology?
What is a schema, and how does it transform our understanding of cultural knowledge and enculturated psychological processes?
How did evolutionary history shape the modern human brain, and how is that brain a producer and product of culture?
How did sociality and tool use drive brain development in humans?
How do cognitive anthropologists explain the presence of complex cultural phenomena like religion?
What is neuroanthropology? How has it bolstered qualitative claims about the cultural impact on mental processes, and how can anthropologists integrate it into ethnography?

Psychological anthropology has come a long way over the past hundred or even fifty years. From prejudicial assumptions about "primitive mentality" and the intellectual and perceptual differences (read: inferiorities) of indigenous and non-Western peoples to valid but simplistic interests in the relationship between culture and personality to attempts to create a science of cultural knowledge and a searchable database of variables in cultures to increasingly perceptive and creative ethnographies of specific psychological issues, the field has shed old paradigms and matured into a diverse subdiscipline with lessons to teach not only anthropology but also psychology, philosophy, and medical professions. During that time, it has also absorbed and digested influences from those disciplines as well as, especially and repeatedly, from linguistics. In recent decades, as will become abundantly clear later, computer science, artificial intelligence, and neuroscience, together with physical anthropology, primatology, and archaeology, have shaped psychological anthropology and drawn it into a potential and profitable confluence of knowledge.

The inseparability of anthropology and psychology should be immanent by now. In fact, Maurice Bloch argues that psychological anthropology is not a peripheral branch of the discipline or one that only some anthropologists specializing in the subject should care about. Rather, he insists that anthropologists are forced, by the very nature of their subject matter, to "do cognitive anthropology" all the time. They, like many other social scientists, are "doing cognitive anthropology" as soon as they claim to represent the knowledge of those they study, as soon as they try to explain the actions of people in terms of that knowledge.

(2012: 7)

Bluntly stated, he and co-author Rita Astuti insist that anthropology is at heart a cognitive science, even if it has appeared superficially to be a fundamentally descriptive or ethnographic enterprise (as if ethnography is nothing more than "bringing back raw data in much the same way as shore scavengers bring back bits of wood and the odd exotic sea creature" [Astuti and Bloch 2012: 459]). Indeed, if we define cognitive anthropology as Roy D'Andrade did, as "the study of the relation between human society and human thought" (1995: 1), there can be little doubt.

This of course does not mean that all anthropologists must or will become practicing psychological or cognitive anthropologists. Much of the work of anthropology can continue with psychological/cognitive concerns in the background. However, the mission of anthropology—of being a comprehensive science of human nature and culture—cannot proceed without an essential commitment to the psychological/cognitive, or for that matter, the biological/embodied, dimension of culture. The challenge for psychological anthropology generally, and cognitive anthropology specifically, is to realize its potential while (a) retaining its distinctness from psychology, (b) integrating findings from evolutionary biology and neuroscience to become a truly biocultural science, and (c) discovering ways to practice ethnography in light of those allied sciences. As we will see, the process is well underway.

Contemporary cognitive anthropology

In the fourth chapter of this book, we learned that anthropology took a cognitive turn as early as the 1950s, largely in reaction to the generalized and nonquantitative claims of the previous culture-and-personality school. Some participants in that intellectual turn even used the term "cognitive anthropology" to name what others called componential analysis or ethnoscience. According to D'Andrade's history, cognitive anthropology went through four periods of development, from its initial formative phase in the work of Lounsbury and Goodenough in the 1950s to the stage of "detailed research in the analysis of cultural knowledge" (1995: 245) by the likes of Tyler and Frake to Eleanor Rosch's suggestion in the 1970s of a psychology of categories to what D'Andrade regarded at the time of his writing as something that was "too new and unformed to be definitely described" (1995: 247–8).

The first generation of cognitive anthropology was born from a marriage of anthropology and linguistics, particularly the theories of Saussure and Jakobson, and the work of Noam Chomsky in his 1957 *Syntactic Structures* and his 1959 obliteration of the behaviorist account of language. (For Lévi-Strauss, another seminal cognitivist, Freud's concept of the unconscious was crucially mixed with structural linguistics.) For both ethnoscience and Lévi-Strauss's structuralism, language was the model of cultural knowledge and of human thought; for the former, culture was basically a vocabulary, stored in the mind of a member of society as a dictionary or outline, while for the latter, culture was basically a grammar or set of transformational rules for a limited kit of cultural elements.

Curiously, while ethnoscientists and structuralists were convinced that cultural knowledge was "in the mind" (and ultimately in the brain), neither had much to say about mental or brain processes; the focus was on content rather than on underlying mental/neural mechanisms. Another source coming along at roughly the same moment portended a better understanding of minds and brains: namely, computer science. Computers consist of a physical substrate (hardware), as brains do, that "had memory, could plan ahead, and could even be constructed to make good guesses about what would happen in situations too complex to calculate exact answers," like minds (D'Andrade 1995: 9–10). The dramatic achievements in computer science, and even more so, the discovery of artificial neural networks that seemed to possess many of the abilities of a mind/brain, led to a computational model of intelligence (human and artificial) championed by scholars like Marvin Minsky in his 1969 *Perceptrons: An Introduction to Computational Geometry* and, more immediately for the social sciences, Jerry Fodor in a series of publications, starting with his 1975 *The Language of Thought* and extending to his 1981 *Representations* and *The Modularity of Mind* and 1983 *Psychosemantics*. Fodor posited that, just as a computer communicates with itself via a machine code or computer language, so the mind operates on the basis of an internal code or "language of thought." As Fodor summarized the position in his 2000 *The Mind Doesn't Work That Way*, "cognitive mental processes are operations defined on syntactically structured mental representations that are much like sentences" (2000: 4). This internal mind/brain language, sometimes also called Mentalese, hypothetically handles primarily propositions or factual information, although Fodor also claimed that it processes lower-level perceptual data, storing "Mentalese symbols in memory locations, manipulating those symbols in accord with mechanical rules" (Rescorla 2016), just as a computer does.

Scholars soon launched two criticisms of this theory. The first problem was that Fodor and other computationalists seemed to imagine this Language of Thought as resembling a natural language. Indeed, as seen throughout this book, anthropologists have leaned heavily on the language analogy (which was sometimes advanced as more than an analogy), but Bloch has long been an opponent of this view. Back in 1991, in an article titled "Language, Anthropology and Cognitive Science," he accused anthropology of relying "upon a psychologically misleading and overly linguistic model of culture," whereas by that time, psychology had already demonstrated "that concepts are principally formed independently of language" (1991: 183). Moreover, the writing of Bourdieu and the practice theorists from the late 1970s on (see Chapter 5) had established the existence and salience of embodied and nonpropositional knowledge "which is not language-like" (183)—whether that language is a natural language like English or a machine language. The second and related problem was reliance on yet another analogy—the computer analogy. "Since computers gave a mechanical example of how a mind *could* work," D'Andrade responded, "they began to serve as a model for how the human mind *did* work" (1995: 10). This included the assumption that one neuron (or perceptron, in Minsky's terminology) in the brain or one byte in computer memory stores one idea or representation and that information processing is a sequential series of neural activation and idea/representation invocation. But that is not even how computers function, except perhaps the most primitive models, and it is certainly not how minds and brains function.

It did not take long for this dissatisfaction to lead to a more sophisticated picture of the mind/brain—and, for that matter, of the computer—with the latter probably driving the former. In a 1975 essay on a "framework for representing knowledge," Minsky moved beyond the one-byte/neuron, one-idea/fact view by introducing the notion of a "frame," defined as "a data-structure for representing a stereotyped situation, like being in a certain kind of living room, or going to a child's birthday party" (1975: 212). This more holistic understanding of knowledge, which even sounds cultural in referring to kinds of room or parties, was accompanied and facilitated by strides in artificial intelligence and robotics that depended on (a) neural networks or parallel processing of many points and paths of data simultaneously and (b) the inadequacy of rules. Precisely as Bourdieu warned, real life was too complex for a set of rules, no matter how elaborate, to prepare the computer, robot, or living being to deal with it. Instead, any entity that was going to act in the world (beyond merely contemplating or generating grammatical statements) would have to possess more complicated and adaptive skills for solving novel problems and integrating new knowledge.

By 1980, cognitive anthropology had also transcended the dictionary/checklist stage of ethnoscience and the unconscious grammar of structuralism with the more pragmatic concept of a "schema" (plural, "schemata"). The idea of schema was not new; psychologists had been using it for some time, with F. C. Bartlett's 1932 book *Remembering* often celebrated as the first extensive exploration in reference to bodily movement and skill. Seminal cognitive and developmental psychologist Jean Piaget also made far-reaching use of the concept, recognizing the maturation of children's knowledge as a matter of acquiring and employing increasingly effective and flexible schemata or intellectual and practical skill sets, built up from practical interaction with the world (pouring liquid from one container to another, following a ball under a couch) and then unleashed to organize future worldly interactions.

The year 1980 began for cognitive anthropology with an article by Elizabeth Rice on "cultural schemata." Acknowledging Bartlett as the source of the idea of a schema as "an active organization of past experiences" that is "regularly used in the reconstruction of past experiences," that is, *remembering*, she characterized a schema as "at the same time both structure and process—a set of rules":

> In perception, schemata have an assimilation function: they work to recognize and process input. In memory, they provide organization for the storage of memories, and they may reorganize these memories in the face of new information or changing goals. In recall, schemata provide the rules of arranging memories, and for determining the "what must have been" for any gaps they detect.
>
> (1980: 153)

But schemata are hardly limited to perception and memory; in fact, their primary presence and effect are found in knowledge and practical skill. A schema constitutes what we know about and can do within a particular aspect of reality. It is a situational understanding and ability, as Piaget intuited, that is constructed from experience, and a schema approach in anthropology recognizes that "people's comprehension of the world is mediated by their prior knowledge of it" (155).

Rice added that a schema, as a complex bundle, frame, or script of knowledge-and-skill, "provides a vehicle for specifying this prior knowledge in a form which goes beyond post hoc description. Specification of schemata yields the possibility of predicting and measuring certain aspects and outcomes of the comprehension process" (155). Stated another way, a schema "functions simultaneously as a data structure and a data processor" (155), that is, as the product of past knowledge and the producer of future knowledge. If this sounds familiar, it is: Bourdieu's concept of *habitus* as structured structures predisposed to serve as structuring structures (see Chapter 5) is basically the same thing. Indeed, he developed his theory of practice and of genetic epistemology (the growth of knowledge-and-skill) in the shadow of Piaget and Merleau-Ponty, as we noted in that chapter, and we can reasonably understand *habitus* as a person's collected schemata. When we listen again to the rest of Bourdieu's definition of *habitus*—

> principles of the generation and structuring of practices and representations which can be objectively "regulated" and "regular" without in any way being the product of obedience to rules, objectively adapted to their goals without presupposing a conscious aiming at ends or an express mastery of the operations necessary to attain them and, being all this, collectively orchestrated without being the product of the orchestrating action of a conductor
>
> (1977: 72)

—we hear both the language of schemata and the repudiation of older models of propositional and rule-governed knowledge and action.

Following previous thinkers, like David Rumelhart and Don Norman (e.g. Rumelhart and Norman 1978), Rice identified four features of a schema—that it has variables, that it can embed within other schemata, that it can vary in its level of abstraction, and that it represents "knowledge, rather than definitions" (154). She illustrated these points by offering a study of how Americans understand and process stories. She found that when presented with unfamiliar, incomplete, or anomalous stories, the listener "recognizes the appropriate schemata in the story"—whether they are there or not—"and then proceeds to assimilate the story to them"; further, the imposition of a cultural schemata (i.e. what the listener expects a story to contain based on previous experiences of stories) forces the new story to conform in specific ways, such as through "simplification and stereotyping," which consequently affects how the story is remembered—"elements required by a schema and not in the story will be constructed, redundancies eliminated, and a simplified, stereotyped recall will result" (156). Thereby, we can virtually see the schema at work, bending new material to fit into the categories of prior experience.

BOX 10.1 ROY D'ANDRADE: COGNITIVE SCHEMAS

D'Andrade's definition of a schema may help clarify a difficult concept:

> the organization of cognitive elements into an abstract mental object capable of being held in working memory with default values or open slots which can be variously filled in with appropriate specifics. For example, most Americans have a well-formed schema for a *commercial transaction* in which a buyer and seller exchange money for the rights over some object.
>
> (1995: 179)

From an action standpoint, a schema is comparable to a "situation" in the sociological theory of symbolic interactionism: members of a society recognize a finite set of situations—workplace, courtroom, first date, party—and hopefully master the norms and roles for each. From an informational standpoint, a schema is like a blank form with specified fields (D'Andrade's "open slots") to be filled: as he explained, a "commercial transaction" involves a buyer, a seller, an object to be exchanged, and a medium of exchange (as well, perhaps, as a setting of exchange, such as a store). From a narrative standpoint, as in Rice's example, a schema includes common genres, plots, characters, and story devices; competent members of a society identify a "fairy tale" when they hear certain elements, such as "Once upon a time," and they expect certain kinds of characters and events to follow. All of these variables—actions, propositions, and narratives—constitute "knowledge."

By 1983, schema theory had progressed sufficiently to merit a discussion in *Annual Review of Anthropology*, drafted by Ronald Casson. Noting first a proliferation of synonyms for schema, including frame, scene, script, "active structural networks," and "memory organization packets" (1983: 429), he explained that schemata are

> conceptual abstractions that mediate between stimuli received by the sense organs and behavioral responses. They are abstractions that serve as the basis for all human information processing, e.g. perception and comprehension, categorization and planning, recognition and recall, and problem-solving and decision-making.
>
> (430)

Rather than isolated bits of knowledge or single entries in a mental encyclopedia or outline, they are "organic wholes comprised of parts" (431); moreover, echoing Rice, they "are not only data structures" (products of the past) but "are also data processors" (producers of the future) and not only patterns of knowledge but patterns of action (438). He differentiated several kinds of schemata—object schemata for various kinds of objects, orientation schemata for spatial orientation, event schemata, and metaphors and narratives (441–52)—and made the important observation that some schemata are cultural while others are not. (The schemata made famous by Piaget were practical and ideally—and hopefully—universal but not exactly cultural as the child learned them individually through encounter with the world.) Some schemata, Casson reasoned, are universal and perhaps even hardwired; others are "idiosyncratic" and "unique to particular individuals as the result of their personal histories and life experiences"; but insofar as individuals share common experiences, and transmit those experiences to each other, then "cultural schemata" are formed and circulated, which become conventional ways of processing experience, constructing knowledge, and generating practice. This third kind of schema was what D'Andrade (1981) had singled out as "the cultural part of cognition" and the province of anthropology in the enterprise of cognitive science, although, we will contend later, it is increasingly difficult if not futile to maintain the separation between culture as content and cognition as process; indeed, there is ample evidence that cultural experience rewires the brain itself.

BOX 10.2 CLAUDIA STRAUSS AND NAOMI QUINN: COGNITIVE THEORY OF CULTURAL MEANING

A key moment in the formulation of schema theory was Claudia Strauss and Naomi Quinn's 1997 *A Cognitive Theory of Cultural Meaning*. They grappled with the persistent issue of meaning, which they contended is a "momentary state" achieved or produced "through the interaction of two sorts of stable structures: *intrapersonal*, mental structures (which we also call 'schemas' or 'understandings' or 'assumptions') and *extrapersonal*, world structures" (1997: 6, emphasis in the original). A *cultural meaning*, then, "is the typical (frequently recurring and widely shared aspects of the) interpretation of some experiences" (6). Evoking Bourdieu and linking his theory of practice to contemporary cognitive science, they argued that the "essence of schema theory in the cognitive sciences is that in large measure information processing is mediated by learned or innate mental structures that organize related pieces of our knowledge"; schemata "are not distinct things but rather collections of elements that work together to process information at a given time" (49). To account for the power to integrate the past (from which schemata are derived), the present (in which schemata are employed), and the future (which schemata anticipate and help create), Strauss and Quinn turned to the model known as *connectionism*, also known, especially in computer science and neuroscience, as "parallel distributed processing" or "neural network modeling" (50). Current designers of computers and robots or modelers of neural systems realize that neurons or bytes of computer memory do not work in isolation but in complex webs; accordingly, knowledge in such systems "is not represented by symbols strung together in sentences, but by simple processing units [e.g. brain neurons or computer transistors] arranged in layers (input, output, and one or more layers in between)" (52). As Bloch and others have insisted, and contra Fodor, knowledge is not (always or usually) language-like or "semantic" in the sense that ethnoscience tried to establish nor is it the formulation and execution of rules; in D'Andrade's words, "there are no rules—explicit or implicit—in a connectionist network, only a set of weights and connections" (1995: 143). In other words, a network of relationships between units is assembled (either intentionally by a computer scientist or pragmatically during social experience) with "weights" (strength of association and likelihood of certain functions) between units. Strauss and Quinn concluded that "the system [a computer or a mind/brain] builds up its knowledge by learning associations (positive or negative correlations) among the features of a number of specific cases, rather than by being taught any explicit rules" (1997: 60); for that reason, knowledge is "well-learned but flexibly adaptive rather than rigidly repetitive" (53), that is, not merely rule-enacting. Mental schemata thus have certain consistent qualities: they are durable in the individual; "can have emotional and motivational force"; tend to be transmitted and reproduced from person to person and generation to generation; are "relatively thematic, in the sense that certain understandings may be repeatedly applied in a wide variety of contexts"—which is also the nature of Piagetian schemata—and can obviously "be more or less widely shared" (85). This reveals what anthropologists mean by "culture": "we do not call an understanding 'cultural' unless it is shared, to some extent, in a social group" (85). Finally, Strauss and Quinn illustrated their point by examining significant American schemata like "marriage."

The evolution of human cognition and culture

If human culture is dependent on human cognitive processes and dispositions, and if those processes and dispositions are dependent on human biology (including but not limited to brain physiology and function), then the next natural question is how humans acquired the biology that makes the cognition that makes the culture. In fact, we might ask how culture—and particular aspects of culture, such as language, morality, or religion—are possible in the first place.

The question of the evolution of cognition and of culture is not an altogether novel one. We witnessed that Clifford Geertz was drawing profound conclusions in the 1960s (see Chapter 5). In his essay "The Impact of the Concept of Culture on the Concept of Man," first published in 1966, he challenged the regnant notion that culture was added onto a biologically complete *Homo sapiens* species late in evolutionary history. Understanding that

> at least some elemental forms of cultural, or if you wish protocultural, activity (simple tool-making, hunting, and so on) seem to have been present among some of the Australopithecines [progenitors of the human species], there was an overlap of, as I say, well over a million years between the beginning of culture and the appearance of man as we know him today.
>
> (1973: 47)

What this means is that culture did not appear *after* human biological traits were settled—indeed, such a belief would leave unanswered the question of *why* those traits evolved at all—but instead that the course of human biology, including but not only brains, occurred entirely in the context of culture. Tools, fire, family, maybe even language and ritual were, in small but expanding ways, part of humanity's evolutionary environment. Consequently,

> Between the cultural pattern, the body, and the brain, a positive feedback system was created in which each shaped the progress of the other, a system in which the interaction among increasing tool use, the changing anatomy of the hand, and the expanding representation of the thumb on the cortex is only one of the more graphic examples. By submitting himself to governance by symbolically mediated programs for producing artifacts, organizing social life, or expressing emotions, man determined, if unwittingly, the culminating stages of his own biological destiny. Quite literally, though quite inadvertently, he created himself.
>
> (47–8)

The full analysis of the biocultural evolution of human cognition requires psychological anthropology to recruit a number of allied disciplines, including physical anthropology, archaeology, and primatology. Beginning with primatology, which studies the biological and behavioral traits of primates (prosimians, monkeys, apes, and humans), that class of species shares a battery of diagnostic features:

* relatively large brains in proportion to body size
* tendency toward erectness or upright posture, with at least some bipedalism (walking on two legs)
* good vision, with forward-facing eyes and an associated reduction in snout
* grasping hands, with opposable thumbs and nails instead of claws (except in the primitive prosimians)
* relatively long lives, with prolonged period of dependent childhood and concomitant relationship between mother and child.

More importantly, since the pioneering observations of Jane Goodall commencing in 1960, primatologists have discovered remarkable mental and cultural capacities, especially in apes (chimpanzees, gorillas, and orangutans) in the wild and in the laboratory. Goodall found wild chimpanzees using and making simple tools, cooperating in hunting, and interacting in distinctly social and emotional ways. In the lab, apes have demonstrated previously unsuspected capabilities to manipulate linguistic symbols via hand gestures or push-buttons or shapes (although not to speak), to use tools in complex combinations (like stacking boxes to reach food), to possess a sense of self (e.g. recognizing themselves in a mirror), to recognize and remember numbers (and much faster than humans, by the way), and to display what can only be called a sense of fairness and "morality." All of this sophisticated cognition is possible, in the case of chimps, with a brain volume of three hundred to five hundred cubic centimeters, roughly one-third the brain of modern humans.

Physical anthropologists investigate, among other things, the evolutionary history of hominids, the family of species that includes pre-humans, early *Homo*, and anatomically modern humans or *Homo sapiens sapiens*. Branching off from their primate ancestors sometime around six or seven million years ago, the first hominids inherited the primate physical and behavioral characteristics just mentioned. The earliest, with brains no larger than chimps but with increasingly upright posture, soon experienced a substantial expansion of brain size and a concurrent gradual expansion in cultural repertoire—exactly as Geertz predicted (see Table 10.1).

Table 10.1 Brain volume and cultural characteristics of hominid species

Hominid species	Earliest known date	Brain volume	Cultural characteristics
Australopithecus afarensis	3.9 million years ago	350–550 cc	No firm evidence of culture
Homo habilis	2.4 million years ago	550–780 cc	Oldowan (simple chopper) stone tools
Homo erectus	1.8 million years ago	700–1,250 cc	Acheulian/Acheulean (hand axe) stone tools made by hitting a core stone with a hammerstone to produce a more finished surface with bilateral symmetry; fire, simple shelters, possibly some language
Neanderthal (*Homo neandertalensis* or *Homo sapiens Neandertal?*)	160–140,000 years ago	1,100–1,700 cc (some calculations of 1,400–1,900)	Mousterian stone tools fashioned from a prepared core yielding a "kit" of tools and some regional variation; ritual burials, probably some language and "religious" beliefs
Homo sapiens (anatomically modern humans)	200–150,000 years ago	1,300–1,400 cc	At first, Mousterian tools. By 40,000 years ago, art, diverse and rapidly changing tool technologies, certainly full language and "religious" beliefs

For comparison, a modern chimpanzee has a brain volume of 300–500 cubic centimeters (cc).

One significant cost but also opportunity associated with brain inflation is that human babies have to be born with highly immature brains. Their large heads already make birth hard, so they are born with very unfinished brains. This means that a great deal of neural growth occurs after birth—and therefore in a social and cultural environment. As those brains grow and mature, they integrate social and cultural experience (which is what anthropologists mean by socialization or enculturation), developing into a very different product than if they had matured with less or no social/cultural input (see the following).

Drivers of cognitive evolution: sociality and tool use

For a while, the dominant explanation of this unprecedented brain growth was environmental— that, as Robin Dunbar put it in a classic article, "brains evolved to process information of ecological relevance" (1998: 178), spurred by changes in the environment (forests drying into savannah) or migration or both. However, Dunbar among others found this hypothesis unconvincing, if only because brains "are exceedingly expensive both to evolve and to maintain" (178). Subsequently—and again, very much consistent with Geertz's opinion—two other factors have been proposed to account for the explosion of brain growth and, as Geertz titled another major essay, the growth of culture and the evolution of mind. These are social life itself and tool use.

Dunbar, as evinced by the title of his article, "The Social Brain Hypothesis," was a champion of the former theory. In a cautious argument, he endorsed the position that "primates' large brains reflect the computational demands of the complex social systems that characterize the order" (178). Living permanently in fairly large social groups with intricate relationships of kinship, dominance, alliance, and cooperation and competition, he reckoned that primate brains were called upon to perform a myriad of social tasks, such as identifying individuals and remembering their faces, understanding and remembering their own relationships and the relationships of others (e.g. who is a parent or offspring of whom), and "process[ing] emotional information, particularly with respect to recognizing and acting on cues to other animals' emotional states" (184). Indeed, as many primatologists and physical anthropologists have determined, primates must not only know whom they can trust for alliance and "coalition-formation" but also whom they cannot trust and whom they can fool ("tactical deception") (178). That is, apes and humans (and some monkeys) seem to possess a theory of mind that enables them to comprehend and anticipate the knowledge and intentions of others; as Dunbar phrased it,

> apes seem to be good psychologists in that they are good at reading minds, whereas monkeys are good ethologists in that they are good at reading behavior—or at least at making inferences about intentions in the everyday sense, even if not in the philosophical sense of belief states.
>
> (188)

In the lab, experimenters have noticed primates apparently understanding what other individuals, including humans, know and do not know and what they need to know, guiding them, for instance, to find useful objects. From all these considerations, Dunbar declared that the only viable explanation for primate and human brain volume "is that the mechanisms involved lie in the ability to manipulate information about social relationships themselves" (185).

Figure 10.1 Neanderthal tools showed considerable advanced mental capacities, such as planning and economy.
The Natural History Museum / Alamy Stock Photo.

Undoubtedly the complex sociality of primates is crucial to neurological and cultural growth, but it is impetuous to call it the only alternative or the only contributor to the evolution of mind and culture. The other likely candidate is tool use. Using and even more so making tools requires a quite advanced set of cognitive and manual skills, as Richard Byrne specified in a chapter in the aptly-titled *The Evolution of Thought*. These skills include "precision handling," "accurate aiming of powerful blows," "bimanual role differentiation" (that is, coordinating the action of two hands), "regular and sequential plan," "hierarchical organization with use of subroutines," "corrective guidance by anticipatory schema," "high individual manual laterality" (i.e. every member of the group uses their hands in the same way), and "population right-handedness" (2004: 34). Extensive future-orientation and foresight (from searching for and carrying raw materials to preparing cores and imagining a finished artifact) as well as perhaps cooperation are also involved, and teaching—whether by observation and example or in words—is definitely needed (Figure 10.1).

At the point where tools appear in the evolutionary record, the work of archaeology begins. Most people think of archaeology as the mere study of artifacts (describing, dating, and classifying them) and of the societies that made them, and much of archaeology does or has done that, but a recent movement in the field strives to identify the mind behind the object. Among its main practitioners are Frederick Coolidge and Thomas Wynn, who define *cognitive archaeology* as the study of

> human cognitive evolution by applying cognitive-science theories and concepts to archaeological remains of the prehistoric past. It is based on the premise that the material traces of past activities can be used as clues to the minds that organized those activities.
>
> (2016: 386)

An early boost to this project came in the form of the concept of *chaîne opératoire* proposed by André Leroi-Gourhan, a student of Marcel Mauss. French for "operational chain," he explained it in 1964 as how the techniques to produce an object, including both gestures or bodily movements and tools, are "organized in a chain by a veritable syntax that simultaneously grants to the operational series their fixity and their flexibility" (1993: 114). In simple terms, manufacturing a material object entails performing specific motions or operations in a specific order, which can be reconstructed by the archaeologist, and those motions or operations also unveil the workings of the mind of the operator.

Following this pregnant suggestion, Colin Renfrew polished the idea of cognitive archaeology in a series of books, from his 1982 *Towards an Archaeology of Mind* and his co-edited 1994 volume (with Ezra Zubrow) *The Ancient Mind: Elements of Cognitive Archaeology* to his 2007 *Prehistory: The Making of the Human Mind*. Reasonably, much of cognitive archaeology has focused on early hominid stone tools, the progress of which evinces key developments in human cognitive capabilities. For instance, in a recent volume titled *Stone Tools and the Evolution of Human Cognition*, Ignacio de la Torre claims that the very oldest stone tools (Oldowan) already "display a good technical control of concepts, principles, and methods associated with the mechanics of stone tool making and show an exponential qualitative leap over the use of tools by any other animal species" (2010: 45). It is no accident that these talents coincided with the first burst of hominid brain growth.

Coolidge and Wynn further determine that two tremendous leaps in human cognition can be seen in the tool record. The first, they opine, occurred less than two million years ago, at the moment when *Homo erectus* appeared. With an average brain volume twice that of Oldowan's *Homo habilis* makers, their Acheulean tools—trimmed, symmetrical, and worked across their entire surface—indicate

> spatial cognitive abilities (the active coordination of dorsal and ventral information from the primary visual cortex) and hierarchical organization of action that also relied on mechanisms of cognitive control whose use was not evident in the stone tools of earlier hominins.
>
> (2016: 387)

Writing elsewhere about the Levallois technique commonly associated with Neanderthals and their Mousterian technology, they judge it to be an "expert performance, indistinguishable in its basic organization from expert performances in the modern world" and dependent on many of the same mental and manual talents (Wynn and Coolidge 2010: 84). They even liken it in some ways to playing chess. The second great step happened less than two hundred thousand years ago as modern *Homo sapiens* was emerging, the breakthrough being an enhancement in working memory, "giving *Homo sapiens* essentially modern thinking" (390). At that moment, not only do we see better and more diverse tools but previously-unknown signs of "personal ornamentation, depictive cave art, ritualized burials, bow-and-arrow technology, and enigmatic figurines" (390).

The concept of working memory is very important to Coolidge and Wynn, which they view as "correlated with a variety of critical cognitive abilities, including reading comprehension, vocabulary learning, language comprehension, language acquisition, second-language learning, spelling, storytelling, logical and emotional reasoning, suppression of designated events, certain types of psychopathology, fluid intelligence, and general intelligence" (Coolidge et al. 2015: 187). Following psychologist A. D. Baddeley and his working memory model, they also emphasize the evolution of a constellation of mental functions, governed by a central executive and featuring phonological storage (speech and vocal or subvocal rehearsal), "visuospatial sketchpad" (holding and integrating visual and spatial information), and episodic memory for recalling narrative or story-like accounts of events (187–9). They even locate important cognitive functions in specific parts of the brain, like the parietal lobe which is responsible for

> the analysis of relationships of space, time, and number; integration of visuospatial and sensory information, including the location of the body in space; planning and execution of motor sequences; creation of 'inner space' representations of external space; and critical language functions, including abilities for comprehending speech and metaphor.
>
> (194)

BOX 10.3 NEANDERTHAL PERSONALITY?

Wynn and Coolidge have used cognitive archaeological concepts and methods to speculate on the personality of a particular prehuman species, the Neanderthals. They theorized that Neanderthal thought was different from that of modern humans, although not unrecognizably so. The main difference, discerned from tools and cultural traces, was Neanderthal's lack of "enhanced working memory," leaving them to rely on "long-term working memory," which Wynn and Coolidge characterized as "a long-term storage that does not fade rapidly and generally takes more trials to establish than for verbal or declarative memories. It consists of skills ... or the ability to replay motor behaviors, techniques, or procedures ... such as stone tool knapping" (2004: 470). They also extrapolated that "the language of Neandertals may have been pragmatically restricted to declarative, imperative, and exclamatory modes of speech" (482), with limited capacity for questions and for humor. If Neanderthals told stories, their stories "might have been simpler and less inventive" (482). The bottom line, they concluded, was that Neanderthal modal personality probably included "stoicism, tolerance for boredom, low levels of harm avoidance, and difficulties in cost benefit judgments" as well as a shorter attention span (483–4).

Finally, the data and the principles of cognitive archaeology adhere to two themes in contemporary psychological anthropology. First, relatively advanced culture in the form of stone tool technologies seems to have preceded language and to have been taught and learned non- or pre-verbally, supporting the claim that knowledge is not always verbal or language-like. Indeed, anthropologists, psychologists, and others have discovered that plenty of learning among modern humans occurs through nonverbal apprenticeship rather than verbal instruction. Second, reminiscent of Alfred Gell's comments about distributed personhood and the personhood of things (see Chapter 5), cognitive archaeology underscores the mutual constitution of humans and objects. Lambros Malafouris put it especially succinctly in his *How Things Shape the Mind: A Theory of Material Engagement*: the human mind "is embodied, extended, and distributed rather than 'brain-bound' and limited by the skin" (2013: 6) nor even by the human body; rather, the things that we make are extensions and materializations of mind, both produced by and producing consciousness and cognition. In a word, artifacts are mind in matter.

The cognitive evolution of religion

Since Edward O. Wilson's epochal but controversial 1975 *Sociobiology* asserted that even the most complex social behaviors had a biological basis, anthropologists and other social and natural scientists have applied evolutionary thinking to all manner of cultural domains. Language and morality have both been extensively treated, but probably no aspect of culture has received more attention than religion, if only because scientists are vexed by a phenomenon that seems to be so counterintuitive and difficult to believe and to practice. There are of course other theories for the existence of religion, but evolutionary theory offers two main scenarios. One possibility is that evolution somehow selected for religion; the argument runs that religion enhanced survival, not necessarily for the individual but for the group (religion being so thoroughly collective). Shared religious beliefs and rituals can and do strengthen group bonds and preserve the group in trying times. Another mechanism that some scholars have posited addresses the enduring problem of "free riders" in society or those who take advantage of the group's benefits without bearing their portion of the burdens. Richard Sosis, Candace Alcorta, and Joseph Bulbulia have collaborated on a series of essays promoting "costly signaling theory" (e.g. Bulbulia and Sosis 2011; Sosis and Alcorta 2003) as the key to religion. The claim is that religion is socially integrative *precisely because* it is expensive and uncomfortable: social living demands cooperation and mutual trust, but there is always the potential of deception in the group. Thus, lazy deceivers find themselves in an evolutionary arms race with their comrades who, as deceiver-detectors, erect ever more onerous tests of honesty and commitment, including and especially apparently impractical and arbitrary ones. "The result of such escalation would be increasingly complex ritual behaviors, as senders attempt to deceive receivers and receivers seek to determine the truthfulness of the sender's signal" (Sosis and Alcorta 2003: 266). In a word, if religion was easy, it would not verify one's social commitment and willingness to cooperate and to conform; anyone could do it—or fake it. The costly signaling idea might help explain some of the extreme ordeals that believers subject themselves and others to, including sacrifice, self-injury, and war.

The other alternative, more immediately germane to psychological anthropology, is that religion was not directly selected by evolution but emanates from other, more general cognitive traits that *were* evolutionarily beneficial. In this view, religion is a cognitive by-product of the kind of brain and personality that Armin Geertz attributes to humans as

> intelligent apes that are highly emotional, easily spooked, very superstitious, extremely sensitive to social norms and virtual realities, and equipped with nervous systems that are vulnerable to influence from conspecifics [i.e. other members of our group or species] and their symbolic worlds. These traits are prerequisites for religious behavior.
>
> (2013: 19)

Such a cognitive-evolutionary theory of religion in anthropology was inaugurated twenty years earlier in Stewart Guthrie's *Faces in the Clouds*, which rooted religion in the evolved human tendency toward anthropomorphism. Because of the profligate sociality of our species and our profound attention to the "influence of conspecifics"—which makes us the greatest practitioners of theory of mind in the planet's history—we are unusually prone to attribute mind to other people *and to other non-human beings and forces* whether mind is present or not. Humans are quick to ascribe human-like minds, thoughts, feelings, and intentions to animals, to plants, and even to inanimate objects like the sun and the moon as well as to forces and phenomena like wind, war, and death (recall from Chapter 5 that not all societies believe that objects and forces are inanimate). As he wrote to open the book,

> we anthropomorphize because guessing that the world is humanlike is a good bet. It is a bet because the world is uncertain, ambiguous, and in need of interpretation. It is a good bet because the most valuable interpretations usually are those that disclose the presence of whatever is most important to us. That usually is other humans.
>
> (1993: 3)

Religion, in Guthrie's estimation, is nothing special in this regard; it is simply projecting human mind or personality or intentionality onto another class of putatively supernatural beings. Accordingly, there is no need to hypothesize that "religion is a separate mode of thought" (194); it is humanity's standard mode of thought turned in a distinct direction.

Justin Barrett took exception to Guthrie's singular focus on anthropomorphism but concurred with him and other cognitive-evolutionary theorists of religion that religious belief "comes from the same mental processes that the vast majority of beliefs come from: the operation of mostly nonconscious mental tools" (2004: 90). The two tools upon which he placed the most emphasis were our susceptibility to "minimally counterintuitive" concepts and our inclination to attribute mind or agency to people and other things. Minimally counterintuitive ideas (or we might better say *optimally* counterintuitive, since if they are not sufficiently counterintuitive, they are not compelling), are those that are "violating just enough" of our expectations and assumptions—that is, in cognitive terminology, of our schemas and frames—"to be attention demanding and to have an unusually captivating ability to assist in the explanation of certain experiences" (22). Religious ideas, particularly ideas about gods, he held, hit the sweet spot of counterintuitiveness—not too little, not too much. On the subject of theory of mind, he did not drift as far from Guthrie as he thought, rather raising the stakes by positing an "agency detection device" (something like Chomsky's language acquisition device) in the mind that wants and tries to find mind or agency in the world. In fact, so overactive is this mechanism that he dubbed it a "hypersensitive agency detection device" or HADD, which interprets almost any behavior that seems intelligent or goal-directed as the sign of an intentional mind—in the case of religion, to a nonhuman and superhuman mind. Barrett and his research team have actually done something that anthropologists seldom do—conduct experiments to study the spontaneous development of religious intuitions, especially in young children who have supposedly not yet been influenced by cultural teachings (e.g. Barrett et al. 2003; Richert and Barrett 2005).

The notion of the appeal of counterintuitive ideas in religion actually came from Pascal Boyer who, inspired by Dan Sperber's thinking about the epidemiology of representations (see Chapter 5), pondered why some religious ideas stick and spread. In his 1994 *The Naturalness of Religious Ideas: A Cognitive Theory of Religion* and more extensively in *Religion Explained: The Evolutionary Origins of Religious Thought*, he began from the well-founded position that the human mind/brain is not a unitary or homogeneous entity but a congeries of multiple inter-operating thought modules, a "confederacy" of explanatory devices, which he called "inference systems." Among these are three with particular significance for religion—concept formation, attention to exception, and agency. Thought proceeds by the creation of concepts and even more abstract "templates"; templates are like blank forms with certain fields to be filled (much as we described schemata earlier), and concepts are the specific way that the templates are completed. For example, "tool" and "animal" would be templates, while "hammer" and "cat" would be concepts. Boyer then reasoned that humans are attracted to exceptions and violations of concepts, and some exceptional ideas have the potential to stick in our minds better because they are minimally or optimally contrary to normal thought. Predictably, "religious concepts *violate* certain expectations from ontological categories [but] they *preserve* other expectations" (2001: 62); for instance, supernatural beings "are not represented as having *human* features in general [like a body] but as having human *minds* which is much more specific" (144, emphasis in the original). As he concluded, religion is constructed out of "mental systems and capacities that are there anyway ... [therefore] the notion of religion as a special domain is not just unfounded but in fact rather ethnocentric" (311). In this view, religion does not require a separate explanation at all but is rather a *product* or *by-product* of how mind in society functions in every, including nonreligious, context. In particular, he pointed to the evolved mental predispositions of humans, the nature of social living, processes of information exchange, and the processes of deriving inferences. If nonhuman agents exist, and they can be engaged as social beings—as "social exchange partners"—this is clearly worth thinking about and acting on.

Scott Atran added greater technicality to this hypothesis. He too asserted that religion involves "the very same cognitive and affective structures as nonreligious belief and practices—and no others—but in (more or less) systematically distinct ways" (2002: ix). Since "there is no such entity as 'religion,'" there is no need to "explain" it in a unique way. Religion is once again a by-product and epiphenomenon of other, generally human processes or modules, of which he identified several: perceptual modules, primary emotional modules (for "unmediated" physiological responses like fear, surprise, anger, and disgust), secondary affective modules (for reactions like anxiety, guilt, and love), and conceptual modules. Agency is also high on his list of human priorities, and we have elaborate and essential processes for detecting and interpreting it, especially because we can be fooled and faked by others. Supernatural agents are a mere and fairly reasonable extrapolation of human and natural agency, "by-products of a naturally selected cognitive mechanism for detecting agents—such as predators, protectors, and prey—and for dealing rapidly and economically with stimulus situations involving people and animals" (15). No wonder, he declared, that "supernatural agency is the most culturally recurrent, cognitively relevant, and evolutionarily compelling concept in religion" (57).

BOX 10.4 HARVEY WHITEHOUSE: TWO MODES OF RELIGIOSITY

The focus on the evolutionary origins and cognitive foundations of religion and Sperber's suggestion about the epidemiology of cultural ideas have sparked an interest in particular psychological processes like attention, motivation, and memory. The question after what kinds of religious ideas get created in the first place is which religious ideas are effectively remembered and thereby reproduced. In 1995, Harvey Whitehouse published his research on religious movements among the Mali Baining, a people of Papua New Guinea, which eventually sparked his thoughts on "modes" of religion. By the 1970s, the Pomio Kivung movement, a kind of cargo cult (cargo cults being a type of culture-change movement in which societies often reject or destroy parts of their traditional culture and embrace parts of modern/foreign culture in expectation of a bonanza of wealth or "cargo"), was widespread among the Mali Baining; however, later, yet another movement, Dadul-Maranagi, arose in the community and largely displaced the first sect. The competition between these two religious formations led Whitehouse to propose his model of two distinct "modes of religiosity." Related to processes of memory and motivation, Whitehouse designated one mode as the "doctrinal mode," while the other is the "imagist mode." The doctrinal mode depends on explicit religious teachings and formal leadership, on frequent repetition of religious behaviors, and on religious centralization, all of which satisfy the more "semantic" or language-based memory processes. The imagistic mode, by contrast, functions through religious behaviors that are "invariably low frequency" but "also, without exception, highly arousing" (2004: 70). These behaviors activate a different kind of memory, "flashbulb memory," and stick in the mind because of their drama and sensory power. Exciting the senses and the emotions, they tend to downplay leadership, centralization, and orthodoxy; they also tend to appeal to small/local and exclusive communities. Whitehouse finally claimed that a religion tends to "gravitate toward" (76) one end of this spectrum or the other, although the two modes are not mutually exclusive.

Neuroanthropology: how brains make culture and culture makes brains

Anthropology seems to have almost fully digested Geertz's admonition that the modern human brain is not only a product of evolutionary history but of the cultural dimension of that history, including both complex social organization and progressive tool use, judging from the pronouncement of Greg Downey and Daniel Lende that the "brain and nervous system are our most cultural organs":

> While virtually all parts of the human body—skeleton, muscles, joints, guts—bear the stamp of our behavioral variety, our nervous system is especially immature at birth, our brain disproportionately small in relation to its adult size and disproportionately susceptible to cultural sculpting.
>
> (2012: 23)

Fully grasping the import of what they call the encultured brain (and, we might add, embrained culture), they inaugurated a blog in late 2007 called Neuroanthropology (https://neuroanthropology.net), on the grounds that cultural and even psychological anthropology have not taken advantage of or even been adequately informed of advances in neuroscience and therefore that anthropological "theories of culture do not sufficiently take into account what we now know about the brain." Older documents continue to be housed at that site, although Lende and Downey have moved their current blog to the science site PLOS (http://blogs.plos.org/neuroanthropology). There they explain that neuroanthropology "places the brain and nervous system at the center of discussions about human nature," setting a four-point agenda for itself:

> (1) exploring the interaction of brain and culture and its implication for our understanding of mind, behavior, and self; (2) examining the role of the nervous system in the creation of social and ideological structures; (3) providing empirical and critical inquiry

into the interplay of neuroscience and ideologies about the brain; and (4) providing novel syntheses and advances in social science theory and the humanities that might also prove useful to brain and behavioral sciences.

Other similar projects and new interdisciplinary sciences include cultural neuroscience, which "aspires to understand how culture as an amalgam of values, meanings, conventions, and artifacts that constitute daily social realities might interact with the mind and its underlying brain pathways of each individual member of the culture" (Kitayama and Park 2010: 111) and cultural neurophenomenology, seeking to bridge the schism between mind and body and to position culture firmly as "*information contained within the memory processes of people's brains and bodies*, information that patterns the adaptational interaction of each individual with his/her local environment and other members of the group" (Laughlin and Throop 2006: 328, emphasis in the original).

It should be unimpeachably certain by now that culture is a product of the human mind/brain, but that is only half of the anthropological tale. The other half is that the mind/brain is a product of culture, *historically and biographically*. That is to say, as we have said, the mind/brain was molded over evolutionary time by the presence and progress of culture, *and it is molded over the course of an individual's lifetime by culture*. If we replace the comparatively mystifying term "culture" with "experience," the neuroanthropological conclusion is that the individual human being's mind/brain is sculpted by experience.

Neuroscientists have only recently understood the extent of the brain's plasticity, "the ability of neurons to be altered by experience" (LeDoux 2002: 137). Indeed, "learning" ultimately means nothing more or less than the imprint of experience on the brain (and body). Not so long ago, scientists believed that the brain did not change much after birth and definitely not after adulthood. However, subsequent research has demonstrated that the brain and nervous system continue to alter in response to experience and that synapses, the junctions between nerve cells, "are changed when we learn" (155). One of the most significant relationships within the complex neural network referred to by the aforementioned cognitive anthropologists is known by scientists as Hebb's law, which proclaims that "cells that fire together wire together" (79)—in other words, over time the functional connections between neurons can become stronger and more durable, resulting in long-lasting mental structures that we call knowledge or schemata. In sum,

> your brain was assembled during childhood by a combination of genetic and environmental influences. Genes dictated that your brain was a human one and that your synaptic connections, though more similar to those of members of your family than to those of members of other families, were nevertheless distinct. *Then, through experiences with the world, your synaptic connections were adjusted* (by selection and/or instruction and construction), further distinguishing you from everyone else.
>
> (307, emphasis added)

We should add, based on similar shared experiences within a society, your synaptic connections were adjusted to resemble those of other members of your group. And we should remind ourselves, as anthropology regularly does, that it is not brains alone that undergo these modifications under conditions of culture but the entire body. As another prominent cultural neuroscientist, Antonio Damasio, phrased it, "The mind is embodied, in the full sense of the term, not just embrained" (1994: 118).

BOX 10.5 MIRROR NEURONS

One of the more fascinating discoveries of contemporary neuroscience is the "mirror neuron," which appears to make possible much of cultural learning and of sociality in general. First identified in monkeys, mirror neurons are nerve cells that fire not only when an individual performs an action but when she sees another individual perform the action. Mirror neurons make primates like humans "imitation-ready," according to Marco Iacoboni, a leader in research on the subject. The behaviors—and emotions—of others are literally felt in our own brains and bodies, allowing us to imagine ourselves doing and feeling what they feel. This feature of the nervous system makes empathy, "the sharing of experiences, needs, and goals across individuals," possible and likely (Iacaboni 2005: 95) and gives substance to anthropological notions of social cognition and theory of mind. We may find someday that Barrett's hypersensitive agency detection device is some such function of mirror neurons. For now, we can say with confidence that a human individual really does have other people in his mind and body, as they have him in theirs.

If "sustained exposure to a set of cultural experiences and behavioral practices will affect neural structure and function" (Park and Huang 2010: 391), growing new cells or building new connections between cells, then the next obvious question is whether neuroscientists have been able to discern differences in brain structure and function across cultures. The short answer is a tantalizing yes. Ethnographic and psychological data have long suggested cognitive differences between cultures, but today brain research is providing concrete evidence and explanation for those variations. Shihui Han and Georg Northoff conclude that "recent transcultural neuroimaging studies have demonstrated that one's cultural background can influence neural activity that underlies both high- and low-level cognitive functions" (2008: 646). Technologies like functional magnetic resonance imaging (fMRI) allow scientists to see the brain working in real time, and Han and Northoff summarize culture-related disparities in brain function in such areas as perception, attention, emotion, language, music, and self-awareness (Figure 10.2).

Much of the investigation of psychological and cognitive differences has concentrated on Western versus Asian people and has consistently shown, for instance, that Westerners are more inclined to focus their attention on foreground objects, while Asians tend to "process scenes more holistically, attending to the context in which objects are embedded" (Jenkins et al. 2010: 236). Lucas Jenkins and his colleagues report actual variance between the two populations in activity in a specific brain region, the lateral occipital complex, when looking at "incongruent scenes" or pictures with objects in unlikely settings (like a television in the desert). The research of Joshua Goh et al. (2010) identifies differences in how Westerners and East Asians process faces, Westerners relying on the left fusiform face area of the ventral visual cortex and East Asian on the right. Coming at the question from another angle, Steven Demorest and associates (2010) compare music memory in American and Turkish subjects and find that culturally familiar and unfamiliar music activates different parts of the brain. Kitayama and Park, mentioned earlier, even marshal evidence that "the structure of the self varies systemically across cultures at the level of brain representations" (2010: 114), with more pronounced activation of the medial prefrontal cortex and the temporal parietal junction in

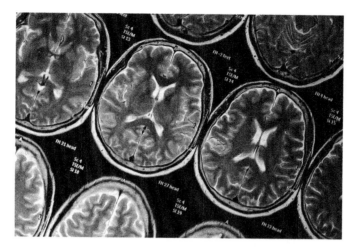

Figure 10.2 Thanks to modern technology, anthropologist have access to precisely what parts of the brain are active during particular cognitive tasks, which sometimes reveals differences across cultures.
toysf400 / Shutterstock.

Americans than in Japanese. Ying Zhu et al. likewise contend that the "Western independent self is mediated by unique neural substrates, whereas East Asian (e.g. Chinese here) interdependent self depends on overlapping of neural substrates for the self and close others" (2007: 1315). Yanhong Wu et al. go so far as to attribute the distinctness of Tibetan brain processing of the self to "the minimal subjective sense of 'I-ness' in Tibetan Buddhists," which supports "the presumed role of culture and religion in shaping the neural substrate of self" (2010: 324).

Neurological study of culture is still in its infancy, and we must be cautious about drawing conclusions, but given the exciting results so far—and the extent to which it concretizes the kinds of claims that psychological anthropologists have been making for decades—the final frontier for anthropology is to integrate contemporary cognitive anthropology and neuroanthropology with the discipline's traditional vocation of ethnography. That this is a worthwhile goal is reflected in Tim Ingold's (2008) useful reminder that anthropology is not—or not only—ethnography. Ethnography, the mostly qualitative description of culture, is one valuable method but is not the whole of anthropology. Accordingly, Juan Domínguez Duque, Robert Turner, E. Douglas Lewis, and Gary Egan call for a *neuroethnography* that "involves embedding neuroscientific experiments in ethnography" (2010: 140). Of course, not all anthropologists are going to or want to become neuroscientists, and carrying MRI machines into the field is not always feasible nor is bringing people under anthropological observation into the lab always desirable. Indeed, Downey and Lende insist that laboratory experiments "cannot offer a complete account of how the human brain works precisely because the nervous system is so crucially embedded in its environment" (2012: 25), which includes its social and cultural environment. If, as they offer alternatively, neuroanthropologists seek "brains in the wild," the point of neuroethnography need not be conducting experiments so much as finding ways to utilize cognitive and neurological concepts to inform ethnographic observations and utilize ethnographic opportunities to measure and test cognitive and neurological hypotheses.

BOX 10.6 DIMITRIS XYGALATAS: ANASTENARIA FIREWALKING RITUAL

Domínguez Duque et al. complained in 2010 that there were no published examples of neuroethnography, but in 2012, Dimitris Xygalatas published a study that meets some of their standards. His topic is a ritual of firewalking among the Anastenaria of rural Greece. The book explicitly combines conventional ethnographic description with examination "of the implicit psychological factors that contribute to the persistence and the transmission of the Anastenaria and other emotionally arousing rituals" (2012: 2). Approaching the ceremony as both practice and knowledge, in a chapter titled "Ritual and Mind" he introduces the cognitive paradigms of Sperber, Guthrie, Boyer, Whitehouse, and others. Subsequently, he runs the Anastenaria tradition through other state-of-the-art perspectives, such as costly signaling theory and issues of physical and emotional arousal, finding support for the Whitehouse's bimodal theory of religiosity, which posits two modes or styles of religion, one with high levels of arousal but low frequency of performance and the other with low levels of arousal but high frequency (see earlier). Interestingly, Xygalatas describes the rural Greek religious field as comprised of both: ordinary Church services are (remarkably) low arousal/high frequency, while the Anastenaria tradition is high arousal/low frequency. The nature of the Anastenaria ritual, thus, not only explains its great salience for participants, but ordinary physio-emotional processes like endorphin release explain the "miracle" of walking on fire without pain or damage as well as the effective of the ritual as a way of knowing. His final plea is for "explanatory pluralism" and a "multilevel analysis of culture" (185) that merges the social and historical with the physical and emotional.

Findings and results

For over a century, anthropologists have asked probing questions about psychological processes in and mental differences between cultural groups, and they have progressed from generalized and often overly simplistic claims to increasingly sensitive and sophisticated observations of mind in culture, ranging from emotions and self-concepts to altered states of consciousness and mental illness. In the past decade or two, influenced by advances in computer science and robotics as well as neuroscience and brain-imaging technologies, psychological anthropologists have developed new ideas and discovered new empirical confirmations of old ideas.

- Cognitive anthropology since the 1980s has abandoned semantic and dictionary-like—often even language-like—models of mind in favor of more holistic and networked models
- Concepts like "schema" have given anthropologists more powerful tools for understanding how cultural knowledge works while adding specific mental and sometimes physiological dimensions to previous ideas of theorists like Bourdieu and Sperber
- Primatology and physical anthropology have contributed to a more complete psychological anthropology that grasps the evolved nature of the human mind/brain

- Both complex social organization and progress in tool technology provided the context for expansion of the brain and the development of advanced cognitive capacities
- Cognitive archaeology offers a glimpse of the mind-in-the-matter of manmade objects like tools and artifacts
- Psychologically oriented anthropologists have applied their terms and concepts to higher-level cultural phenomena like language, morality, and especially religion, commonly arguing that religion is a manifestation of ordinary evolved mental tendencies like agency detection and theory of mind
- New technologies to observe the brain at work have spawned neuroanthropology, which aims to understand the reciprocal relationship between brains (and bodies) and cultural experience
- Exciting discoveries of culture-based differences in brain structure and function support ethnographic accounts of cultural variations in perception, thought and emotion and suggest the value of neuroethnography or integrating cognitive/neurological perspectives in ethnographic fieldwork.

Bibliography

Abramowitz, Sharon A. 2014. *Searching for Normal in the Wake of the Liberian War.* Philadelphia: University of Pennsylvania Press.

Abu-Lughod, Lila. 1986. *Veiled Sentiments: Honor and Poetry in a Bedouin Society.* Berkeley: University of California Press.

Ackerman, Susan E. 1981. "The Language of Religious Innovation: Spirit Possession and Exorcism in a Malaysian Catholic Pentecostal Movement." *Journal of Anthropological Research* 37 (1): 90–100.

Adcock, Cyril J. and James E. Ritchie. 1958. "Intercultural Use of Rorschach." *American Anthropologist* 60 (5): 881–92.

Adorno, Theodor W., Else Frenkel-Brunswick, Daniel J. Levinson, and R. Nevitt Sanford. *The Authoritarian Personality.* 1950. New York: Harper & Row.

Aggarwal, Neil K. 2013. "Cultural Psychiatry, Medical Anthropology, and the DSM-5 Field Trials. *Medical Anthropology* 32 (5): 393–8.

Allerton, Catherine. 2013. *Potent Landscapes: Place and Mobility in Eastern Indonesia.* Honolulu: University of Hawai'i Press.

American Psychiatric Association. 2013. *Diagnostic and Statistical Manual of Mental Disorders: DSM-5.* Washington, DC: American Psychiatric Association.

Ammar, Hamed. 2002 [1954]. *Growing up in an Egyptian Village.* London: Routledge & Kegan Paul.

Appadurai, Arjun, ed. 1986. *The Social Life of Things: Commodities in Cultural Perspective.* Cambridge: Cambridge University Press.

Astuti, Rita and Maurice Bloch. 2012. "Anthropologists as Cognitive Scientists." *Topics in Cognitive Science* 4 (3): 453–61.

Atran, Scott. 2002. *In Gods We Trust: The Evolutionary Landscape of Religion.* Oxford: Oxford University Press.

Bacchiddu, Giovanna. 2011. "Holding the Saint in One's Arms: Miracles in Apiao, Southern Chile." In Anna Fedele and Ruy Llera Blanes, eds. *Encounters of Body and Soul in Contemporary Religious Practices: Anthropological Reflections.* New York and London: Berghahn Books, pp. 23–42.

Barnouw, Victor. 1973 [1963]. *Culture and Personality.* Homewood, IL: The Dorsey Press.

Barrett, Justin L. 2004. *Why Would Anyone Believe in God?* Lanham, MD: AltaMira Press.

Barrett, Justin L., Roxanne M. Newman, and Rebekah A. Richert. 2003. "When Seeing is Not Believing: Children's Understanding of Humans' and Non-Humans' Use of Background Knowledge in Interpreting Visual Displays." *Journal of Cognition and Culture* 3 (1): 91–108.

Barry, Herbert, Irvin L. Child, and Margaret K. Bacon. 1959. "Relation of Child Training to Subsistence Economy." *American Anthropologist* 61 (1): 51–63.

Baruss, Imants. 1992. "Contemporary Issues Concerning the Scientific Study of Consciousness." *Anthropology of Consciousness* 3 (3–4): 28–35.

Bateson, Gregory. 1936. *Naven: A Survey of Problems Suggested by a Composite Picture of the Culture of a New Guinea Tribe Drawn from Three Points of View.* London: Cambridge University Press.

———. 1975. "Some Components of Socialization for Trance." *Ethos* 3 (2): 143–55.

Bateson, Gregory and Margaret Mead. 1942. *Balinese Character: A Photographic Analysis*. New York: Special Publication of the New York Academy of Science, volume II.

Belo, Jane. 1935–6. "The Balinese Temper." *Character and Personality* 4: 120–46.

———. 1937. "Balinese Children's Drawings." *Djawa* 17 (5–6): 1–13.

Bender, Andrea, Hans Spada, Stefan Seitz, Hannah Swoboda, and Simone Traber. 2007. "Anger and Rank in Tonga and Germany: Cognition, Emotion, and Context." *Ethos* 35 (2): 196–234.

Benedict, Ruth. 1922. "The Vision in Plains Culture." *American Anthropologist* 24 (1): 1–23.

———. 1932. "Configurations of Culture in North America." *American Anthropologist* 34 (1): 1–27.

———. 1934. "Anthropology and the Abnormal." *Journal of General Psychology* 10 (2): 59–82.

———. 1959 [1934]. *Patterns of Culture*. Cambridge, MA: The Riverside Press.

———. 1972 [1946]. *The Chrysanthemum and the Sword: Patterns of Japanese Culture*. New York: The World Publishing Company.

Berlin, Brent and Paul Kay. 1969. *Basic Color Terms: Their Universality and Evolution*. Berkeley: University of California Press.

Berry, John W., Ype H. Poortings, Marshall H. Segall, and Pierre R. Dasen. 2002. *Cross-Cultural Psychology: Research and Applications*, 2nd ed. Cambridge and New York: Cambridge University Press.

Bird-David, Nurit. 1999. "'Animism' Revisited: Personhood, Environment, and Relational Epistemology." *Current Anthropology* 40: S67–91.

Bloch, Maurice. 1991. "Language, Anthropology and Cognitive Science." *Man* (n.s.) 26 (2): 183–98.

———. 2012. *Anthropology and the Cognitive Challenge*. Cambridge and New York: Cambridge University Press.

Blount, Ben. 2011. "A History of Cognitive Anthropology." In David B. Kronenfeld, Giovanni Bennardo, Victor C. de Munck, and Michael D. Fischer, eds. *A Companion to Cognitive Anthropology*. Malden, MA and Oxford: Blackwell, pp. 11–29.

Boas, Franz. 1901. "The Mind of Primitive Man." *The Journal of American Folklore* 14 (52): 1–11.

———. 1910. "Psychological Problems in Anthropology." *The American Journal of Psychology* 21 (3): 371–84.

———. 1938 [1911]. *The Mind of Primitive Man*. New York: The Macmillan Company.

Boddy, Janice. 1988. "Spirits and Selves in Northern Sudan: The Cultural Therapeutics of Possession and Trance." *American Ethnologist* 15 (1): 4–27.

Boggs, Stephen T. 1958. "Culture Change and the Personality of Ojibwa Children." *American Anthropologist* 60 (1): 47–58.

Bourdieu, Pierre. 1977 [1972]. *Outline of a Theory of Practice*. Richard Nice, trans. Cambridge and New York: Cambridge University Press.

———. 1990 [1980]. *The Logic of Practice*. Richard Nice, trans. Stanford, CA: Stanford University Press.

Bourguignon, Erika. 1954. "Dreams and Dream Interpretation in Haiti." *American Anthropologist* 56 (2, part 1): 262–8.

———. 1973a. "Introduction: A Framework for the Comparative Study of Altered States of Consciousness." In Erika Bourguignon, ed. *Religion, Altered States of Consciousness, and Social Change*. Columbus: Ohio State University Press, pp. 3–35.

———, ed. 1973b. *Religion, Altered States of Consciousness, and Social Change*. Columbus: Ohio State University Press.

———. 1976. *Possession*. San Francisco, CA: Chandler & Sharp Publishers.

Boyer, Pascal. 1994. *The Naturalness of Religious Ideas: A Cognitive Theory of Religion*. Berkeley and Los Angeles, CA: University of California Press.

———. 2001. *Religion Explained: The Evolutionary Origins of Religious Thought*. New York: Basic Books.

Briggs, Jean. 1970. *Never in Anger: Portrait of an Eskimo Family*. Cambridge: Harvard University Press.

Brown, Judith K. 1963. "A Cross-Cultural Study of Female Initiation Rites." *American Anthropologist* 65 (4): 837–53.

Brown, Penelope. 2006. "Cognitive Anthropology." In C. Jourdan and K. Tuite, eds. *Studies in the So-cial and Cultural Foundations of Language 23: Language, Culture, and Society*. Cambridge: Cambridge University Press, pp. 96–114.

Bulbulia, Joseph and Richard Sosis. 2011. "Signalling Theory and the Evolution of Religious Cooper-ation." *Religion* 41 (3): 363–88.

Busby, Cecilia. 1997. "Permeable and Partible Persons: A comparative Analysis of Gender and Body in South India and Melanesia." *The Journal of the Royal Anthropological Institute* 3 (2): 261–78.

Byrne, Richard W. 2004. "The Manual Skills and Cognition that Lie Behind Hominid Tool Use." In Anne E. Russon and David R. Begun, eds. *The Evolution of Thought: Evolutionary Origins of Great Ape Intelligence*. Cambridge: Cambridge University Press, pp. 31–44.

Carbaugh, Donal, Michael Berry, and Marjatta Nurmikari-Berry. 2006. "Coding Personhood through Cultural Terms and Practices: Silence and Quietude as a Finnish 'Natural Way of Being.'" *Journal of Language and Social Psychology* 25 (3): 203–20.

Carpenter, Sandra and Zahide Karakitapoglu-Aygün. 2005. "Importance and Descriptiveness of Self Aspects: A Cross-Cultural Comparison." *Cross-Cultural Research* 39 (3): 293–321.

Carroll, John B., ed. 1956. *Language, Thought, and Reality: Selected Writings of Benjamin Lee Whorf*. Cambridge, MA: The Technology Press of Massachusetts Institute of Technology; New York: John Wiley & Sons.

Cartwright, Samuel A. 1851. "Diseases and Peculiarities of the Negro Race." *De Bow's Review* 11. www.pbs.org/wgbh/aia/part4/4h3106t.html, accessed December 8, 2016.

Cassaniti, Julia. 2015. *Living Buddhism: Mind, Self, and Emotion in a Thai Community*. Ithaca, NY and London: Cornell University Press.

Casson, Ronald W. 1983. "Schemata in Cognitive Anthropology." *Annual Review of Anthropology* 12: 429–62.

Chance, Norman A. 1965. "Acculturation, Self-Identification, and Personality Adjustment." *American Anthropologist* 67 (2): 372–93.

Child, Charles M. 1927. *The Unconscious: A Symposium*. New York: Alfred A. Knopf.

Chomsky, Noam. 1959. "Review of *Verbal Behavior* by B. F. Skinner." *Language* 35 (1): 26–58.

Chowdhury, Uma. 1960. "An Indian Modification of the Thematic Apperception Test." *The Journal of Social Psychology* 51: 245–63.

Coolidge, Frederick L. and Thomas Wynn. 2016. "An Introduction to Cognitive Archaeology." *Current Directions in Psychological Science* 25 (6): 386–92.

Coolidge, Frederick L., Thomas Wynn, Karenleigh A. Overmann, and James M. Hicks. "Cognitive Archaeology and the Cognitive Sciences." In Emiliano Bruner, ed. *Human Paleoneurology*. Cham, Switzerland: Springer, pp. 177–206.

Course, Magnus. 2011. *Becoming Mapuche: Person and Ritual in Indigenous Chile*. Urbana: University of Illinois Press.

———. 2014. "The End of Me: The Role of Destiny in Mapuche Narratives of the Person." In Suzanne Oakdale and Magnus Course, eds. *Fluent Selves: Autobiography, Person, and History in Lowland South America*. Lincoln and London: University of Nebraska Press, pp. 144–62.

Coy, Michael W. 1989a. "From Theory." In Michael W. Coy, ed. *Apprenticeship: From Theory to Method and Back Again*. Albany, NY: State University of New York Press, pp. 1–11.

———. 1989b. "Introduction." In Michael W. Coy, ed. *Apprenticeship: From Theory to Method and Back Again*. Albany, NY: State University of New York Press, pp. xi–xv.

Csordas, Thomas J. 1990. "Embodiment as a Paradigm for Anthropology." *Ethos* 18 (1): 5–47.

———. 1993. "Somatic Modes of Attention." *Cultural Anthropology* 8 (2): 135–56.

———. 2002. *Body/Meaning/Healing*. Basingstoke, UK and New York: Palgrave Macmillan.

Dahl, Shayne A. P. 2011. "The Vision Quest as a Progressive Self-Sacrifice: The Permeable Agency of a Blackfoot Medicine Man." Montreal, Quebec: Paper presented to American Anthropological Association Annual Meeting.

Damasio, Antonio R. 1994. *Descartes' Error: Emotion, Reason, and the Human Brain*. New York: G. P. Putnam's Sons.

D'Andrade, Roy. 1961. "Anthropological Studies of Dreams." In Francis L. K. Hsu, ed. *Psychological Anthropology*. Homewood, IL: Dorsey Press, pp. 296–332.

———. 1981. "The Cultural Part of Cognition." *Cognitive Science* 5 (3): 179–95.

———. 1995. *The Development of Cognitive Anthropology*. Cambridge: Cambridge University Press.

Davis, Elizabeth A. 2012. *Bad Souls: Madness and Responsibility in Modern Greece*. Durham, NC and London: Duke University Press.

de la Torre, Ignacio. 2010. "Insights on the Technical Competence of the Early Oldowan." In April Nowell and Iain Davidson, eds. *Stone Tools and the Evolution of Human Cognition*. Boulder: University Press of Colorado, pp. 45–65.

Demorest, Steven M., Steven J. Morrison, Laura A. Stambaugh, Münir Beken, Todd L. Richards, and Clark Johnson. 2010. "An fMRI Investigation of the Cultural Specificity of Music Memory." *Social Cognitive and Affective Neuroscience* 5 (2–3): 282–91.

de Munck, Victor C. 2008. "Self, Other, and the Love Dyad in Lithuania: Romantic Love as Fantasy and Reality (Or, When Culture Does and Doesn't Matter." In William R. Jankowiak, ed. *Intimacies: Love + Sex Across Cultures*. New York: Columbia University Press, pp. 65–94.

Dentan, Robert K. 2008. *Overwhelming Terror: Love, Fear, Peace, and Violence among the Semai of Malaysia*. Lanham, MD: Rowman & Littlefield.

de Rougemont, Denis. 1940. *Love in the Western World*. New York: Pantheon.

De Silva, Ravi, Neil Krishan Aggarwal, and Roberto Lewis-Fernández. 2015. "The DSM-5 Cultural Formulation Interview and the Evolution of Cultural Assessment in Psychiatry." www.psychiatrictimes.com/special-reports/dsm-5-cultural-formulation-interview-and-evolution-cultural-assessment-psychiatry, accessed December 10, 2016.

Desjarlais, Robert. 1999. "The Makings of Personhood in a Shelter for People Considered Homeless and Mentally Ill." *Ethos* 27 (4): 466–89.

Devereux, George. 1957. "Dream Learning and Individual Ritual Differences in Mohave Shamanism." *American Anthropologist* 59 (6): 1036–45.

Diriwachter, Rainer. 2004. "*Völkerpsychologie*: The Synthesis that Never Was." *Culture Psychology* 10 (1): 85–109.

Domínguez Duque, Juan F., Robert Turner, E. Douglas Lewis, and Gary Egan. 2010. "Neuroanthropology: A Humanistic Science for the Study of the Culture-Brain Nexus." *Social Cognitive and Affective Neuroscience* 5 (2–3): 138–47.

Douglas, Mary. 1988 [1966]. *Purity and Danger: An Analysis of the Concepts of Pollution and Taboo*. London and New York: Ark Paperbacks.

———. 1996 [1970]. *Natural Symbols: Explorations in Cosmology*. London and New York: Routledge.

Downey, Greg and Daniel H. Lende. 2012. "Neuroanthropology and the Encultured Brain." In Daniel H. Lende and Greg Downey, eds. *The Encultured Brain: An Introduction to Neuroanthropology*. Cambridge, MA: Massachusetts Institute of Technology Press, pp. 23–66.

Drazin, Adam and Susanne Küchler, eds. 2015. *The Social Life of Materials: Studies in Material and Society*. London and New York: Bloomsbury Academic.

Du, Shanshan. 2008. "'With One Word and One Strength: Intimacy among the Lahu of Southwest China." In William R. Jankowiak, ed. *Intimacies: Love + Sex Across Cultures*. New York: Columbia University Press, pp. 95–121.

Du Bois, Cora. 1960 [1944]. *The People of Alor: A Social-Psychological Study of an East Indian Island*. Cambridge, MA: Harvard University Press.

Dumont, Louis. 1970. *Homo Hierarchicus*. London: Weidenfeld and Nicolson.

Dunbar, Robin I. M. 1998. "The Social Brain Hypothesis." *Evolutionary Anthropology* 6 (5): 178–90.

Duncan, Whitney L. 2014. "Transnational Disorders: Returned Migrants at Oaxaca's Psychiatric Hospital." *Medical Anthropology Quarterly* 29 (1): 24–41.

Durkheim, Émile. 1965 [1912]. *The Elementary Forms of the Religious Life*. New York: The Free Press.

Edgar, Iain R. 2011. *The Dream in Islam: From Qur'anic Tradition to Jihadist Inspiration*. New York and Oxford: Berghahn.

Edgerton, Robert. 1966. "Conceptions of Psychosis in Four East African Societies." *American Anthropologist* 68 (2, part 1): 408–25.

———. 1971. *The Individual in Cultural Adaptation: A Study of Four East African Peoples*. Berkeley: University of California Press.

Edwards, Carolyn P. and Marianne Bloch. 2010. "The Whitings' Concepts of Culture and How They Have Fared in Contemporary Psychology and Anthropology." *Journal of Cross-Cultural Psychology* 41 (4): 485–98.

Eggan, Dorothy. 1949. "The Significance of Dreams for Anthropological Research." *American Anthropologist* 51 (2): 177–98.

Eissler, Kurt. 1944. "Balinese Character." *Psychiatry* 7 (2): 139–44.

Eliade, Mircea. 1972 [1964]. *Shamanism: Archaic Techniques of Ecstasy*. Willard R. Trask, trans. Princeton, NJ: Princeton University Press.

Erikson, Erik H. 1962. *Young Man Luther: A Study in Psychoanalysis and History*. New York: W. W. Norton.

———. 1969. *Gandhi's Truth: On the Origins of Militant Nonviolence*. New York: W. W. Norton.

Evans-Pritchard, Edward E. 1940. *The Nuer*. London: Oxford University Press.

Ewing, Katherine P. 1990. "The Illusion of Wholeness: Culture, Self, and the Experience of Inconsistency." *Ethos* 18 (3): 251–78.

Feld, Steven. 2012 [1982]. Sound and Sentiment: Birds, Weeping, Poetics, and Song in Kaluli Expression, 3rd ed. Durham, NC and London: Duke University Press.

Firth, Raymond. 1936. *We, the Tikopia*. New York: American Book.

Fodor, Jerry. 2000. *The Mind Doesn't Work That Way: The Scope and Limits of Computational Psychology*. Cambridge, MA: Massachusetts Institute of Technology Press.

Ford, Clellan S. 1945. "A Comparative Study of Human Reproduction." *Yale University Publications in Anthropology* 32: 1–111.

Fortes, Meyer. 1938. *Social and Psychological Aspects of Education in Taleland*. London: International African Institute Memorandum XVII.

———. 1987. *Religion, Morality and the Person: Essays on Tallensi Religion*. Cambridge and New York: Cambridge University Press.

Foucault, Michel. 1965. *Madness and Civilization: A History of Insanity in the Age of Reason*. New York: Random House.

———. 1988. "Technologies of the Self." In Luther H. Martin, Huck Gutman, and Patrick H. Hutton, eds. *Technologies of the Self: A Seminar with Michel Foucault*. Amherst: University of Massachusetts Press, pp. 16–49.

Frake, Charles O. 1961. "The Diagnosis of Disease among the Subanun of Mindanao." *American Anthropologist* 63 (1): 113–32.

———. 1969. "The Ethnographic Study of Cognitive Systems." In Tyler, Stephen A., ed. *Cognitive Anthropology*. New York: Holt, Rinehart, and Winston, Inc., pp. 28–41.

Freeman, Derek. 1983. *Margaret Mead and Samoa: The Making and Unmaking of an Anthropological Myth*. Cambridge: Harvard University Press.

Freud, Sigmund. 1965 [1900]. *The Interpretation of Dreams*. James Strachey, trans. New York: Discus/Avon Books.

———. 2001 [1913]. *Totem and Taboo: Some Points of Agreement between the Mental Lives of Savages and Neurotics*. James Strachey, trans. London and New York: Routledge.

Galanek, Joseph D. 2014. "Correctional Officers and the Incarcerated Mentally Ill: Responses to Psychiatric Illness in Prison." *Medical Anthropology Quarterly* 29 (1): 116–36.

Gallup, Gordon G., Jr. 1970. "Chimpanzee Self-Recognition." *Science* 167: 86–87.

Gardner, Peter M. 1976. "Birds, Words, and a Requiem for the Omniscient Informant." *American Ethnologist* 3 (3): 446–68.

Gask, Linda. 2004. *A Short Introduction to Psychiatry.* London and Thousand Oaks, CA: Sage.

Geertz, Armin W. 2013. "Whence Religion? How the Brain Constructs the World and What This Might Tell Us About the Origins of Religion, Cognition and Culture." In Armin W. Geertz, ed. *Origins of Religion, Cognition and Culture.* Durham, UK and Bristol, CT: Acumen, pp. 17–70.

Geertz, Clifford. 1973. *The Interpretation of Cultures.* New York: Basic Books.

———. 1974. "'From the Native's Point of View': On the Nature of Anthropological Understanding." *Bulletin of the American Academy of Arts and Sciences* 28 (1): 26–45.

Geertz, Hildred. 1961. *The Javanese Family: A Study of Kinship and Socialization.* New York: Free Press.

Gell, Alfred. 1998. *Art and Agency: An Anthropological Theory.* Oxford: Clarendon Press.

Gewertz, Deborah. 1984. "The Tchambuli View of Persons: A Critique of Individualism in the Works of Mead and Chodorow." *American Anthropologist* 86 (3): 615–29.

Gillin, John. 1942. "Acquired Drives in Culture Contact." *American Anthropologist* 44 (4): 545–54.

Gladwin, Thomas and Seymour B. Sarason. 1953. *Truk: Man in Paradise.* Viking Fund Publications in Anthropology, no. 20. New York: Wenner-Gren Foundation for Anthropological Research.

Glaskin, Katie. 2005. "Innovation and Ancestral Revelation: The Case of Dreams." *The Journal of the Royal Anthropological Institute* 11 (2): 297–314.

Goddard, Cliff. 1991. "Anger in the Western Desert: A Case Study in the Cross-Cultural Semantics of Emotion." *Man* (n.s.) 26 (2): 265–79.

Goh, Joshua O. S., Eric D. Leshikar, Bradley P. Sutton, Jiat Chow Tan, Sam K. Y. Sim, Andrew C. Hebrank, and Denise C. Park. 2010. "Culture Differences in Neural Processing of Faces and Houses in the Ventral Visual Cortex." *Social Cognitive and Affective Neuroscience* 5 (2–3): 227–35.

Goode, William J. 1959. "The Theoretical Importance of Love." *American Sociological Review* 24 (1): 38–47.

Goodman, Feliticas D. 1999. "Ritual Body Postures, Channeling, and the Ecstatic Body Trance." *Anthropology of Consciousness* 10 (1): 54–9.

Goodenough, Ward H. 1956. "Componential Analysis and the Study of Meaning." *Language* 32 (1): 195–216.

———. 1957. "Cultural Anthropology and Linguistics." In P. Garvin, ed. *Report of the Seventh Annual Round Table on Linguistics and Language Study.* Georgetown University Monograph Series on Language and Linguistics 9. Washington, DC: Georgetown University.Gordillo, Gastón. 2002. "The Breath of the Devils: Memories and Places of an Experience of Terror." *American Ethnologist* 29 (1): 33–57.

Gorer, Geoffrey. 1948. *The American People: A Study in National Character.* New York: W. W. Norton.

Gorer, Geoffrey and John Rickman. 1962 [1949]. *The People of Great Russia: A Psychological Study.* New York: W. W. Norton.

Govindama, Yolande. 2006. "Mental Disorders and the Symbolic Function of Therapeutic Rites in the Réunion Island Hindu Environment." *Transcultural Psychiatry* 43 (3): 488–511.

Gow, Peter. 2014. "'This Happened to Me': Exemplary Personal Experience Narratives among the Piro (Yine) People of Peruvian Amazonia." In Suzanne Oakdale and Magnus Course, eds. *Fluent Selves: Autobiography, Person, and History in Lowland South America.* Lincoln and London: University of Nebraska Press, pp. 69–92.

Gray, Chris H. 2007. "Consciousness Studies: The Emerging Military-Industrial-Spiritual Scientific Complex." *Anthropology of Consciousness* 18 (1): 3–19.

Green, Linda. 1994. "Fear as a Way of Life." *Cultural Anthropology* 9 (2): 227–56.

———. 1999. *Fear as a Way of Life: Mayan Widows in Rural Guatemala.* New York: Columbia University Press.

Gregor, Thomas. 1981. "'Far, Far Away My Shadow Wandered…': The Dream Symbolism and Dream Theories of the Mehinaku Indians of Brazil." *American Ethnologist* 8 (4): 709–20.

Groark, Kevin P. 2008. "Social Opacity and the Dynamics of Empathic In-Sight among the Tzotzil Maya of Chiapas, Mexico." *Ethos* 36 (4): 427–48.

———. 2010. "Willful Souls: Dreaming and the Dialectics of Self-Experience among the Tzotzil Maya of Highland Chiapas, Mexico." In Keith M. Murphy and C. Jason Throop, eds. *Toward an Anthropology of the Will*. Stanford, CA: Stanford University Press, pp. 101–22.

Guthrie, Stewart. 1993. *Faces in the Clouds: A New Theory of Religion*. New York and Oxford: Oxford University Press.

Hall, G. Stanley. 1904. *Adolescence: Its Psychology and Its Relation to Physiology, Anthropology, Sociology, Sex, Crime, Religion, and Education*, vol. I and II. Englewood Cliffs, NJ: Prentice-Hall.

Hallowell, A. Irving. 1945. "The Rorschach Technique in the Study of Personality and Culture." *American Anthropologist* 47 (2): 195–210.

———. 1955. *Culture and Experience*. Philadelphia: University of Pennsylvania Press.

———. 1976. "Ojibwa Ontology, Behavior, and World View." In Paul Radin, ed. *Contributions to Anthropology: Selected Papers of A. Irving Hallowell*. Chicago: The University of Chicago Press, pp. 357–90.

Halloy, Arnaud. 2012. "Gods in the Flesh: Learning Emotions in the Xangô Possession Cult (Brazil)." *Ethnos* 77 (2): 177–202.

Halloy, Arnaud and Vlad Naumescu. 2012. "Learning Spirit Possession: An Introduction." *Ethnos* 77 (2): 155–76.

Hamer, John and Irene Hamer. 1966. "Spirit Possession and Its Socio-Psychological Implications among the Sidamo of Southwest Ethiopia." *Ethnology* 5 (4): 392–408.

Han, Shihui and Georg Northoff. 2008. "Culture-Sensitive Neural Substrates of Human Cognition: A Transcultural Neuroimaging Approach." *Nature Reviews: Neuroscience* 9 (August): 646–54.

Harrington, Charles. 1968. "Sexual Differentiation in Socialization and Some Male Genital Mutilations." *American Anthropologist* 70 (5): 951–6.

Harris, Helen. 1995. "Rethinking Polynesian Heterosexual Relationships: A Case Study on Mangaia, Cook Islands." In William R. Jankowiak, ed. *Romantic Passion: A Universal Experience?* New York: Columbia University Press, pp. 95–127.

Harrison, Simon. 1985. "Concepts of the Person in Avatip Religious Thought." *Man* (n.s.) 20 (1): 115–30.

Harvey, Graham. 2006. *Animism: Respecting the Living World*. New York: Columbia University Press.

Hay, Thomas H. 1977. "The Development of Some Aspects of the Ojibwa Self and Its Behavioral Environment." *Ethos* 5 (1): 71–89.

Heald, Suzette. 1986. "The Ritual Use of Violence: Circumcision among the Gisu of Uganda." In David Riches, ed. *The Anthropology of Violence*. Oxford: Basil Blackwell, pp. 70–85.

Heath, Chip and Dan Heath. 2007. *Made to Stick: Why Some Ideas Survive and Others Die*. New York: Random House.

Helman, Cecil. 2007. *Culture, Health and Illness: An Introduction for Health Professionals*, 5th ed. London: Hodder Arnold.

Henry, Jules, Siegfried F. Nadel, William Caudill, John J. Honigmann, Melford E. Spiro, Donald W. Fiske, George Spindler, and A. Irving Hallowell. 1955. "Symposium: Projective Testing in Ethnography." *American Anthropologist* 57 (2, part 1): 245–70.

Herbst, Franziska A. 2016. *Biomedical Entanglements: Conceptions of Personhood in a Papua New Guinea Society*. New York and Oxford: Berghahn.

Herskovits, Melville J. 1937. "The Significance of the Study of Acculturation for Anthropology." *American Anthropologist* 39 (2): 259–64.

Hinton, Devon, Ha Chau, Lim Nguyen, Mai Nguyen, Thang Pham, Sarah Quinn, and Minh Tran. 2001. "Panic Disorder among Vietnamese Refugees Attending a Psychiatric Clinic: Prevalence and Subtypes." *General Hospital Psychiatry* 23 (6): 337–44.

Hippler, Arthur E. 1973. "The Athabascans of Interior Alaska: A Culture and Personality Perspective." *American Anthropologist* 75 (5): 1529–41.

Hollan, Douglas. 1989. "The Personal Use of Dream Beliefs in the Toraja Highlands." *Ethos* 17 (2): 166–86.

———. 1992. "Cross-Cultural Differences in the Self." *Journal of Anthropological Research* 48 (4): 283–300.

Holland, William R. and Roland G. Tharp. 1964. "Highland Maya Psychotherapy." *American Anthropologist* 66 (1): 41–52.

Honigmann, John J. 1959. "Psychocultural Studies." *Biennial Review of Anthropology* 1: 67–106.

Horton, Donald. 1943. "The Functions of Alcohol in Primitive Societies: A Cross-Cultural Study." *Quarterly Journal of Studies of Alcohol* 4: 199–320.

Hsu, Francis L. K. 1972a [1953]. *Americans and Chinese: Reflections on Two Cultures and Their People.* Garden City, NY: Doubleday Natural History Press.

———. 1972b [1961]. *Psychological Anthropology.* Cambridge, MA: Schenkman Publishing Company.

Iacoboni, Marco. 2005. "Understanding Others: Imitation, Language, and Empathy." In Susan Hurley and Nick Chater, eds. *Perspectives on Imitation: From Neuroscience to Social Science. Volume 1: Mechanisms of Imitation and Imitation in Animals.* Cambridge, MA: Massachusetts Institute of Technology Press, pp. 77–100.

Ingold, Tim. 2008. "Anthropology is *Not* Ethnography." *Proceedings of the British Academy* 154: 69–92.

James, Doris J. and Lauren E. Glaze. 2006. *Mental Health Problems of Prison and Jail Inmates.* Washington, DC: U.S. Department of Justice.

Jankowiak, William R. and Edward F. Fischer. 1992. "A Cross-Cultural Perspective on Romantic Love." *Ethnology* 31 (2): 149–55.

Jenkins, Lucas J., Yung-Jui Yang, Joshua Goh, Ying-Yi Hong, and Denise C. Park, 2010. "Cultural Differences in the Lateral Occipital Complex while Viewing Incongruent Scenes." *Social Cognitive and Affective Neuroscience* 5 (2–3): 236–41.

Jokic, Zeljko. 2015. *The Living Ancestors: Shamanism, Cosmos, and Cultural Change among the Yanomani of the Upper Orinoco.* New York and Oxford: Berghahn.

Junker, Marie-Odile and Louise Blacksmith. 2006. "Are There Emotional Universals? Evidence from the Native American Language East Cree." *Culture & Psychology* 12 (3): 275–303.

Kane, Steven M. 1974. "Ritual Possession in a Southern Appalachian Religious Sect." *The Journal of American Folklore* 87 (346): 293–302.

Kant, Immanuel. 2006 [1798]. *Anthropology from a Pragmatic Point of View.* Robert B. Louden, trans. and ed. Cambridge and New York: Cambridge University Press.

Kardiner, Abram. 1939. *The Individual and His Society: The Psychodynamics of Primitive Social Organization.* New York: Columbia University Press.

———. 1945. *The Psychological Frontiers of Society.* New York: Columbia University Press.

Katz, Richard. 1982. *Boiling Energy: Community Healing Among the Kalahari Kung.* Cambridge, MA and London: Harvard University Press.

Kaye, Barrington. 1962. *Bringing Up Children in Ghana.* London: Allen & Unwin.

Keller, Heidi. 2007. *Cultures of Infancy.* Mahwah, NJ: Lawrence Erlbaum.

Kidd, Dudley. 1906. *Savage Childhood: A Study of Kafir Children.* London: Adam and Charles Black.

Kirmayer, Laurence J. 2001. "Sapir's Vision of Culture and Personality." *Psychiatry* 64 (1): 23–31.

Kitayama, Shinobu and Jiyoung Park. 2010. "Cultural Neuroscience of the Self: Understanding the Social Grounding of the Brain." *Social Cognitive and Affective Neuroscience* 5 (2–3): 111–29.

Kleinman, Arthur. 1978. "Concepts and a Model for the Comparison of Medical Systems as Cultural Systems." *Social Science & Medicine* 12: 85–93.

———. 1980. *Patients and Healers in the Context of Culture: An Exploration of the Borderland between Anthropology, Medicine, and Psychiatry.* Berkeley and London: University of California Press.

Kohn, Eduardo. 2007. "How Dogs Dream: Amazonian Natures and the Politics of Transspecies Engagement." *American Ethnologist* 34 (1): 3–24.

Kondo, Dorinne K. 1987. "Creating an Ideal Self: Theories of Selfhood and Pedagogy at a Japanese Ethics Retreat." *Ethos* 15 (3): 241–72.

Krippner, Stanley. 1987. "Cross-Cultural Approaches to Multiple Personality Disorder: Practices in Brazilian Spiritism." *Ethos* 15 (3): 273–95.

Kroeber, Alfred L. 1917. "The Superorganic." *American Anthropologist* 19 (2): 163–213.

———. 1919. "On the Principle of Order in Civilization as Exemplified by Changes in Fashion." *American Anthropologist* 21 (3): 235–63.

Kusserow, Adrie S. 1999. "Crossing the Great Divide: Anthropological Theories of the Western Self." *Journal of Anthropological Research* 55 (4): 541–62.

Laing, Ronald D. 1967. *The Politics of Experience.* New York: Ballantine Books.

Lakoff, George and Mark Johnson. 1999. *Philosophy in the Flesh: The Embodied Mind and Its Challenge to Western Thought.* New York: Basic Books.

Lambek, Michael. 1980. "Spirits and Spouses: Possession as a System of Communication among the Malagasy Speakers of Mayotte." *American Ethnologist* 7 (2): 318–31.

Lang, Claudia and Eva Jansen. 2013. "Appropriating Depression: Biomedicalizing Ayurvedic Psychiatry in Kerala, India." *Medical Anthropology: Cross-Cultural Studies in Health and Illness* 32 (1): 25–45.

Langer, Suzanne K. 1942. *Philosophy in a New Key: A Study in the Symbolism of Reason, Rite, and Art.* New York: Mentor Books.

Latour, Bruno. 1987. *Science in Action: How to Follow Scientists and Engineers Through Society.* Cambridge, MA: Harvard University Press.

Laughlin, Charles D. and C. Jason Throop. 2006. "Cultural Neurophenomenology: Integrating Experience, Culture and Reality through Fisher Information." *Culture & Psychology* 12 (3): 305–37.

Leach, Edmund. 1969. *Genesis as Myth and Other Essays.* London: Jonathan Cape.

———. 1981. "A Poetics of Power." *The New Republic* 184 (14): 30–2.

Leavitt, John. 1996. "Meaning and Feeling in the Anthropology of Emotions." *American Ethnologist* 23 (3): 514–39.

LeDoux, Joseph. 2002. *The Synaptic Self: How Our Brains Become Who We Are.* New York: Penguin Books.

Lee, Dorothy. 1959. *Freedom and Culture.* Englewood Cliffs NJ: Prentice-Hall, Inc.

Leenhardt, Maurice. 1979. *Do Kamo: Person and Myth in the Melanesian World.* Chicago: The University of Chicago Press.

Leheny, David. 2006. *Think Global, Fear Local: Sex, Violence, and Anxiety in Contemporary Japan.* Ithaca, NY and London: Cornell University Press.

Leighton, Alexander H. and Dorothea C. Leighton. 1942. "Some Types of Uneasiness and Fear in a Navaho Indian Community." *American Anthropologist* 44 (2): 194–209.

Leighton, Dorothea and Clyde Kluckhohn. 1948. *Children of the People: The Navajo Individual and His Development.* Cambridge, MA: Harvard University Press.

Lepowsky, Maria. 2011. "The Boundaries of Personhood, the Problem of Empathy, and 'the Native's Point of View' in the Outer Islands." In Douglas W. Hollan and C. Jason Throop, eds. *The Anthropology of Empathy: Experiencing the Lives of Others in Pacific Societies.* New York and Oxford: Berghahn, pp. 43–65.

Leroi-Gourhan, André. 1993 [1964]. *Gesture and Speech.* Cambridge, MA: Massachusetts Institute of Technology Press.

Lévi-Strauss, Claude. 1963 [1958]. *Structural Anthropology.* Claire Jacobson and Brooke Grundfest Schoepf, trans. New York and London: Basic Books.

———. 1966 [1962]. *The Savage Mind.* George Weidenfeld, trans. Chicago: The University of Chicago Press.

———. 1969 [1949]. *The Elementary Structures of Kinship.* Hames Harle Bell and John Richard von Sturmer, trans. Boston, MA: Beacon Pres.

LeVine, Robert A. 1973. *Culture, Behavior, and Personality: An Introduction to the Comparative Study of Psychosocial Adaptation*. Chicago: Aldine Publishing Company.

———. 2010. "The Six Cultures Study: Prologue to a History of a Landmark Project." *Journal of Cross Cultural Psychology* 41 (4): 513–21.

Levy, Robert I. 1973. *Tahitians: Mind and Experience in the Society Islands*. Chicago and London: The University of Chicago Press.

Lévy-Bruhl, Lucien. 1966 [1910]. *How Natives Think*. Lilian A. Clare, trans. New York: Washington Square Press.

Lewis, Ioan M. 1966. "Spirit Possession and Deprivation Cults." *Man* (n.s.) 1 (3): 307–29.

Lewis-Williams, David. 2002. *The Mind in the Cave: Consciousness and the Origins of Art*. London: Thames & Hudson.

Lewis-Williams, David and Thomas A. Dowson. 1988. "The Signs of All Times: Entoptic Phenomena in Upper Palaeolithic Art." *Current Anthropology* 29 (2): 201–45.

Lincoln, Jackson S. 1935. *The Dream in Primitive Cultures*. London: Cresset Press.

Lindholm, Charles. 2005. "Anthropology of Emotion." In Conerly Casey and Robert B. Edgerton, eds. 2005. *A Companion to Psychological Anthropology: Modernity and Psychocultural Change*. Malden, MA and Oxford: Blackwell, pp. 30–47.

———. 2006. "Romantic Love and Anthropology." *Etnofoor* 19 (1): 5–21.

Linton, Ralph. 1945. *The Cultural Background of Personality*. New York: Appleton-Century Crofts.

LiPuma, Edward. 2000. *Encompassing Others: The Magic of Modernity in Melanesia*. Ann Arbor: University of Michigan Press.

Littlewood, Roland. 1992. "DSM-IV and Culture: Is the Classification Internationally Valid?" *Psychiatric Bulletin* 16 (May): 257–61.

———. 1998. "Mental Illness as Ritual Theatre." *Performance Research* 3 (3): 41–52.

Littlewood, Roland and Maurice Lipsedge. 2005 [1982]. *Aliens and Alienists: Ethnic Minorities and Psychiatry*, 3rd ed. London: Taylor & Francis e-Library.

Lohmann, Roger I. 2011. "Empathic Perception and Imagination among the Asabano: Lessons for Anthropology." In Douglas W. Hollan and C. Jason Throop, eds. *The Anthropology of Empathy: Experiencing the Lives of Others in Pacific Societies*. New York and Oxford: Berghahn, pp. 95–116.

Londono Sulkin, Carlos D. 2012. *People of Substance: An Ethnography of Morality in the Colombian Amazon*. Toronto: University of Toronto Press.

Lounsbury, Floyd G. 1956. "A Semantic Analysis of the Pawnee Kinship Usage." *Language* 32 (1): 158–94.

Low, Setha M. 1997. "Urban Fear: Building the Fortress City." *City & Society* 9 (1): 53–71.

Ludwig, Arnold M. 1990. "Altered States of Consciousness." In Charles Tart, ed. *Altered States of Consciousness*, 3rd ed. New York: HarperCollins, pp. 18–33.

Luria, Alexander R. and Lev S. Vygotsky. 1992 [1930]. *Ape, Primitive, Man, and Child: Essays in the History of Behavior*. Evelyn Rossiter, trans. New York: Harvester Wheatsheaf.

Lutz, Catherine A. 1998. *Unnatural Emotions: Everyday Sentiments on a Micronesian Atoll and Their Challenge to Western Theory*. Chicago and London: The University of Chicago Press.

Lyon, Margot L. 1995: "Missing Emotion: The Limitations of Cultural Constructionism in the Study of Emotion." *Current Anthropology* 10 (2): 244–63.

Mageo, Jeannette M. 1991. "Ma'i Aitu: The Cultural Logic of Possession in Samoa." *Ethnos* 19 (3): 352–83.

———. 2011. "Empathy and 'As-If' Attachment in Samoa." In Douglas W. Hollan and C. Jason Throop, eds. *The Anthropology of Empathy: Experiencing the Lives of Others in Pacific Societies*. New York and Oxford: Berghahn, pp. 69–93.

Maggi, Wynne. 2006. "'Heart-Struck': Love Marriage as a Marker of Ethnic Identity among the Kalasha of Northwest Pakistan." In Jennifer Hirsch and Holly Wardlow, eds. *Modern Loves: The Anthropology of Romantic Courtship and Companionate Marriage*. Ann Arbor: University of Michigan Press, pp. 78–91.

Malafouris, Lambros. 2013. *How Things Shape the Mind: A Theory of Material Engagement*. Cambridge, MA: Massachusetts Institute of Technology Press.

Malinowski, Bronislaw. 1927. *Sex and Repression in Savage Society*. Chicago: The University of Chicago Press.

———. 1929. *The Sexual Life of Savages in North-Western Melanesia*. New York: Eugenics Publishing Company.

———. 1984 [1922]. *Argonauts of the Western Pacific*. Long Grove, IL: Waveland Press.

Manschreck, Theo C., and Arthur Kleinman. 1979. "Psychiatry's Identity Crisis: A Critical Rational Remedy." *General Hospital Psychiatry* 1 (2): 166–73.

Margold, Jane A. 1999. "From 'Cultures of Fear and Terror' to the Normalization of Violence: An Ethnographic Case." *Critique of Anthropology* 19 (1): 63–88.

Marriott, McKim and Ronald B. Inden. 1977. "Toward an Ethnosociology of South Asian Caste Systems." In Kenneth A. David, ed. *The New Wind: Changing Identities in South Asia*. The Hague: Mouton, pp. 277–38.

Martínez, David. 2004. "The Soul of the Indian: Lakota Philosophy and the Vision Quest." *Wicazo Sa Review* 19 (2): 79–104.

Mauss, Marcel. 1985 [1938] "A Category of the Human Mind: The Notion of Person; The Notion of Self." W. D. Halls, trans. In Michael Carrithers, Steven Collins, and Steven Lukes, eds. *The Category of the Person: Anthropology, Philosophy, History*. Cambridge and New York: Cambridge University Press, pp. 1–25.

———. 1992 [1934]. "Techniques of the Body." In Jonathan Crary and Sanford Kwinter, eds. *Incorporations*. New York: Zone, pp. 455–77.

McCallum, Cecilia. 1996. "The Body that Knows: From Cashinahua Epistemology to a Medical Anthropology of Lowland South America." *Medical Anthropology Quarterly* 10 (3): 347–72.

McGranahan, Carole. 2005. "Truth, Fear, and Lies: Exile Politics and Arrested Histories of the Tibetan Resistance." *Cultural Anthropology* 20 (4): 570–600.

Mead, George H. 1934. *Mind, Self, and Society*. Charles W. Morris, ed. Chicago: The University of Chicago Press.

Mead, Margaret. 1926. "The Methodology of Racial Testing: Its Significance for Sociology." *American Journal of Sociology* 31 (5): 657–67.

———. 1928. *Coming of Age in Samoa: A Psychological Study of Primitive Youth for Western Civilization*. New York: William Morrow & Company.

———. 1930. *Growing Up in New Guinea: A Comparative Study of Primitive Education*. New York: Blue Ribbon Books.

———. 1932. "Investigation of the Thought of Primitive Children, with Special Reference to Animism." *The Journal of the Royal Anthropological Institute of Great Britain and Ireland* 62 (Jan–Jun.): 173–90.

———. 1953. "National Character." In Alfred L. Kroeber, ed. *Anthropology Today: An Encyclopedic Inventory*. Chicago: The University of Chicago Press, pp. 642–67.

———. 1963 [1935]. *Sex and Temperament in Three Primitive Societies*. New York: William Morrow & Company.

Mead, Margaret and Rhoda Métraux, eds. 1953. *The Study of Culture as a Distance*. Chicago and London: The Chicago University Press.

Meggitt, Mervyn J. 1962. "Dream Interpretation among the Mae Enga of New Guinea." *Southwestern Journal of Anthropology* 18 (3): 216–29.

Mikkelsen, Henrik H. 2016. "Chaosmology: Shamanism and Personhood among the Bugkalot." *Hau: Journal of Ethnographic Theory* 6 (1): 189–205.

Miller, Jeremy. 2015. *Sticky Branding: 12.5 Principles to Stand Out, Attract Customers, and Grow an Incredible Brand*. Toronto: Dundurn Press.

Minsky, Marvin. 1975. "A Framework for Representing Knowledge." In Patrick H. Winston, ed. *The Psychology of Computer Vision*. New York: McGraw-Hill, pp. 211–77.

Minturn, Leigh and William W. Lambert. 1964. *Mother of Six Cultures: Antecedents of Child Rearing*. New York: John Wiley.

Moreira-Almeida, Alexander and Francisco Lotufo Neto. 2005. "Spiritist Views of Mental Disorders in Brazil." *Transcultural Psychiatry* 42 (4): 570–95.

Murdock, George P. 1957. "World Ethnographic Sample." *American Anthropologist* 59 (4): 664–87.

Murdock, George P., Clellan S. Ford, Alfred E. Hudson, Raymond Kennedy, Leo W. Simmons, and John W. M. Whiting. 1961. *Outline of Cultural Materials*, 4th revised ed. New Haven, CT: Human Relations Area Files.

Murdock, George P. and Douglas R. White. 1969. "Standard Cross-Cultural Sample." *Ethnology* 8 (4): 329–69.

Murphy, Dominic. 2015. "'Deviant Deviance': Cultural Diversity in DSM-5." In Steeves Demazeux and Patrick Singy, eds. *The DSM-5 in Perspective*. History, Philosophy and Theory of the Life Sciences 10. Dordrecht: Springer Science+Business Media, pp. 97–110.

Murphy, Robert F. 1990 [1987]. *The Body Silent: The Different World of the Disabled*. New York: W. W. Norton.

Musharbash, Yasmine. 2014. "Introduction: Monsters, Anthropology, and Monster Studies." In Yasmine Musharbash and Gier Henning Presterudstuen, eds. *Monster Anthropology in Australasia and Beyond*. New York: Palgrave Macmillan, pp. 1–24.

Nadel, Siegfried F. 1951. *The Foundations of Social Anthropology*. Glencoe, IL: The Free Press.

Naroll, Raoul. 1970. "What Have We Learned from Cross-Cultural Surveys?" *American Anthropologist* 72 (6): 1227–88.

Noll, Richard. 1983. "Shamanism and Schizophrenia: A State-Specific Approach to the 'Schizophrenia Metaphor' of Shamanic States." *American Ethnologist* 10 (3): 443–59.

Obeyesekere, Gananath. 1981. *Medusa's Hair: An Essay on Personal Symbols and Religious Experience*. Chicago: The University of Chicago Press.

Obiechina, Emmanuel. 1973. *An African Popular Literature: A Study of Onitsha Market Pamphlets*. Cambridge: Cambridge University Press.

Ochs, Elinor and Lisa Capps. 1996. "Narrating the Self." *Annual Review of Anthropology* 25: 19–43.

Ohnuki-Tierney, Emiko. 1974. *The Ainu of the Northwest Coast of Southern Sakhalin*. New York: Holt, Rinehart, and Winston.

Okello, Elialilia S. and Solvig Ekblad. 2006. "Lay Concepts of Depression among the Baganda of Uganda: A Pilot Study." *Transcultural Psychiatry* 43 (2): 287–313.

Opler, Morris E. 1945. "Themes as Dynamic Forces in Culture." *American Journal of Sociology* 51 (3): 198–206.

Osborne, Larry. 2010. *Sticky Teams: Keeping Your Leadership Team and Staff on the Same Page*. Grand Rapids, MI: Zondervan.

Overing, Joanne. 1986. "Images of Cannibalism, Death, and Domination in a 'Non-Violent' Society." In David Riches, ed. *The Anthropology of Violence*. Oxford: Basil Blackwell, pp. 86–102.

Owens, James O. 1884. *Omaha Sociology*. Washington, DC: Smithsonian Institution, Bureau of American Ethnology annual report, no.3.

Pálsson, Gísli. 1994. "Enskilment at Sea." *Man* (n.s.) 29 (4): 901–27.

Park, Denise C. and Chih-Mao Huang. 2010. "Culture Wires the Brain: A Cognitive Neuroscience Perspective." *Perspectives on Psychological Science* 5 (4): 391–400.

Park, Robert E. 1928. "Human Migration and the Marginal Man." *American Journal of Sociology* 33 (6): 881–93.

Parsons, Talcott. 1951. *The Social System*. Glencoe, IL: The Free Press of Glencoe.

Pedersen, Morten A. 2011. *Not Quite Shamans: Spirit Worlds and Political Lives in Northern Mongolia*. Ithaca, NY and London: Cornell University Press.

Penny, H. Glenn. 2002. *Objects of Culture: Ethnology and Ethnographic Museums in Imperial Germany*. Chapel Hill: University of North Carolina Press.

Peters, Larry G. 1982. "Trance, Initiation, and Psychotherapy in Tamang Shamanism." *American Ethnologist* 9 (1): 21–46.

Porath, Nathan. 2013. "'Not to be Aware Anymore': Indigenous Sumatran Ideas and Shamanic Experiences of Changed States of Awareness/Consciousness." *Anthropology of Consciousness* 24 (1): 7–31.

Porteus, Stanley D. 1917. "Mental Tests with Delinquents and Australian Aboriginal Children." *Psychological Review* 24 (1): 32–42.

———. 1931. *The Psychology of a Primitive People.* London: Arnold & Co., London; New York: Longmans Green.

———. 1933. "Mentality of Australian Aboriginals." *Oceania* 4 (1): 30–6.

Powell, Kara E. and Chap Clark. 2011. *Sticky Faith: Everyday Ideas to Build Lasting Faith in Your Kids.* Grand Rapids, MI: Zondervan.

Prothro, Edwin T. 1961. "Child Rearing in the Lebanon." *Harvard Middle Eastern Monographs* 8. Cambridge, MA: Harvard University Press.

Pruett, Chris. 2010. "The Anthropology of Fear: Learning about Japan through Horror Games." *Interface: The Journal of Education, Community and Values* 10: 1–16.

Radcliffe-Brown, Alfred R. 1957. *A Natural Science of Society.* Glencoe, IL: The Free Press.

Rahimi, Sadeq. 2014. "Power, Change, and 'The Culture of Psychiatry.'" *Anthropology & Medicine* 21 (3): 312–24.

Ram, Kalpana. 2013. *Fertile Disorder: Spirit Possession and Its Provocation of the Modern.* Honolulu: University of Hawai'i Press.

Ramirez, Michelle, Andrea Altschular, Carmit McMullen, Marcia Grant, Mark Hornbrook, and Robert Krouse. 2014. "'I Didn't Feel Like I Was a Person Anymore': Realigning Full Adult Personhood after Ostomy Surgery." *Medical Anthropology Quarterly* 28 (2): 242–59.

Ramsay, Rosalind. 1999. "Roland Littlewood: In Conversation with Rosalind Ramsay." *Psychiatric Bulletin* 23: 733–9.

Read, Ursula M., Victor C. K. Doku, and Ama De-Graft Aikins. 2015. "Schizophrenia and Psychosis in West Africa." In Emmanuel Akyeampong, Allan G. Hill & Arthur Kleinman, eds. *The Culture of Mental Illness and Psychiatric Practice in Africa.* Bloomington and Indianapolis: Indiana University Press, pp. 73–111.

Rebhun, Linda A. 1994. "Swallowing Frogs: Anger and Illness in Northeast Brazil." *Medical Anthropology Quarterly* 8 (4): 360–82.

———. 1995. "The Language of Love in Northeast Brazil." In William R. Jankowiak, ed. *Romantic Passion: A Universal Experience?* New York: Columbia University Press, pp. 239–61.

Redfield, Robert, Ralph Linton, and Melville Herskovits. 1936. "Memorandum for the Study of Acculturation." *American Anthropologist* 38 (1): 149–52.

Regis, Helen A. 1995. "The Madness of Excess: Love among the Fulbe of North Cameroon." In William R. Jankowiak, ed. *Romantic Passion: A Universal Experience?* New York: Columbia University Press, pp. 141–51.

Rescorla, Michael. 2016. "The Computational Theory of Mind." In Edward N. Zalta, ed. *The Stanford Encyclopedia of Philosophy* (Winter 2016 Edition). https://plato.stanford.edu/archives/ win2016/entries/computational-mind, accessed December 26, 2016.

Rice, G. Elizabeth. 1980. "On Cultural Schemata." *American Ethnologist* 7 (1): 152–71.

Richert, Rebekah A. and Justin L. Barrett. 2005. "Do You See What I See? Young Children's Assumptions about God's Perceptual Abilities." *The International Journal for the Psychology of Religion* 15 (4): 283–95.

Ridington, Robin. 1982. "Telling Stories: Stories of the Vision Quest." *The Canadian Journal of Native Studies* 2 (2): 213–9.

Rivers, William H. R. 1924a. *Medicine, Magic, and Religion.* London: Kegan Paul, Trench, and Trübner.

———. 1924b. *Social Organization.* London: Kegan Paul, Trench, and Trübner.

———. 1999 [1926]. *Psychology and Ethnology.* London: Routledge.

Robarchek, Clayton A. 1979. "Learning to Fear: A Case Study of Emotional Conditioning." *American Ethnologist* 6 (3): 555–67.

———. 1986. "Helplessness, Fearfulness, and Peacefulness: The Emotional and Motivational Contexts of Semai Social Relations." *Anthropological Quarterly* 59 (4): 177–83 + 200–4.

Robbins, Joel and Alan Rumsey. 2008. "Introduction: Cultural and Linguistic Anthropology and the Opacity of Other Minds." *Anthropological Quarterly* 81 (2): 407–20.

Rohde, Joy. 2013. *Armed with Expertise: The Militarization of American Social Research during the Cold War*. Ithaca, NY and London: Cornell University Press.

Róheim, Géza. 1925. *Australian Totemism: A Psycho-analytic Study in Anthropology*. London: Frank Cass.

———. 1932. "Animism and Religion." *Psychoanalytic Quarterly* 6: 59–112.

———. 1934. *The Riddle of the Sphinx*. London: Institute of Psychoanalysis.

———. 1945. *The Eternal Ones of the Dream: A Psychoanalytic Interpretation of Australian Myth and Ritual*. New York: International Universities Press.

Rosaldo, Michelle. 1980. *Knowledge and Passion: Ilongot Notions of Self and Social Life*. Cambridge: Cambridge University Press.

———. 1984. "Toward an Anthropology of Self and Feeling." In Richard Shweder and Robert LeVine, eds. *Culture Theory: Essays on Mind, Self and Emotion*. Cambridge: Cambridge University Press, pp. 137–57.

Röttger-Rössler, Birgitt. 2008. "Voice Intimacies: Verbalized Experiences of Love and Sexuality in an Indonesian Society." In William R. Jankowiak, ed. *Intimacies: Love + Sex Across Cultures*. New York: Columbia University Press, pp. 148–73.

Rudnyckyj, Daromir. 2010. *Spiritual Economies: Islam, Globalization, and the Afterlife of Development*. Ithaca, NY and London: Cornell University Press.

Rumelhart, David E. and Don A. Norman. 1978. "Accretion, Tuning, and Restructuring: Three Modes of Learning." In John W. Cotton and Roberta L. Klatzky, eds. *Semantic Factors in Cognition*. Hillsdale, NJ: Lawrence Erlbaum Associates, pp. 37–53.

Rushkoff, Douglas. 1994. *Media Virus!: Hidden Agendas in Popular Culture*. New York: Ballantine Books.

Ryle, Gilbert. 1970 [1949]. *The Concept of Mind*. Harmondsworth, UK: Penguin Books.

Saglio-Yatzimirsky, Marie C. and Brigitte Sébastia. 2015. "Mixing Tīrttam and Tablets: A Healing Proposal for Mentally Ill Patients in Gunaseelam (South India)." *Anthropology & Medicine* 22 (2): 127–137.

Sakauye, Kenneth. 2015. "Diversity and Cultural Competence: Part 2: Cultural Issues in Treating Geriatric Patients with Mental Illness." *Psychiatric Times* 32 (7): 16.

Sapir, Edward. 1917. "Do We Need a 'Superorganic'?" *American Anthropologist* 19 (3): 441–7.

———. 1921. *Language: An Introduction to the Study of Speech*. New York: Harcourt, Brace.

———. 1929. "The Status of Linguistics as a Science." *Language* 5 (4): 207–14.

———. 1932. "Cultural Anthropology and Psychiatry." *The Journal of Abnormal and Social Psychology* 27 (3): 229–42.

———. 1934. "The Emergence of the Study of Personality in a Study of Cultures." *Journal of Social Psychology* 5 (3): 408–15.

———. 2001 [1938]. "Why Cultural Anthropology Needs the Psychiatrist." *Psychiatry* 64 (1): 2–10.

Saussure, Ferdinand de. 1959 [1916]. *Course in General Linguistics*. Charles Bally and Albert Sechehaye, eds. New York: Philosophical Library.

Schäuble, Michaela. 2014. *Narrating Victimhood: Gender, Religion, and the Making of Place in Post War Croatia*. New York and Oxford: Berghahn.

Scheper-Hughes, Nancy. 1992. *Death without Weeping: The Violence of Everyday Life in Brazil*. Berkeley: University of California Press.

Schieffelin, Bambi B. 2008. "Speaking Only Your Own Mind: Reflections on Talk, Gossip, and Intentionality in Bosavi (PNG)." *Anthropological Quarterly* 81 (2): 431–41.

Schieffelin, Edward L. 1983. "Anger and Shame in the Tropical Forest: On Affect as a Cultural System in Papua New Guinea." *Ethos* 11 (3): 181–91.

Schulz, Priscilla M., L. Christian Huber, and Patricia A. Resick. 2006. "Practical Adaptations of Cognitive Processing Therapy with Bosnian Refugees: Implications for Adapting Practice to a Multicultural Clientele." *Cognitive and Behavioral Practice* 13 (4): 310–21.

Segall, Marshall H., Donald T. Campbell, and Melville J. Herskovits. 1966. *The Influence of Culture on Visual Perception.* Indianapolis, IN: The Bobbs-Merrill Company.

Shamoon, Deborah. 2012. *Passionate Friendships: The Aesthetics of Girls' Culture in Japan.* Honolulu: University of Hawai'i Press.

Shirley, Rodney W. and A. Kimball Romney. 1962. "Love Magic and Socialization Anxiety." *American Anthropologist* 64 (5, part 1): 1028–31.

Shweder, Richard A. 1980. "Rethinking Culture and Personality Theory Part III: From Genesis and Typology to Hermeneutics and Dynamics." *Ethos* 8 (1): 60–94.

Sillitoe, Paul. 2002. "Contested Knowledge, Contingent Classification: Animals in the Highlands of Papua New Guinea." *American Anthropologist* 104 (4): 1162–71.

Simmons, Leo, ed. 1942. *Sun Chief: The Autobiography of a Hopi Indian.* New Haven, CT and London: Yale University Press.

Simons, Ronald C. and Charles C. Hughes, eds. 1985. *The Culture-Bound Syndromes: Folk Illnesses of Psychiatric and Anthropological Interest.* Dordrecht: D. Reidel.

Simova, Bobbie, Tara Robertson, and Duke Beasley. 2009. "Cognitive Anthropology." Http://anthropology.ua.edu/cultures/cultures.php?culture=Cognitive%20Anthropology, accessed October 3, 2016.

Singleton, John. 1989. "Japanese Folkcraft Pottery Apprenticeship: Cultural Patterns of an Educational Institution." In Michael W. Coy, ed. *Apprenticeship: From Theory to Method and Back Again.* Albany, NY: State University of New York Press, pp. 13–30.

Skidmore, Monique. 2003. "Darker than Midnight: Fear, Vulnerability, and Terror Making in Urban Burma (Myanmar)." *American Ethnologist* 30 (1): 5–21.

Skultans, Vieda. 1987. "The Management of Mental Illness Among Maharashtrian Families: A Case Study of a Mahanubhav Healing Temple." *Man* (n.s.) 22 (4): 661–79.

Slotkin, James S., ed. 1965. *Readings in Early Anthropology.* London: Methuen & Co. Ltd.

Smith, Karl. 2012. "From Dividual and Individual Selves to Porous Subjects." *The Australian Journal of Anthropology* 23: 50–64.

Society for Medical Anthropology. 2017. "What is Medical Anthropology?" www.medanthro.net/about/about-medical-anthropology, accessed November 7, 2017.

Solomon, Robert C. 2002. "Back to Basics: On the Very Idea of 'Basic Emotions.'" *Journal for the Theory of Social Behavior* 32 (2): 115–44.

Sosis, Richard and Candace Alcorta. 2003. "Signaling, Solidarity, and the Sacred: The Evolution of Religious Behavior." *Evolutionary Anthropology* 12: 264–74.

Spencer, Baldwin and Francis J. Gillen. 1968 [1899]. *The Native Tribes of Central Australia.* New York: Dover Publications.

Sperber, Dan. 1979 [1974]. *Rethinking Symbolism.* Alice L. Morton, trans. Cambridge: Cambridge University Press.

———. 1985. "Anthropology and Psychology: Towards an Epidemiology of Representations." *Man* 20 (1): 73–89.

Spiegel, David, Richard J. Loewenstein, Roberto Lewis-Fernández, Vedat Sar, Daphne Simeon, Eric Vermetten, Etzel Cardeña, and Paul F. Dell. 2011. "Dissociative Disorders in DSM-5." *Depression and Anxiety* 28: 824–52.

Spindler, George D. 1955. *Sociocultural and Psychological Processes in Menomini Acculturation.* Berkeley: University of California Press.

Spiro, Melford. 1951. "Culture and Personality: The Natural History of a False Dichotomy." *Psychiatry* 15: 19–46.

———. 1993. "Is the Western Conception of the Self 'Peculiar' within the Context of the World Cultures?" *Ethos* 21 (2): 107–53.

Srivastava, Vinay K. 2002. "Some Thoughts on the Anthropology of Mental Health and Illness with Special Reference to India." *Anthropos* 97 (2): 529–41.

Staal, Frits. 1979. "The Meaningless of Ritual." *Numen* 26 (1): 2–22.

Stanner, William E. H. 2010 [2009]. *The Dreaming & Other Essays.* Collingwood, Victoria, Australia: Black Inc. Agenda.

Stephens, William N. "A Cross-Cultural Study of Menstrual Taboos." *Genetic Psychology Monographs* 64: 385–416.

Stern, Pamela R. and Richard G. Condon. 1995. "A Good Spouse is Hard to Find: Marriage, Spouse Exchange, and Infatuation among the Copper Inuit." In William R. Jankowiak, ed. *Romantic Passion: A Universal Experience?* New York: Columbia University Press. pp. 196–218.

Strathern, Marilyn. 1988. *The Gender of the Gift: Problems with Women and Problems with Society in Melanesia.* Berkeley: University of California Press.

Strauss, Claudia and Naomi Quinn. 1997. *A Cognitive Theory of Cultural Meaning.* Cambridge: Cambridge University Press.

Sturtevant, William C. 1964. "Studies in Ethnoscience." *American Anthropologist* 66 (3, part 2): 99–131.

Szasz, Thomas S. 1961. *The Myth of Mental Illness: Foundations of a Theory of Personal Conduct.* New York: Dell Publishing.

Taussig, Michael. 1986. *Shamanism, Colonialism, and the Wild Man: A Study in Terror and Healing.* Chicago: The University of Chicago Press.

Tedlock, Barbara. 1981. "Quiché Maya Dream Interpretation." *Ethos* 9 (4): 313–30.

Teuton, Joanna, Richard Bentall, and Chris Dowrick. 2007. "Conceptualizing Psychosis in Uganda: The Perspective of Indigenous and Religious Healers." *Transcultural Psychiatry* 44 (1): 79–114.

Throop, C. Jason. 2011. "Suffering, Empathy, and Ethical Modalities of Being in Yap (Waqab), Federated States of Micronesia." In Douglas W. Hollan and C. Jason Throop, eds. *The Anthropology of Empathy: Experiencing the Lives of Others in Pacific Societies.* New York and Oxford: Berghahn, pp. 119–49.

Thurman, Joanne. 2014. "Cave Men, Luminoids, and Dragons: Monstrous Creatures Mediating Relationships between People and Country in Aboriginal Northern Australia." In Yasmine Musharbash and Gier Henning Presterudstuen, eds. *Monster Anthropology in Australasia and Beyond.* New York: Palgrave Macmillan, pp. 25–38.

Thurnwald, Richard. 1932. "The Psychology of Acculturation." *American Anthropologist* 34 (4): 557–69.

Topinard, Paul. 1890 [1876]. *Anthropology.* London: Chapman and Hall.

Tyler, Stephen A. 1969. "Introduction." In Stephen A. Tyler, ed. *Cognitive Anthropology.* New York: Holt, Rinehart, and Winston, Inc., pp. 1–23.

Tylor, Edward B. 1958 [1871]. *Primitive Culture.* New York: Harper Torchbooks.

University of Pennsylvania Collaborative on Community Integration. N.d. "Cultural Competence in Mental Health." http://tucollaborative.org/pdfs/Toolkits_Monographs_Guidebooks/community_inclusion/Cultural_Competence_in_MH.pdf, accessed December 16, 2016.

van Dujil, Marjolein, Etzel Cardeña, and Joop T. V. M. de Jong. 2005. "The Validity of DSM-IV Dissociative Disorders Categories in South-West Uganda." *Transcultural Psychiatry* 42 (2): 219–41.

Varma, Saiba. 2016. "Disappearing the Asylum: Modernizing Psychiatry and Generating Manpower in India." *Transcultural Psychiatry* 53 (6): 783–803.

Vivieros de Castro, Eduardo. 1998. "Cosmological Deixis and Amerindian Perspectivism." *The Journal of the Royal Anthropological Institute* 4 (3): 469–88.

Voget, Fred. 1951. "Acculturation at Caughnawaga: A Note on the Native-Modified Group." *American Anthropologist* 53 (2): 220–31.

Voss, Susan M. 1977. "Claude Levi-Strauss: The Man and His Works." *Nebraska Anthropologist* Paper 145: 21–38.

Waitz, Theodor. 1863. *Introduction to Anthropology*. London: Longman, Green, Longman, and Roberts.

Wallace, Anthony F. C. 1956. "Revitalization Movements." *American Anthropologist* 58 (2): 264–81.

———. 1964 [1961]. *Culture and Personality*. New York: Random House.

Wardlow, Holly. 2006. "All's Fair When Love is War: Romantic Passion and Companionate Marriage among the Huli of Papua New Guinea." In Jennifer S. Hirsch and Holly Wardlow, eds. *Modern Loves: The Anthropology of Romantic Courtship and Companionate Marriage*. Ann Arbor: University of Michigan Press, pp. 51–77.

Weller, Susan C. and A. Kimball Romney. 1988. *Systematic Data Collection*. Newbury Park, CA and London: Sage.

White, Leslie A. 1959a. "The Concept of Culture." *American Anthropologist* 61 (2): 227–51.

———. 1959b. *The Evolution of Culture: The Development of Civilization to the Fall of Rome*. New York: McGraw-Hill.

Whitehead, Amy. 2013. *Religious Statues and Personhood: Testing the Role of Materiality*. London: Bloomsbury.

Whitehouse, Harvey. 2004. *Modes of Religiosity: A Cognitive Theory of Religious Transmission*. Lanham, MD: AltaMira Press.

Whiting, Beatrice. 1950. *Paiute Sorcery*. New York: Viking Fund Publications in Anthropology, no. 15.

———, ed. 1963. *Six Cultures: Studies in Child Rearing*. New York: John Wiley and Sons.

Whiting, Beatrice and John W. M. Whiting. 1975. *Children of Six Cultures: A Psycho-cultural Analysis*. Cambridge, MA: Harvard University Press.

Whiting, John W. M. 1941. *Becoming a Kwoma: Teaching and Learning in a New Guinea Tribe*. New Haven, CT: Yale University Press.

Whiting, John W. M. and Irvin L. Child. 1953. *Child Training and Personality: A Cross-Cultural Study*. New Haven, CT: Yale University Press.

Whiting, John W. M., Irvin L. Child, William W. Lambert, Ann M. Fischer, John L. Fischer, and Corinne Nydegger 1966. *Field Guide for a Study of Socialization*. New York: John Wiley.

Whiting, John W. M., Richard Kluckhohn, and Albert Anthony. 1958. "The Function of Male Initiation Ceremonies at Puberty." In Eleanor E. Maccoby, Theodore M. Newcomb, and Eugene L. Hartley (eds.) *Readings in Social Psychology*, 3rd ed. New York: Henry Holt, pp. 359–70.

Wierzbicka, Anna. 1986. "Human Emotions: Universal or Culture-Specific?" *American Anthropologist* 88 (3): 584–94.

———. 1999. *Emotions across Languages and Cultures: Diversity and Universals*. Cambridge: Cambridge University Press.

Wikan, Unni. 1987. "Public Grace and Private Fears: Gaiety, Offense, and Sorcery in Northern Bali." *Ethos* 15 (4):337–65.

Wilson, Edward O. 1975. *Sociobiology: The New Synthesis*. Cambridge, MA: Harvard University Press.

Winkelman, Michael. 1986. "Trance States: A Theoretical Model and Cross-Cultural Analysis." *Ethos* 14 (2): 174–203.

———. 2013. "Shamanism in Cross-Cultural Perspective." *International Journal of Transpersonal Studies* 31 (2): 47–62.

Wu, Yanhong, Cheng Wang, Xi He, Lihua Mao, and Li Zhanga. 2010. "Religious Beliefs Influence Neural Substrates of Self-Reflection in Tibetans." *Social Cognitive and Affective Neuroscience* 5 (2–3): 324–31.

Wolf, Eric. 1994. "Perilous Ideas: Race, Culture, People." *Current Anthropology* 35 (1): 1–12.

Wynn, Thomas and Frederick L. Coolidge. 2004. "The Expert Neandertal Mind." *Journal of Human Evolution* 46 (4): 467–87.

———. 2010. "How Levallois Reduction is Similar to, and Not Similar to, Playing Chess." In April Nowell and Iain Davidson, eds. *Stone Tools and the Evolution of Human Cognition*. Boulder: University Press of Colorado, pp. 83–103.

Xygalatas, Dimitris. 2012. *The Burning Saints: Cognition and Culture in the Fire-Walking Rituals of the Anastenaria*. Sheffield, UK and Bristol, CT: Equinox Publishing.

Ye, Zhengdao. 2004. "The Chinese Folk Model of Facial Expressions: A Linguistic Perspective." *Culture & Psychology* 10 (2): 195–222.

Zane, Wallace W. 1995. "Ritual States of Consciousness: A Way of Accounting for Anomalies in the Observation and Explanation of Spirit Possession." *Anthropology of Consciousness* 6 (4): 18–29.

Zhu, Ying, Li Zhang, Jin Fan, and Shihui Hana. 2007. "Neural Basis of Cultural Influence on Self Representation." *NeuroImage* 34 (3): 1310–6.

Index